AN ASOR MOSAIC

*Philip J. King, Honorary Editor
ASOR President 1976–1982.*

An ASOR Mosaic

A Centennial History of the
American Schools of Oriental Research
1900–2000

Contributing Authors
Jeffrey A. Blakely
Nancy Lapp
Eric M. Meyers
Joe D. Seger
Stuart Swiny

Edited by
Joe D. Seger

Honorary Editor
Philip J. King

American Schools of Oriental Research
Boston, MA

An ASOR Mosaic

A Centennial History of the
American Schools of Oriental Research
1900–2000

edited by
Joe D. Seger

book design by
Patty O. Seger
NewIDEAS, Inc.

Copyright © 2001
The American Schools of Oriental Research

ACKNOWLEDGMENT

This volume was prepared and published with financial assistance from Richard J. Scheuer. His instrumental support of this and many other ASOR projects and activities through the years is greatly appreciated and very warmly acknowledged.

DEDICATION

The ASOR community along with his family and a large host of friends mourn the loss of The Reverend Charles Upchurch Harris, Jr. who died peacefully at his Virginia farm home on Sunday September 16, 2001. A long-time trustee, Harris served ASOR as Treasurer from 1985–1988 and was its Chairman of the Board from 1992-1994, after which he continued as Life Trustee and Honorary Chairman. He was instrumental in the founding of CAARI on Cyprus, serving as its President from 1984–1991 and as its Board Chairman from 1991 until his death. He enjoyed a distinguished career as an Anglican divine and was a formative presence within ASOR circles as is aptly recorded in this history. In grateful recognition of his substantive support, firm leadership, wise counsel, and always consummate good humor this volume is specially dedicated to his memory.

Library of Congress Cataloging-in-Publication Data

An ASOR mosaic : a centennial history of the American Schools of Oriental Research, 1900-2000 / edited by Joe D. Seger ; contributing authors Jeffrey A. Blakely ... [et al.].
     p. cm.
Includes bibliographical references.
    ISBN 0-89757-033-2 (alk. paper)
  1. American Schools of Oriental Research—History. 2. Middle East—Antiquities. 3. Middle East—History—To 622—Study and teaching. I. Title: American Schools of Oriental Research mosaic. II. Seger, Joe D. III. Blakely, Jeffrey A., 1952-
   DS41 .A78 2001
   939'.4—dc21
                                                2001005825

Contents

Foreword, *P. E. MacAllister*	vi
Editor's Preface, *Joe D. Seger*	vii
Key Sources	ix
About the Authors	x
Tabula Congratulatoria	xi
Centennial Keynote Address, *Hon. Thomas R. Pickering*	xiii

ASOR: A History of the American Schools of Oriental Research 1900–2000

Part One: The First Eight Decades, *Eric M. Meyers*	3
Part Two: The New ASOR 1975–2000, *Joe D. Seger*	34
Part Three: Celebrating a Century, *Joe D. Seger*	78
ASOR Appended Lists: *Officers, Board of Trustees, Staff, Institutional Members, Appointees 1970–2000, CAP Affiliated Projects 1970–2000*	104

AIAR: A History of the W.F. Albright Institute of Archaeological Research, Jerusalem, Israel 1967–2000

Rebuilding the House that Albright Built, *Jeffrey A. Blakely*	125
AIAR Appended Lists: *Officers, Board of Trustees, Staff, Appointees, Assisted Research Projects*	218

ACOR: A History of the American Center of Oriental Research, Amman, Jordan 1968–2000

The ACOR Odyssey, *Nancy Lapp*	239
ACOR Appended Lists: *Officers, Board of Trustees, Staff, Appointees, Assisted Research Projects*	301

CAARI: A History of the Cyprus American Archaeological Research Institute, Nicosia, Cyprus 1978–2000

The House of the Dancing Bird, *Stuart Swiny*	319
CAARI Appended Lists: *Officers, Board of Trustees, Staff, Appointees, Assisted Research Projects*	368

FOREWORD

ASOR has negotiated its first century and established itself as the premier interpreter of life in the ancient Middle East — sometimes correcting and corroborating existing history, occasionally refuting and rewriting it. Our search is finding truth, and as we've done so, we have been a contributor to understanding our nature as a species, and as a culture. But if the past is ineluctably locked in place, ASOR in the present continues to change — to improve its technique, broaden its exploratory scope, become more precise in its interpretation, find new types of evidence; learning infinitely more in a given baulk than was possible a few decades ago. ASOR is still propelled by a self-generated, internal initiative sending hundreds of teams into the field while simultaneously attending an administrative structure, sometimes a bit disheveled, but stubbornly enduring as it publishes countless findings, refines its technology, expands its associations, exercises precise discipline in the field, and cooperates with host countries in conformance to its charter and purposes.

It would be well for us if indeed "the past is prologue to the future" since the past has been an adventure — productive, rewarding, informative, and (we think) successful. But it was also "different." Through the past century the climate has changed. Now new demands are imposed and new challenges await. The future beckons with its allure even as it portends with challenge and threat. Just as we have changed techniques in the field, it is time also to review the organization's game plan; to change modes and models of structure in order to prepare ASOR for resolving the enigmatic financial dilemma athwart the path; the nonchalance about archaeology in academe; time to reappraise our publishing role and function; time to under-shore our three overseas centers and other initiatives in Middle East countries. The next century surely requires a new agenda for ASOR, incorporating the best of the old and equipping us with the contemporary vehicle we need to make the next hundred years as glorious as the last. The fate of ASOR in the twenty-first century "lies not in our stars, but in ourselves." We need to gird our loins for the trial.

P. E. MacAllister, ASOR Board Chairman, August 2001

EDITOR'S PREFACE

In 1983, following a period of greatly expanded archaeological activity and of formative ASOR growth and development, just retired ASOR President Philip J. King produced the first comprehensive history of the American Schools of Oriental Research under the title *American Archaeology in the Mideast*. (ASOR: Philadelphia 1983. Cited throughout the volume as KING).

This completed a charge that King had accepted a decade earlier from President G. Ernest Wright and the ASOR Board of Trustees, to prepare such a work in celebration of ASOR's seventy-fifth anniversary in 1975. At that juncture, coupled with necessities and opportunities occasioned by political circumstances, ASOR initiatives had provided for the establishment of three active overseas research centers; the W. F. Albright Institute (AIAR) in Jerusalem, Israel, representing ASOR's continuing presence there, the American Center of Oriental Research (ACOR) in Amman, Jordan, and the Cyprus American Archaeological Research Institute (CAARI) in Nicosia, Cyprus. By the close of the century each of these centers was well-established, enjoying independent development under separate governance. By this time ASOR, on its own part, had also experienced significant growth and change.

As plans for the celebration of ASOR's centennial developed it thus seemed most appropriate that the story of ASOR and of each of the affiliated overseas centers be brought up to date.

It was also deemed fitting that due respect be given to the earlier efforts of Philip King both for his service to the organization and for his pioneering work in documenting its history. Accordingly, and with most sincere appreciation, Philip J. King is acknowledged as Honorary Editor of this volume.

The Mosaic Simile

At the conclusion of Mildred Freed Alberg's film "The Royal Archives at Ebla," produced in the late 1970s, UCLA Professor Georgio Buccelati explains, "Archaeology is a mosaic, a mosaic of a variety of things that we put together today as we find them in the ground … It is a way of seeing patterns emerge in front of us and as they do we can understand better the processes of civilizations and what causes them to flourish and decay." While this is a volume not so much about archaeology as about archaeologists, the simile is apt. From the outset the committee of authors and consultants was concerned to avoid duplication of earlier efforts to record the organization's history (in addition to writings by King see the list of Key Sources that follows), while at the same time providing cohesive story lines. With this came the decision to specially emphasize graphic content in the volume. At the same time it was necessary to contemplate the likelihood that others who have lived this history will have other views and might wish for different emphases and alternative images. The volume title, "An ASOR Mosaic," was thus chosen to acknowledge recognition that this record, like many mosaic carpets found in excavation work, is incomplete, with missing tesserae. To this extent the volume is presented as a work in progress. While the authors and editor have worked deliberately to be faithful to their charge, to "see the patterns that emerged" through the century, and are confident that both the broad framework and many details of these histories are accurately presented, there is no claim to completeness or finality. This is evident for example, in captions where images of persons unknown ("persons uk") remain, and necessarily true for an organization like ASOR where work and achievements are so dependent on an extremely large cast of volunteer scholars, members, students and other associates who labor on its behalf. Accordingly, with the presentation of the volume comes also an open invitation to readers to submit notes of addition and correction to be shared as "ASOR Mosaic Updates" in future issues of the *ASOR Newsletter*.

Special Acknowledgments and Credits

At an early stage of planning for this project impetus was provided by a gift of financial assistance from Richard J. Scheuer, and this is most gratefully acknowledged. His support enabled travel and research activities by the authors, and provided for the preparation of a finished digital camera ready manuscript. Supplementary support for printing the volume was provided by other contributors to centennial funding, including especially those on the list of pre-subscribers in the Tabula Congratulatoria which follows.

In addition to the named authors and editor, many others participated in efforts to prepare this work. These include the directors and staff members from offices of each of the overseas centers and of ASOR, and a large number of other individual ASOR members and associates who helped research archives and cooperated in providing photographs and graphic images. Many of these are acknowledged more deliberately in introductory materials for the several sections. In addition, recognition is due a number of individuals who provided assistance with editorial work. Principal among these are Patty Seger, President of NewIDEAS, Inc. and Billie Jean Collins, Director of Publications for ASOR. Mrs. Seger designed the book and prepared the camera ready document. She labored incessantly to enhance photographic images and to accommodate the authors and editor through numerous manuscript editions and corrections. Dr. Collins served as a consultant to the editor throughout the preparation period and, with the help of Publications Assistant Chris Madell, copyedited the final manuscript. Others providing special editing assistance include AIAR Director Sy Gitin (for the sections on AIAR history and AIAR centennial activities), ASOR and AIAR Trustee Lydie Shufro (for the sections on AIAR and CAARI histories and the AIAR centennial activities), CAARI Director Robert Merrillees (for parts of the CAARI history and the CAARI centennial activities), and Mississippi State University, Cobb Institute of Archaeology, Student Research Assistant Justine Warren who read and rechecked all of the several editions of each of the section manuscripts. The efforts of all these individuals contributed immeasurably to the shaping of the final work and the editor is sincerely appreciative of their formative assistance.

An ASOR Mosaic was prepared to illustrate the vital course followed through the century by ASOR and its affiliates in pursuit of their common mission and dedication to archaeology and to cultural understanding of the civilizations of the ancient Near East. It is our hope that the volume will also prove useful in supporting the organization's continuing mission and pursuit of service in scholarly research and educational outreach into the twenty-first century.

Joe D. Seger, Editor, August 2001

KEY SOURCES

Branwen Denton and Patricia Bikai, Eds.

1993 ACOR: *The First Twenty Five Years; The American Center of Oriental Research, 1968–1993.* Amman, Jordan: American Center of Oriental Research.

Bert de Vries

1991 ACOR: Past, Present and Future *ACOR Newsletter* 4: 1–8.

Seymour Gitin

1997 W. F. Albright Institute of Archaeological Research. Pp. 62–63 in *Oxford Encyclopedia of Archaeology in the Near East*, Vol. 1. New York: Oxford University.

Charles U. Harris

1989 The Role of CAARI on Cyprus. *Biblical Archaeologist* 52:4: 157–62

Philip J. King

1975a Archaeology at the Albright Institute. *Biblical Archaeologist* 38:3-4: 79–88

1975b The American Archaeological Heritage in the Near East. *Bulletin of the American Schools of Oriental Research* 217: 55–65.

1983 *American Archaeology in the Mideast: A History of the American Schools of Oriental Research.* Philadelphia: American Schools of Oriental Research. (Cited throughout as KING)

David McCreery

1997 American Center of Oriental Research. Pp. 89–90 in *Oxford Encyclopedia of Archaeology in the Near East*, Vol. 1. New York: Oxford University.

Eric M. Meyers

1997 American Schools of Oriental Research. Pp. 94–98 in *Oxford Encyclopedia of Archaeology in the Near East*, Vol. 1. New York: Oxford University.

Stuart Swiny

1997 Cyprus American Archaeological Research Institute. Pp. 96–97 in *Oxford Encyclopedia of Archaeology in the Near East*, Vol. 2. New York: Oxford University.

ABOUT THE AUTHORS

Jeffrey A. Blakely

Jeff Blakely is a Research Archaeologist working with Archeological Assessments, Inc. of Nashville, AR. He is a long-time member of ASOR and has served for many years as a member of the Committee on Archaeological Policy. He served as Annual Professor at AIAR in 1996/1997. He is currently an elected ASOR Trustee.

Nancy Lapp

Nancy Lapp is the recently retired Curator of the Pittsburgh Theological Seminary Museum. She is a long time member of ASOR and served during several terms as a member of the Committee on Archaeological Policy. She was Assistant to the Director at AIAR during the term of her husband there from 1961–1965. She has been a Trustee of ACOR since 1976 and served as Board Secretary for a number of years. She currently chairs the ACOR Fellowship Committee.

Eric M. Meyers

Eric Meyers is currently the Bernice and Morton Lerner Professor of Religion at Duke University. A long-time member of ASOR, he has served the organization in myriad ways. Most notable are his terms as First Vice-President for Publications and Editor of *Biblical Archaeologist* from 1983–1989 and as President from 1990–1996. He is currently an elected ASOR Trustee. He served for a long time as a Trustee of AIAR, of which he is a past Director, and is now an Honorary Trustee. He has also served several terms as a Trustee of CAARI.

Joe D. Seger

Joe Seger is currently the Director of the Cobb Institute of Archaeology and Professor of Religion at Mississippi State University. A long-time member of ASOR he served as Chairman of the Committee on Archaeological Policy from 1994–1996 and has been President since 1996. He was a long-time Trustee of the AIAR and served as President from 1988–1994. He is now an AIAR Honorary Trustee.

Stuart Swiny

Stuart Swiny is currently Director of the Institute of Cypriot Studies and Professor in the Department of Classics of the University at Albany. He served as Director of CAARI from 1980–1995. A long-time member of ASOR he served for many years as a member of the Committee on Archaeological Policy. He is currently an elected Trustee of ASOR as well as of CAARI.

TABULA CONGRATULATORIA

Congratulations to the American Schools of Oriental Research and support for the publication of this commemorative volume celebrating ASOR's Centennial have been extended by the following individuals, institutions and foundations.

Astrid B. Beck — La Jolla, CA
Sheila T. Bishop — Goldboro, NC
Oded Borowski — Atlanta, GA
Robin M. Brown — Watertown, MA
Robert and Vivian Bull — McMinville, OR
Sara T. Callaway — Athens, GA
Central Baptist Theological Seminary Library — Kansas City, KS
Lillian W. Craig — Nicosia, Cyprus
Sidnie White Crawford — Lincoln, NE
Frank M. Cross — Lexington, MA
Cobb Institute of Archaeology, Mississippi State University — Mississippi State, MS
Currents in Theology and Mission — Chicago, IL
David A. Detrich — Mattituck, NY
Rudolph H. and Meredith Dornemann — West Roxbury, MA
Dorot Foundation — Providence, RI
James A. and Joy Devine Durlesser — New Wilmington, PA
Erick R. Egerston — Fremont, NE
Raymond C. Ewing — Annendale, VA
Peter Feinman — Port Chester, NY
Nan Frederick — West River, MD
Harold O. Forshey — Oxford, OH
David Noel Freedman — La Jolla, CA
Juergen Friede — Essen, Germany
Patty Gerstenblith — Wilmette, IL
Glass Memorial Library, Johnson Bible College — Knoxville, TN
Lawrence T. Geraty — Riverside, CA
Lois R. Glock — Madison, NJ
Victor Roland Gold — Berkeley, CA
Eugene M. Grant — New York, NY
Elliot Greenberg — Tucson, AZ
Lowell K. Handy — Evanston, IL
Ellen Herscher — Washington DC
Ulrich Hubner — Mainz, Germany

Curtis M. Hutt — Teaneck, NJ
Artemis and Martha Joukowsky — Providence, RI
Ann E. Killebrew — Santa Ana, CA
Wade Kotter — Ogden, UT
Oystein S. LaBianca — Berrien Springs, MI
George M. Landes — New York, NY
George Hans Lievenow — Cincinnati, OH
P.E. MacAllister — Indianapolis, IN
David W. and Linda S. McCreery — Salem, OR
Barbara Miley — La Jolla, CA
Melissa G. Muendel — Knoxville, TN
Beth Alpert Nakhai — Tucson, AZ
John Oleson — Victoria, BC, Canada
Thomas R. Pickering — Alexandria, VA
Dana M. Pike — Provo, UT
Princeton Theological Seminary — Princeton, NJ
B.W. Ruffner — Signal Mountain, TN
R. Thomas and Marilyn Schaub — Pittsburgh, PA
Richard J. and Joan G. Scheuer — Larchmont, NY
Joe D. and Patricia Seger — Starkville, MS
Lee R. Seeman. — Great Neck, NY
Nancy Serwint — Phoenix. AZ
Leila Sharaf — Amman, Jordan
Abraham and Marian Scheuer Sofaer — Palo Alto, CA
Arnold Spaer, Spaer, Sitton, and Co. — Jerusalem, Israel
Richard L. Spees — Washington DC
John R. Spencer — University Heights, OH
Olin J. Storvick — Moorhead, MN
Carolyn and James F. Strange — Tampa, FL
Jean Sulzberger — New York, NY
Gough W. Thompson Jr. — La Jolla, CA
Bryan Wilkins — Washinton, D.C.
Prescott H. and Jane M. Williams, Jr. — Austin, TX
Ingrid E. Wood — Boston, MA
Keeley and J. Edward Wright — Tucson, AZ
Patricia Plum Wylde — Wareham, MA

Keynote Address
Centennial Gala Celebration of the
American Schools of Oriental Research

By the Honorable Thomas R. Pickering
Under Secretary of State for Political Affairs

The Benjamin Franklin Room, U.S. Department of State
Washington, DC, April 14, 2000

Diplomacy and Archaeology: Past, Present and Future

Thank you, Mr. MacAllister, for that generous introduction, and I join you in extending a special welcome to the distinguished members of the diplomatic corps present tonight, and to Senator and Mrs. Moynihan.

Let me also express my thanks to President Joe Seger, Dr. Rudy Dornemann, and all the others who worked so long and hard to organize this wonderful event.

I know something about what you went through to get here. It makes Indiana Jones' adventures look like a tea party!

On behalf of the Department of State, welcome to the Benjamin Franklin Room. The age of these beautiful objects may not overly impress this gathering, but whenever I enter here, I am reminded that we in the Department are engaged in an enterprise far greater than our individual preoccupations. I suspect that this is a familiar thought to most of you as well.

Alice and I are deeply honored to be asked to be part of your centennial celebrations, and to have the honor of welcoming you here.

My one contribution as an ardent amateur to the literature of archaeology unfortunately has only found its way into Reader's Digest and People magazine.

In early 1986 at the Sea of Galilee, when some of your colleagues were excavating an early fishing boat, a local journalist asked me to compare archaeology and diplomacy.

The best I could do was to say that archaeology was uncovering the unknown, and diplomacy almost certainly was the opposite!

Nevertheless, Alice and I both take great pride in our amateur status and our personal association with this remarkable organization. Like so many others who have breathed the excitement and dust of a major dig, we have found no other experience in the world that can provide such a combination of intellectual challenge and physical discomfort.

This evening, we celebrate not merely the centennial of a remarkable organization, but of a century of extraordinary scientific exploration. The American Schools of Oriental Research (ASOR) was present at the creation of an era that has profoundly transformed our understanding of the ancient worlds of the Middle East and Mediterranean.

Consider just three milestones of the last half-century in which ASOR participated: discovery of the Dead Sea Scrolls at Qumran, recovery of ancient Petra's Nabatean and Byzantine civilizations, and excavation of pygmy hippopotamus bones from Neolithic era on Cyprus.

*The Honorable Thomas R. Pickering
Under Secretary of State for
Political Affairs*

These are not simply monuments, but monumental additions to the storehouse of knowledge about a region that gave birth to civilization and shaped the Western world.

They are achievements of painstaking scholarship, creative imagination, and sheer backbreaking labor.

ASOR's individual members and member institutions have enriched the world, and transformed our understanding of it in ways that are as fundamental as Edwin Hubble's discovery that we live in an expanding universe.

At the same time, ASOR — through its three major centers in Jerusalem, Amman, and Nicosia — has not simply survived the ethnic and religious conflicts of the region, but served as a model of inclusive, politically neutral scholarship.

Through times of political turbulence and conflict, ASOR has built institutions of intellectual excellence — and thereby demonstrated the power of international cooperation to achieve a common purpose.

These lessons did not pass unnoticed by the political leaders of the region, and serve as excellent models for what success in the peace process can (and has) created.

Securing a just, lasting and comprehensive Arab-Israeli peace is at the center of our work at the State Department. It is never easy, and yet we can also trace how our efforts over the years have made a real difference for people throughout the region.

All tracks of the peace process are active. Israeli Prime Minister Barak was just in Washington and chairman Arafat is scheduled to visit soon. We also are encouraged by Israel's decision to withdraw its forces completely from south Lebanon in accordance with the relevant UN resolutions.

At the same time, we hope to find ways to resolve the small but significant gaps that remain between Syria and Israel. All of this demands very hard work, but we are committed to achieving peace.

You have played an historic role in America's determination to find peace in the region. Archaeology has never respected modern boundaries. Indeed, it has helped us transcend those boundaries.

Having had the pleasure of serving both in Jordan and Israel, I know that the archaeologists on both sides of the Jordan River have much to say to each other. And there is real joy in learning that old friends in the field of archaeology on both sides are now working more closely together than ever before. This kind of cooperation has helped to build the public support and backing for peace that the region so urgently needs.

With your commitment to preservation and protection of sites, fact finding, truth telling, and scientific inquiry, you embody the core values of this county, and strengthen our relationships with nations throughout the region.

This new century offers you many challenges, not the least of which is to match the achievements of your own past.

I have little doubt that ASOR's future holds many more exciting insights into our human past. They may be found in the Vasilikos Valley of Cyprus, the Madaba Plains of Jordan, the Caesarea excavations of Israel — or most likely in many places yet unknown.

This evening, I would like to talk about several challenges facing archaeology, especially those that intersect with diplomacy and U.S. foreign policy.

My first point is both an obvious and fundamental one: the importance of partnership. Just as ASOR's scholarly integrity can strengthen the foundations of trust among people, so the U.S. commitment to fostering dialogue can nourish the work of international researchers.

Let me give you an example, one whose last chapter has yet to be written. A collection of 10,000 year old animal bones — of wild goats, cattle, gazelles, and dogs — currently resides inside drawers at the Smithsonian's Museum of natural History. As described in a recent National Public Radio report, they offer a striking picture of one of the most important events in human history: the Neolithic revolution that led to the invention of agriculture and domestication of animals.

The tale these bones seem to tell is that the Neolithic people, rather than having been forced by hunger into animal domestication, may have been experimenting with creative ways of managing resources and maximizing gain.

However, there is a problem: these bones were found years ago at a site in Iran that is no longer generally open to the scholarly community.

Suddenly, past and present are joined, and the political conflicts of today are inescapably connected to the lives of human beings ten centuries ago.

Two years ago, President Khatami of Iran spoke of opening a "dialogue of civilizations." Last month, Secretary Albright announced a set of major new initiatives toward Iran — motivated, and I quote:

"Solely by a realistic interest in taking this relationship to a higher level so that we may use diplomacy to solve problems and benefit the people of both countries."

In taking this initiative, the United States is affirming its belief in the proposition that expanded dialogue and exchanges among nations are in everyone's interest. Make no mistake, serious political differences between the United States and Iran remain.

Nevertheless, the Secretary made clear our commitment to encourage cultural exchanges of scholars, scientists, artists, athletes, and others, to serve as a bridge between our two countries. It is not hard to imagine that this opening may one day — soon, we hope — lead to new opportunities for expanded archaeological research in Iran — and a better understanding of the moment in human history when hunters became herders — and then found the spare time to create something we now can call civilization.

But we don't need to speculate about the positive aspects of public-private partnerships in international archaeology. We have many concrete examples.

In Jordan, the United States, along with ASOR and other private donors, has provided decades of support for the excavation and preservation of one of the most evocative archaeological sites in the world — Petra.

I take some pride in being a part of this process when some years ago we asked the Agency for International Development (USAID) to apply U.S. standards of good environmental practice. As standard procedure, our development projects now survey — and avoid — archaeological resources whenever possible, and conduct salvage archaeology only as a last resort.

And we found that support for archaeology in Jordan has meant support for greater economic development through enriched tourism.

So USAID over the years helped fund development of a master plan for Petra, a dam to control periodic flooding, and an innovative shelter for the display of a Byzantine mosaics. To meet the infrastructure demands of local residents and tourists, USAID is now helping fund a wastewater treatment facility for the Wadi Musa community located outside Petra.

USAID is also continuing its long partnership with the Jordan American Center of Oriental Research (ACOR) through a grant for archaeology and site preservation not only at Petra, but also at the Madaba Archaeological park, Aqaba, and the Citadel in Amman.

Elsewhere in the region, in Egypt, the challenge is not simply to protect archaeological sites, but to manage an unparalleled cultural heritage.

In cooperation with such institutions as the American Research Center in Egypt and the Egyptian Supreme Council for Antiquities, USAID has helped fund conservation projects that reflect Egypt's diverse heritage. To note just a few:

- *Conservation of Greco-Roman mosaics at the Kom El Kikka archaeological park in Alexandria;*
- *The tomb of Seti I in Luxor, the largest decorated tomb in the Valley of the Kings;*
- *Queseir fort, built by Sultan Sclim on the Red Sea; and*
- *Monasteries of St. Anthony and St. Paul, which contain Coptic wall paintings from the 13th century.*

We are also providing Egyptians with training in the core archaeological disciplines of excavation, documentation, conservation, and museum management.

A second critical intersection between archaeology and diplomacy is that of protection. Whether as a nation, as scientists, or simply as a people anxious to understand our past - we all are victimized by the looting of archaeological sites and the trafficking in illegal or stolen artifacts.

The United States was the first major art-importing country to ratify the 1970 UNESCO Convention on Cultural property. We now have entered into agreements or taken emergency actions with eight nations to protect an array of archaeological treasures. These include:

- *Khmer stone sculptures and architectural pieces from Cambodia;*
- *Artifacts of Canada's aboriginal cultures;*
- *Byzantine ecclesiastical and liturgical objects from Cyprus;*
- *Both pre-Columbian and colonial materials from Peru;*
- *Pre-Columbian objects from El Salvador;*
- *Mayan artifacts from Guatemala;*
- *Artifacts from the highland and Niger River regions of Mali; and*
- *Aymara Indian textiles from Bolivia*

Before the State Department reaches a decision to protect artifacts through import controls or restrictions, the foreign government's request goes before the Cultural Property Advisory Committee, which comprises distinguished experts in the fields of archaeology, anthropology, cultural property law, and museum management.

One of the newest members of the Advisory committee is a Trustee of ASOR as well — and she is here tonight — Dr. Patty Gerstenblith of the DePaul University College of Law.

Dr. Gerstenblith is an expert in the field of the law and cultural heritage and the arts. She also serves as editor-in-chief of the *International Journal of Cultural Property*.

Law enforcement is the other side of the protection equation, and both the U.S. Customs Service and FBI play major roles in investigating the trafficking in illegal antiquities.

We recognize that, as one of the principle markets for stolen antiquities, the United States carries a particularly heavy responsibility for building systems of protection and incentives to halt the traffic in illegal antiquities. And frankly, if looted or stolen artifacts appear in U.S. museums and auction houses, they can harm our bilateral relations with other countries.

The United States is taking decisive action in this area.

On March 1, for example, a two-year investigation conducted in cooperation with the government of Turkey culminated in the return of more than 100 stolen or looted artifacts representing a panoply of ancient cultures: Assyrian, Hittite, Phoenician, Greek, Roman, and Byzantine.

Our participation in exploring and protecting Turkey's past is hardly new, I might add. American and Ottoman archaeologists first explored a site at Assos in 1881, and a well-known Princeton University expedition looked at Ottoman Syria and Jordan before the end of the 19th century.

Last November, the First Lady, Hillary Rodham Clinton, announced a grant to exchange archaeological knowledge between Turkey and Greece about their shared Mediterranean heritage — and incidentally to promote a new spirit of cooperation between these two countries.

Despite its heavy responsibilities for interdicting drugs and other contraband, the U.S. Customs Service has worked vigorously to halt the smuggling of archaeological artifacts.

Just last month, federal authorities blocked the sale of a marble wall sculpture stolen from a 10th century tomb in China's Hebei province. In February, the Customs Service arranged for the return to Italy of two irreplaceable if quite different items: a collection of Paleolithic bones, and a gold bowl, or phiale, dating from 450 B.C. and worth an estimated $1.2 million.

By stemming the traffic in undocumented and stolen artifacts, we seek to strengthen the bonds of international scholarship, to encourage research, and to expand opportunities for the exchange and display of historic and cultural artifacts worldwide.

A third point of connection between diplomacy and archaeology is that of stewardship. I hardly need to expand on a concept that is absolutely core to both archaeology as a profession and ASOR as an organization.

What I can do is cite an example close to home, here at the Department of State.

The Department has long recognized the need to undertake a systematic assessment of its own historic and culturally important sites overseas. Now, under the leadership of the Under Secretary for Management, Bonnie Cohen, we have begun to assemble and document such an inventory.

The United States owns or holds long-term leases to more than 3,500 properties at 265 locations worldwide. Among them we estimate there are about 150 properties that are significant for historical, architectural, or cultural reasons. Let me cite just two

"Mediterranean" examples:

> - *In 1821, Sultan Moulay Suliman of Morocco presented the United States with its first property, the Tangier Old Legation.*
>
> - *Our embassy in Rome is located in Palazzo Margherita, a veritable treasure trove of history, encompassing late Roman fresco paintings, the 17th century residence of Cardinal Ludovico Ludovisi, and the royal chambers of the Queen Mother Margherita which, during Mussolini's dictatorship, were partitioned into offices for the national Fascist Confederation of Farmers.*

In the near future, we plan to complete the assessment process and formally announce the Secretary of State's first "Register of Culturally Significant Properties." Our hope is that the Secretary's register will give these sites greater visibility and protection — and highlight their historic or cultural designations as genuine assets for the United States.

Another tangible example of the U.S. commitment to stewardship of the past is our participation in the World Heritage Convention, largely through the National Park Service and ICOMOS — the United States Committee, International Council on monuments and Sites.

There are now 22 World Heritage sites in the United States. Some are as large and familiar as Yellowstone National Park and Florida's Everglades. Others are less familiar, but no less irreplaceable — such as the Cahokia Mound outside St. Louis, once the location of one of the great population centers of Mesoamerica.

Domestically, efforts to protect historic sites on federal lands go back to the Antiquities Act of 1906. Today, the Federal Archaeology Program encompasses a wide range of research and conservation efforts, collections of artifacts and data, site protection, and public education and outreach efforts.

Virtually every federal agency with "on-the-ground" responsibilities — the National Park and Forest Services, Bureau of Land Management, Army Corps of Engineers — have archaeological programs integrated into their activities.

Outside federal lands, cultural preservation is a state and local responsibility, and the federal role is one of advice and consultation.

One must always take care in extrapolating our domestic experience internationally, but I think the concepts of integration and local decision-making are broadly applicable elsewhere. Archaeology, however specialized, is a public endeavor, requiring understanding and support from the people who find themselves living in a region with a significant past.

A fourth intersection of archaeology and diplomacy is the complicated issue of how we value the past.

In one sense, archaeology is the victim of its own successes. Archaeology's grip on the public imagination is nothing new, dating back at least to the novels of H. Rider Haggard in the 1880s. More recently, however, discoveries such as the Dead Sea Scrolls and Petra have seized the imagination of people around the world.

Archaeology is no longer the monopoly of academics. It is now part of the larger culture. Let's admit it, there are worse fates than being portrayed by Harrison Ford. And I'm told that the most popular digital character on the Internet is Lara Croft, heroine of the best-selling computer game, "*Tomb Raider.*"

But popularity is a two-edged sword, encouraging trivialization, and threatening to turn archaeological sites into theme parks.

We arrive, finally, at a set of very difficult questions.

How do we place a value on the human heritage embodied in the ruins and objects of the ancient world?

Should they be measured chiefly for their economic value, or because they illuminate the human condition?

Is our model the visitor's center at an excavation site, a museum display — or the "Antiques Road Show?"

One answer, it seems to me, is to connect archaeology and historic preservation with two very powerful concepts that have widespread national and international support: sustainable development and biodiversity.

For archaeology to be sustainable, it must be anchored in the local economy as well as in the priorities of national governments. The benefits — whether knowledge and insight, tourism, partnerships, education, or jobs — must be as tangible as the shards and stones that workers excavate.

Biodiversity, we now know, is essential to the life and health of the natural environment. So too is a diverse human environment, one that allows people to become rooted in their heritage and past, even as they seek a better future.

The increasing use of science in archaeology, the marriages with botany and new technologies of dating historic objects, are all indicators, too, of how a better future supports archaeology.

In the end, however, what captures the imagination and intellect of people is not the monetary value of the artifacts that emerge from the sands and seas of the world. It is, instead, the promise of the encounter with the real, the authentic — the gripping capacity of your science to tell us the story of our common history and heritage which otherwise we would never know.

The people may come for the show. But they will stay for the truth.

You are not simply digging up the past, but excavating the human soul.

As you do so, you reveal our future as well. For archaeologists understand one great truth that they are often reluctant to utter: In the end, all human works will be reduced to rubble. Not because of war or natural catastrophe, but simply because we are human.

And for human beings, in the words of the poet Delmore Schwartz, "Time is the fire in which we burn."

Just as you, today, sift through pottery shards of past centuries, so too, will archaeologists of the future sift through the remains of our time.

And no doubt they will wonder at a civilization whose emblematic buildings seemed to be sports stadiums and shopping malls, and whose inhabitants often wore T-shirts emblazoned with tribal or regligious symbols that have not yet been deciphered.

So as ASOR begins its second century, I have little doubt that great discoveries await you - that one day you, too, will clear out a rubble-filled passageway and peer into a dark space.

And when someone says, "What do you see?" you — like Howard Carter on that day in the Valley of the Kings when he found the tomb of Tutenkhamen — can answer:

"Wonderful things. I see wonderful things."

Thank you.

ASOR

A History of the
AMERICAN SCHOOLS OF ORIENTAL RESEARCH

by Eric M. Meyers
and
Joe D. Seger

The ASOR Logo

In 1923, the ASOR trustees approved the organization's corporate seal, which combines the Egyptian *ankh*, the sign of life, and the Babylonian *dingir*, the eight pointed star formed by four cuneiform wedges, the sign for deity. Today this unique *ankh* and *dingir* symbol continues to represent the broad scope of ASOR's geographic and chronological interests in the greater Middle East.

Credits

In the preparation of this history of ASOR, the authors relied on a number of critical sources. Along with the pioneer volume on ASOR history, *American Archaeology in the Mideast*, by Philip J. King (cited herein as KING), these include minutes and reports in *BASOR*, materials published in *Biblical Archaeologist* and the *ASOR Newsletter* and minutes of Executive Committee and Board of Trustees meetings. The Board Minutes so carefully prepared by Secretary George Landes during his years in office from 1972 to 1994 proved to be an especially good resource for preparing the review of those crucial decades. The archive of records and reports on the work of the 1979 Presidential Task Force, lead by its Chairman Edward F. Campbell, Jr. were similarly useful. We warmly acknowledge the special assistance of the staff in the ASOR Boston office, Rudolph Dornemann, Holly Andrews and Britt Hartenberger in accessing these and other records, together with photographic files from office archives. All pictures not otherwise referenced come from these ASOR archives.

We also aknowledge with appreciatation the following sources for other photographic images. These are: Virginia Ben Arie (VBA), Boston University Photo Services (BU), the Nelson Glueck Archive (NG), Nancy Lapp (NL), Eric M. Meyers (EMM), Joe D. Seger (JDS), Patty O. Seger (POS), The W. F. Albright Institute Archives (AIAR) and the W. F. Albright Family Archives (WFAF). Pictures are referenced as indicated in parentheses.

ASOR
A History of the American Schools of Oriental Research 1900–2000

Part One: The First Eight Decades
by Eric Meyers

The American Schools of Oriental Research (ASOR) was founded in 1900. Its goals were to encourage research, especially archaeological, about the history, geography, languages, literatures, and religions of the societies of the ancient Near East. With this volume we celebrate the centennial of the organization and commemorate one hundred years of dramatic successes in aiding the recovery of the history of the ancient Near East and eastern Mediterranean worlds, and in exposing the ancient cultural landscapes wherein the origins of western civilization were shaped.

Nineteenth Century Origins

The history and traditions of ASOR are linked to the parent societies that called for its founding more than a century ago. The first academic organization to press for the establishment of a new society with an archaeological focus was the Society of Biblical Literature (SBL), originally founded as the Society for Biblical Literature and Exegesis in 1880. On June 13, 1895, its president, J. Henry Thayer, a specialist in the New Testament at Harvard University, urged the society to establish a school in Palestine that would be able to promote the study of scripture in the very land in which it had taken shape. It was to be called an American School for Oriental Study and Research. Others, notably Henry W. Hulbert, wanted such a school to be located in Beirut and had referred to it as a school of biblical archaeology and philology in the East.

> *The Founders' Goals* . . . *to enable properly qualified biblical, linguistic, archaeological, historical, and other kindred studies and researches under more favorable conditions than can be secured at a distance from the Holy Land,* . . .
>
> *(From founding resolutions 1900)*
>
> . . . *organized exclusively for* . . . *such purposes to include the initiation, encouragement and support of research into and public understanding of the peoples and cultures of the Near East and their wider spheres of interaction from earliest times to the modern period* . . .
>
> *(From Article Three of ASOR's Articles of Incorporation 1921)*

Thayer's suggestion to establish a school in Palestine was referred to committee, which consequently published a circular to win the support and confidence of both theological schools and universities. In that document Thayer's colleagues expressed the rationale for establishing an overseas center in this way:

The object of the school would be to afford graduates of American theological seminaries, and other similarly qualified persons, the opportunity to prosecute biblical and linguistic investigations under more favorable conditions than can be secured at a distance from the Holy land; . . . to gather material for the illustration of the biblical narratives; to settle doubtful points in biblical topography; to identify historic localities; to explore and, if possible, excavate sacred sites. (King, p. 26)

Additional strong support for the idea of establishing an overseas research center in the Near East was soon provided by the American Oriental Society (AOS), which formally endorsed the idea in 1896, and in 1898, the Archaeological Institute of America (AIA) not only endorsed the proposal, but also pledged an annual subsidy. The AIA had established its own American School of Classical Studies at Athens in 1882 and a comparable school in Rome in 1895. The president of the AIA in 1899 was Charles Eliot Norton, professor of Fine Arts at Harvard. Norton pledged his complete support to a school of biblical studies soon to be established in Jerusalem on the model of the Athens and Rome institutes.

While the tone and direction of SBL's 1895 circular clearly expressed the overriding interest of the founding fathers in biblically related investigations, with AOS and AIA interests and influences, ASOR's purpose was soon broadened to also include wider and non-biblical aspects of Near Eastern studies. During the late 1890s eleven institutions and individuals pledged one hundred dollars each annually, for a period of five years, until a plan for a new school could be implemented. In 1900, under the name the "American School of Oriental Study and Research in Palestine," the organization was born.

Founded 1880

Founded 1842

Founded 1879

> **The Charter Member Institutions of the American Schools of Oriental Research**
>
> Andover Theological Seminary
> Auburn Theological Seminary
> Boston University
> Brown University
> Bryn Mawr College
> Colgate University
> Columbia University
> Cornell University
> Episcopal Theological School (Cambridge, MA)
> Episcopal Divinity School (Philadelphia)
> General Theological Seminary (New York)
> Harvard University
> Hebrew Union College (Cincinnati)
> Johns Hopkins University
> New York University
> University of Pennsylvania
> Princeton University
> Princeton Theological Seminary
> Trinity College (Hartford)
> Union Theological Seminary (New York)
> Yale University

At its founding twenty-one institutions of higher learning — including two colleges, eight seminaries, and eleven universities — had been organized into ASOR's first academic consortium. Although most of those institutions were secular universities, theological interest and support were key from the outset. The organizing committee's restatement of goals and objectives, which became the basis of ASOR's future bylaws, reflected a broadened intellectual horizon that would enable ASOR to extend its purview beyond the Levant into the greater Near East and to extend its historical reach and interest beyond the mere "biblical." Its founding resolutions also contained an inclusive statement that resonates with an entirely modern spirit:

The School shall be open to duly qualified applicants of all races and both sexes, and shall be kept wholly free from obligations or preferences as respects any religious denomination or literary institution. (KING p. 27)

ASOR's ties with the AIA and the SBL were so strong that in the early years all research studies conducted under ASOR auspices were to be published in the journal of either affiliated society — the former publishing the archaeological and non-biblical material, and the latter the biblical.

American School for Oriental Study and Research in Palestine

FIRST ANNUAL REPORT OF THE DIRECTOR OF THE AMERICAN SCHOOL FOR ORIENTAL STUDY AND RESEARCH IN PALESTINE

To the Managing Committee of the American School in Palestine:

GENTLEMEN, — I have the honor to present the following report of my administration of the affairs of the American School in Palestine during the first year of its existence; namely, the year beginning October 1, 1900.

Acting upon the advice of your Committee, and after consultation with Mr. Oscar Straus, United States Minister to Turkey, I proceeded first to Constantincple, in order to acquaint the Turkish Government with the character and aims of the proposed American School for Oriental Study and Research in Palestine, and to secure, if possible, the official permit, or firman, for its establishment. In addition to my credentials as Director of the School, and copies of the various printed circulars, etc., previously issued by your Committee, I was provided with letters from Minister Straus and from our Secretary of State, John Hay. Arriving in Constantinople, September 21, I was at once assured of the hearty coöperation of the representative of our Government there, Mr. Lloyd C. Griscom, chargé d'affaires at the United States Legation during the absence of Mr. Straus in America. During the whole course of the negotiations with the Turkish Government on behalf of our enterprise, Mr. Griscom manifested a keen interest in the projected School, and showed himself an untiring and efficient helper.

Page one of the first ASOR Director Charles C. Torrey's first annual report. From the **Journal of the Archaeological Institute of America** *Vol. V (1901) p. 45.*

Beginnings in Jerusalem

ASOR's first presence overseas was established in 1900 in Jerusalem, with Charles C. Torrey, an Old Testament scholar at Yale University, serving as the director for that year. Torrey, supported by the U.S. consul in Jerusalem Selah Merrill, himself a distinguished Orientalist, established ASOR's initial headquarters in a large room in the Grand New Hotel inside the Jaffa Gate area. He launched a lecture program, and in 1901 he began ASOR's first archaeological field work project with the excavation of tombs at Sidon. These activities became hallmarks of the School's future programs. Without a permanent ASOR facility, American scholars in Jerusalem at the time were dependent on other institutes, among them the Ecole Biblique, for library resources.

In 1906 under Annual Director Benjamin Bacon, the school's headquarters were moved outside the Old City to 6 Ethiopia Street, and in 1908 another move was made to a house opposite the German Archaeological Institute. In 1909, Director Robert Harper purchased vacant property between the Ecole Biblique and Saint George's Cathedral to provide for a permanent residence for the institute. Funds for building construction were not yet available, however, and the school continued to rent space through 1924.

Doorway of house at 6 Ethiopia Street
(AIAR)

The Jerusalem property in 1920 on which the ASOR School was later constructed.

The view to the Old City from the ASOR property in 1920.

Palestine's unstable political situation at the beginning of the twentieth century — with the emergence of Arab nationalism clashing with Zionism and signaling the collapse of the Ottoman Empire — made significant progress for the Jerusalem School difficult. The political instability, lack of a permanent facility, and annual rotation of directors meant that a program of activities along the lines established by Torrey and his successors was the correct and most stable course for the school. ASOR's first major field project in the years prior to World War I was the expedition to Samaria supported by funds raised by Episcopal Minister James B. Nies. Excavations were led in 1908 by Gottlieb Schumacher, and in 1909–1910 by George A. Reisner, Clarence S. Fisher, and David G. Lyon. The report of this project, delayed by the War, appeared in 1924.

The Reverend James B. Nies, Ph.D. 1856–1922

During those years, the Jerusalem school was governed in the United States by a managing committee. Reports on the school's activities and research were given at special meetings or at ASOR meetings held in conjunction with the annual meeting of the SBL or AIA. To all intents and purposes, the "American School of Oriental Study and Research in Palestine" was the Jerusalem Institute. In 1907 the Ottoman government recognized it as the "American School of Archae-ology at Jerusalem," and in 1910 the U.S. managing committee changed its official name to "The American School of Oriental Research in Jerusa-lem." With this, the acronym "ASOR" was established. In December 1914, with the onset of World War I, Annual Director James Montgomery closed the School's doors and they remained so until after hostilities ceased.

The War Years

However, efforts on behalf of the School continued in the interim. In 1917 Torrey announced the promise of a gift of $50,000 by Mrs. James B. Nies (the former Jane Dows Orr) to erect a permanent facility on the land that had been purchased in Jerusalem by Robert Harper in 1909. James A. Montgomery of the University of Pennsylvania and the Protestant Episcopal Divinity School, the Jerusalem School's annual director in 1914–1915, became the chairman of ASOR's managing committee in 1918. At its annual meeting that year the committee voted to reopen the Jerusalem school again in 1919. Also at that meeting, W. F. Albright was elected to be Thayer Fellow for 1919–1920. The school reopened in October with William H. Worrell as director. The first issue of the *Bulletin of the American School of Oriental Research (BASOR)*, the journal that was to become the central organ of scholarly communication for ASOR, also appeared in that year. The first volume of the *ASOR Annual*, edited by four former directors of the Jerusalem school, appeared in 1920.

ASOR is Formally Incorporated

In 1921 ASOR was legally incorporated in the U.S. in the District of Columbia and James A. Mongomery of the University of Pennsylvania was named its first President. With the incorporation process the name of the organization was modestly but deliberately altered to signal a major broadening of its mission and intent. Spurred on specifically by the imminent start of another school in Baghdad, this was accomplished by the simple addition of an "s," changing "American School of Oriental Research" to "American Schools of Oriental Research." This important change was suggestive of the expansion of geographical interests and the development of other research institutes which would mark ASOR's progress through the rest of the century. Symbolizing this broad geographical scope of interest was the adoption, in 1923, of ASOR's identifying mark with the Egyptian ankh hieroglyph, the symbol of life, containing within it the Babylonian dinger, the eight-pointed star formed by four cuneiform wedges, signifying deity.

The original ASOR seal.

Establishing a Permanent Home in Jerusalem
The W. F. Albright Era

William Foxwell Albright was appointed as ASOR's first long-term director in Jerusalem in 1920, serving until 1929, and then again from 1933 to 1936. Albright's first task involved the building of a new facility with monies from the Nies bequest on the land purchased in 1909. Using an architectural plan acquired as the winning entry in a contest among students in the Yale School of Architecture, the structure took shape in several phases. Builder Elias T. Gelat first completed the Annual Professor's building in 1924, then the main building shortly after, and finally the Director's house in 1931. A proposed fourth building unit to complete the quadrangle was never constructed. With comfortable housing for a Director and Annual Professor, and with ten more rooms for students and visiting scholars, the stage was set for a major increase of participation and activity.

Dedicatory plaque commemorating the visionary efforts of Joseph Henry Thayer installed at the Jerusalem school entrance after its completion.
(POS)

An ASOR Mosaic: A Centennial History of the American Schools of Oriental Research

Builder Elias T. Gelat overseeing construction work in the early 1920s.

The front of the building and left wing nearing completion.

The rear of the building with unfinished right wing in foreground.

Under Albright's leadership archaeological and other activities expanded and the school's future was secured in a way that had not been possible before. In 1922 he led fellows at the school in excavations at Tell el-Fûl, just north of Jerusalem, and in 1923 he worked at the four mounds of Malhah, to Jerusalem's southwest. One of the senior fellows at the School at this time was Melvin Grove Kyle, President of Xenia Theological Seminary (later Pittsburgh Theological Seminary). A friendship developed and Kyle was able to raise funds to pay for another modest excavation project. Kyle and Albright chose the site of Tell Beit Mirsim and excavations were pursued in four seasons between 1926 and 1932. Due to Albright's scholarly aptitudes, this project became one of the most significant excavations of the period, and established Albright as one of its leading archaeologists. The final reports, published as *ASOR Annuals*, set new standards for the discipline, especially with respect to ceramic chronology.

Tell Beit Mirsim staff in 1932: Standing (left to right) William Gad (surveyor), Cyrus Gordon (ASOR Baghdad), Henry Detweiler (architect), John Bright (Union Seminary), W.F. Stinespring (Yale University), Rev. Eugene Liggit (Pittsburgh-Xenia Seminary), Rev. Vernon Broyles (Union Seminary), Aage Schmidt (Danish Shiloh Expedition); Front row (left to right) James L. Kelso (Pittsburgh-Xenia Seminary), W. F. Albright (John Hopkins University), Melvin G. Kyle (Pittsburgh-Xenia Seminary), Nelson Glueck (ASOR).

Albright left the Jerusalem School in July 1929 to assume the post of W. W. Spence Professor of Semitic Languages at Johns Hopkins University in Baltimore. While his departure signaled a great loss for the Jerusalem Institute, what he left behind was a well founded and firmly rooted establishment, represented not only in the stones and mortar of the new building but also in the traditions of high scholarship and academic prestige that he pioneered.

W. F. Albright at his desk at Johns Hopkins ca. 1958.

The completed Jerusalem School ca. 1930.

Nuzi. View from the North 1928–29.

The Baghdad School is Founded

During this era ASOR also extended its horizons to Mesopotamia where a Baghdad School, originally called the American School of Mesopotamian Archaeology, officially opened offices in Baghdad in 1923. This was the first American academic institution in the city; and it was housed in a space provided by the American consulate. The Baghdad School, although not a full-fledged institute, had an outstanding library, and from its inception provided an important base from which researchers conducted field surveys and on-site examination of the most important sites in Mesopotamia. Among the best-known excavations conducted from the school were the ASOR-Harvard excavations at Nuzi, lead by Edward Chiera and Robert Pfeiffer from 1925 to 1931. Other noteworthy excavations included Tell Billa, Tepe Gawra, Tarkhalan, and Tel Oman. The Baghdad School's first publication, Edward Chiera's The Joint Expedition with the Iraq Museum at Nuzi, appeared in 1927.

Tablet from Nuzi, showing a map of the city.

George A. Barton was appointed first director of the Baghdad School at its founding in 1921 with offices at that time in the U.S. Barton, a professor at Bryn Mawr College and the University of Pennsylvania, was among the early leaders of ASOR, serving as its third director in Jerusalem in 1902–1903.

The cover plate from Barton's A Year's Wandering in the Holy Land published in 1904 and based on his experiences as the Jerusalem School Director.

A First Endowment Fund

In December 1929 at the Annual Meeting of the Trustees and Corporation, a momentous announcement was made that both encouraged and challenged the ASOR leadership. This was in the form of a half million dollar pledge from the Rockefeller Foundation, half of which was offered as a challenge that ASOR was to match dollar for dollar to build its endowment. The challenge was to continue for a seven year period during which time the outright portion would be provided in annual increments for operations. Faced with this opportunity ASOR's academic managing committee was accordingly reorganized. Henceforth an enlarged Executive Committee would include non-academic "men of affairs" to provide help to establish its financial base.

Over the following years, the Rockefeller operations subsidy formed a major component in annual budgets. However, the challenge portion, having been received in the vanguard of the Depression era, was not fully satisfied. By 1936, as the end of the challenge period approached, only $65,000 had been raised. With Rockefeller additions, the endowment was $130,000. At that juncture the Rockefeller foundation generously revised terms for the distribution of the remaining $185,000, extending the term of contributions through 1939, offering $35,000 as outright support during those years, and agreeing to match two for one all endowment dollars raised to the limit of the remaining $150,000. A rigorous campaign was conducted in the ensuing years. In the Thirty Eighth Annual Report of the President presented by Millar Burrows in November 1940 the successful completion of the Endowment Campaign was announced. Nelson Glueck was specially cited for his strenuous efforts in making this come to pass. The Annual Financial Report of June 30 that year showed the General Endowment Fund to be $319,861.89.

Albright's place in Jerusalem in 1929 was taken by Chester C. McCown, a Dean at the Pacific School of Religion in Berkeley, who, it was hoped, would provide another period of long-term leadership. However, he returned to the U.S. after two years and Millar Burrows of Yale University was appointed Annual Director for 1931–1932. A remark made by Burrows that year provides insight into the period between the world wars and is remarkably relevant. Noting the dearth of American archaeologists and the plethora of archaeological activities in Palestine, he observed that most of the funding was American, but that most of the leadership of excavations was non-American, and asserted that chief among ASOR's goals should be to raise a cadre of "young Americans who would like to take up the fascinating work."

Millar Burrows (right) with Nusrallah in front of the Jerusalem School, July 30, 1936.

A Second Long-Term Director — Nelson Glueck

A major figure to emerge during the 1930s was Nelson Glueck, explorer *par excellence*. Trained in biblical studies at Jena in Germany, Glueck came under the influence of Albright in the late 1920s while digging at Tell Beit Mirsim. There he learned the essentials of stratigraphic archaeology and the basis of ceramic typology. Glueck succeeded Millar Burrows as Annual Director for 1932–1933. Then, for the next three years, Albright arranged to split his own yearly activities spending half time at Johns Hopkins and the other half once more serving as director in Jerusalem. In 1936 Glueck returned to the Jerusalem post, which he held until 1940 and again — after a one year leave in the U.S. — from 1942 to 1947. Glueck's major contribution to work in the region involved the extensive explorations in Transjordan and the Negev desert, which he conducted while serving as the School's Director. As a result of this enterprise he became fascinated with the history and material culture of the Nabateans.

(left to right) Nelson Glueck, Jerusalem School Director with Sir Flinders Petrie, Director of the British School of Archaeology in Egypt, and P.L.O. Guy, Director of the British School of Archaeology in Palestine, July 1937. (NG)

Nelson and Helen Glueck at the Jerusalem School in 1937. The Gluecks were married on March 26, 1931. As reported by W.F. Albright, during the previous summer at Tell Beit Mirsin Nelson had sworn to marry the first girl he met after returning to Cincinnati in order not to become "as crusty a character as an old bachelor who was known to both of us." (NG)
(See L. G. Running and D. N. Freedman *William Foxwell Albright, A Twentieth Century Genius* — New York: Morgan, 1975, p. 423.)

Nelson Glueck (right) with Yusef Musa of Siloam at the Khan by Solomon's Pools, July 1936.

During the 1940–1941 hiatus in Glueck's tenure, Clarence S. Fisher assumed responsibilities as Acting Director at the School. Fisher, trained as an architect at the University of Pennsylvania, had participated in virtually every American excavation conducted during the century, beginning at Samaria in 1908 and including the major projects at Beth-shan, Megiddo, Jerash and Beth-Shemesh. He was a much lauded mentor in fieldwork methods for Albright, Glueck and many others. It was Fisher, who in 1939, recruited Omar Jibrin to service on the staff. From 1925 until his death in 1941 Fisher was professor of archaeology at the School in Jerusalem.

(left to right) Thayer Fellow Avraham Bergman (Biran); Professor of Archaeology, Clarence S. Fisher; Director, Nelson Glueck; and ASOR President Millar Burrows on tour in the summer of 1936. (NG)

Activities in Mesopotamia

From the late 1920s the Baghdad school continued to attract a series of distinguished scholars as annual professors. Notable among those who worked out of Baghdad through to the 1960s were Ephraim Speiser (1926–1927, 1931–1932), Nelson Glueck (1933–1934, 1942–1946), Samuel Noah Kramer (1946–1947), Thorkild Jacobsen (1953–1954, 1968–1969), Robert McCormack Adams (1968–1969), Albrecht Goetze (1955–1956), and McGuire Gibson (1969–1970). From 1947 to 1956 Goetze served as director of the school; among his most significant achievements was the founding of the *Journal of Cuneiform Studies* in 1947.

E.F. Speiser (1902–1965)

Journal of Cuneiform Studies Volume 1, Number 1 (1947).

ASOR: A History of the American Schools of Oriental Research by Eric M. Meyers and Joe D. Seger

The Middle East Scene after World War II *

During the years of World War II programs at the Jerusalem School were put on hold as travel by professors and students was not possible. Then the aftermath of the war signaled major upheavals in the politics of the Middle East. In 1948, the end of the British Mandate saw the establishment of the State of Israel and the Hashemite Kingdom of Jordan. Just after World War II had ended in 1946, the Jerusalem School, still under Glueck's leadership, had attempted to resumed more normal activities, but the rising tensions made this difficult. Later that year Glueck retired to Cincinnati to take up reponsibilities as President of Hebrew Union College where he had held a faculty post since 1928.

Nelson Glueck June 4, 1900–February 12, 1971.

> *While Nelson Glueck had conducted his surveys during his service as director of the Jerusalem School, he sharpened his expertise in Nabatean studies further during the years from 1952–1964, while President at HUC in Cincinnati. One of his major accomplishments as HUC's chief administrator was the building of a new school campus in Jerusalem. This opened in 1963 with an archaeological component he envisioned as the successor to ASOR's Jerusalem School, which had been cut off from Israel as a result of the 1948 War of Independence.*

*Editor's Note: During the Post World War II era, from 1946 into the early 1970s, the histories of ASOR and of its Jerusalem School, which becomes the W. F. Albright Institute, are intimately intertwined. The editor and authors of the ASOR and AIAR histories in this volume have worked deliberately to minimize redundancies in reporting on these overlapping years while preserving a coherent story line for each section. Readers will of course find the fullest picture by reviewing both.

The original building of the Nelson Glueck School of Biblical Archaeology at 13 King David Street, Jerusalem. (VBA)

The irony of the situation cannot be overstated. Glueck had explored the territories that largely became part of the Kingdom of Jordan. Now he was president of a theological school for training American Reform rabbis. He founded an archaeological school in Israeli Jerusalem after 1948 in order to provide for continuing American involvement in archaeological work in Israel. Thus it happened that following the 1967 war and the reunification of Jerusalem, there were two major American institutes in the city devoted to archaeological work, ASOR's Jerusalem school and the Hebrew Union College Biblical and Archaeological School (HUCBAS), later to be renamed the Nelson Glueck School of Biblical Archaeology.

The Jerusalem School and the Dead Sea Scrolls

The Jerusalem directorship for 1947–1948 was assumed by Millar Burrows, who was at that time also serving his fourteenth and final year as President of ASOR. Burrows attempted to reinstate a full program. However, continuing tensions caused two senior appointees to abort their terms. Nonetheless three fellows, including John Trever and William H. Brownlee, remained with him. It was Trever, left in charge while Burrows was away on an official visit to the Baghdad School during the winter, who first received and recognized the antiquity of the Dead Sea Scroll manuscripts. These were brought to the school by Father Butros Sowmi, a representative of the Syrian Archbishop Mar Athanasius Yeshue Samuel. Trever had the foresight to photograph the manuscripts, a few prints of which were then sent to Albright at Johns Hopkins for further authentication. Albright's immediate response was received in Jerusalem on March 15, 1948.

> *My heartiest congratulations on the greatest manuscript discovery of modern times! There is no doubt in my mind that the script is more archaic than that of the Nash Papyrus. I should prefer a date around 100 B.C. ... What an absolutely incredible find! And there can happily not be the slightest doubt in the world about genuineness of the manuscript.* BA 11 (1948) p. 55.

(See also the AIAR history section and KING pp. 113–118 for further discussion of ASOR's involvement with the Dead Sea Scrolls research.)

ASOR: A History of the American Schools of Oriental Research by Eric M. Meyers and Joe D. Seger

The Isaiah Scroll (DSIa) on display at Duke University Chapel, 1950. (EMM)

Millar Burrows with ASOR vehicle in Jerusalem, July 1936.

The manuscript of IQpHab, the Habakkuk Commentary, open to columns x and xi. IQpHab was one of the scrolls acquired by the Syrian Orthodox Metropolititan of St. Mark's Monastery in Jerusalem and photographed by John Trever in February 1948. Along with IQIs^a, the St. Mark's Isaiah manuscript, the Habakkuk Commentary was the first scroll to be published in 1950. See The Dead Sea Scrolls of St. Mark's Monastery, Vol. I, edited by Millar Burrows, John C. Trever and William H. Brownlee, ASOR, New Haven.

Mar Athanasius Samuel, Archbishop of the Syrian Orthodox Church, Jerusalem, presenting an exhibition of the original scrolls identified by ASOR scholars, Duke University Chapel, 1950. (EMM)

John C. Trever with photos of the Isaiah Scroll and Qumran artifacts.

The political and military situation in Jerusalem deteriorated dramatically in 1948 and the School's position near the front lines of the conflict made its situation precarious. No appointments were made for 1948–49 except for that of the Annual Director Ovid R. Sellers. He arrived in the summer and with consummate bravery worked hard to maintain the School premises during the ensuing months of conflict. In July 1948 much of the building was rented by the United States consulate as a headquarters for services to Arab Jerusalem. It also served to house war refugees. The consulate continued to use the building until April, 1951.

The Period of Hashemite Control 1949–1967

In 1949, Carl H. Kraeling of the University of Chicago succeeded Millar Burrows as ASOR President. In the following year he was appointed Director of the University's Oriental Institute. During his career Kraeling made significant contributions to the excavation and publication of the major classical period sites of Gerasa (Jerash) in Jordan, and Dura Europos in Syria. His service as ASOR President during the critical years from 1949 to 1954 was lauded by W. F. Albright for his ability to "take a neutral position of political and other critical issues".

(BASOR 198 [1970] 6)

Kraeling was succeeded in 1955 by A. Henry Detweiler of Cornell University who served as President for ten years. Detweiler was an architect with broad interests and mainly a classical period scholar who worked with many ASOR affiliated projects in Palestine and Mesopotamia in the 1930s and 1940s. In 1948 his *A Manual of Archaeological Surveying* was published by ASOR. In 1958, he assisted George M. A. Hanfmann of Harvard in launching the long-term joint expedition to Sardis, in Turkey. These were vital years which saw ASOR field activities in the Middle East expand and grow, putting Detweiler's considerable administrative skills to full test. In 1966 Detweiler was appointed by ASOR as a Life Trustee and, until his death in 1970, he continued to participate actively on the ASOR Board.

The conclusion of hostilities in 1948 left the Jerusalem School within the boundaries of the city under Jordanian control, and cut off from continuing direct contact with scholars and activities in the new state of Israel to the west. Annual Director James L. Kelso was joined by a few appointees at the school that year and a few new projects were initiated. Most notable were those by Annual Professor Kenneth W. Clark and Fellow Howard Kee who photographed Greek and Armenian manuscripts in

Jerusalem and at St. Catherine's Monastery in Sinai, and the excavation work by Kelso at sites near Jericho in support of United Nations relief efforts. During this and following years the annual directors and officers of ASOR also concentrated on plant repairs and on making improvements in the building's furnishings. Annual trips to sites in Syria, Turkey, Lebanon and Iraq were also resumed as were visits to sites throughout Jordan and West Bank areas as part of the regular school "curriculum." Routinely these included Petra as well as Tell Dothan north of Samaria where Wheaton College conducted work.

From 1950 on the pace of archaeological activity from the school increased steadily. Between 1950 and 1967 ASOR sponsored, co-sponsored or supported projects at Tulul el-'Alayiq, Dhiban, Tell es-Sultan, Khirbet Qumran, Bethel, the Buqe'ah, Petra, el-Jib, Shechem, Beth-Zur, Pella, Ghassul, Araq el-Emir, Ta'anach, Wadi edh-Daliyeh, Dhahr Mirzbaneh, Ai, Tell er-Rumeith, Tell es-Saidiyeh, Bab edh-Dhra' and even on the grounds of the school itself. Oleg Grabar also conducted work at various Islamic sites in Syria. Even another brief flare up of Middle East politics during the Suez Crisis in 1956 did not interrupt the lively growth of the school's program of activity for long.

During these years Dead Sea Scrolls research also continued with at least several school appointees each year attached to the project. As the excavations by Pére de Vaux at Khirbet Qumran were underway, both formal and clandestine explorations of the region continued, and a steady stream of manuscript fragments accumulated. Many derived from an active antiquities market. ASOR Trustee Elizabeth Hay Bechtel assisted in providing funds for purchase of many of these materials, which were given to the Palestine Archaeological Museum (the Rockefeller Museum).

Elizabeth Bechtel with Yusef Saad, the last curator of the Palestine Archaeological Museum which became the Rockefeller Museum in 1947.

Dead Sea Scrolls research was to occupy many scholars at the Jerusalem School through to the end of the century. Prominent among these is John Strugnell of Harvard University seen here studying the ancient text 4Q394 as an Albright Institute National Endowment for the Humanities Fellow in 1981–82.

Staffs of the Shechem and El Jib excavations with King Hussein of Jordan and other dignitaries in 1960. H.R.H. Hussein in center. To the right Vivian and Robert Bull, Lee Ellenberger, person uk, John McKenzie, Asia Hallaby, Clint Morrison, Edward F. Campbell and Dan P. Cole. To the left person uk, Nancy Lapp, person uk, Awni Dajani (Director of Antiquities of Jordan), Joseph Callaway, Paul Lapp, Rafiq Dajani, James Ross, Jack Irwin, person uk, person uk. (NL)

(left to right) Joseph Callaway and G. Ernest Wright with Kathleen Kenyon at excavations in Jerusalem in 1964. (JDS)

A New Generation of Scholars and New Digging Methods

From the late 1950s, as international air travel improved, American participants on excavation teams increased, including growing contingents of new and younger scholars and graduate students. Residence facilities in the school hostel became increasingly stressed, especially through the spring and summer dig seasons. Utilization of digging equipment managed by the school, and the use of storage space between seasons, likewise became increasingly contentious.

This period saw the appointment in Jerusalem of another long-term director, Paul W. Lapp, who served in the post from 1961 to 1965. A student of Albright at Johns Hopkins, he received his Ph.D. from Harvard under G. Ernest Wright with whom he excavated at Shechem in 1957. In the traditions of his predecessors Lapp, was an energetic field archaeologist. He directed excavations at Araq el-Emir, Tell er-Rumeith, Wadi ed-Daliyeh, Tell el-Ful, Bab edh-Dhra' and Dhahr Mirzbaneh. From 1963–1968 he headed up the major ASOR-Concordia Seminary expedition to Tell Taanach. As was the case with other projects during the early 1960s, and in particular the work at Shechem under George Ernest Wright, and at et-Tell (Ai) led by Joseph Callaway, excavation efforts at Taanach brought together a vigorous young leadership team, and introduced new field methods and recording techniques. This included application of the Wheeler-Kenyon methods of debris analysis that Lawrence Toombs and Joe Callaway, both of whom worked with Kathleen Kenyon at Jericho, had first introduced into American work at Shechem. In 1964 Lapp took a brief leave from his directorship to head up a USAID project to help the Jordanian government develop sites for tourism. When he returned to the school in 1965 it was not as Director but as Professor of Archaeology, a post in which he remained till 1968. During these years the administration of the school was again guided by a series of Annual Directors.

Paul W. Lapp in 1968. Lapp was Director of the school in Jerusalem from 1961–1965 and Professor of Archaeology there until 1968. In that year he returned to the U.S. to assume a position at Pittsburgh Theological Seminary. The following year he laid plans to begin new excavations at the site of Idalion on Cyprus. In 1970 his career ended tragically when he died in a swimming accident off the North coast of Cyprus East of Kyrenia, just as he was about to initiate the Idalion field work.
(NL)

THE
BIBLICAL ARCHAEOLOGIST

Published by
The American Schools of Oriental Research
(Jerusalem and Baghdad)
409 Prospect St., New Haven, Conn.

Vol. I   February, 1938   No. 1

Fig. 1. A Cherub of Raphael, from his Sistine Madonna.

Fig. 2. A Cherub of Biblical Times, supporting the throne of King Hiram of Byblus.

WHAT WERE THE CHERUBIM?

Today we think of a cherub as a tiny winged boy, following the tradition of Renaissance artists (see Fig. 1). This conception was directly borrowed from pictures of Graeco-Roman "loves" or Erotes, familiar to us from the excavations of Pompeii. The actual appearance of the cherubim of the Old Testament was already forgotten before the time of Christ, and Josephus (1st century A.D.) says that "no one can tell what they were like."

The Biblical Archaeologist was inaugurated with G. E. Wright as its editor in 1938. Its first editorial board consisted of W. F. Albright (Johns Hopkins), Millar Burrows (Yale) and E. A. Speiser (University of Pennsylvania). It was to be published quarterly at an initial subscription price of fifty cents per year.

Formal portrait of G. Ernest Wright by Paul Kolby

The G. E. Wright Presidency

In 1965 the ASOR presidency and leadership in the U.S. passed from the hands of A. Henry Detweiler to G. Ernest Wright of Harvard. Wright knew first hand of the pressures being experienced with regard to the use of the facilities in Jerusalem and recognized that these were in many ways becoming inadequate to the needs of appointees. He also observed, with others, the way the school's immediate neighborhood had grown and developed as a busy commercial center, which served to increase its property value. Faced with ASOR's always precarious financial situation, he and the Trustees hit upon an optimal solution: sell the school property and use the proceeds to buy more adequate space in a less developed part of the city, and hopefully pocket some excess for continuing support. An estimated worth of $1,000,000 was determined for the property, and in 1966 Annual Director John Marks was instructed to proceed with negotiations. By early 1967 a good offer was in hand, rental space for two years had been arranged, land to purchase had been identified, and an architect was engaged to prepare plans for a new structure. At the April 1967 meeting of the ASOR Board it was voted to implement the plan and sell the property.

G. Ernest Wright (right) with Lester E. Williams in Jerusalem as staff of the Bethel Excavations in 1934.

The Jerusalem School in its urban setting in the late 1960s.

The plan was never consummated. During 1966–1967 tensions between Israel and its Arab neighbors escalated. By spring 1967 both sides were girding for war. The prospective buyer was finding it difficult to generate the needed money. However, in June Director Marks had a check in his hands and considered the property sold. But people were being hastily evacuated from the city and on Monday June 5 in the late morning shelling in the city commenced. The school was evacuated by everyone except for Omar Jibrin, major-domo and cook, who stayed on by himself to guard the facilities. The hostilities were brief and by June 7 the School's neighborhood and the Old City were in Israeli hands. Avraham Biran, Director of the Israel Department of Antiquities was the first to greet Omar that Wednesday. Biran, a student of Albright, had been Thayer Fellow at the School in 1935–36. Biran reported his visit to William Dever, then serving as Director of the Hebrew Union College Biblical and Archaeological School, and Dever, on authority from President Wright, as was done in 1948, turned the property over to the American Consulate General for their temporary use.

A week later Nelson Glueck arrived in Israel and reached the school, taking official control. Within a few days, on June 16, 1967 William Van Etten Casey, the year's appointee as Annual Director, also arrived and took up formal residence. Casey swiftly determined that the property had not been sold; the check had not been cashed and the buyer had stopped payment. Faced with the confusing circumstances the ASOR Executive Committee decided that a moratorium of a year or more would be needed before further decisions on the future of the Jerusalem school and property could be made.

G. E. Wright on his first visit to Tell Beit Mirsim, seen rising in the background, Spring 1969. (JDS)

Nelson Glueck in Field V at Gezer, April 1968. (JDS)

ASOR and Its Overseas Expansion: The 1967–1978 Transition

One of the major results of the 1967 war was the Arab boycott of all scholars working in Israel, its former or newly-held territory. This effectively meant that archaeologists and Near Eastern specialists in other disciplines had to decide whether to continue to work in Israel. If they had worked in Israel or West Bank areas they could still choose to work in Arab lands, especially in the Hashemite Kingdom of Jordan or in Syria, but could not then continue to work in Israel as well. The war also made any future significant ASOR presence in Iraq doubtful. ASOR's last field project there prior to the war had been in 1963 and the Baghdad operation was already moribund. Accordingly, the ASOR Board of Trustees, headed by G. Ernest Wright, decided that the only way for ASOR scholars to continue working on both sides of the Jordan River was to create separate institutes. At the December 1969 ASOR Annual Meeting both the Board of Trustees and the ASOR Corporation voted in support of such action. In the April 1970 issue of the *ASOR Newsletter* Wright summarized the resolution as follows:

> *ASOR suggests to its Amman, Baghdad, Beirut and Jerusalem Committees that, if they desire, they incorporate themselves as independent institutes in the various national states in the Near East, over which neither the Trustees nor the Officers of ASOR will have any control. These institutes may apply for such grants toward budgets as ASOR can provide, and their individual members may serve in ASOR councils and even control its Executive Committee, but individually they must now make their own decisions and manage their own budgets.*

By the spring of 1970 actions had been taken. The Jerusalem school was incorporated and renamed the W.F. Albright Institute of Archaeological Research (AIAR). A new center was started in Amman, Jordan and incorporated under the name the American Center of Oriental Research (ACOR). Both institutes were dedicated to the continuation of ASOR's historic goals and aims.

In Baghdad during this time politics inhibited continuing activity. Fieldwork in Iraq was resumed only in the 1980s, and the 1991 Gulf War ended that activity as well. However a Baghdad Committee continued to function. Once physical presence in Baghdad was terminated, the annual professorship, supported in part by continuing funds from a bequest by the estate of James B. Nies, was converted to a Mesopotamian fellowship. Today, the Baghdad Committee supervises ASOR's interests in the region and oversees the continuing publication of the *Journal of Cuneiform Studies*.

Expanding Regional Interests in the 1970s

During the tumultuous period in the region between the 1967 War and 1973 Yom Kippur conflict, and in the years immediately following, ASOR's leadership, including successive presidents G. E. Wright, Frank Moore Cross, and Philip J. King, embraced an expanded vision for activities in the Middle East and Eastern Mediterranean region.

(Left to right) AIAR President Philip King, ASOR President Frank Cross, Norma Dever and AIAR Director William Dever in the courtyard of the Albright Institute in June, 1975 on the occasion of the seventy-fifth anniversary of the founding of ASOR.

During this era ASOR entertained the idea of establishing a center in Beirut, one that would focus scholarly attention on Lebanon's special heritage of Phoenician culture and other history. Although the Civil War in Lebanon and ASOR's increased financial responsibilities ultimately precluded undertaking the project, interests in Phoenicia led ASOR scholars to look west to two of Phoenicia's principal colonies, Cyprus and Carthage.

At Carthage, ASOR fulfilled its field objectives from 1975 to 1979 by sponsoring a series of excavations, financed with U.S. federal funds, at Punic and Roman Carthage. During this limited period ASOR supported a new center nearby, the Carthage Research Institute, which served as a base for the excavation and survey work at the site. The western Mediterranean region could not maintain its hold on ASOR's historic constituency, however, which was oriented more to the east, and the Institute closed upon the completion of fieldwork.

Frank Moore Cross in his Harvard study (mid 1980s). Cross became ASOR's sixth president upon the death of Ernest Wright in 1974. A scholar of international acclaim and a member of the team of experts responsible for the editing of the Dead Sea Scrolls, Cross led ASOR through crucial years of the expansion of projects on Cyprus and in Tunisia. He chaired the public sessions in Jerusalem in 1975 that celebrated ASOR's Seventy-Fifth Anniversary.

Philip J. King working in his room at AIAR (1988). King was elected to replace Frank Cross in 1976 when Cross resigned to devote more time to his scholarship. King served for two three-year terms through 1982. (POS)

Cyprus, the other important Phoenician center, had attracted ASOR's attention from the early 1970s. President Wright actively encouraged ASOR scholars to engage in fieldwork that would shed further light on Phoenician culture and help to establish a definitive typology of Cypriot ceramics. Accordingly Paul Lapp initiated plans for excavations at ancient Idalion to begin in 1970. His untimely death that summer caused the cancellation of the 1970 season but Wright and two former students, Lawrence Stager and Anita Walker, began excavation work in 1971. Wright's interest in establishing a permanent ASOR facility away from the center of the ancient Near Eastern mainland was greatly stimulated by this Idalion work. Wright died in 1974, but interest in establishing a Cyprus center was carried forward by his successors Frank Cross and Philip King. By 1978 formal steps to establish the Cyprus American Archaeological Research Institute (CAARI) in Nicosia had been taken.

Task Force Goals

I. To initiate, encourage and support research into, and public understanding of, the peoples and cultures of the Near East and their wider spheres of interaction, from earliest times to the modern period, especially archaeologically informed projects which are integrative and interdisciplinary.

II. To improve the existing institutes in Jerusalem and Amman, and to continue developing the institute in Nicosia, so as to enhance their usefulness in the service of Goal I, as centers for historical research in its broadest sense.

III. To respond to the changing as well as growing needs of Near Eastern peoples and governments for assistance in the conservation and disciplined study of their cultural heritage.

IV. To explore the possibilities of ASOR's expanding its research work to countries within ASOR's range of interest where there is no ASOR-associated institute.

V. To develop means of responding more effectively to the diverse interests of ASOR's membership, and to foster greater communication and participation throughout the organization.

VI. To improve and accelerate the dissemination of the results of scholarly research, including that which serves the emphases in Goal I.

VII. To develop and sustain a program for communicating to the general public the results and significance of research within ASOR's fields of interest, including influencing the educational system at all levels to expand attention to the roots of the human heritage that lie in the ancient Near East.

The report also included a series of suggested actions for implementation of the respective goals. Among these, in reference to Goal V, was a mandate immediately to establish a Presidential Search Committee. While president King's term of office would run through June 1982, this recommendation by the committee recognized that the report embraced an agenda for ASOR that would need also to be pursued under the next administration. While some of the report's suggestions were only partly or never implemented, it nonetheless provided substantive guidance for ASOR's future course, not only for immediate five year period it envisioned, but throughout the rest of the century.

Some Recommendations for Implementation

A. in reference to Goal I — to expand the mandate for CAP to cover projects other than purely field-related ones and to change its name to the Committee on Research Projects (CORP);

B. for Goal II — to develop legal statements clarifying and updating the relationship of ASOR with the overseas centers;

C. for Goal III — to collaborate in efforts to educate and provide field training for host country students;

D. for Goal V — to define clearly with respect to fees, rights and benefits, the forms of memberships for both corporate and individual members;

E. for Goal VI — to continue and enhance the work of COP and to encourage the Program Committee to develop and schedule forums for ASOR with the annual meetings of SBL/AAR, AOS, and AIA; and

F. for goal VII — to initiate and activate a Committee on Public Information with a broad mandate for public relations and outreach education work.

Fund Raising Efforts in the 1980s

By the end of the 1970s opportunities for support of overseas projects from the U.S. government counterpart and Smithsonian PL 480 fund programs for the Middle East drew to a close. By this time ASOR's financial resources were severely stressed and its ability to provide direct support to the overseas centers was rapidly diminishing. Accordingly ASOR and each of the respective centers had to mobilize to seek new fund sources for program and maintenance support.

In 1979 a "Friends of Near East Archaeology" initiative was put forward by President King as a first step in a long term ASOR financial development program. In that year more than one hundred individuals contributed a total of over $10,000 in much needed unrestricted operating funds. Also in 1979, ASOR was successful in securing a three year National Endowment for the Humanities fellowship award in the amount of $120,000. This was for support of research activity by several scholars each year at the overseas institutes. The first to utilize these funds in 1980–81 were James Flanagan, Robert Gordeon, Gary Rollefson and David Graf at ACOR in Amman, and Cheryl Exum, Miriam Balmuth, and Robert Bull at AIAR in Jerusalem. These NEH fellowship opportunities were soon expanded to include CAARI, and support of this kind was solicited by ASOR, and renewed by NEH, throughout the 1980s. By the end of the decade, however, efforts to continue these and other fellowship supports were taken over directly by the respective centers for themselves. During this same period a fellowship in the name of W. F. Albright was initiated from ASOR's own funds. This could be used by recipients for travel and research work at any of the affiliated centers.

In late January 1980, in concert with the work of the Presidential Task Force, President King and Executive Director Beale, also submitted a proposal to the NEH for a $2,520,000 Challenge Grant the objectives of which were

> *to strengthen the financial base and resources for ASOR's present programs; to increase ASOR's capacity to serve and inform a broader public; and to enable ASOR to develop long-range fund-raising capabilities with which to meet future demands for expansion.*
>
> (NEH Proposal Abstract January 30, 1980)

More specifically these grant monies were designated to support its publications program; to help increase the endowments for each of the overseas institutes; and to help purchase land and build new facilities for the Amman, Jordan center. The grant application was successful, but the total award, announced by the NEH December 15, 1980, was reduced to $800,000, including $200,000 in NEH monies to match 1 for 3, hence $600,000 to be raised by ASOR. The grant term, which extended to June 30, 1984, was retroactive back to October 1, 1979 so monies already contributed by Friends of Near East Archaeology and from other sources since that date gave an initial impetus to the program. Supporting this grant's funding objectives was also a major campaign for capital support that had been launched by the ACOR trustees in January 1980.

The success of this initial Challenge Grant through 1984 lead to the submission in early 1986 of a follow up application by President Jim Sauer and Executive Director Mitchell Rothman. This resulted in a second award from NEH in December 1986 totaling $2,076,752, the matching portion of $1,557,564 to be raised by ASOR within the period December 1, 1985 to July 31, 1990. The purposes and goals itemized in this second grant were broadly the same as those for the first one, with significant portions targeted for the support of ACOR's building program and for the establishment of an independent endowment fund for the Albright Institute. Deliberate efforts by ASOR trustees and by the Boards of the respective centers produced some very positive results and the main portion of the needed funds were realized. But at the transition of officers and administrations during the final years of the grant period management difficulties and disputes arose and the full matching objective was not reached.

The Administration of James A. Sauer 1982–88

President King had acted promptly on the recommendation of the Planning Committee to establish a Presidential Search Committee, appointing Joy Ungerleider Mayerson as committee chair. Committee work resulted in the election of James A. Sauer, then Director of ACOR in Amman. Sauer, as ASOR's eighth president, took up responsibilities in July 1982 and moved aggressively to maintain the momentum in programming and development that had been initiated by President King and the Planning Committee. Not only did he press forward with a continuing program of NEH grants for excavation project assistance, fellowships and challenge supports, but he also forged formidable alliances with other federal agencies with Middle East interests. Among these were the USIA, USAID and ASHA with which he had established contacts during his tenure as the Director of ACOR.

As he inaugurated his term as ASOR President, Sauer also assumed a professional post at the University of Pennsylvania, and among other early initiatives of his administration was the move of ASOR offices from Cambridge to Philadelphia. This followed the pattern established by his immediate predecessors. From the presidency of Millar Burrows in the 1940s ASOR offices had been in New Haven under the management of Gladys R. Walton and remained there for several years after her retirement in 1963. Then, at the start of his term as president in 1966, G. E. Wright made his office at the Harvard Semitic Museum the ASOR headquarters. Soon after, in August, 1967, ASOR's publications activities were consolidated nearby in Cambridge at 625 Mount Auburn Street, with Mrs. Dorothea Willcomb as Executive Secretary. But already by early 1968 these offices had been moved to 126 Inman Street under the direction of Thomas D. Newman, newly appointed Administrative Director. The Inman Street office continued in use during the terms of presidents Cross and King. Thomas Newman remained Administrative Director until 1977. Then, after a brief period when Paul Misner served as Assistant to President King, Thomas Beale became Executive Director in 1979. For much of this period the Cambridge office was personified by Helen Estey who, through her personal and professional skills, contributed formidably to the advancement of ASOR's goals.

ASOR President James A. Sauer (right) with Trustee Elizabeth Moynihan in front of the new ASOR administration office in Philadelphia in 1983.

Sauer's experiences at ACOR were carried along as he established the Philadelphia offices. He initially hoped to create a kind of U.S. resident institute on the overseas models. He believed that this would allow for scholar exchanges and research for which the University of Pennsylvania provided an apt environment. This prompted the selection in 1982 of a facility at 4243 Spruce Street for the administrative center. At the same time Sauer assembled a new staff including Mitchel Rothman as Executive Director, Susan Wing as Assistant to the Treasurer, and Cynthia Eisemann as Development Officer. The early success of initiatives by this team were highlighted by the 1984 announcement of a special NEH award of $200,000 to fund the operation of Summer Institutes in Near East Archaeology by ASOR in cooperation with the University Museum and the University of Pennsylvania. The ASOR headquarters was to be used as the administrative base. The first seminar program "The Ancient Near East as the Cradle of Civilization" was conducted between June 3 and July 12, 1985 led by David O'Connor, McGuire Gibson, Paul Zimansky, William Dever and Jim Sauer with nineteen participants. A second successful program "An Archaeological History of Palestine" led by Gary Rollefson, Renata Holod, William Dever and Jim Sauer, was held in 1986 and involved twenty other scholars.

ASOR: A History of the American Schools of Oriental Research by Eric M. Meyers and Joe D. Seger

ASOR/NEH Seminar Group at the University of Pennsylvania in 1986. (standing left to right) W. G. Dever, J. A. Sauer, J. M. Bullard, C. L. Waltz, G. Verbrugghe, W. R. McFadden, R. Holod, J.C. Moyer, S. L. McKenzie, G. Oller, K.V. Mull, J.R. Spencer, A. Lichtenstein, O.A. Soltes, J. Peterson, M. Martin. (seated left to right) T. Longman, J. M. Russell, B. Vivolta, L.L. Bronner, R. S. Frick, L. Greenspoon, G. O. Rollefson, S. Epstein.

During his term Sauer also paid special attention to increasing membership supports. To build the endowment, he forged a special initiative to establish Life Memberships through a one-time contribution of $1000. By August 1983 some thirty-four individuals had joined this support group and the number continued to grow throughout his term. At the same time he also continued Phil King's program to increase the number of institutions participating as Corporation Members and in this he was likewise very successful. In the spring of 1982 the Corporation was 143 strong and by the May 7, 1984 meeting of the trustees the total of institutional members had risen to 162. By July 1986 it was 171, which represents the all-time high for participation in Corporation membership.

Elizabeth Moynihan becomes ASOR's First Board Chair

Notable also from the outset of Sauer's term was the involvement of trustee Elizabeth Moynihan. Moynihan became an ASOR trustee in 1980. Her early involvement included pursuit of initiatives to establish CAORC (the Council of American Overseas Research Centers), an organization for advocacy of the interests of America's foreign research institutes. These efforts were fully supported by President King and all the officers of ASOR, AIAR, ACOR and CAARI. In 1981, in cooperation with Robert McCormick Adams, trustee and member of the ASOR Planning Task Force, a spring meeting was arranged at the Smithsonian Institution for all the ASOR center constituents, principals of the American Academy at Rome, the American School of Classical Studies in Athens and the American Research Center in Egypt, along with others from more recently formed centers. This planning effort resulted in the chartering of CAORC within the umbrella of the Smithsonian Institution. Initially, from 1982–1985 the Smithsonian Institute Office of Fellowships and Grants, led by Francine Berkowitz, served as the CAORC secretariat. In 1986 Mary Ellen Lane was appointed as Executive Director and since then CAORC, under her leadership, has continued its work on behalf of its member institutes abroad with increasingly positive results. These and other initiatives by Moynihan in support of ASOR development activities lead to her appointment as ASOR's first Chairman of the Board in the summer of 1984. The establishment of this new office had been recommended by President King as part of the Task Force discussions at the close of his term.

With Sauer's election in 1982 came also a transition in other major officers within ASOR. Eric Meyers succeeded Noel Freedman as First Vice President (for Publications) and William Dever succeeded Edward Campbell as Second Vice President (for Archaeological Policy). They held these offices to the close of the decade, each carrying forward and augmenting the mandates of their respective orbits of responsibility.

Elizabeth Moynihan, ASOR's first Chair of the Board of Trustees 1984–1986.

(left to right) ASOR officers William Dever, James Sauer and Eric Meyers in 1984 at the World Congress of Biblical Archaeology in Jerusalem.

In 1979 Robert McCormick Adams co-edited a report document *Corners of a Foreign Field: Discussions about American Overseas Advanced Research Centers in the Humanities and Social Sciences*. This report helped significantly to encourage the formation of CAORC. In 1984 Adams left his post as Provost of the University of Chicago to succeeded S. Dillon Ripley as Secretary of the Smithsonian Institution, a position he held till 1994.

COP — The Committee on Publications

As First Vice President and Chairman of COP, Eric Meyers assumed responsibility for one of ASOR's most dynamic and demanding service enterprises. Through the brilliant and energetic oversight of David Noel Freedman through the late 1970s ASOR's publications program had grown almost exponentially. In 1974 as editor of *BASOR*, Freedman had instituted the first format change in its over fifty year life (*BASOR* 215) and with the March 1976 issue of *Biblical Archaeologist* that publication also appeared in a larger and more elegant form. In addition to managing, and even for a brief time editing, the *Journal of Cuneiform Studies*, Freedman edited and produced a regular schedule of volumes in the *ASOR Annual* series, and promoted a number of more general works, including especially several volumes of the *Biblical Archaeology Reader*. Early in Freedman's term, ASOR publications were moved to the new Center for Scholarly Publishing and Services (later Scholars Press) at the University of Montana in Missoula, MT. Working with Scholars Press at the University of Montana at that time was James Flanagan, who also served as editor of the *ASOR Newsletter*. Flanagan would subsequently succeed Eric Meyers as Vice President and COP Chairman.

Freedman was aware that his ambitious publications agenda posed challenges and difficulties for ASOR. He viewed the enterprise as a partner to the work going on in the field, in the laboratory and at the scholar's desk. In a report to the Trustees in April 1976 he emphasized two objectives:

> *first, to achieve self-support so that the entire publications program can fund its operations out of its income; and second, to go beyond that and contribute significantly to those equally important activities of ASOR which are not self-supporting and which require continued assistance.*
> (Board of Trustees Minutes, April 1976)

The first of these objectives still challenges the work of COP to this day.

Eric Meyers assumed the mantle of publications work and accepted its responsibilities with great vigor. During the last half of Freedman's term, arrangements with the Center for Scholarly Publishing in Montana proved unsatisfactory, and in 1978 ASOR withdrew from its partnership in the Scholars Press enterprise and the publications office was moved to Ann Arbor, Michigan. With the move to Philadelphia in 1982 the subscription and fulfilment services also moved there. Meyers, at the same time, had negotiated for space at Duke University to provide headquarters for management of COP's production activity in Durham, NC.

As well as chairing COP, in 1982 Meyers also became editor of *Biblical Archaeologist*. He continued Freedman's aggressive promotion of the journal and worked deliberately to enhance its appearance through the application of more color and new design features. The 50th anniversary of the magazine was celebrated in the spring of 1987, with the March issue. Volume 50:1 presented a special "Salute to the Founder of BA," George Ernest Wright. Wright had served as BA editor from its beginning in 1937 until 1963. He had worked tirelessly to assure that its scholarship represented the best in the field, and that its appeal would reach beyond the academic community to the wider public. These goals were emulated by his successors Edward Campbell (1963–75), H. Darrell Lance (co-editor with Campbell 1972–75), David Noel Freedman (1976–1982) and Meyers himself (from 1982–1992). In the anniversary issue, Meyers eulogizes Wright as follows:

> *G. Ernest Wright lives on not only in the pages of this magazine and in the legacy of ASOR, he continues to be a central and vital force in biblical archaeology through his students, dozens and dozens of them, including all the current senior officers of ASOR, he was not only a mentor but a dear friend to those of us who were privileged to study with him.*

Meyers continued to serve as Vice President for Publications until 1990 at which time he took office as ASOR's tenth president. He remained *BA* editor continued till 1992.

CAP — The Committee on Archaeological Policy

In 1982 William G. Dever, former Director of the AIAR in Jerusalem and by then well-established at the University of Arizona, became ASOR's Second Vice President for Archaeological Policy succeeding Edward Campbell. Campbell and the CAP committee had worked deliberately to articulate a "Statement of Standards" for ASOR project affiliations and initiated a program of reviews through annual reports and summer in-field visits. In 1977 field and publications projects affiliated with ASOR/CAP numbered twenty. Under Dever's leadership CAP's program of evaluations was pursued vigorously with the issue of timely publication becoming acute for several longer-term excavation teams. At the start of his term Dever also continued as the editor of *BASOR* a position that he had assumed in 1978, and wearing that hat he continued strongly to encourage the early presentation of reports on digs. Throughout the 1980s he remained at the center of the "biblical archaeology" controversy, continuing to press forward his support for the discipline of "Syro-Palestinian Archaeology" as an equal in the dialogue with biblical scholarship. Upon completion of his term in 1988 Dever reported that ASOR affiliated projects had doubled in number to forty.

(left to right) ASOR Second Vice President William G. Dever with President James A. Sauer and AIAR Director Sy Gitin on a tour of Tel Miqne in 1985.

ASOR: A History of the American Schools of Oriental Research by Eric M. Meyers and Joe D. Seger

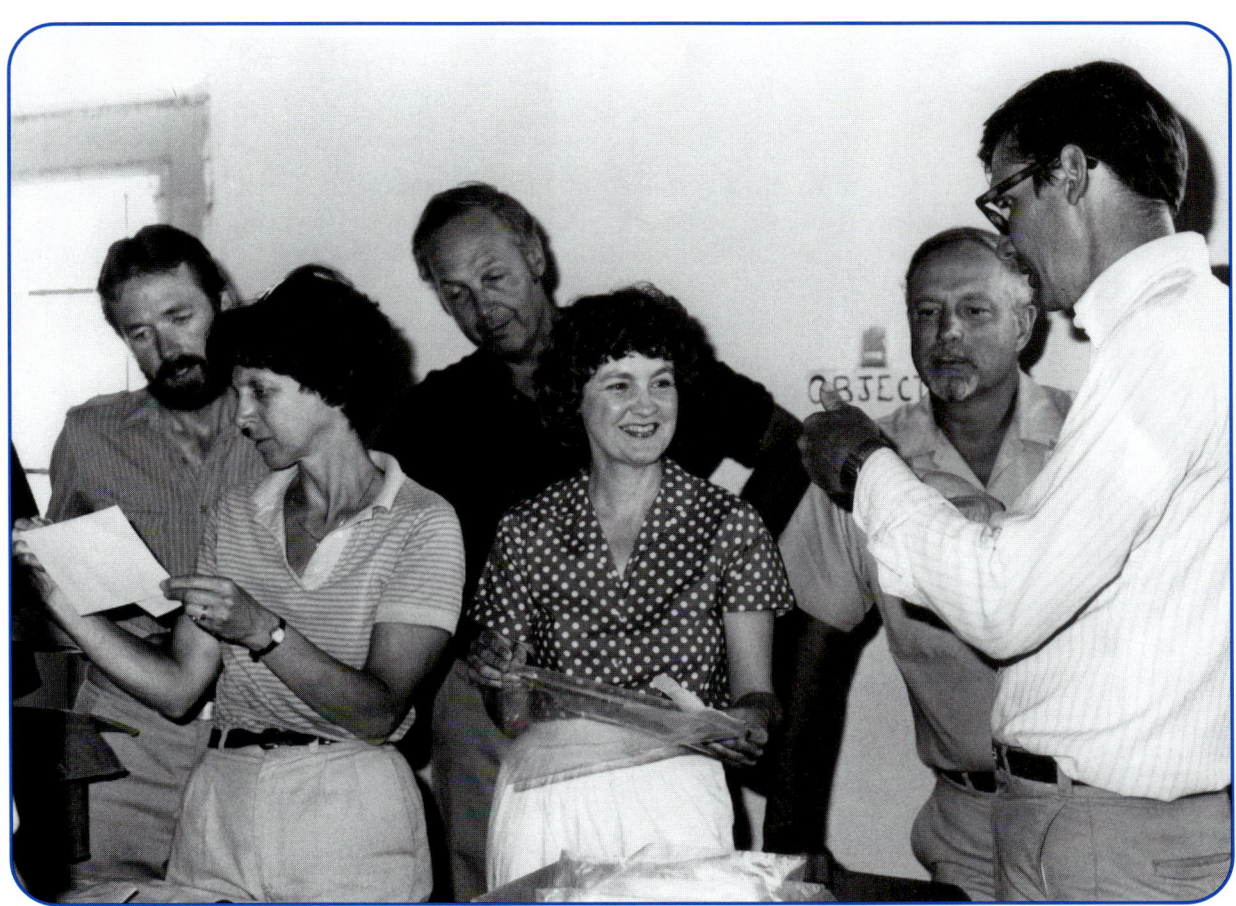

In the summer of 1984 the ASOR CAP tour of Middle East excavations visited 45 Field projects in Israel, Jordan, Syria and Cyprus. At the Tall al-Umeiri base camp, tour members examine the object registration system with Madaba Plains Project Director Lawrence Geraty (left) and Umeiri Registrar E. E. Platt (center). Tour members (left to right) include AIAR Vice President Carol Meyers, ASOR First Vice President Eric Meyers, ASOR Second Vice President William Dever and ASOR President James Sauer.

The Transition in ASOR governance of the late 1980s

The election of Elizabeth Moynihan as the first Chair of the ASOR Board of Trustees in 1984 initiated a new era in ASOR leadership and governance. The Board Chair position was configured to provide leadership in development initiatives and Moynihan had already provided formative help in these efforts. In April 1985 she helped organize a special program to celebrate ASOR's 85th Anniversary in Washington. This was followed in late April and May by a Trustees and Friends Tour of the Middle East. The tour group was led by President Sauer and visited each of the affiliated centers as well as other archaeological sites in North Yemen, Egypt and Syria. In addition to celebrating ASOR's birthday, these 1985 events signaled the start of another three-year fund-raising effort. This was in connection with the second NEH Challenge Grant for which application was made at that time. Announcing the anniversary program, the January, 1985 issue of the *ASOR Newsletter* concluded as follows:

> At 85, ASOR needs to build on its strong past so that it can look forward, as a healthy and vibrant organization, to its 100th anniversary in only fifteen years.

In the early 1980s Jim Sauer served as Chief Archaeologist for the American Foundation for the Study of Man's Wadi al-Jubah Archaeological Project, in the Yemen Arab Republic. Seated on the porch of the Saba School's headquarters in the village of Jubah al Jadidah during the 1982 season, he awaits the start of field work while Epigrapher, Albert Jamme (in foreground) of the Catholic University of America, makes a morning entry in the expedition's log.
(Photo by Stephen Bald)

Jim Sauer with Marilyn Phillips Hodgson, of the American Foundation for the Study of Man, reviewing an expedition report volume at the spring meeting of ASOR Trustees in Washington DC in 1985. (U.S. Senate photo)

Gough Thompson becomes Board Chair

Elizabeth Moynihan was succeeded as Board Chair by Gough W. Thompson, Jr in 1986. Thompson, President and CEO of Cavendish Development Company, headquartered in Princeton, New Jersey, had just completed a four year term as President of the ACOR Board and had been instrumental in developing corporate and foundation support for the building fund program in Amman. He was of course also familiar with Sauer's leadership and initiatives as ACOR director and was accordingly able to immediately affirm and help carry forward the program of ASOR development Sauer already had underway.

Gough W. Thompson, Jr. ASOR Board Chairman 1986–1992.

P. Kyle McCarter, Jr. ASOR President 1988–1990.

McCarter becomes Eighth President

In 1987, as Jim Sauer's term was drawing to a close, a presidential nominating committee was appointed by Chairman Thompson under the leadership of Trustee Shelby White. In March 1988 the committee brought forward a full slate of officers for the new term and by early April their election was confirmed by mail ballot. The name of P. Kyle McCarter, Jr. was presented to succeed Sauer as President. In 1985 McCarter had been appointed to the distinguished post of William Foxwell Albright Professor of Biblical and Ancient Near Eastern Studies at Johns Hopkins University in Baltimore, and at the time of his ASOR election in 1988 he also served there as Associate Dean of Arts and Sciences.

Also elected were Eric M. Meyers for continuing service as First Vice President for Publications and Walter E. Rast, as Second Vice President for Archaeological Policy succeeding William Dever. Rast, Professor of Old Testament and Palestinian Archaeology in the Theology department at Valparaiso University had been President of ACOR from 1979–1982 and since 1984 had been the editor of *BASOR*. George M. Landes, Professor of Old Testament at Union Theological Seminary in New York was elected to continue as Secretary. Landes had already provided excellent service in this position since 1972 and he would continue as Secretary until 1994. His full and deliberate maintenance of the ASOR Board and Corporation minutes for these years provides a solid record of ASOR's fitful pilgrimage from the critical decades of the 1970s into the early 1990s. In 1988 Kevin G. O'Connell, S.J., was also re-elected as Assistant Secretary and Parliamentarian. Finally, W. H. Holden Gibbs, Vice President of the Mercantile Safe Deposit & Trust Company in Baltimore was named Treasurer. Gibbs succeeded Charles U. Harris of Delaplane, Virginia. In 1985 Charles Harris had replaced long term Treasurer Harry W. Fowler of New York City. At this point in the mid-1980s the centrifugal energies and needs of the rapidly developing programs of the overseas centers were bringing an increasing challenge to ASOR's fiscal stability. With the help of Assistant Treasurer Anne Ogilvy, Harris was able to hold the line and maintain balance in ASOR operations throughout his tenure.

The election of McCarter as President and Gibbs as Treasurer coincided with initiatives by Chairman Thompson to move the ASOR headquarters from Philadelphia to Baltimore. There, the Johns Hopkins administration had pledged help in providing office space near its Homewood campus. In July 1988, with financial support from the Mercantile Trust Company, administrative offices were established in The Rotunda, at 711 W. 40th Street in Baltimore. This was adjacent to the Johns Hopkins University Press which by this time was handling production of most of ASOR's publications. Under mandate from the Trustees, President McCarter moved swiftly to assemble a new office staff. Included were Executive Director Susan Foster Krombholz and Administrative Assistant Pam Turner. Additional part time support was provided by Kathryn Gould as Accountant, Debra Katz as Administrator of Academic Exchange Services, and Mark Gallagher, Administrator of Grants and Fellowships. Pam Turner would continue in her post until 1996 when the offices moved from Baltimore to Boston. Mark Gallagher served as Administrative Director from 1990 to 1991 providing continuity for operations during the several transition situations in this period.

Walter E. Rast, ASOR Second Vice President for Archaeological Policy 1988–1994, 1996–1998.

George M. Landes, ASOR Secretary 1972–1994.

The staff of the Baltimore Office 1989. (left to right back row) Susan Foster Kromholz, Executive Director; Pam Turner, Administrative Assistant; (front row) Purnell Kelly, Assistant; Katheryn Gould, Accountant; Mark Gallagher, Administrator of Grants and Fellowships.

Kevin G. O'Connell, S.J. ASOR Assistant Secretary and Parliamentarian 1988–1994. In 1994–95 O'Connell served as Vice Chairman of the Board.

McCarter's term as president was, from the start, beset with very serious challenges. Despite the efforts of his predecessors to move ASOR toward greater financial stability, the growth of its maturing overseas affiliates continued to hamper its ability to provide them with needed financial help and at the same time maintain other operations. Budget numbers for direct support allocations to the centers were increasingly cut back. The cash flow situation in the organization remained perilous. At the Trustees' meeting in May of 1988 Treasurer Gibbs reported that "the loss for the year will probably increase to around $50,000..." When the preliminary audit figures were assessed in June, Gibbs announced that the corporation loss for the year was in fact $190,000. At the same time serious governance issues with respect to the relationships of ASOR with the centers were emerging. In addition the administrative office was being seriously distracted by the burden of paper work as final reports on federal grant commitments came due.

McCarter's presidency was nonetheless initiated with great energy and considerable optimism.

Shelby White and Leon Levy (center right) with (left to right) Douglas Esse, Philip King and Barry Gittlin visiting Tell Miqne with AIAR and Excavation Director Sy Gitin (right) in 1984. (AIAR)

New efforts in fund raising were announced by Development Committee Chair Shelby White, and the Baltimore staff began to implement new public relations initiatives. McCarter and Gibbs also instituted a practice of trying to insulate budget line allocations from encroachment and use to cover other budget line needs within the organization. This was intended to help build confidence regarding fiscal integrity within ASOR and to obviate further squabbles concerning donor intentions of a type that the financial situation had erstwhile exacerbated. While this policy was often dishonored, and did not resolve problems of income deficits, it did instill renewed confidence in ASOR efforts and helped promote energies toward self-support by the affiliated centers.

CASOR is Founded

In May 1989 McCarter announced an initiative to help establish ASOR as a tax exempt corporation in Canada. This was to provide a vehicle for ASOR members and friends in Canada to be able to participate in raising fund support for the organization. By fall 1990 this effort had borne fruit. On October 3, *Les Ecoles Americaine de Recherche Orientale au Canada* (CASOR) was incorporated by Letters Patent under the Canada Corporations Act. Its original institutions included Brock University, the University of Toronto, McGill University, Concordia University in Alberta, the University of Lethbridge and Wilfrid Laurier University. Its first corporation directors were Walter Aufrecht, Baruch Halpern, Michele Daviau, John Holladay and Clifford Goldfarb. Later the University of Victoria in British Columbia also joined. The purposes and goals of the corporation parallel those of ASOR and representatives of its member schools hold franchise among the institutional membership of ASOR. CASOR past-presidents include Walter Aufrecht, Baruch Halpern, and Michele Daviau. The current officers are Larry Herr, President; Mary-Louise Mussel, Vice President and Secretary; Burton MacDonald, Treasurer; and Cliff Goldfarb, Legal Counsel.

The Scheuer Medal Announced

In April 1989, Chairman Thompson, with Johns Hopkins University Provost John V. Lombardi, hosted a special gala dinner with the trustees of ASOR and of all the overseas centers in the historical Peabody Library on Mount Vernon Place in Baltimore. At this event ASOR president McCarter, joined at the podium by AIAR Board Chairman Edward E. Cohen, presented Trustee Richard J. Scheuer with a special medal prepared in his honor. Scheuer's long-term service as a trustee, his outstanding generosity in supporting ASOR and all of its overseas institutes, along with his vital lay interest in the objectives of the ASOR mission, were cited as an inspirational model of support for the organization. Accordingly it was announced that henceforth an award to be designated "the Richard J. Scheuer Medal" would be given to those ASOR notables who on occasion are seen to emulate these ideals.

Richard J. Scheuer, ASOR Life Trustee.

The Scheuer Medal introduced in 1989.

EBR Fellowships Continue

In November 1989 it was announced that the Endowment for Biblical Research (EBR) once again had agreed to continue its program of scholarship grant supports for undergraduate and graduate students and seminarians to enable their participation on summer digs. EBR was founded in Boston as the Zion Research Foundation in 1929 with the goal of facilitating scholarly research and public study of the Bible and Christian church history. From the late 1970s ASOR had received annual EBR support for various publication efforts, for conferences, for digs and library programs overseas, and for student scholarships. This support was a vital component in enabling ASOR to fulfill its mission to promote public interest in Near Eastern archaeology, and to enable a new generation of student/scholars to participate in excavation work. EBR support was continued until 1996 at which juncture its directors announced a redirection of program initiatives. By this time ASOR had received upwards from one million dollars in program support from EBR funds.

Steps Toward Better Governance

From the outset of McCarter's term it was evident that efforts to review ASOR's governance structures and reconsider the scope of membership on the Board needed to continue. In 1989 a Nominating Committee chaired by Robert Johnston was appointed to review the makeup of Board membership. At the November meeting that year the committee recommended to the Trustees that the category of Associate Trustees be abolished and that in its place members of the Corporation be appointed to serve as "observers". Appropriately this recommendation was referred to the Corporation but other events intervened before it could be considered and acted upon. In the same meeting Charles Harris proposed the appointment of a "blue ribbon" governance committee to undertake a broader review of the ASOR administrative structure and this was voted. In his report at the same meeting President McCarter announced the resignation of Executive Director Kromholz to be effective March 1, 1990. During the ensuing months, citing personal reasons, McCarter also presented his own resignation to Chairman Thompson.

An ASOR Mosaic: A Centennial History of the American Schools of Oriental Research

The Presidency of Eric Meyers

In the late winter of 1990 the Executive Committee met and, serving as a Nominating Committee with Joe Seger as Chair, resolved to present the name of Eric Meyers to the Board as ASOR's next president. At the same time James Flanagan was nominated to replace Meyers as First Vice President for Publications. These nominations were presented and confirmed at the April 30, 1990 Board of Trustees meeting.

Despite ASOR's notable successes with the NEH challenge programs and other grant initiatives through the 1980s, its entry into the last decade of the century was fraught with fiscal peril. On assuming the presidency in April 1990 Eric Meyers struck a positive tone quipping: "Our finances may be a wreck but our future lies in ruins." In his fuller remarks to the Trustees he continued:

> *It is disheartening that archaeology of all the human sciences is today imperiled because of economic conditions impacting the university and the nation in which we work. The literary field is flourishing but it hardly needs operating funds. The AAR and SBL membership lists have never been larger, ASOR's has never been shorter. And yet the public and media seem to have an insatiable appetite for archaeology.*

Eric M. Meyers, ASOR President 1990–1996.
(EMM)

> *I believe that we have the academic constituency in ASOR that can articulate such a vision and who can individually and collectively express themselves through ASOR as a learned society of men and women, joined by a loyal and dedicated cadre of lay followers who know the importance of ASOR and the mute stones we uncover. Together we can make the stones speak and it will not take a miracle — it will take a lot of good will and hard work.* (Newsletter 40:3 p. 2)

Meyers' term opened with a flourish of activities. As Acting-President in the spring of 1990 Meyers had already moved forward on a number of agenda items. With Mark Gallagher as interim administrator the search for a new Executive Director was continued. At the same time Frank Cross and Noel Freedman were appointed to help organize a celebration on the centenary of W. F. Albright's birth in 1991, James Moyers and Victor Matthew of Southwest Missouri State University were appointed to be co-editors of the *Newsletter*, and David Hopkins of Wesley Theological Seminary was appointed the Associate Editor of *BA*.

James Flanagan, ASOR First Vice President 1990–1993.

At the same time, the Governance Committee, chaired by Kevin O'Connell, was also carrying forward its work. At a special retreat meeting held in Durham, NC proposals for streamlining ASOR Board membership were discussed. The results as reported to the Trustees at the April 30 meeting included the following:

1. Reduce Board membership to 34 or 35 to include 15 term trustees (16 if the Board Chairman is not in a class); eight trustees from the Corporation, eight trustees from the overseas institutes, and three representing the President and Vice Presidential offices.

2. Establish the position of Vice President for Development to be held by a lay trustee.

3. Authorize the President to establish regions within the Corporation for promotional purposes.

These proposals were approved. The Executive Committee was charged with making requisite changes in the by-laws in preparation for further Board and Corporation action at the November, 1990 meeting. In the April meeting an increase of Institutional Dues to $600 was also proposed and approved.

During the summer of 1990 the momentum continued with the hiring in July of Stephen Wilhelm, reported to be a fund raising specialist, as Executive Director. Trustee Lydie Shufro was appointed as Chair of the Development Committee. By early fall the outlines of a joint fund campaign to seek support for ASOR and all of the three of the overseas centers was in hand. In October the campaign titled "A Tenth Decade to Preserve Ten Millennia" was launched by Chairman Thompson and the Committee. The 1990–91 goal was projected as $400,000. At the Annual Meeting in New Orleans in November it was reported that almost 17% ($67,487) had been given or pledged. *ASOR Newsletter* 41:1 in the spring of 1991 announced that the campaign total was at $252,015.

At the 1990 November meeting both the Corporation and the Board acted to ratify the several proposals for governance change. At the same time the Corporation also voted to establish a new position of Vice President for the Corporation. Paul F. Jacobs of Mississippi State University was elected to fill the post. At the meeting, ASOR also celebrated its ninetieth year with a program of "Retrospective and Prospective" talks. These featured ASOR past-president Philip King and overseas institute directors Sy Gitin (AIAR), Bert de Vries (ACOR) and Stuart Swiny (CAARI). President Meyers used the occasion of the meetings to extend honors to several trustees for their outstanding service and participation in the ASOR organization and among its center affiliates. Included were Norma Kershaw, Gough W. Thompson, Jr., Joy Ungerleider Mayerson, Prince Ra'ad bin Zeid and Charles U. Harris.

(left to right) ASOR Trustees Joy Ungerleider Mayerson, Richard J. Scheuer and Ann C. Ogilvy at a reception during meetings in Philadelphia in May 1984.

The Gulf War Interegnum

As 1991 began the Persian Gulf crisis blossomed into open war. This had serious impact on programs at each of the overseas institutes: ACOR closed for the duration, and AIAR and CAARI maintained only "housebound" activities. In response President Meyers had immediately established a "Post Gulf War Task Force" to review the implications of the crisis for ASOR's future work. At its April meeting the Trustees received a report from the Task Force and resolved the following:

> The American Schools of Oriental Research, through its Board of Trustees, reaffirms its historic mission to encourage and facilitate scholarship dedicated to the recovery and preservation of the heritage of the lands of the Middle East and the Mediterranean Basin. In support of this mission, ASOR continues in partnership with the three permanent overseas centers —Jerusalem, Amman and Nicosia — and supports research elsewhere in the Middle East through its Baghdad and Damascus Committees. The publications of ASOR reflect this diversity of ASOR's historic mission.
>
> (Board Minutes, April 29, 1991)

Dornemann becomes Executive Director

In the late spring of 1991 the abrupt resignation of Executive Director Wilhelm was announced. President Meyers had already reported in the April meeting that Mark Gallagher would leave ASOR's service in the summer and that Rudolph Dornemann, recently retired as Curator of History at the Milwaukee Public Museum in Milwaukee, Wisconsin, would replace him as Administrative Director. With Wilhelm's departure Dornemann was immediately promoted to the post of Executive Director. His long history within ASOR, which included service as the first Director of ACOR in Amman, provided excellent credentials for the appointment. In taking the post Dornemann indicated his plans to also continue excavation work at Tell Qarqur in Syria where ASOR had initiated project efforts in the 1980s. At the same time Gough Thompson stepped down as Board Chairman. Assistant Chairman Robert Johnston assumed the interim role of Acting Chairman as the search for a new chair was underway. In September, shortly after Dornemann arrived in Baltimore, the ASOR office moved from The Rotunda to the corner of 33rd and North Charles Streets, just opposite the main entrance to the Johns Hopkins Homewood Campus. The building had just been newly renovated by the University and was connected to its computer system. ASOR enjoyed use of its third floor, sharing the facility with the office of JHU Alumni Affairs.

ASOR Baltimore offices at the corner of 33rd and North Charles Streets.

Rudolph H. Dornemann, ASOR Executive Director 1991–present.

(left to right) Zooarchaeologist Susan Arter, and ASOR Vice President for Archaeological Policy Walter Rast with Excavation Director Rudolph Dornemann at Tell Qarqur in 1994. (JDS)

By the summer of 1991 First Vice President Flanagan had also taken firm hold of the publications program. A new schedule of membership and subscription rates, voted by the Trustees in their spring meeting, was implemented on July 1. At the same time ASOR's publishing program together with membership and subscription services were moved to relocated once again with Scholars Press in Atlanta, Georgia. The shift to Scholars Press was fully supported by Treasurer Gibbs who saw it as a move to promote and protect the fiscal integrity of the publications activity within ASOR. It was accompanied by several other significant developments;

1. Victor Matthews succeeded as sole editor of the *ASOR Newsletter*;

2. Responsibility for the Annual Meeting program was assigned to the Vice President for Publications;

3. Frank S. Frick of Albion College was assigned Chairperson of an ASOR Academic Planning Committee to review the program units of the Annual Meeting;

4. A first time forum was announced for the November 1991 Annual Meeting for business and discussion by ASOR's individual members.

In the early fall a transition in the editorship of *JCS* was also announced. Professor Erle Leichte, who took over responsibilities for the journal at the death of the founding editor Albrecht Goetze, stepped down. William L. Moran was appointed to succeed him.

While the Gulf War crisis muted plans for excavation activities during 1991, the activities of the CAP Committee continued apace. At the April Board meeting a report was received by a subcommittee assigned to review CAP efforts. Headed by Lawrence Stager, it recommended that the term of CAP Chairman Walter Rast be extended for another three years to 1994 and that CAP remain the sole ASOR committee for reviewing and approving archaeological projects for ASOR affiliation. In addition, it recommended that CAP consider approving proposals for more than one year terms, and that it be more engaged in initiating symposia, workshops and other colloquia for annual meeting programs.

At the Board meeting in November 1991 Rast reported on a total of forty seven projects. Twelve were approved for field work in 1992 and another twenty one for publication phase efforts. In addition, five other field projects were approved in principle pending submission of further information, two projects were reported as completed, and seven others, which had been previously affiliated but for which reports had not been received in 1991, were also noted. Included were projects working in Cyprus, Egypt, Israel, Jordan, the Palestinian West Bank, Tunisia and Yemen.

Rast also reported that the committee had initiated discussions on several policy matters. These focused on issues related to the protection and preservation of historic remains, on proprietorial rights to ancient remains and on responsibilities for seeing to their accessibility through publication. The committee was in part responding to a statement prepared by ASOR's Ancient Manuscripts Committee reflecting concerns raised in the debate over the rights of publication and public access to Dead Sea Scroll documents, which was being waged at that time. CAP supported a motion made to the Board by the chairman of the Ancient Manuscripts Committee, James C. VanderKam, advising that an open symposium on these issues be organized as part of the Annual Meeting program the following year. That discussion took place at the San Francisco meetings in November 1992, and the Manuscripts Committee statement was formally adopted at that time by the trustees. ASOR's policy took into account both written and non-written archaeological remains and deliberately reaffirmed the rights of the host countries to regulate access and guarantee proper artifact and site preservation.

Chairman Walter Rast (right) on the 1994 CAP tour at Tall Jawa with excavation Director Michéle Daviau (left). (JDS)

The ASOR Policy on Preservation and Access

We the members of ASOR affirm the priority of national antiquities authorities to manage and regulate cultural remains. As an organization of scholars devoted to recovery of the cultures of Middle and Near Eastern lands, we reaffirm the principles of scholarly integrity and ethics with respect to retrieval, preparation, preservation, and timely publication of material remains, including texts.

1. Publication

Before assignment of finds to an excavator(s) or editor(s) by the responsible authorities (be they the licensed excavator(s) or the antiquities authority) and their scholarly advisors, these groups should determine what constitutes a reasonable time for publication. In the case of major finds, it is desirable that preliminary editions be promptly published. In the interval between assignment and publication, the excavator(s) or editor(s) should be encouraged to cooperate with interested scholarly parties.

2. Access

a. Recognizing that the responsible antiquities authorities and their scholarly advisors will be concerned with securing and preserving the finds, it is likely that scholarly access to the originals, after publication, will still be necessary. Such access will be regulated by the responsible antiquities authorities and their scholarly advisors.

b. After the reasonable time limit (see no. 1 above) has passed, the materials, photographs, and documentation should be made generally accessible within the limits of the requirements for preservation and laws of the host country.

(Resolution of the ASOR Board, November 1992)

The Ancient Manuscripts Committee

Since the discovery of the first of the Dead Sea Scrolls in 1947, ASOR and the Jerusalem School had maintained an active profile in connection with the ongoing program of research and publication of the scroll materials. From the 1960s ASOR's interests in these and other epigraphic discoveries were monitored through its Dead Sea Scrolls Committee. Following the deliberations of the Campbell task force in 1979, it was redesignated the Ancient Manuscripts Committee, to embrace the broader scope of epigraphic research then underway. The Committee's leading members included, among others, Philip King, Frank Cross, David Noel Freedman, James Sanders, James Robinson, William Moran, John Strugnell, James Charlesworth and James VanderKam.

Charles Harris is elected ASOR Board Chair

After a prolonged search, The Reverend Charles U. Harris was elected as ASOR's third Board Chairman in the spring of 1992. As Dean and President of Seabury-Western Theological Seminary in the 1960s, Harris had served as its corporate representative to ASOR and was instrumental in forming the consortium of schools to support the Tell el-Hesi excavation project. Later he served as an ASOR trustee and, from 1985–1988, as its Treasurer. He was one of the founding members of the CAARI Board, becoming its President in 1984. He served throughout the 1990s as its Board Chairman. In accepting the ASOR post Harris commented:

> ASOR is an old, respected, learned society. Its international mission of archaeology, research, education and publication is incredibly valuable. I hope that all of its activities may be strengthened for even greater service to the scholarly world. (ASOR Newsletter 42:1)

Robert Johnston continued to serve as Vice Chairman of the Board until 1995 when Kevin G. O'Connell assumed the position for a short period.

The Reverend Charles Upchurch Harris, Chairman of the ASOR Board 1992–1994.

The Endowment Fund for Biblical Archaeological Research

Many generous contributions through the years were made by Charles Harris and his late wife Janet both to ASOR and to the overseas centers. Among their efforts to support ASOR they secured a fund that led to the establishment of the Endowment Fund for Biblical Archaeological Research. In May of 1994, a gift of $100,000 was provided as an irrevocable endowment, the interest proceeds to be used to support the activities of field archaeologists and their related research. Through the 1990s and to this day these funds, distributed through CAP, have provided small grants to five or more projects each year, providing new incentives for excavation efforts, and thus serving to fulfill ASOR's historic mission of encouragement and support for Middle East field research.

The Annual Meeting 1992

The 1992 Annual Meeting in San Francisco signaled several new departures for ASOR. At the end of 1991, Academy International Travel Services based in Atlanta, Georgia, had been appointed ASOR's designated travel agent. Working with Vice President Flanagan and with the AAR/SBL Joint Ventures convention organizers, Julene Miller, President of Academy Travel, was able to have the Sir Francis Drake Hotel in San Francisco designated specially for ASOR use, with a room block for members, and meeting space for its related boards and committees. Plans to have such an "official ASOR hotel" were projected also for the years ahead.

The San Francisco meeting also saw the introduction of a new Outreach Education Section to ASOR's program. The goal of this program section was to interface with K–12 classroom teachers and others in public education fields in order to provide exposure and instruction regarding resources and applications available for archaeological study. The inaugural session was chaired by Carolyn Draper with welcoming remarks by President Meyers.

ASOR's Annual Meeting: a Brief History

Until the 1950s ASOR's committees and officers had met on a convenience basis at sessions of one or another of its Founding Society partners, AIA, AOS and SBL. By the late 1950s a pattern of association with the year end meetings of SBL, and together in turn with the newly-founded National Association of Biblical Instructors (NABI), had been established. To this point formal ASOR activity involved only business sessions, although individual scholar members participated in the program sessions of the other societies. This situation began to change modestly in the early 1960s when, in the wake of increasing excavation activity, a single afternoon session was set aside by SBL program organizers for "dig reports." Through the 1960s and into the 1970s ASOR member participation in these annual programs grew exponentially. By this time, with the explosion of programs in religion especially on state university campuses, NABI had been transformed into the American Academy of Religion (AAR).

During the 1960s and 1970s opportunities for international travel also increased and participation in excavations fostered a major growth of interest in Middle East archaeological work. Accordingly more program sessions with a special archaeological focus were introduced into both the SBL and AAR schedules. In the mid-1970s the planning for the annual meetings for SBL, AAR and ASOR was coordinated through the Missoula Montana Center for Scholarly Publications and Services (Scholars Press). Despite the hiatus in ASOR's formal association with Scholars Press from the late 1970s until 1992, ASOR remained a partner, through SBL, in the rapidly growing annual meeting enterprise. This enterprise took form in the 1980s as a separate facet of the Scholars Press operation called Joint Ventures. During this period ASOR responded by means of its Program Committee that worked to organize and coordinate archaeological program sessions. In the late 1970s Kevin G. O'Connell chaired this committee's efforts. He was succeeded by Roger Boraas (1978–1982), James D. Muhly (1983–1987) and Barry Gittlin (1988–1991). In 1991 responsibility for the annual meeting program was assigned to the office of the First Vice President. Barry Gittlin continued to help in developing the program for 1992, along with Frank Frick whom Jim Flanagan had assigned to chair a planning committee to review the annual meeting processes.

In the spring meeting of the trustees in 1993 Jim Flanagan stepped down as Vice President. Chairman Harris established a nomination committee, with Richard Scheuer as chair, to seek an appropriate successor. In a letter to the trustees dated June 24, 1993 Harris announced the appointment of R. Thomas Schaub, Professor of Religious Studies at Indiana University of Pennsylvania as ASOR First Vice President. Also during 1993 new co-editors were appointed for *BASOR* — Albert Leonard Jr., Professor of Classics at the University of Arizona and James Weinstein, Senior Editor at CBORD Group, Inc. in Ithaca, New York. They began their assignment in January, 1994. During Schaub's term several stages of transition took place in publications operations. At the outset David Hopkins, who had succeeded Eric Meyers as sole editor of *BA* a year earlier, made a smooth transfer of its production activities from the Duke headquarters to the Baltimore–Washington area. For a brief period other activities continued to be coordinated by Carolyn Steele at Case Western Reserve University but plans to move operations to Scholars Press in Atlanta were soon under serious consideration. At that time Scholars Press was promoting plans to build a new multi-tenant facility for itself, affiliated societies and sponsors near its headquarters at Emory University. In 1994 ASOR pledged a contribution to the project in exchange for future publication office space. In 1995, anticipating the eventual move into the new space, the offices of publications operations were moved to Atlanta. At the same time applications for the new position of Director of Publications were solicited and Billie Jean Collins, a specialist in Hittite studies with a Ph.D. from Yale, was appointed. Collins came with over five years experience in publishing, having worked one year for Doubleday in New York City and subsequently as a Research Associate on the Chicago Hittite Dictionary Project at the University of Chicago. She assumed her new responsibilities on July 1, 1995 and subsequently also took over the task of editing the *ASOR Newsletter* from Victor Matthews.

R. Thomas Schaub, ASOR First Vice President 1993–1996.

R. Thomas Schaub (left) at excavations in the Jerusalem Old City with Ronnie Reich on the CAP tour in 1995. (JDS)

In 1994 other transitions in ASOR leadership also occurred. Walter Rast finished his second term as Second Vice President for CAP and was succeeded by Joe Seger. Seger had just completed two terms as president of the AIAR and in the summer of 1994 he joined Rast in leading the annual summer tour of ASOR/CAP affiliated projects. According to the established practice they visited sites with active field projects in Jordan, Israel, Cyprus and Syria where they were fully supported by the directors and staff members of ACOR, AIAR and CAARI, and by ASOR Executive Director Dornemann at Tell Qarqur. Visits were also scheduled with principals of the antiquities departments in each of these countries. A similar program of visits was carried out by Seger in 1995 and 1996.

Within the CAP Committee work also continued at an increasing rate. Fifty projects were vetted and approved for 1995 and fifty eight for 1996. The first solicitation by CAP of applications for Charles U. Harris Fund for Biblical Archaeology grants also began in 1995 and these provided new incentive for ASOR/CAP affiliation. Work was also continued by a sub-committee, assigned by Rast and chaired by Ellen Herscher, to further investigate issues of ethics and standards related to the preservation and protection of archaeological remains. The draft of a policy statement on the Preservation of Archaeological Resources was received by CAP and published in the Winter 1994 issue of the *ASOR Newsletter* (44: 4 p. 2–3). The policy statement was approved by the Board at its November 1995 meeting. The final text of the statement appeared subsequently in *BASOR* 309 (1998):1–2.

On the CAP Tour in the summer of 1996 ASOR Second Vice President and President-elect Joe D. Seger (right) and CAMP Chairman-elect Paul F. Jacobs (left) at the Tell Miqne Excavations in Israel with (left to right center) Co-Directors Trudy Dothan and Sy Gitin, and ASOR/AIAR Trustee Lydie Shufro. (AIAR)

More Governance Changes

In the early 1990s, in addition to the three Vice Presidents (for COP, CAP and for the Corporation) a number of ASOR notables were appointed to special Vice Presidential posts for a variety of task oriented purposes. Among these were Lydie Shufro who served first as Vice President for Development, and later, in 1993, as Vice President for Public Affairs; W. H. Holden Gibbs who served as Vice President for Finance; and Ernest S. Frerichs who served as Vice President-at-large. Through these same years issues regarding ASOR's governance structures continued to be discussed vigorously and further re-evaluations were carried forward under the leadership of Kevin O'Connell. O'Connell became Vice Chairman of the Board in 1994 and in that year another set of amendments to the bylaws were passed. But it was already evident that more radical changes were called for and O'Connell's committee continued as a Long Range Planning group.

The New ASOR — 1995

At the Trustees' meeting in April 1995 the plan for a broad-scale restructuring, along with amendments to the bylaws and to the Articles of Incorporation, were put forward and approved.

Central to the new organizational plan was the transformation of the old "Corporation," wherein only the representatives of the member institutions had the privilege to vote, into a "General Membership" body in which both institutional member representatives and individual ASOR members held voting rights. The Board of Trustees was to be constituted of three groups of nine trustees each, to be elected respectively by the Institutional Members, the Individual Members, and the Board itself. In addition the Board would include one representative from each of the overseas center affiliates AIAR, ACOR and CAARI. By subsequent action each of the organization's Founding Societies AOS, AIA and SBL were also provided this option. The organization's officers, including a Board Chairman, President, Vice President, Secretary and Treasurer, were to be elected by the Board of Trustees. They would serve as ex-officio voting members of the Board. In addition the offices of the former First and Second Vice Presidents were newly designated as Chairs of Operations Committees continuing with responsibilities for publications (COP) and archaeological policy (CAP). The office of Vice President for the Corporation was abolished and in its place a third Operations Committee (acronym CAMP) was created to oversee the annual meeting and program activities. It was decided that these chairs were to be elected by the General Membership body. By later action they also became ex-officio voting members of the Board. The new structure also provided for an Executive Committee to be composed of the officers and of trustees appointed by the Board Chair. In subsequent action the chairs of the Operations Committees were likewise added as ex-officio voting members of this body.

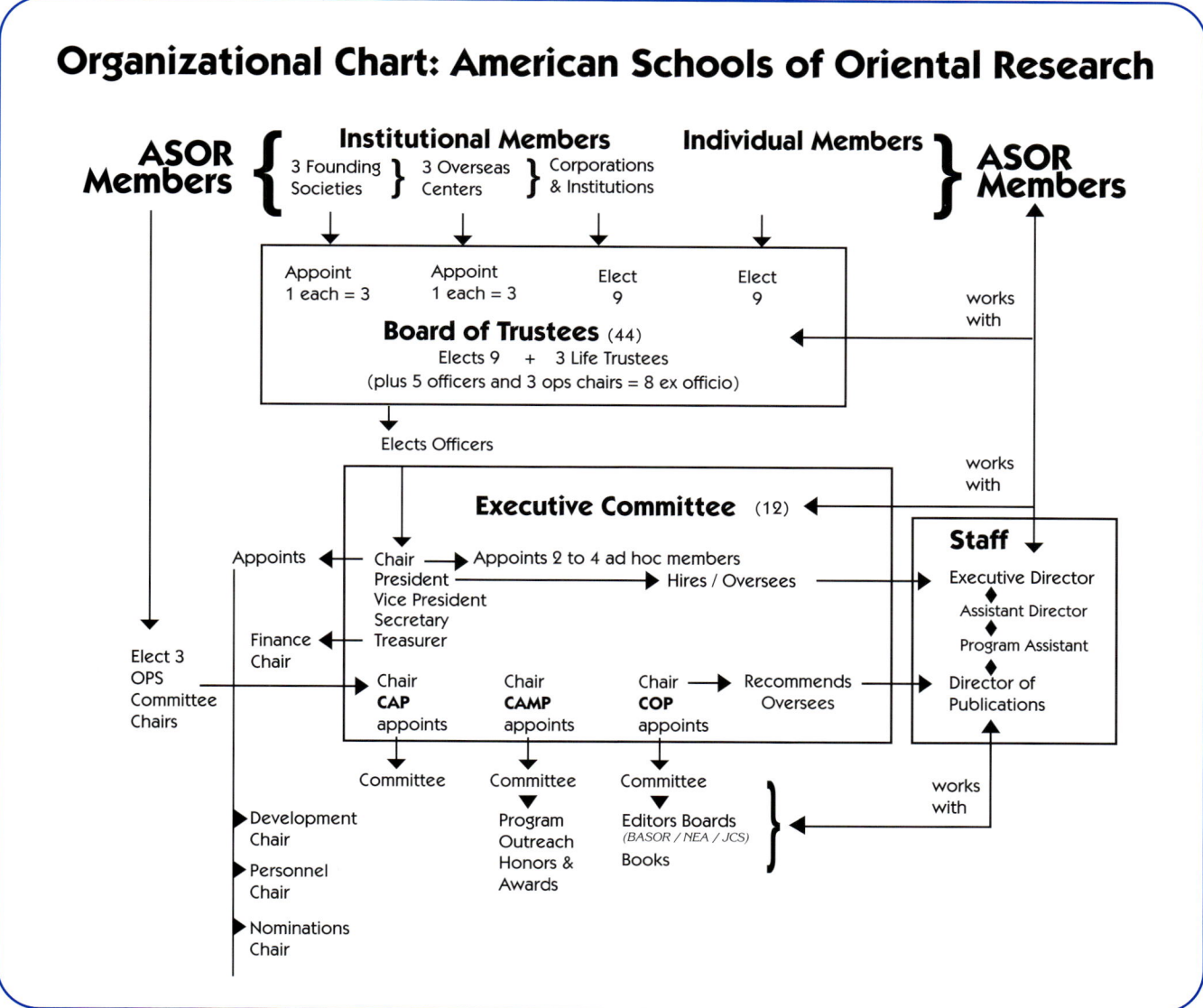

At the meeting of the Corporation in November of 1995 the amendments to the bylaws and Articles of Incorporation enabling these changes were ratified. However, a related proposal, to change the organization's name to the American Society of Oriental Research, was roundly defeated. While proponents believed that "Society" would better reflect the new character of the organization with its individual member franchise, the sentiment to preserve the original "American Schools" name prevailed.

ASOR Joins ACLS

The 1995 revisions of ASOR's bylaws established it as a member-based society and provided the catalyst for making application to join the American Council of Learned Societies. ACLS is a private non-profit federation of national scholarly organizations with a mission to "advance humanistic studies in all fields of learning in the humanities and related social sciences, and to maintain and strengthen relations among the national societies devoted to such studies." ASOR's historical focus on Near Eastern archaeology and culture, and on biblical studies and history, fell well within the parameters of ACLS concerns. On May 7, 1998 ASOR received formal notification of its acceptance as the 61st member of the Council.

MacAllister elected Board Chairman

As the new organizational structure was being put in place, another transition of officers occurred. In the spring of 1994 Charles Harris had announced his intention to step down as Board Chair. At the Board Meeting in November of that year P.E. MacAllister was elected to succeed him. MacAllister, CEO of MacAllister Machinery Company, Inc. in Indianapolis, Indiana, was a long time student of the ancient world having written a book on the Old Testament entitled, *Tongue of the Nursling* (Von Hoffman Press, Inc.: St Louis, Missouri) in 1974. He held leadership positions on the boards of both the Christian Theological Seminary and of Carroll College. He was nominated to the ASOR Board in the early 1970s by Edward F. Campbell of McCormick Theological Seminary and had served faithfully as a trustee for more than twenty years. MacAllister's initial term as Chairman was scheduled to run through June 1996, coinciding with that of President Meyers. However, with the new bylaws in place, he was nominated and elected again in 1995, and also in 1998 and continued in the office as Board Chairman as the new century began.

P.E. MacAllister, Chairman of the ASOR Board 1994–present.

ASOR Board Chairs

1984–86 — Elizabeth Moynihan

1986–92 — Gough W. Thompson Jr.

1992–94 — Charles U. Harris

1994–   — P.E. MacAllister

Harris becomes Honorary Chairman

In 1994 when Charles Harris completed his term as Board Chairman he was immediately nominated to continuing service as Honorary Chairman of ASOR. In putting forward the nomination, which the Board voted by acclamation, Vice President-at-large Ernest Frerichs commented:

> ASOR owes an unending debt to Charles U. Harris. He accepted the chairmanship of the ASOR Board when many felt that the tide was running out for ASOR... This Chairman has taken us across the threshold of a new year, a new age... He showed us that time was not primarily chronological, but rather kairotic. Time was opportunity — to be filled with a heritage of grandeur and prepared for a life of service to which we had been called. He convinced us that this was true and carried us into that new age with skill, wisdom, and a wit hewn from the rich treasury of an Anglican divine.
>
> Fortunately, he has made the chairmanship so attractive that he is succeeded by a man who also possesses great vision, courage, and commitment (i.e., P.E. MacAllister). Retirement need not mean removal and we can have the continuing pleasure of Charles' company and the continuing wisdom of his judgment. We can do this by electing Charles U. Harris as ASOR's Honorary Chairman.
>
> (ASOR Newsletter 44:4 [1994] p. 1)

More New Officers

At the November 1995 annual meeting in Philadelphia, in accord with the new governance plan, the processes for the elections of officers and leaders for the regular rotation scheduled for July 1996 were initiated. During the Board meeting, in addition to the reelection of Chairman MacAllister, the name of Joe D. Seger was brought forward to succeed Eric Meyers as president. Seger, Professor of Religion and Director of the Cobb Institute of Archaeology at Mississippi State University, had served as President of the AIAR Board from 1988–94 and was ASOR's current Second Vice President for Archaeological Policy. Concurrent with Seger's election Secretary James Ross and Treasurer W. H. Holden Gibbs were reelected to continue in their positions. In the Corporation/General Membership session plans to solicit nominations for the new Operations Committee Chairs were presented, and mechanisms for conduct of a mail ballot vote in the following spring were adopted. These procedures resulted in the election of Albert Leonard Jr. of the University of Arizona as the Chair of COP (succeeding R. Thomas Schaub), of Walter Rast of Valparaiso University as the Chair of CAP (succeeding Joe Seger), and of Paul F. Jacobs of Mississippi State University as the Chair of CAMP. Jacobs had served as Vice President for the Corporation from 1991–94. During this period Corporation Membership recovered to a peak of 143 institutions. Jacobs was succeeded in 1994 by Donald Wimmer of Seton Hall University. Under the new 1995 bylaws, however, that position was discontinued.

Joe D. Seger, ASOR President 1996–present.

ASOR Presidents through the Twentieth Century.

1921–1933	James A. Montgomery	University of Pennsylvania
1934–1948	Millar Burrows	Yale University
1949–1954	Carl H. Kraeling	University of Chicago
1955–1965	A. Henry Detweiler	Cornell University
1966–1974	G. Ernest Wright	Harvard University
1975–1976	Frank Moore Cross	Harvard University
1976–1982	Philip J. King	Boston College
1982–1988	James A. Sauer	University of Pennsylvania
1988–1990	P. Kyle McCarter	Johns Hopkins University
1990–1996	Eric M. Meyers	Duke University
1996–present	Joe D. Seger	Mississippi State University

Albert Leonard, Jr., Chairman, ASOR Committee on Publications 1996–present.

Paul F. Jacobs, Chairman, ASOR Committee on Annual Meeting and Program 1996–1998.

ASOR Headquarters Move to Boston

In 1994, as P.E. MacAllister began his chairmanship, ASOR's arrangements for courtesy use of office space at Johns Hopkins were nearing an end and a search for rental space in Baltimore was already underway. At this point MacAllister made a generous contribution establishing a fund to see ASOR through the transition to a new location for its offices. In the fall of 1995, before the move from the Johns Hopkins space became necessary, President Meyers announced that negotiations were underway with Boston University for use of space being developed at 656 Beacon Street where the headquarters of the Archaeological Institute of America were located. The overtures to BU had been initiated by Artemis Joukowsky, President of ACOR, and were embraced and encouraged by Boston University President Jon Wesley. By the spring of 1996 Chairman MacAllister and President Meyers had confirmed the details of the arrangements. With support from the MacAllister transition fund, Executive Director Dornemann organized the move to Boston in the early summer. By mid-July he was settled into the new Beacon Street quarters. The era of ASOR "at Boston University" was thus initiated.

ASOR Boston office staff in 1999 (left to right) Britt Hartenberger, Program Assistant, Holly Andrews, Assistant Director and Rudolph Dornemann, Executive Director. (BU)

The "656 Associates" Group is Formed

The arrangements for use of the BU space included an understanding that the facilities would be shared with ACOR, AIAR and CAARI. In the fall of 1996, in order to facilitate negotiations and enable equitable resolves in this and other matters of mutual interest, President Seger convened a Committee of Chairs, Presidents and Directors of ASOR, ACOR, AIAR and CAARI. Among the committee's first actions was an agreement to establish a limited not-for-profit association designated "656 Associates" to legally acknowledge cooperative arrangements for the distribution and management of space among the parties. A draft of the "656 Associates" proposal was presented to the ASOR Board in April 1997 and subsequently reviewed by ASOR legal counsul. In November 1997 the proposal was ratified by vote of the ASOR Board and by the boards of each of the overseas center partners. As of this writing the Chairs, Presidents and Directors Committee continues to meet annually to discuss matters of common concern to the partners.

ASOR's Search for New Identity

By the early 1990s ASOR's overseas center "children" had fully come of age. Each was enjoying robust development under strong and determined leadership. In his inaugural statement in 1990 President Meyers had envisioned the day "when all of the ACOR family can gather for a mid-day seminar or lecture at the Albright Institute in Jerusalem and the AIAR family can return to ACOR for a late supper on the veranda in Jebel Amman, and then move on to the island of Aphrodite the next day for a Spring Trustees Meeting at CAARI in Nicosia" (ASOR Newsletter 46:3). In the wake of the 1995 Mideast peace accords this vision became reality and as Meyers completed his term as president in 1996 a spirit of optimism resonated throughout the organization.

But as the centers took firm hold of the overseas mission, ASOR itself was challenged to find and renew its own focus for the future. This was partly to take shape in connection with the expanding scope and character of the Annual Meeting program. By special agreement with SBL and Joint Ventures, for the meeting in Philadelphia in 1995 ASOR discontinued the previous practice of having its own headquarters hotel. ASOR members were again treated as part of the general population of the convention. Similar arrangements continued in place for the meeting in New Orleans in 1996. But as the new CAMP Committee was formed under Paul Jacobs' leadership, dissatisfaction with the meeting situation was growing. After lively discussion at the Members Meeting in New Orleans in 1996 it was decided that ASOR should hold its own independent annual meeting, but as close as possible in time and place to the Joint Ventures sessions of SBL/AAR. Accordingly, Jacobs and the CAMP Committee arranged for a separate venue in 1997 in Napa, California for the week prior to the SBL/AAR meetings held that year in San Francisco. The Napa program proved very successful with expanded sections on work in Anatolia and Cyprus and with over 350 registered participants. However, proposals brought by CAMP for a more complete separation in time and location from the Joint Ventures convention for 1998 were rejected. Because of this, arrangements for ASOR's 1998 meetings were again scheduled to be just prior to the AAR/SBL sessions in Orlando, Florida. A similar pattern was continued for the 1999 meeting in Cambridge, Massachusetts and for the 2000 meeting in Nashville, Tennessee. Each of the successive meetings witnessed further expansion in the geographical and chronological scope represented in paper sessions and registration peaked in 1999 with over 500 participants. During each of these years outreach education programs and workshops were also conducted.

Victor Matthews, Chairman, ASOR Committee on Annual Meeting and Program 1998–2001.

David McCreery, Chairman, ASOR Committee on Archaeological Policy 1998–present.

In the spring of 1998, citing personal concerns, Paul Jacobs resigned as CAMP Chair. He was succeeded in the fall of that year by Victor Matthews of Southwestern Missouri State University. In that same year Walter Rast stepped down as Chairman of CAP and David McCreery of Willamette University was elected to the position. As the independence of the overseas centers became established, the role of CAP as monitor of ASOR's member interests in overseas locations was further highlighted. While CAP continued its traditional practice of reviewing projects for affiliate status, and was able to provide some modest financial support to a few each year from the Harris Fund, it began also to evaluate its own procedures and to consider opportunities for the promotion of work by ASOR scholars more widely in the region. Through this period CAP worked closely with the Damascus Committee and its Chair, Michael Fuller to maintain contact with the several American initiatives operating in Syria, and with the Baghdad Committee and its Chair, Paul Zimansky. Although Iraq had remained closed to field work following the Gulf War in 1991, the Baghdad Committee, through monies provided by part of the Nies Trust, was able to offer grants to researchers studying materials from Mesopotamia on an annual basis.

With Al Leonard's election as Chairman of COP in 1996, James Weinstein became sole editor of *BASOR* and by this time Billie Jean Collins was established as Director of Publications in offices at Emory University. Meanwhile a survey of members, initiated by Tom Schaub and *BA* editor David Hopkins, to assess the advantages and disadvantages of changing the name of the magazine had been concluded. Based on the results a motion to rename the journal *Near Eastern Archaeology* was brought to the Board at the 1996 meeting in New Orleans. Proponents argued that *NEA* better reflected the wider nature and scope of ASOR's archaeological interests. However the motion was tabled at that time. After further review and study the proposal was reconsidered at the April 1997 Board meeting and passed. The first journal issue under the new name appeared in the fall of that year. During this same period the publications office established ASOR's web presence at *www.asor.org*. Among the first material presented on-line was a report on 1996 CAP affiliated projects titled *ASOR Digs 1996*. Support for this special project was provided by Richard Scheuer with materials edited by Paul Jacobs. It was subsequently distributed in a CD edition. The ASOR web site has continued to develop to the present time with the addition of major information sections on membership, annual meeting programs, on-line *ASOR Newsletters*, outreach education and other features.

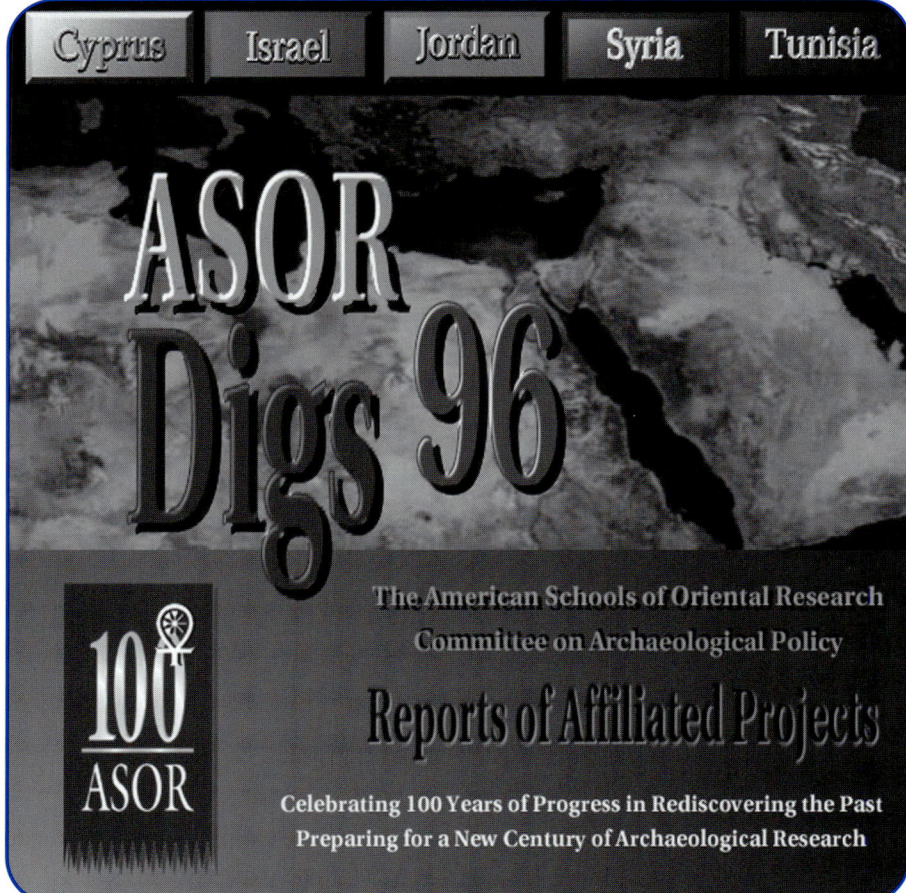

James Weinstein, **BASOR** editor 1996–present. (JDS)

Honors and Awards

With the introduction of the Scheuer Medal in 1989 ASOR began a tradition of "honoring its own." At the Annual Meeting in 1990 President Meyers presented Certificates of Merit to five notables, each for special long-term service to ASOR and the centers. Included were retiring Board Chairman, Gough Thompson; Prince Ra'ad bin Zeid, Chair of the Jordanian Administrative Committee of ACOR; Joy Ungerleider Mayerson, AIAR Board Chair; and Norma Kershaw and Charles U. Harris, both long term ASOR Trustees and former officers of CAARI. In May of 1994, as their terms as Board Chairs respectively of ASOR and AIAR were drawing to a close, both Charles Harris and Joy Mayerson were further honored as recipients of ASOR's highest award, the Scheuer Medal. In a special banquet at the May 1996 Board Meeting retiring President Meyers himself was accorded special honors for his long-term and dedicated service, as Trustee, *BA* Editor, Vice President and President.

Billie Jean Collins, ASOR Director of Publications 1995–present.

The tradition of giving special recognitions was continued at the November 1996 Annual Meetings in New Orleans in connection with a special Centennial Kick-off Reception. As part of the ceremony President Seger, acting on behalf of the ASOR trustees, honored P. E. MacAllister by awarding him the Scheuer Medal, citing his significant contributions to ASOR as a trustee for more than twenty years and his vital and energetic leadership as its current Board Chairman. At the same time Charles Harris was again honored by his appointment as an ASOR's Life Trustee, a designation that was also accorded to both Richard Scheuer and P. E. MacAllister as they subsequently completed their elected terms. Certificates of merit were also given to retiring Secretary George Landes and to Treasurer W. H. Holden Gibbs for their respective long terms of service on behalf the organization. Fully appropriate and sentimental honors were likewise given to James A. Sauer, Director of ACOR from 1975–1981 and Past-President of both ACOR and ASOR. In failing health, Jim Sauer made a special effort to be present at the meeting. In addition to the ASOR honors, he also was awarded the "Order of the Star" from His Majesty King Hussein of Jordan in a presentation by Jordan's Royal Prince Ra'ad bin Zeid.

(left to right) Honorees Charles U. Harris (as Life Trustee) and Board Chairman P. E. MacAllister (Scheuer Medal recipient) at the Centennial Kickoff Celebration in New Orleans, November 23, 1996. (POS)

(left to right) Honoree James A Sauer, with ASOR President Joe D. Seger and ACOR President Artemis Joukowsky, at the presentation of the "Order of the Star" by Jordan Royal Prince Ra'ad bin Zeid in New Orleans November 23, 1996. (POS)

These ceremonies also included announcement of the completion of the *Oxford Encyclopedia of Archaeology in the Near East*, a joint enterprise of Oxford University Press and ASOR. Noting that the five volumes serve as a special legacy of work by Eric Meyers President Seger commented:

> The presentation of the *Oxford Encyclopedia of Archaeology in the Near East* represents a most significant milestone is ASOR history. ASOR Past-President and encyclopedia editor Eric Meyers, along with his editorial staff, and Jeff Edelstein and the staff of Oxford University Press, all deserve the highest honors for preparation of a most handsome and truly formative resource for students and scholars in Near Eastern studies and archaeology. *(Newsletter 46:4, p. 2)*

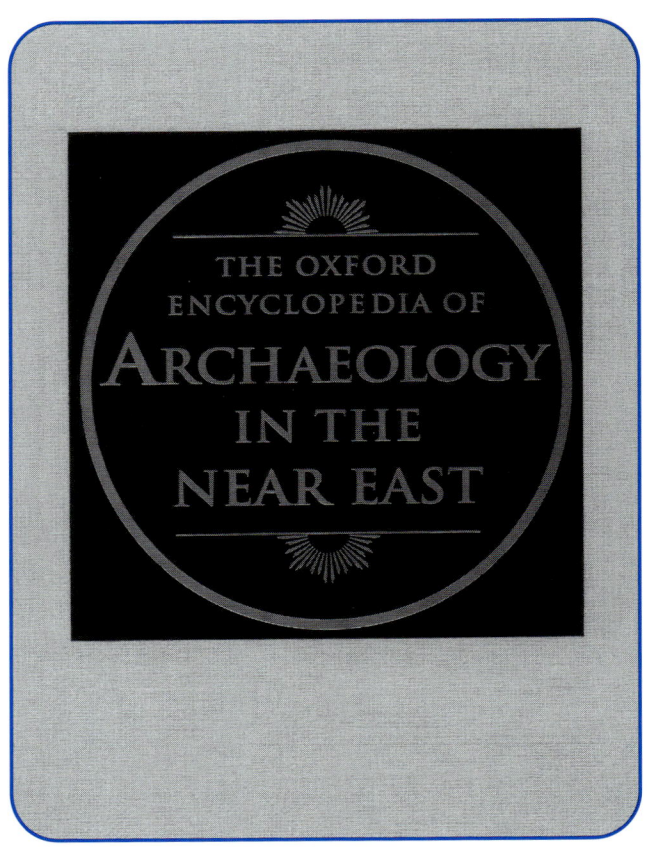

*Book cover of the **Oxford Encyclopedia of Archaeology in the Near East.***

Senior editorial staff for the Oxford Encyclopedia project. (left to right) Jeffrey Edelstein, James A. Sauer, Carol Meyers, Eric M. Meyers, James Muhly and William G. Dever. (POS)

Charles U. Harris Service Award.

P. E. MacAllister Field Archaeology Award.

G. Ernest Wright Award for the best recent publication on archaeological results.

Frank Moore Cross Award for the best recent publication on epigraphy.

W. F. Albright Awards for special support service contributions to affiliated centers.

Building on these precedents President Seger and the CAMP Committee organized an ongoing program of awards that was initiated at the Napa meetings in 1997. In addition to the Scheuer Medal several other awards named for ASOR notables were announced. Included were the Charles U. Harris Service Award for distinguished service to the organization, the P.E. MacAllister Field Archaeology Award for distinguished contributions in Near Eastern archaeology, the G. Ernest Wright Award for the best recent publication of archaeological results, the Frank Moore Cross Award for the best recent publication on epigraphy, text and tradition, and the W. F. Albright Awards for special support service contributions to one of the affiliated centers. Included also were ASOR Membership Service Awards to recognize those making special contributions to ASOR through committee, editorial or office services. An "Honors and Awards" sub-committee of CAMP was organized to solicit nominations from the general membership and to handle the awards processes.

Honors were awarded to a distinguished slate of recipients in Napa. Most notable among these was the presentation of the fifth Scheuer Medal to Norma Kershaw. In addition to her numerous service contributions to ASOR and the centers, she was cited also for the wider range of her philanthropic contributions to art history and archaeology, and for work with AIA and ARCE. Specially noted was her initiation in 1998 of the Kershaw Near Eastern Archaeology Lectures program jointly sponsored by AIA and ASOR. Other award recipients included Ernest Frerichs (Harris Service Award), William G. Dever (MacAllister Award), Eric Meyers (Wright Award for archaeological publication), James Charlesworth (Cross Award for epigraphic publication), Artemis Joukowsky (Albright Award for service to ACOR), and Stuart Swiny (Albright Award for Service to CAARI). Member Service Awards were given to R. Thomas Schaub specially for his efforts as Vice President for COP and Carolyn Draper-Rivers for the initiation of outreach education programs. The annual presentation of awards was continued in 1998 at the Orlando Annual Meeting. Awards for 1999 were presented in connection with the centennial year celebrations in Washington, DC in April 2000 and those for 2000 in November at the Nashville Annual Meeting.

Honors and Awards Recipients 1997–2000

1997

Richard J. Scheuer Medal — Norma Kershaw
Charles U. Harris Service Award — Ernest S. Frerichs
P.E. MacAllister Field Archaeology Award — William G. Dever
G. Ernest Wright Publication Award — Eric M. Meyers
Frank Moore Cross Publication Award — James H. Charlesworth
W. F. Albright Award — ACOR — Artemis A. W. Joukowsky
W. F. Albright Award — CAARI — Stuart Swiny
Membership Service Award — Carolyn Draper-Rivers
Membership Service Award — R. Thomas Schaub

1998

Charles U. Harris Service Award — Walter E. Rast
P.E. MacAllister Field Archaeology Award — Lawrence E. Toombs
G. Ernest Wright Publication Award — Steven A. Rosen
Frank Moore Cross Publication Award — Ronald S. Hendel
W. F. Albright Award — ACOR — Nancy L. Lapp
W. F. Albright Award — CAARI — Giraud V. Foster
W. F. Albright Award — AIAR — James F. Ross
Membership Service Award — Anne Ogilvy
Membership Service Award — David C. Hopkins
Membership Service Award — Jonathan N. Tubb

1999 (awarded spring 2000)

Charles U. Harris Service Award — Robert Hohlfelder
P.E. MacAllister Field Archaeology Award — Martha Sharp Joukowsky
W. F. Albright Award — AIAR — Patty Gerstenblith
Membership Service Award — James Weinstein
Membership Service Award — Norma Dever

2000

Charles U. Harris Service Award — Philip J. King
P.E. MacAllister Field Archaeology Award — Lawrence Geraty
W. F. Albright Award — ACOR — Pierre Bikai
W. F. Albright Award — AIAR — Sy Gitin
Membership Service Award — Billie Jean Collins
Membership Service Award — Lydie Shufro
Membership Service Award — Robert J. Bull

William G. Dever (left) receives the first MacAllister Award for distinguished career accomplishments in Field Archaeology from Joe Seger at the 1997 Napa banquet. *(POS)*

(left to right) Honors and Awards Committee Chair Lydie Shufro, with President Joe Seger, presenting the Scheuer Medal to Norma Kershaw at the Annual Meeting Centennial Banquet in Napa California in November 1997. *(POS)*

Presenters and honorees at the Orlando Meeting in November 1998. (left to right) James F. Ross, Nancy L. Lapp, Walter E. Rast, P.E. MacAllister (Board Chair), Anne Ogilvy, Ron S. Hendel, David C. Hopkins, Lydie Shufro (Honors and Awards Committee Chair), Joe D. Seger (President). *(POS)*

Renewing ASOR's Mission for the 21st Century

Through the final years of the 1990s, as plans for celebration of the organization's Centennial took shape, the leadership of ASOR focused attention on establishing its vision for the future. In 1997 President Seger initiated an open on-line dialogue with members that culminated in an "ASOR Vision 2000" program of roundtable discussions at the 1998 Annual Meeting in Orlando. At the same time the Development Committee under the leadership of Vice President Holland Hendrix was also organizing plans for a major fund raising campaign. These efforts and discussions helped to shape a new Mission Statement intended to provide a concise iteration of ASOR's goals and objectives, to assist in development efforts and to serve as a reminder of the organization's purposes for its membership. The new statement was formally approved at the Board of Trustees' spring meeting in New York City on May 1, 1999.

The ASOR Mission

ASOR's mission is to initiate, encourage and support research into and public understanding of the peoples and cultures of the Near East from the earliest times:

By fostering original research, archaeological excavations and explorations,

By encouraging scholarship in basic languages, cultural histories and traditions of the Near Eastern world,

By promoting the educational goals of Near Eastern studies disciplines and advocating high academic standards in teaching and interdisciplinary research,

By maintaining an active program of timely dissemination of research results and conclusions,

By offering educational opportunities in Near Eastern history and archaeology to undergraduates and graduates in North American colleges, university and seminaries, and through outreach activities to secondary schools and the general public.

ASOR's Future: Challenge and Promise

As the twentieth century closed, ASOR remained vital and continued to pursue its historic vision. The hundred years of its history had witnessed an ever-increasing demand throughout America and the world for more information about the ancient and contemporary Near Eastern region. From its birth in 1900, ASOR, through its wide-ranging programs of research and support of scholarship, helped to satisfy this curiosity for knowledge about the human past, serving to increase global awareness and to promote a better understanding of the foundations of western society.

Supported by more than 1300 individual members and by one hundred ten institutions ASOR made its entrance into the twenty-first century looking forward to a productive future in pursuit of its mission. Through its support of scholars and scholarship, and in partnership with Overseas Center affiliates and regional committees, ASOR's resolve to maintain its highly respected programs of exploration and discovery throughout the Middle East and eastern Mediterranean area remained constant. Its Committee on Archaeological Policy continued to nurture and encourage excavations and other research work in key locations in Cyprus, Israel and Jordan and to maintain and expand its attentions to activities in other countries throughout the region. Maintenance of efforts to assist the overseas centers in building their libraries through book and journal exchanges, in communicating with trustees and scholars through its newsletter and other publications, and in support of public relations and fund-raising efforts, were also ongoing through ASOR's home office.

In North America the organization also faced exciting new opportunities and challenges. Within the academic world a fresh generation of scholars was emerging, broadening the ASOR mission by reaching beyond the traditional fields of biblical studies, languages and history into a broad range of disciplines including anthropology, ethnography and environmental science, along with museum and preservation studies. Today ASOR remains the premier international scholarly organization dedicated to fostering research in the ancient and modern Near East and its scholar members hold distinguished positions in academic institutions throughout North America and beyond. Through its Committees on Publication and Annual Meetings and Programs ASOR has in place dynamic programs for facilitating interactions among the scholars themselves, for disseminating the results of research broadly to the academic community and for sharing more widely these results with the general public.

Passing the Torch

At the November 1999 meeting of the ASOR Board in Cambridge, Massachusetts, the Development Committee presented the case statement for a three-year fundraising effort entitled "Passing the Torch." Citing the need for ASOR to secure financially its passage into the new century the goal proposed for the campaign was set at $3 million. This included $2 million for endowment and another $1 million to cover annual operations support and program enhancements for the three years, as well as costs for centennial year activities. The Board approved these plans without dissent and plans to launch the campaign were scheduled to coincide with special centennial programs the following year. Formal announcement of the Torch Campaign took place at the November 2000 Annual Meeting of the organization in Nashville, Tennessee at which time gifts and pledges of almost $1 million were announced. ASOR thus brought its first century to a close with vigor and enthusiasm, looking forward with optimism to its future.

Part Three: Celebrating a Century
by Joe D. Seger

Prelude

Celebration of ASOR's Centennial was initiated by a "Centennial Kickoff Reception" at the Annual Meeting of the organization in New Orleans in 1996.

> *Altogether those honored in New Orleans provide us with models of service, and help explain why ASOR has remained vibrant and successful through almost a full century. I hope that their example will encourage us each likewise to rededicate ourselves to the work of the organization as we prepare for our Centennial, and look forward to the continuation of active programs in Near Eastern archaeology and related research into the next millennium.*
>
> President Joe Seger commenting on recipients of ASOR Honors and Awards at the 1996 Annual Meeting. ASOR Newsletter 46:4

By this time a working committee under the leadership of Past-President Eric Meyers had been established and planning for centennial year activities was underway. The committee included representatives from each of the overseas centers and other constituent groups. Initial planning involved consideration of several program facets. These included a possible exhibition, the writing of an updated history of the organization and the preparation of a TV/video series on ASOR digs, together with lectures, various other academic sessions and gala events. From the outset centennial planning also included active participation by the Development Committee, chaired by then Vice President Holland Hendrix, which was engaged in both centennial and longer range fund raising initiatives. In an effort to be as inclusive as possible a "Long Lists" project was initiated under the leadership of Norma Dever. This was to insure that the names and addresses of all members of the extended ASOR family would be at hand for distribution of centennial program information and invitations.

The Centennial countdown was continued during the Napa, California meeting in 1997 with a special Centennial Fund Raising Banquet. This featured a memorable talk by senior ASOR scholar Avraham Biran, titled "Biblical Archaeology Then and Now." Planning initiatives were pursued throughout 1998 and during the October meeting of the Executive Committee in Boston contact was established with Elizabeth Moynihan, ASOR's first Board Chairperson, who agreed to serve with Eric Meyers as a Co-Chair of a Centennial Honorary Committee. At that point Joe Seger assumed responsibilities for chairing the working committee.

Avraham Biran, Thayer Fellow at the Jerusalem School from 1935 to 1937 and current Director of the Nelson Glueck School of Biblical Archaeology at Hebrew Union College in Jerusalem. (POS)

ASOR Centennial Committee

Eric M. Meyers Co-Chair Honorary Committee
Elizabeth Moynihan Co-Chair Honorary Committee
Joe D. Seger Chair Working Committee
P. E. MacAllister Board Chair
Nan Frederick ACOR liaison
Walter Rast ACOR liaison
Lydie Shufro AIAR liaison
Jerry Vincent CAARI liaison
Ed Gilbert CAARI liaison
Holland Hendrix Development liaison
Gus Van Beek Member at large
Joe Greene Member at large
Alice Pickering Member at large
John Spencer Member at large
Lawrence Stager Member at large
Rudy Dornemann (Staff ex officio)
Holly Andrews (Staff ex officio)
Billie Jean Collins (Staff ex officio)

Final decisions on the scope of the year 2000 celebration activities were made during committee and trustee sessions at the November 1998 Annual Meeting in Orlando, Florida. Washington DC was established as the venue for a major program in mid-April 2000 and a schedule was set for subsequent events at each of the overseas centers in late May and early June. Special year-ending activities were also planned for the November 2000 Annual Meeting in Nashville, Tennessee and in conjunction with the Archeological Institute of America, for early January 2001 during its Annual Meeting in San Diego, California. In Orlando, P. E. MacAllister announced good progress on the preparation of the ASOR digs TV/Video series and final plans for preparation of this volume on ASOR history were coordinated by the committee of authors and editors. AIAR representatives also announced plans for special sessions on the Jerusalem School and AIAR beginnings titled "The House that Albright Built" at the 1999 Annual Meeting in Cambridge Massachusetts.

Beginning in the spring of 1999 deliberate efforts to arrange for all the various event activities commenced. In Washington the Public Forum Institute, a local planning group, was contracted to assist with program and development work and fruitful negotiations were undertaken with The Smithsonian Associates for a major public program segment. These efforts were aided in most significant ways by the participation of Alice Pickering and Under Secretary of State Thomas Pickering, long-time friends of ASOR and of Middle East archaeology.

A Program of Reminiscences.

The buildup to the centennial year was concluded with the special mini-symposium "The House that Albright Built" at the Cambridge Annual Meeting in 1999. The program was organized as part of the ASOR/AIAR Centennial celebration by the Chair of the Albright Institute's Centennial Committee Lydie Shufro. In afternoon sessions past Albright Institute Fellows and the Institute Director spoke on topics that had been of interest to W. F. Albright, and to which he himself had made major contributions. The presenters were Paul-Alain Beaulieu, Aaron Brody, Sidnie White Crawford, J. P. Dessel, Sy Gitin, Gordon Hamilton, Lawrence Herr, Carolyn Higgenbotham, Jodi Magness, David Schloen, Mark Smith and J. Edward Wright. Wright and Walter Aufrecht participated as respondents. Lydie Shufro presided.

Trude Dothan honoring her departed friend Joy Ungerleider Mayerson at the Cambridge banquet in 1999.

These were followed in the evening by the ASOR annual banquet and a program of reminiscences about Albright and the Jerusalem School by senior ASOR and Albright scholars with Walter Aufrecht as moderator. The principal speakers were Avraham Biran, Vivian Bull, Trude Dothan, Ernest S. Frerichs and Carol Meyers. In addition Robert Bull, William Dever, Norma Dever, Eric Meyers and Joe Seger, together with other members of the audience, also contributed stories. The day's program was specially dedicated to the memory of the late Joy Ungerleider Mayerson, who served as Chair of the AIAR Board of Trustees from 1988–1994.

Avraham Biran celebrating his 90th birthday with the ASOR/AIAR family at the Cambridge meeting in 1999. The cake's inscription reads "In celebration of the AIAR/ASOR centennial and with warmest congratulations to the 90 years young Avraham Biran."

ASOR at 100

The Washington Event

The main celebration of ASOR's centennial took place in spring 2000 in Washington, DC from Friday to Sunday April 14–16 with a full range of program features. These included a formal Gala at the State Department on Friday evening, an outstanding public program in conjunction with The Smithsonian Associates through the day Saturday and a no-holds barred reception Saturday evening. It concluded with a wonderful series of academic papers and a closing luncheon on Sunday.

The Friday Gala was replete with all the pomp appropriate to the occasion. Hosted by the Under Secretary of State for Political Affairs Honorable Thomas R. Pickering and Mrs. Alice Pickering, the evening began with a champagne reception featuring music by the "Celebrated String Quartet." This was followed by a wonderful gourmet dinner in the regal environs of the Benjamin Franklin Dining Room. As Master of Ceremonies, ASOR Chairman P.E. MacAllister opened the evening program by acknowledging the Honorary Patronage of the First Lady, Hillary Rodham Clinton, and by extending greetings to members of the Centennial Honorary Committee and all in attendance. With his usual eloquent style he underscored the significance of ASOR's successful work through its 100 years of activity, and noted its arrival at a critical juncture, facing the challenges of continuing efforts in a new century. He then introduced the evening's Keynote Speaker, Under Secretary of State Thomas Pickering.

Overview of the Centennial Banquet underway in the Benjamin Franklin Dining Room with the head table in the middle foreground.

An ASOR Mosaic: A Centennial History of the American Schools of Oriental Research

ASOR CENTENNIAL HONORARY PATRON

First Lady Hillary Rodham Clinton

ASOR CENTENNIAL HONORARY COMMITTEE

Co-Chairpersons
Mrs. Elizabeth Moynihan
Dr. Eric M. Meyers

Ambassador Abdulwahab Al-Hajjri (Yemen)
Ambassador Erato Kozakou-Marcoullis (Cyprus)
Ambassador Marwan Muasher (Jordan)
Ambassador Hasan Abdel Rahman (Palestinian Authority)
Ambassador Raymond Chrétien (Canada)
Ambassador H. E. David Ivry (Israel)
H.R.H. Ra'ad bin Zeid, (The Hashemite Kingdom of Jordan)
Ambassador Farid Abboud (Lebanon)

Senator Daniel Patrick Moynihan and Elizabeth Moynihan, Past Chairman of the Board and Honorary Trustee, ASOR
Under Secretary of State for Political Affairs Thomas Pickering and Alice Pickering
Senator Paul Sarbanes and Christine Sarbanes
John D'Arms, President, American Council of Learned Societies (ACLS)
Adele Berlin, President, Society of Biblical Literature (SBL)
Miguel Civil, President, American Oriental Society (AOS)
Richard Lariviere, President, Council of American Overseas Research Centers (CAORC)
Jon Westling, President, Boston University
Nancy Wilkie, President, Archaeological Institute of America (AIA)

Avraham Biran, Thayer Fellow Emeritus, ASOR
Frank Moore Cross, Past President and Honorary Trustee, ASOR
David Noel Freedman, Past First Vice President, ASOR
Patty Gerstenblith, President, AIAR
Edward Gilbert, President, CAARI
Charles U. Harris, Honorary Chairman of the Board and Life Trustee, ASOR and Janet Harris*
Artemis Joukowsky, President, ACOR and Martha Joukowsky
Norma Kershaw, Honorary Trustee, ASOR
Philip King, Past President and Honorary Trustee, ASOR
Leon Levy, Honorary Trustee, ASOR and Shelby White
P.E. MacAllister, Chairman of the Board and Life Trustee, ASOR and Rebecca MacAllister
P. Kyle McCarter, Past President and Trustee, ASOR
Eric Meyers, Past President and Trustee, ASOR and Carol Meyers
James Sauer*, Past President, ASOR
Richard Scheuer, Life Trustee, ASOR and Joan Scheuer
Gough Thompson, Past Chairman of the Board and Honorary Trustee, ASOR
Daniel Wolk, Chairman of the Board, AIAR
*in memoriam

ASOR Board Chairman P.E. MacAllister, Master of Ceremonies at the Centenial Banquet.

Under Secretary Pickering's talk was clearly the highlight of the weekend. Drawing on his vast diplomatic experience, his own special interests in history and antiquity and the special opportunities he had for firsthand involvement in ASOR's and the overseas centers' efforts while he served respectively as Ambassador to Israel and then to Jordan, he provided a unique perspective on the backgrounds and importance of ASOR's contributions to cultural development and scholarship in the Middle East region. The full text of his comments are presented as a special preface to this volume.

The Honorable Thomas R. Pickering, Under Secretary of State for Political Affairs delivering his address as Centennial keynote speaker.

The evening closed with a series of Toasts by President Joe Seger to members of the Centennial Honorary Committee; to ASOR's three Life Trustees, Richard J. Scheuer, Charles U. Harris and P.E. MacAllister; to its Founding Societies and affiliated overseas centers and boards; and to all the representatives of the wider community of associates and associations providing support for the organization.

(left to right) Under Secretary of State Thomas Pickering and ASOR Board Chairman P.E. MacAllister in the Benjamin Franklin Room of the U.S Department of State building.

Notables at the Centennial Banquet. (Left to right) Charles U. Harris, ASOR Life Trustee and Honorary Board Chairman; P.E. MacAllister, ASOR Life Trustee and Board Chairman; Marion Scheuer Sofaer, AIAR Trustee (representing Richard J. Scheuer ASOR Life Trustee and AIAR Trustee); Honorable Thomas R. Pickering, Under Secretary of State and Keynote Speaker; Joe D. Seger, ASOR President; Eric M. Meyers, ASOR Past-President and Co-Chair of the Centennial Honorary Committee.

ASOR: A History of the American Schools of Oriental Research by Eric M. Meyers and Joe D. Seger

ASOR President Joe Seger with Mrs. Alice Pickering at the Gala Reception. Mrs. Pickering was most instrumental in helping the Centennial Committee prepare for the Washington events.

During the day on Saturday the public program of "ASOR at 100" lectures in cooperation with The Smithsonian Associates was held at the U.S. Department of Agriculture, Jefferson Auditorium. Titled "A Century of Discoveries in the Ancient Near East" it drew a crowd of more than four hundred attendees. The five speakers represented the work of ASOR and of the three overseas centers. The topics were organized to represent both the chronological and geographical range of ASOR's Near Eastern work and interests. The talks were interspersed with lively question and answer sessions. President Seger opened and closed the program with comments on ASOR's successful journey through the past century and with an optimistic view of its prospects at the start of a new millennium.

ASOR at 100 Lecture Speakers

William G. Dever
University of Arizona. "Israelite Origins in Context -Abraham to Moses."

Seymour Gitin
W. F. Albright Institute of Archaeological Research, Jerusalem. "The Israelites and their Neighbors -Canaanites and Philistines."

Robert Merrillees
Cyprus American Archaeological Research Institute, Nicosia. "The Greek Emergence in the Eastern Mediterranean -Cyprus and Phonecia."

Eric Meyers
Duke University. "Judaism and Christianity: Origins and Transformations -A View from Qumran."

Pierre Bikai
American Center of Oriental Research, Amman. "Byzantine Petra in Jordan -Churches and Scrolls."

Joe D. Seger
Mississippi State University. "Near Eastern Archaeology in the 21st Century -New Perspectives and New Horizons."

On Saturday evening, ASOR members and friends were given the opportunity to "cut loose" with a lively Grand Buffet Reception featuring good food and a fun-filled program of "Roasts, Toasts, and Boasts." Attendees were first challenged to a game of "ASOR Mosaic Bingo" to win a variety of special centennial prizes, with an ASOR-monogrammed pullover shirt toping the list. The program, with Rudy Dornemann and Joe Seger sharing the podium as Masters of Ceremonies, proceeded with a monologue by President Seger roasting members. This was followed by presentations of Centennial Year Honors and Awards presided over by CAMP Awards Subcommittee Chairman Harold Forshey. A good Middle East touch to the evening was provided by the appearance of belly dancer Nancy Coll from Brooklyn, NY, whose performance in two separate segments clearly left some attendees "in a whirl." The program also featured a series of toasts to memorialize and honor special members from ASOR's past and present; drawings for additional prize handouts; and the presentation of an ASOR 100 special birthday cake replete with the singing of "Happy Birthday" to ASOR. For the late night hangers' on, Joe Seger, assisted by Barbara (Babs) Miley, took the stage as "Kornact," a la Johnny Carson, and sought to mystify the audience by answering questions before they were asked, poking more fun at ASOR notables.

The program continued more soberly on Sunday morning with a series of concurrent seminar sessions on "Archaeological Periods in Perspective." Each of these sessions featured the present state respectively of research in Bronze Age, Iron Age, Hellenistic/Roman, and Byzantine/Islamic archaeology in the Near East. Speakers were: Bronze Age — Al Leonard, Jonathan Tubb, Ellen Herscher, Eric Cline and Elizabeth Stone; Iron Age — Elizabeth Bloch-Smith, Rudolph Dornemann, Dan Master, Bruce Routledge, Ian Morris and David Schloen; Hellenistic/Roman — Andrea Berlin, Jane Waldbaum, Sharon Herbert, Eric Lapp and Elise Friedland; Byzantine/Islamic — Jodi Magness, Kenneth Holum, James Strange and Renata Holod. They all received rave reviews from participants and attendees alike. These proceedings will be published as a special ASOR volume.

The Sunday program closed with a "Digs Luncheon" featuring a backdrop of slides organized by Rudy Dornemann, showing special finds from ASOR-affiliated dig projects, and a few closing words by President Seger. In these he praised the good efforts of the Centennial Committee, the ASOR Staff and the program participants for their work in organizing and expediting the weekend's celebration events. Those ASOR members and friends who attended the Washington program carried forward wonderful memories of these century-closing festivities.

"Kicking up some Dust" at the Grand Buffet Reception, Saturday April 15.

Opposite page

1. President Seger closing the evening program as the Great Kornact.

2. Executive Director Dornemann making introductions at the podium.

3. ASOR Trustee and AIAR Vice President John Spencer presenting an ASOR Service Award to Norma Dever.

4. (left to right) ASOR Trustee William Dever, AIAR Director Sy Gitin, and Jeff Zorn engrossed in the roasts, toasts and boasts program.

5. ASOR Board Chairman P.E. MacAllister lifts a toast to the memory of W. F. Albright.

6. CAMP Awards Sub-committee Chairman Harold Forshey presides over Award presentations at the podium.

7. Ernest Frericks (at keyboard) with Eric Meyers and William Dever (out of frame right) lead in singing "Happy Birthday" to ASOR.

Page following

8. ACOR President Artemis Joukowsky accepts a special toast made in his honor by Nan Frederick.

9. Dancer Nancy Coll flirts with President Seger.

10. (left to right) Former ASOR First Vice President David Noel Freedman receives a toast from AIAR Trustee Carol Meyers.

11. Martha Joukowski receives a P.E. MacAllister Field Archaeology Award for 2000.

12. (left to right) ASOR Executive Director Rudy Dornemann, Meredith Dornemann, ASOR and CAARI Trustee Jerry Vincent with Ian Morris, Eric Cline and James Hardin at the Mosaic Bingo table.

13. (left to right) ASOR Trustee and former CAARI Director Stuart Swiny, with Harold Forshey, presenting a G.E. Wright Publications Award for 2000 to Robert Hohlfelder.

14. (left to right) CAORC Executive Director Mary Ellen Lane, person UK, Martha Joukowsky, Nan Frederick and ACOR Director Pierre Bikai enjoy the program.

15. Former ASOR Board Chairman Gough Thompson lifts a toast to former presidents Philip J. King and James Sauer.

16. AIAR Trustee Norma Dever accepting an ASOR Service Award for 2000 from presenter John Spencer (in background).

ASOR: A History of the American Schools of Oriental Research by Eric M. Meyers and Joe D. Seger

An ASOR Mosaic: A Centennial History of the American Schools of Oriental Research

Celebrations Overseas

A second round of Centennial festivities took place at the affiliated centers overseas from May 29 to June 7.

These included programs in Jerusalem May 29–31, in Nicosia June 5 and in Amman June 7.

AIAR/ASOR Centennial Symposium — Jerusalem

The celebration in Jerusalem from May 29–31 featured a major international symposium held at the Israel Museum and a closing reception in the historic garden of the Albright Institute. The program was organized by Symposium Program Committee Chairman William G. Dever, AIAR Director Sy Gitin and Albright Centennial Committee Chair Lydie Shufro. AIAR Trustee Mark Smith and Sy Gitin developed the theme and titles of the program. Sy Gitin, Lydie Shufro and Helene Roumani, Assistant to the AIAR Director, handled the logistics. Other AIAR Trustees who served on the AIAR Centennial Committee included Walter Aufrecht, Sidnie White Crawford, Barry Gittlen, Jodi Magness, Larry Stager, Jane Waldbaum and Edward Wright. The symposium received generous support from ASOR, the Albright Institute's grant from the United States Information Agency, the Horace W. Goldsmith, the Samuel H. Kress and the Lucius N. Littauer foundations, along with special gifts from Eugene Grant, Austin and Norma Ritterspach, Jonathan and Jeannette Rosen, Herschel Shanks and Lydie Shufro.

(left to right) AIAR Director Sy Gitin with Lydie Shufro, AIAR and ASOR Trustee, and AIAR Centennial Committee Chairperson, and William G. Dever, ASOR Trustee and AIAR Centennial Program Committee Chairman at the Jerusalem celebration.

The symposium program opened on Monday May 29 with greetings from AIAR Director Sy Gitin, Joe Seger, President of ASOR, Sidnie White Crawford, President-elect of AIAR (for AIAR President Patty Gerstenblith) and Albright Centennial Chair Lydie Shufro (for Ernest S. Frerichs, AIAR Past President and Trustee, and Director of the Dorot Foundation). Entitled *Symbiosis, Symbolism, and the Power of the Past: Canaan, Ancient Israel and their Neighbors from the Late Bronze Age through Roman Palestinae*, the program had three main themes: Historical and Political Landscape — The Levant and Beyond, Religion and Distinction, and The History of the Family — Continuity and Change. A total of thirty-seven papers were presented by international scholars from Austria, Belgium, Cyprus, Finland, France, Great Britain, Greece, Israel, the Netherlands and the United States. Respondents and questions from the audience initiated lively exchanges and discussion following each session. The proceedings will be published as a special volume by the Albright Institute.

Centennial Program Participants (left to right from front) Row 1: Osnat Mische-Brandl, Aren Maeir, Shalom Paul, Trude Dothan, William G. Dever, Lydie Shufro, Seymour Gitin, Sarah Morris, Susan Sheratt, Ziony Zevit. Row 2: Peter Machinist, Baruch Halpern, Carol Meyers, Eliat Mazar, Vassos Karageorghis, David Stronach, Hugh Williamson, Avraham Faust. Row 3: Edouard Lipinski, David Ussishkin, Manfred Bietak, Joseph Aviram, Susan Ackerman, Charles Harris, Sidnie White Crawford, Holly Pittman, Karel Van der Toorn, Anne Caubet. Row 4: Mordechai Cogan, Joe Seger, Eliezer Oren, Simo Parpola, Anson Rainey. Row 5: Eric Meyers, Edward Wright, Amihai Mazar, Kenneth Kitchen, Dan Masters, Israel Finkelstein, James Muhly, John Collins, Mark Smith. Participants not in the photograph: Michael Artzy, Dan Bahat, Amnon Ben-Tor, Avraham Biran, Shlomo Bunimovitz, Moshe Kochavi, Baruch Levine, Jodi Magness, Avraham Malamat, Doron Mendels, Jerome Murphy O'Connor, Sari Nusseibeh, James Snyder, Ephraim Stern and Daniel Wolk. Official participants not able to attend: Ernest S. Frerichs, Patty Gerstenblith and P. E. MacAllister.

Following the Monday afternoon sessions James Snyder, Director of the Israel Museum, welcomed the symposium participants at the opening of a special exhibit, *Thunder on High: Images of the Canaanite Storm God*. The exhibit was organized in honor of the AIAR/ASOR Centennial by Osnat Misch-Brandl, Curator of the Israel Museum Department of Chalcolithic and Early Bronze Culture. The day concluded with a reception hosted by the Israel Exploration Society, on behalf of the Archaeological Institutions in Israel. Words of greeting and reminiscences were offered by Joseph Aviram, President of the IES, Avraham Biran, Avraham Malamat, Trude Dothan and Sy Gitin.

On Tuesday May 30, during a special evening session, papers by William Dever and David Ussishkin were presented as public lectures. Both invited eager responses and a lively exchange with the audience. On Wednesday afternoon, William Dever, as Program Chair, also provided remarks closing the symposium. During the three days a sustained audience of more than three hundred and fifty people attended the sessions.

(left to right) Sari Nusseibeh, President of Al-Quds University, William G. Dever, University of Arizona, Hamdan Taha, Director of the Palestinian Department of Antiquities, Seymour Gitin, AIAR Director and David Ussishkin, Tel Aviv University, at the Albright Institute Centennial reception.

An ASOR Mosaic: A Centennial History of the American Schools of Oriental Research

(left to right) AIAR Director Sy Gitin introduces ASOR President Joe Seger to reception guests. ASOR Honorary Board Chairman Charles U. Harris stands by to extend formal greetings on behalf of ASOR.

(left to right) AIAR Director Gitin with Hisham M'farreh at the schwarma stand.

Enjoying the Centennial reception. (left to right) Kenneth Kitchen, University of Liverpool, Nadav Na'aman, Tel Aviv University, and Daphna Ben-Tor of the Israel Museum.

Appropriately, the Albright Institute itself was the venue of a closing buffet-reception on Wednesday evening. This was indeed a memorable event. The garden of the Albright, recently renamed and dedicated as "The Kershaw Garden," was truly "The Meeting Place" in Jerusalem that evening. Offering greetings were AIAR Director Sy Gitin, Charles U. Harris, ASOR Life Trustee and past Chairman of the Board (for ASOR Board Chairman P. E. MacAllister), Sari Nusseibeh, President Al-Quds University and Dan Wolk, Chairman of the AIAR Board. Nadia Bandak, the Institute Manager, and Hisham M'farreh, the Albright Chef, organized an unforgettable feast, which even included *schwarma* and "Ben & Jerry" ice cream. In addition to the many Americans representing the ASOR and AIAR constituency, and the international scholars that participated in the symposium, the gathering included a wide cross section of scholars and friends from the twenty-five Honorary Sponsoring Institutions including all of the Israeli and Palestinian archaeological institutions and museums. This was worthy testimony to the inclusive spirit of the Albright and a fit climax to ASOR's and AIAR's century long role of leadership in promoting archaeological and historical scholarship in Jerusalem and the Middle East.

(left to right) AIAR Trustee Lee Seeman, AIAR Board Chairman Dan Wolk and AIAR and ASOR Trustee Lydie Shufro viewing the pillar marking the dedication of the AIAR courtyard as "The Kershaw Garden."

Lecture and Reception — Nicosia

On Sunday and Monday June 4 and 5 the celebration moved to Cyprus and CAARI where Director Robert Merrillees and his staff had arranged a lecture and reception program to celebrate the occasion. On June 4 a buffet dinner at the Institute served as a welcoming event for visiting trustees from ASOR, residents and other guests. This climaxed in the ceremonial cutting of the "ASOR 100th" birthday cakes tastefully prepared by CAARI Trustee Lillian Craig in honor of the occasion.

Guests dining on CAARI's hostel veranda in welcoming celebration of ASOR's Centennial.

Happy Birthday cakes at the CAARI welcoming dinner.

ASOR President Joe Seger cuts the birthday cakes while Executive Director Rudolph Dornemann stands by to help serve.

The Cyprus American
Archaeological Research Institute

invites you to an illustrated lecture
to celebrate the Centennial of ASOR
(American Schools of Oriental Research)

by

Dr. Gloria London
NEH Fellow

**From Person, Place to Thing:
The Changing Meaning of Pottery**

Monday, 5th June 2000

11 Andreas Demetriou   CAARI Library
1066 Nicosia   7:30 p.m.

Reception to follow

The program continued Monday, June 5 with an evening public lecture by NEH Fellow Gloria London in the CAARI library. Director Merrillees opened the proceedings by drawing attention to ASOR's Centennial and its significance for CAARI. He then introduced ASOR President Joe Seger who offered greetings on behalf of ASOR Chairman P.E. MacAllister and the ASOR Board. Next followed Dr. London's illustrated lecture titled "From Person, Place to Thing: The Changing Meaning of Pottery." She dedicated the talk to the potters of Cyprus with whom she had worked, several of whom were in the audience. After a period of questions and comments the audience of more than one hundred retired to the CAARI garden for a gala reception. Included among the evening's attendees, in addition to ASOR and CAARI Trustees, were scholars from the University of Cyprus, representatives of the Cyprus Department of Antiquities, members of American and other foreign excavation teams, several foreign service diplomats and other local CAARI friends.

Members of the official party at the reception in the CAARI garden. (left to right) CAARI Director Robert Merrillees, CAARI Administrative Assistant Vathoulla Moustoukki, ASOR Trustee Austin Ritterspach, Lecturer and NEH Fellow Gloria London, ASOR President Joe Seger, ASOR Executive Director Rudolph Dornemann.

Reception Celebration — Amman

The final Middle East event took place in Amman, Jordan on the evening of June 7. Following a day long meeting of the ACOR Board of Trustees, ACOR Director Pierre Bikai, with his wife Patricia and ACOR President Artemis Joukowsky, hosted a grand reception for ACOR and ASOR trustees and for the many foreign and local friends and affiliates of the Center. As part of the ceremony the group was first greeted warmly by H.R.H. Ra'ad bin Zeid who congratulated the ACOR Board and its leadership for the excellent status of ACOR affairs and noted ASOR's century of achievements. In response ASOR President Seger extended special centennial greetings to the assembly on behalf of the ASOR Board and its Chairman P. E. MacAllister and commented on the "living connections" between ACOR and ASOR vested in the persons of Mohammad Adawi and Rudy Dornemann. Mohammad, once on the ASOR staff, has served over twenty-five years as the head chef for ACOR. Rudy Dornemann, the first Director at ACOR, now serves ASOR as its Executive Director. President Joukowsky responded warmly, citing ASOR's initiatives in founding and promoting ACOR's development, and noting its assistance in helping ACOR to move to its present state of healthy independence.

ACOR notables (left to right) ACOR Director Pierre Bikai, ACOR Trustee H.R.H. Ra'ad bin Zeid, ACOR President Artemis A. W. Joukowsky, ACOR Associate Director Patricia Bikai.

ASOR: A History of the American Schools of Oriental Research by Eric M. Meyers and Joe D. Seger

Patricia Bikai and Martha Joukowsky talking with H.R.H. Ra'ad bin Zeid at the reception on the ACOR veranda.

H.R.H. Ra'ad bin Zeid greeting the guests at the ACOR reception.

ASOR President Joe Seger (left) greeting guests and honoring ACOR's first Director, now ASOR Executive Director, Rudolph Dornemann (right).

Mohammad Adawi, beloved long-term ACOR Chef.

ACOR President Artemis A.W. Joukowsky (center right) with (left to right) Martha Joukowski, ASOR President Joe Seger and ASOR Executive Director Rudolph Dornemann at the ACOR reception.

ASOR: A History of the American Schools of Oriental Research by Eric M. Meyers and Joe D. Seger

ASOR 2000 in Nashville

ASOR held its 2000 Annual Meeting on November 15–18 in Nashville, Tennessee. Centennial year activities were concluded with its Members Meeting and a Centennial Closing Reception at the Nashville Parthenon on November 17. In addition to the usual business, the meeting featured presentations of Centennial Year Honors and Awards and special recognitions of each of ASOR's Founding Societies, the American Oriental Society (AOS), the Archaeological Institute of America (AIA) and the Society of Biblical Literature (SBL). Representatives of these Founding Societies were each presented with plaques affirming resolutions by the ASOR Executive Committee and Board of Trustees remembering their initiative and support in bringing ASOR into existence in 1900, and expressing appreciation for their respective service contributions to American scholarship from the mid-1800s.

1900-2000

Commemorating its Centennial
the
American Schools of Oriental Research
remembers the initiative and support of
the
Society of Biblical Literature
in appreciation of its service to
American scholarship since 1880 and
honoring it as one of ASOR's Founding Societies.

by resolution of the
ASOR Executive Committee and
Board of Trustees

November 18, 2000

P. E. MacAllister, *Board Chairman*   Joe D. Seger, *President*

1900-2000

The meeting closed with announcement of the formal launch of the "Passing the Torch" Centennial Fund Raising Campaign seeking three million dollars in support of ASOR programs and endowments. Leadership gifts and pledges for the three year appeal in the amount of $950,000 were announced. All members were urged to give generous support to help meet the campaign goals and to help prepare the organization to meet the challenges for its second century.

The meeting session was followed immediately by a sumptuous Centennial Year Closing Reception. Provision for the reception was supported in part by special contributions from the Chairman's Circle of the Board of Trustees in honor of Board Chairman P.E. MacAllister in recognition of his excellent and continuing leadership and for his outstanding support of the organization and its mission.

Nashville 2000 Members Meeting and Centennial Closing Reception.

1. Peter Warnock enjoys the reception fare.

2. Sy Gitin (right) is congratulated on receipt of an ASOR W. F. Albright Award for service to the Albright Institute (right to left) by Harold Forshey, Chairman of the CAMP Honors and Awards Subcommittee, President Joe Seger, Board Chairman P.E. MacAllister and Secretary James Strange.

3. CAP Chairman David McCreery (right) and Michele Daviau in conversation at the reception.

4. Pierre Bikai (right) comes forward to receive an ASOR W.F. Albright Award for service to ACOR presented by former ACOR Director, Bert de Vries.

5. Walter Rast and Carol Meyer in conversation at the reception.

6. ASOR members and guests enjoy the sumptous fare at the Centennial Year Closing Reception. (center right to left) Norma Ritterspach and Richard J. Scheuer.

7. Lydie Shufro graciously accepts an ASOR Member Service Award for her many contributions to ASOR and its affiliated centers.

8. Board Chairman P.E. MacAllister opens the 2000 Members Meeting with greetings.

"Passing the Torch"

"There is no choice. We need to ensure that ASOR can pass the torch to new generations of scholars. The survival of ASOR in the region where civilization began is vital to American interest in the Middle East and essential for a mature understanding of our culture. The ancient Near East is where Judaism, Christianity and Islam took root. In order to truly understand these cultures, we must be sensitive to their literatures and also recognize the true extent of their cultural achievements. In short, we must continue to make the stones speak to us so that the human race can discover more about itself."

Dr. Eric M. Meyers, ASOR Past President and Bernice and Morton Lerner Professor of Religion, Duke University.

ASOR: A History of the American Schools of Oriental Research by Eric M. Meyers and Joe D. Seger

Final Event in San Diego

The final event of the centennial year involved a celebration with the Archaeological Institute of America at its Annual Meeting January 4–7, 2001 in San Diego, California. For the first time ever the AIA and ASOR convened a joint colloquium session. Titled "Sunken Ships and Submerged Cities: Recent Maritime Archaeology in the Eastern Mediterranean" the program was organized by Eric Cline and co-chaired by Joe Seger, ASOR President, and Jane Waldbaum, First Vice-President of AIA. The session included excellent papers by Dan Masters (for Lawrence Stager), Cemal Pulak, Avner Raban, Robert Hohlfelder and Shelly Wachsmann. The program was a major success with a standing room only crowd of 250 attendees.

At the AIA Council Meeting that followed, ASOR President Seger again ceremonially presented the plaque recognizing AIA's role as one of ASOR's Founding Societies to AIA President Nancy Wilke, and commented on the century long tradition of partnership between AIA and ASOR in support of archaeological scholarship. This was followed by an ASOR-sponsored reception honoring AIA officers and members for the organization's role in helping to found ASOR at the start of the twentieth century.

ASOR President Joe Seger (right) presenting the plaque, honoring the AIA as one of ASOR's Founding Societies, to AIA President Nancy Wilke at the meeting of the AIA Council in San Diego.

An ASOR Mosaic: A Centennial History of the American Schools of Oriental Research

ASOR APPENDED LISTS

Officers

Board of Trustees

Staff

Institution Members

Appointees 1970–2000

CAP Affiliated Projects 1970–2000
in countires other than Cyprus, Israel, and Jordan

ASOR: A History of the American Schools of Oriental Research by Eric M. Meyers and Joe D. Seger

ASOR

Celebrating 100 Years of Exploration & Discovery in the Middle East

1900 – 2000

Epilogue: The Continuing Mission

Since it first opened its doors in Jerusalem in 1900, the American Schools of Oriental Research, with its member scholars, associated excavation projects, and affiliated overseas centers, has been partner to many of the greatest archaeological explorations and discoveries in the Middle East region. Throughout the twentieth century it has served to encourage and facilitate academic research and public interest in the rich history of the ancient Near East and its cultures.

Now, as its second century begins, ASOR scholars actively continue their research and rigorously pursue the task of recapturing the past throughout the Middle East and eastern Mediterranean regions. With its thriving, separately incorporated affiliated centers in Israel, Jordan and Cyprus, and through its many approved research projects, ASOR continues to be the principal American organization providing encouragement and support for archaeological and historical research throughout the area. Through ASOR's Committee on Archaeological Policy numerous affiliated projects with multi-disciplinary interests continue to explore traces of the region's past civilizations. These span the more than ten thousand years of Near Eastern cultural development, from distant prehistory into the present. Through its Committee on Publications and the Committee on Annual Meetings and Program the fruits of these researches continue to enlighten and educate a broad spectrum of Americans, and others throughout the world, about the Near Eastern roots of our cultural heritage.

The twentieth century witnessed an ever-increasing demand for greater information about the ancient and contemporary Near East. From its birth in 1900, ASOR's purpose was to help satisfy this thirst for knowledge about the human past and the public's hunger for better understanding of the foundations of our western society. With this volume, the American Schools of Oriental Research proudly celebrates a century of dynamic activity and prepares to continue its program of highly respected research and educational outreach in pursuit of its mission into the new century that lies ahead.

ASOR Board Chairpersons 1984–2000

Elizabeth Moynihan	1984–1986
Gough W. Thompson, Jr.	1986–1992
Charles U. Harris	1992–1994
P. E. MacAllister	1994–

ASOR Presidents 1921–2000

James A. Montgomery	1921–1933
Millar Burrows	1924–1948
Carl H. Kraeling	1949–1954
A. Henry Detweiler	1955–1965
G. Ernest Wright	1966–1974
Frank Moore Cross	1974–1976
Philip J. King	1976–1982
James A. Sauer	1982–1988
P. Kyle McCarter	1988–1990
Eric M. Meyers	1990–1996
Joe D. Seger	1996–

ASOR Officers (Current during 2000)

Chairman	P. E. MacAllister
President	Joe D. Seger
Vice President	Holland Hendrix
Secretary	James F. Strange
Treasurer	Ingrid Wood
Chairman COP	Albert Leonard, Jr.
Chairman CAP	David McCreery
Chairman CAMP	Victor H. Matthews

ASOR Staff (Current during 2000)

Executive Director	Rudolph H. Dornemann
Assistant Director	Holly Andrews
Program Assistant	Britt Hartenberger
Accounting Assistant	Selma Omerefendic
Director of Publications	Billie Jean Collins
Publications Assistant	Chris Madell

ASOR Board of Trustees

(Members during 2000)

Walter E. Aufrecht	Individual Member	University of Lethbridge
Andrea Berlin	Individual Member	University of Minnesota
Kent Bermingham	Board Elected	Powell, Ohio
Jeffrey A. Blakely	Individual Member	Madison, Wisconsin
Oded Borowski	Institutional Member	Emory University
John Camp	Board Elected	Lakeland Shores, Minnesota
Sidnie White Crawford	AIAR Representative	University of Nebraska-Lincoln
William G. Dever	Institutional Member	University of Arizona
Nan Frederick	Individual Member	West River, Maryland
Patty Gerstenblith	AIAR Representative	DePaul University
Edward G. Gilbert	Board Elected	Scottsdale, Arizona
Julie Hansen	Individual Member	Boston University
Charles U. Harris	Life Trustee	Delaplane, Virginia
Timothy P. Harrison	Institutional Member	University of Toronto
Holland Hendrix	Vice President	New York, New York
Oystein S. LaBianca	Individual Member	Andrews University
Albert Leonard, Jr.	COP Chairman	University of Arizona
P. E. MacAllister	Chairman	Indianapolis, Indiana
Burton MacDonald	Individual Member	St. Francis Xavier University
Jodi Magness	Institutional Member	Tufts University
Victor H. Matthews	CAMP Chairman	Southwest Missouri State University
David McCreery	CAP Chairman	Willamette University
Eric M. Meyers	Board Elected	Duke University
P. Kyle McCarter, Jr.	Individual Member	Johns Hopkins University
Robert D. Miller II	Individual Member	Mount St. Mary's Seminary
Andrew M. T. Moore	AIA Representative	Rochester Institute of Technology
Andrew Oliver	CAARI Representative	Chevy Chase, Maryland
Anne Ogilvy	ACOR Representative	Philadelphia, Pennsylvania
Austin Ritterspach	Board Elected	Indianapolis, Indiana
James F. Ross	Individual Member	Gaithersburg, Maryland
Bruce Routledge	Institutional Member	University of Pennsylvania
B. Winfred Ruffner, Jr.	Board Elected	Chattanooga, Tennessee
R. Thomas Schaub	Vice President	Edgewood, Pennsylvania
Richard J. Scheuer	Life Trustee	Larchmont, New York
Brian G. Schmidt	AOS Representative	University of Michigan
Tammi Schneider	Institutional Member	Claremont Graduate University
Joe D. Seger	President	Mississippi State University
Lydie Shufro	Board Elected	New York, New York
John Spencer	Institutional Member	John Carroll University
Deborah Stern	Board Elected	New York, New York
James F. Strange	Secretary	University of South Florida
Stuart Swiny	Individual Member	University of Albany
Gerald Vincent	Board Elected	Cortez, Colorado
Ingrid Wood	Treasurer	Boston, Massachusetts
Randall Younker	Institutional Member	Andrews University

ASOR Trustees 2000

Life Trustees

P.E. MacAllister
Board Chairman

Charles U. Harris

Richard J. Scheuer

Officers

P.E. MacAllister
Board Chairman

Joe D. Seger
President

Holland Hendrix
Vice President

James F. Strange
Secretary

Ingrid Wood
Treasurer

Albert Leonard, Jr.
Chair, Committee
on Publications

David McCreery
Chair, Committee on
Archaeological Policy

Victor H. Matthews
Chair, Committee on
Annual Meeting

Class of 2000

Julie Hansen

James F. Ross

Burton McDonald

Jodi Magness

John Spencer

Randall Younker

Gerald Vincent

Deborah Stern

Class of 2001

Nan Frederick

Andrea Berlin

P. Kyle McCarter, Jr.

Oded Borowski

Tammi Schneider

R. Thomas Schaub

Kent Birmingham

Class of 2002

 Walter F. Aufrecht
 Jeffrey A. Blakely
 Stuart Swiny
 Patty Gerstenblith, AIAR

 William G. Dever
 Timothy P. Harrison
 Bruce Routledge
 Sidnie White Crawford, AIAR

 Lydie Shufro
 Eric M. Meyers
 John Camp

Overseas Institute Trustees 2000

 Ann Ogilvy, ACOR
 Edward G. Gilbert, CAARI

 Andrew Oliver, CAARI

Founding Society Trustees

 Andrew M. T. Moore, AIA
 Brian Schmidt, AOS

Class of 2003

 James F. Ross
 Robert D. Miller II
 Oystein S. La Bianca

 Jodi Magness
 John Spencer
 Randall Younker

 Austin Ritterspach
 B. Winfred Ruffner, Jr.
 Gerald Vincent

ASOR: A History of the American Schools of Oriental Research by Eric M. Meyers and Joe D. Seger

ASOR Offices

Main Headquarters
ASOR
at Boston University
656 Beacon Street, Fifth Floor
Boston, MA 02215-2010

Phone: 617 353 6570
Fax: 617 353 6575
E-mail: asor@bu.edu
Web address: www.asor.org

Publications Office
ASOR Publications
825 Houston Mill Road
Suite 330
Atlanta, GA 30329

Phone: 404 727 0807
Fax: 404 727 4719
E-mail: bcollin@emory.edu

The "Mona Lisa" mosaic detail from the fourth century A.D. Dionysos Mansion at Sepphoris in Israel. EMM

ASOR Member Institutions and Representatives
*(Current during 2000 * Indicates Founding Members for a New Century)*

American Research Center in Egypt	Susanne Thomas
Andrews University	Randall Younker
Asbury Theological Seminary	Bill T. Arnold
Austin Presbyterian Theological Seminary	Andrew Dearman
Baltimore Hebrew University	Barry Gittlen
Baptist Bible College and Seminary	Alan Ingalls
Baylor University	Marilyn McKinney
Birzeit University	Khaled Nashef
Boston College	David Vanderhooft
Boston University	Simon Parker
*Brigham Young University	Dana M. Pike
Brown University	Ernest Frerichs
Bryn Mawr College	Richard Ellis
Calvin College and Seminary	Bert de Vries
Carroll College	Lamar Cope
Case Western Reserve Uiversity	James Flanagan
Catholic University of America	Douglass Gropp
Christian Theological Seminary	Marti J. Steussey
*Claremont Graduate University	Tammi Schneider
Colgate Rochester Divinity School	Werner Lemke
Concordia College	Barbara McCauley
Concordia Lutheran Seminary	Edward Kettner
Concordia Seminary	Lee Maxwell
Converse College	Byron McCane
Cornell University	David Owen
Drew University	Herbert Huffman
Duke Universioty	Carol Meyers
Dumbarton Oaks	Edward L. Keenan
Emmanuel School of Religion	Chris Rollston
Emory University, Candler School of Theology	J. Maxwell Miller
Emory University	Oded Borowski
Fernbank Museum	J. Maxwell Miller
Florida Baptist Theological Seminary	J. W. Lee
Gannon University	Suzanne Richard
General Theological Seminary	Judith Newman
Georgetown University	Robert Lawton, S.J.
Golden Gate Baptist Theological Seminary	Gary Arbino
Gordon-Conwell Theological Seminary	Gary Pratico
Grace Theological Seminary	John J. Davis
Harvard Divinity School	Gary Anderson
Harvard Semitic Museum	Lawrence Stager

Hebrew Union College	Sheldon Zimmerman
Hong Kong Baptist Theological Seminary	Alfred Kong
Illinois Wesleyan University	Dennis E. Groh
John Carroll University	John Spencer
Johns Hopkins University	P. Kyle McCarter
La Sierra University	John Jones
Louisville Presbyterian Seminary	W. Eugene March
Loyola Marymount University	William J. Fulco, S.J.
Lutheran School of Theology	Barbara Rossing
Lycoming College	Robin DeWitt Knauth
McCormick Theological Seminary	Melody Knowles
McGill University	B. Barry Levy
Metropolitan Museum of Art	Prudence Harper
*Miami University, Ohio	Harold Forshey
Midwestern Baptist Theological Seminary	Stephen J. Andrews
*Mississippi State University	Paul F. Jacobs
Mount Holyoke College	Robert Berkey
New Orleans Baptist Theological Seminary	R. Dennis Cole
New York Public Library	John M. Lundquist
New York University	Baruch Levine
North Carolina State University	S. Thomas Parker
Pacific Lutheran Theological Seminary	Victor Gold
Pacific School of Religion	Kevin Kaiser
Pennsylvania State University	Raymond Lombra
Pepperdine University	John Wilson
Pittsburgh Theological Seminary	Ron Tappy
Princeton Theological Seminary	J. J. M. Roberts
Protestant Episcopal Seminary in Virginia	William S. Stafford
Sardis Expedition	Holly Hutchinson
Seton Hall University	Donald Wimmer
Smith College	Karl Donfried
Southeastern Baptist Theological Seminary	L. Russ Bush III
Southern Adventist University	Michael G. Hasel
Southern Baptist Theological Seminary	Joel Drinkard
Southern Methodist University	Roy. L. Heller
Southwest Missouri State University	James Moyer
St. John's Seminary	John Sullivan
St. John's University	Alberic Culhane
St. Mary's University	Thomas Bolin
State University of New York at Binghampton	Glenn Bartle Library
State University of New York at Buffalo	Samuel Paley
Texas A&M University	Shelly Wachsmann
Trinity College	Martha Risser

Trinity Lutheran Seminary	Rodney Hutton
*Tufts University	Jodi Magness
Union Theological Seminary, Richmond	Dean of Faculty
University of Arizona	William G. Dever
University of California-Berkely	Carol Redmount
University of Chicago	David Schloen
University of Cincinnati	Getzel Choen
University of Judiasm	Ziony Zevit
University of Kansas	James Seaver
University of La Verne	Jonathan Reed
University of Lethbridge	Walter E. Aufrecht
University of Mary Hardin-Baylor	Stephen Von Wyrick
University of Maryland	Kenneth Holum
University of Michigan	John F. Cherry
University of Missouri-Columbia	Marcus Rautman
University of Notre Dame	Hugh Page
University of Southern California	School of Religion
University of Toronto	Timothy Harrison
University of Victoria	John Oleson
Valparaiso University	Mark Bartusch
Vanderbilt University Divinity School	Office of the Dean
Wake Forest University	Fred Horton
Wellesley College	Edward Hobbs
Wesley Theological Seminary	David Hopkins
Western Theological Seminary	Carol M. Bechtel
Willamette University	David McCreery
Yale Divinity School	Robert Wilson

ASOR Appointees 1970–2000

Abbreviations for Fellowships offered:

W. F. Albright	ASOR W. F. Albright
EBR	Endowment for Biblical Research (until 1984 - Zion Research Foundation)
Mesopotamian	Neis Fellow in Mesopotamian Civilization
Shell	Shell Companies Foundation Fellowship in Ancient Near Eastern Civilization
Dorot/AM	Dorot Foundation Annual Meeting Participation
Kress/AM	Kress Foundation Annual Meeting Participation
Lindstrom	Lindstrom Foundation Student Service

APPOINTEES

Name	Institution	Year	Fellowship
Uzi Avner	Arava Institute for Environmental Studies	2000	Dorot/AM
Zainab Bahrani	New York University	1986–87	Mesopotamian
Edward Banning	University of Toronto	1981–82	W. F. Albright
Tristan Barako	Harvard University	2000	Dorot/AM
Andrew Bauer	University of Akron	1999	Lindstrom
Joanne Besonen	Tufts University	1998	Lindstrom
Julye Bidmead	Vanderbilt University	1997	Lindstrom
		1998	Dorot/AM
Dianna Bolt	University of California-Berkeley	1987–88	Mesopotamian
Michelle Bonogofsky	University of California-Berkeley	1999	Dorot/AM
Karen Borstad	University of Arizona	1998	Dorot/AM
Aaron Burke	University of Chicago	2000	Dorot/AM
Robin M. Brown	University of Michigan	1986–87	W. F. Albright
Brian F. Byrd	University of Arizona	1984–85	Shell
Ryan Byrne	Johns Hopkins University	1998	Lindstrom
		2000	Dorot/AM
Daniel Casey, Jr.	Colgate Rochester Divinity School	1998	Lindstrom
	Tantur Ecumenical Institute	1999	Lindstrom
David Chatford	Clark University of London	1999	Dorot/AM
Vincent A. Clark		1979–80	W. F. Albright
Elizabeth Carter	University of Chicago	1971–72	Mesopotamian
Felicity Cobbing	Palestine Exploration Fund	1999	Kress/AM
Andrew Cohen	Bryn Mawr College	2000	Dorot/AM
Sarah Kielt Costello	State University of New York-Binghampton	2000	Dorot/AM
Cheryl Coursey	State University of New York-Binghampton	1997–98	Mesopotamian
Eleonora Cussini	Johns Hopkins University	1993–94	Mesopotamian
Michael Danti	University of Pennsylvania	1996–97	Mesopotamian
Jennie Ebeling	University of Arizona	1997	Lindstrom
		1999	Dorot/AM
Christopher Edens	University of Pennsylvania	1998–99	Mesopotamian
Patricia L. Fall	University of Arizona	1989–90	W. F. Albright
Alysia Fischer	University of Arizona	1998	Dorot/AM

Rebecca Foote	Harvard University	1991–92	W. F. Albright
Benjamin Foster	Yale University	1976–77	W. F. Albright
Elizabeth Friedman	University of Chicago	1999	Dorot/AM
Glenda Friend	Baltimore Hebrew University	1997	Dorot/AM
Timothy Frier	Graduate Theological Union	2000	Lindstrom
Sarah Gardner	University of Arizona	1998	Dorot/AM
Mary Henriette Gates	Belkent University, Turkey	2000	Kress/AM
Herman Genz	German Archaeological Institute, Turkey	1999	Kress/AM
Michael Given	University of Glasgow	2000	Kress/AM
Shmuel Givon	Tel Aviv University	1998–99	Dorot/AM
Gabriella C. Gressner	State University of New York-Binghamton	2000	Lindstrom
Barry Gittlen	University of Pennsylvania	1969–70	W. F. Albright
Jennifer Lynn Groves	University of Arizona	1997	Dorot/AM
James W. Hardin	Mississippi State University	1997	Dorot/AM
Britt Hartenberger	Boston University	1998	Lindstrom
		2000–01	Mesopotamian
Mini Hunter Harauch	California Institute	1999	Dorot/AM
Nancy Hocking	Triskelion Pottery	1999	Kress/AM
Chris Holland	Mississippi State University	1997	Lindstrom
Alice Hunt Hudiburg	Vanderbilt University	1997	Lindstrom
David Inbar	Bar Ilan University	2000	Dorot/AM
Cara Jaffe	Occidental College	1997	Lindstrom
Thomas James	Mississippi State University	2000	Lindstrom
Elizabeth Jewell	University of Pennsylvania	1974–75	Mesopotamian
Christina Kahrl	Texas Tech University	1999	Lindstrom
Judith Kenworthy	Texas A&M University	1997	Lindstrom
Kevin Kaiser	University of California-Berkeley	2000	Dorot/AM
Maureen Kaplan	Unaffiliated	1995–96	W. F. Albright
Judy Kenworthy	Texas A&M University	2000	Dorot/AM
Barbara Kling	University of Pennsylvania	1983–84	W. F. Albright
A. Bernard Knapp	University of Glasgow	1999	Kress/AM
Oystein LaBianca	Andrews University	1980–81	W. F. Albright
Jonathan Lawrence	University of Notre Dame	1997–99	Lindstrom
		2000	Dorot/AM
Cherie Lenzen	Drew University	1982–83	W. F. Albright
Stephen Lieberman	Harvard University	1970–71	Mesopotamian
Edward M. Luby	State University of New York-Stoney Brook	1985–86	Mesopotamian
Stephen Lumsden	University of California-Berkeley	1992–93	Mesopotamian
Kate Mackay	University of Arizona	1998	Dorot/AM
Kimberley Maeyama	Katholieke Universiteit Leuven	2000	Dorot/AM
Andrew McCarthy	University of Edinburgh	2000	Dorot/AM
David McCreery	Pittsburgh Theological Seminary	1977–78	W. F. Albright
Suzanne Meek	New York University	1969–70	Mesopotamian

Chantel Nizon	McMaster University	2000	Lindstrom
Asli Ozyar	Bryn Mawr College	1990–91	Mesopotamian
Bradley J. Parker	University of California-Los Angeles	1994–95	Mesopotamian
Daniella Parks	University of Missouri	1997	Dorot/AM
Susan Pollock	University of Michigan	1983–84	Mesopotamian
Melody PopeState	University of New York-Binghampton	1991–92	Mesopotamian
Daniel T. Potts	Harvard University	1980–81	Mesopotamian
Leslie Quintero	University of California-Riverside	1997	Dorot/AM
Wendy Raver	New York University	1999	Dorot/AM
Carol A. Redmount	University of Chicago	1981–82	Shell
Shane Reed	Mississippi State University	1999	Lindstrom
David Reese	University of Cambridge	1983–84	Shell
Seth Richardson	Columbia University	1999–00	Mesopotamian
Gary O. Rollefson	University of Arizona	1978–79	W. F. Albright
Chris Rollston	John Hopkins University	1997	Dorot/AM
David Rupp	Brock University	1987–88	W. F. Albright
John M. Russell	Columbia University	1989–90	Mesopotamian
Hamed Salem	Birzeit University	2000	Dorot/AM
Seth L. Sanders	Johns Hopkins University	1997	Dorot/AM
Daniella Saltz	Harvard University	1974–75	W. F. Albright
James A. Sauer	Harvard University	1971–72	W. F. Albright
Kathryn Salanski	Harvard University	1995–96	Mesopotamian
Sandra Arnold Scham	Catholic University and the Pontifical Biblical Institute	1997	Dorot/AM
Tonia Sharlach	Harvard University	1998–99	Mesopotamian
Glenn Schwartz	Yale University	1982–83	Mesopotamian
Andrew M. Smith II	University of Maryland	2000	Dorot/AM
Diana L. Stein	Harvard Semitic Museum	1984–85	Mesopotamian
Sophia Stos-Gale	University of Oxford	2000	Kress/AM
Laurel Taylor	University of Pennsylvania	1997	Dorot/AM
Christine Thompson	University of California-Los Angeles	1999	Lindstrom
Jason Ur	University of Chicago	2000–01	Mesopotamian
Jackie Villnave	State University of New York-Cortland	1998	Lindstrom
Klaas Vansteenhuyse	Universite de Louvaine-la-Neuve	2000	Dorot/AM
Bert de Vries	Calvin College	1972–73	W. F. Albright
Justine Warren	Mississippi State University	2000	Lindstrom
Harvey Weiss	University of Pennsylvania	1973–74	Mesopotamian
Elizabeth Willett	University of Arizona	1997	Dorot/AM
Assaf Yasur-Landau	Tel Aviv University	1999	Dorot/AM
Norman Yoffee	Yale University	1972–74	Mesopotamian
Richard L. Zettler		1979–80	Mesopotamian

Zion Research Foundation Endowment for Biblical Research
Appointees 1968–1998 Research and Travel Grants

1968
Travel
Lawrence T. Geraty
Conrad E. L'Heureux
James A. Rimbach
James A. Sauer
William R. Sladek
Ziony Zevit

1969
Travel
James Flanagan
James Kautz
Harold Liebowitz
Robert Rogers
Thomas Tappan

1970
Research
Phyllis A. Bird
John C. Lawrenz
David L. Newlands
Dennis G. Pardee
Lawrence E. Stager

1971
Research
John Collins
David Levenson
Marvin Meyer
Sharon Ridgeway

1972
Research
Yechiel Michael Lehavy
Leon Marfoe
Dianella Saltz
Travel
Oded Borowski
Dorthea Brooks
Anne V. Carter
Mary Ann Davitt
Harold A. Liebowitz
John W. Niewold
Anna D. Sophocles
Marilyn J. Spirt
Lawrence E. Stager

1973
Research
Alan Mark Bieber, Jr
James A. Sauer
Travel
John W. Betylon
Peter K. H. Jenkins
William Alan Hartfelder
Cherie Joice Howard
Oystein S. LaBianca
John M. Lundquist
John M. Mathers
John Paul Orton
David Elmer Palmer
Jeffrey H. Schwartz
Marilyn J. Spirt

1974
Travel
Anne Arenstein
Richard J. Bamrick
James R. Battenfield
David A. Denyer
Valerie M. Fargo
Patty Gerstenblith
Larry G. Herr
David McCreery
Kathleen Anne Mitchell
Paul G. Mosca
Frank R. Ostertag
Gary D. Pratico
Suzanne R. Richard
Anna Sophocles

1975
List not available

1976
Research
John W. Betylon
Duane L. Christensen
Oystein S. LaBianca
Holly M. Alderman
Travel
Patricia L. Crawford
Alice M. Greenwald
Larissa S. Hordynsky
Christine Kondoleon
Terrance M. Kerestes
Patricia A. Lombard
John M. Lundquist
Timothy J. McNiven
Naomi J. Norman
David S. Reese
Jerome Schaeffer
Dennis E. Smith
Jarvis Streeter

1977–79
Lists not available

1980
Research
Jane Barlow
Miriam Chernoff
Gary Pratico
Travel
Shelley C. Arwe
Peter T. Baxter
William D. Glanzman
Nikki Lee Hammond
Claudia A. Hartmann
David O. Jenkins
Clayton M. Lehmann
James D. Mayberry
Mary L. Mussell
Joyce Raynor
Joaquin P. Silva
Rachel Sternberg
Lynn W. Tatum
Samuel Wolff
Ellen Zahn

Donna Lynn Belcher
Rohonda Burnette
Meredith S. Chesson
Lauren E. Ebin
Neal Galley
Aletha M. Hilton
Janice F. King
Brigitta Ann Lee
Janet Melnyk
Cynthia K. Rauh
Jennifer Carol Ross
Ada Smolin
Paul Douglas
Bruce Lee White

1994
Research
Susan Vida Grubisha
Travel
Dena Bauer,
Jennifer Blakeslee
Karen Borstad
Mary P. Boyd
Mark Chancery
Kelley N. Coblentz.
Diane Flores
David Gray.
Kenneth Harrington
Naomi Leah Horowitz
Michael Jon Horstmanshof
David Palmer
Michelle Sousa
Tracy Wilson.
Sho Yamada

1995
Research
Caroline Davies
Betsey Robinson
Travel
Stephanie Baker
Wade Clack

Carlos Cordova
Kristi Dahm
Vanessa Davies
Peter Flint
Phil Goldstein
Jennifer Jones
Rita Kingston
Elizabeth Koop
Mary Reeves
Jennifer Ross

1996
Research
Melissa M. Aubin
Travel
Alexander Bauer
James Blankespoor
Theodore William Burgh
Diane L. Douglas
Jonathan David Lawrence
Elizabeth Ann Pollard Lisi
Jeanne McCoy
Jeri Moskala
Charles W. Viets

1997
Research
Jennie R. Ebeling
Kate Mackay
Travel
Joel Bacha
Megan A. Perry
Laura Brian
Ralph K. Hawkins
Allen Katic
Jeffrey M. R. Kentel
M. Barbara Reeves
Michael G. VanZant

1998
Research
Christine Thompson

Travel
Yiyi Chen
Valerie Johnson
John McCarthy
Donna Petter
Thomas Petter
Iman Saca
Gregory Smith
Andrew Torget
Mark Ziese

ASOR/CAP Affiliated Projects 1970–2000
(in countries other than Cyprus, Israel and Jordan)

Egypt

1977–	Wadi Tumilat Project	John S. Holladay, Jr.	*University of Toronto*
1989	Wadi Arba Survey	A. H. Bomann	*Florida, unaffiliated*
1995–96	Eastern Desert Survey	A. H. Bomann	*Florida, unaffiliated*

Italy

1981	Venosa Catacomb Project	Eric Meyers	*Duke University*

North Yemen

1982–94	Wadi al-Jubah	Jeffrey Blakely	
		James A. Sauer	*American Foundation for the Study of Man*

Syria

1977–79	East Jordan Valley Survey	James A. Sauer	*ASOR*
1979–84	North Orontes Valley Expedition	John M. Lundquist	*Brigham Young University*
1989	Tell Qarqur	Patricia Bikai	
		Pierre Bikai	*University of California-Berkley*
1993–	Tell Qarqur Excavation	Rudolph Dornemann	*ASOR*

Tunisia

1975–1980	Carthage Roman Project	John H. Humphrey	
		John H. Pedley	*University of Michigan*
1976–	Carthage Punic Project	Lawrence E. Stager	*University of Chicago*
		Joseph Greene	*Harvard Semitic Museum*

Turkey

2000–	Tell Atchana/Alalakh	K. Aslihan Yener	*University of Chicago*

Mosaic detail from the "Bearing of Gifts to Dionysos" panel of the fourth century A. D. Dionysos Mansion at Sepphoris in Israel. EMM

AIAR

Rebuilding the School that Albright Built

A History of the
W. F. ALBRIGHT
INSTITUTE OF ARCHAEOLOGICAL RESEARCH

Jerusalem, Israel

by Jeffrey A. Blakely

1967–2000

The AIAR logo

The logo of the W. F. Albright Institute was adopted shortly after the Institute's reincorporation as AIAR in 1970. It is taken from a Judahite stamp seal of the late eighth century B.C. The upper register of the scaraboid depicts a four-winged flying beetle with the forelegs grasping a dung ball and flanked by two birds. In Egypt, the dung beetle (Latin: *scarabaeus sacer*) was a symbol of perpetual existence and resurrection, and the bird motif was common in Ammonite iconography. The lower registers provide in old Hebrew script the personal name *Hannanyahu* ("Yahu is gracious") *emet* ("trustworthy") read as *Hananyahu* (son of) *Emet*. The logo symbolizes the breadth of the Institute's interests in rediscovering and preserving the rich heritage of archaeological and textual traditions from the ancient Near East.

Credits

A number of people deserve acknowledgment for their special assistance in the preparation of this section on the history of the Albright Institute. These include a group of individuals with historic connections to the Institute whom the author interviewed during 1999. They are Walter Aufrecht, Josef Aviram, Abraham Biran, Robert J. Bull, Sidnie White Crawford, William G. Dever, Ernest Frerichs, Patty Gerstenblith, Lois Glock, Robert Haak, Omar Jibrin, Jodi Magness, Munira Said, Richard J. Scheuer, Joe D. Seger, Fr. Marcel Sigrist and John Spencer. Their contributions are reflected not only in selected side bars, but throughout the document. Particular thanks are due to AIAR Trustee Lydie Shufro and to Director Sy Gitin. Their special editorial help and constant attention to the details of the historical materials have greatly enhanced the presentation. Director Gitin was also instrumental in helping to search the AIAR photographic archives, and in helping to select and provide captions for the many images from that source used with this section. All pictures not otherwise referenced come from the AIAR archives.

We also acknowledge with appreciation other sources for photographic images as follows: The American Schools of Oriental Research Archives (ASOR), John C. Trever (JT), Norma Dever (ND), the Nelson Glueck Archive (NG), Nancy Lapp (NL), Richard J. Scheuer (RJS), Joe D. Seger (JDS), Patty O. Seger (POS), Sidnie White Crawford (SWC) and the W. F. Albright Family Archives (WFAF). Pictures are referenced as indicated in parentheses.

AIAR

Rebuilding the School that Albright Built
A History of the W. F. Albright Institute of Archaeological Research
Jerusalem, Israel

Highlighting the Period from 1967 to 2000

by Jeffrey A. Blakely

W. F. Albright
May 24, 1891 – September 19, 1971 (WFAF)

Introduction

In the twilight of his illustrious career, William Foxwell Albright received two of his life's most prized awards. On March 23, 1969, he became the first non-Jerusalemite and the first gentile to be named "Worthy of Jerusalem" in a ceremony hosted by Mayor Teddy Kollek at Jerusalem's City Hall. The second award occurred on the same trip when he was presented with a *Festschrift* in the *Eretz-Israel* series, Volume 9, the *Albright Volume*, during a festive dinner and reception at Beit Hanassi in the presence of Israeli President Shazar and of Israel's foremost archaeologists. These were not the sole highlights of Albright's final visit to Israel. He gave lectures, he visited Khirbet Qumran and Masada by helicopter with Masada's excavator Yigael Yadin, he toured the excavations at the Western Wall with Benjamin Mazar, he saw Gezer with William G. Dever and the Gezer staff, and he visited the Jaffa Museum with Jacob Kaplan. He also wanted to make one final visit to the American School of Oriental Research (ASOR) in Jerusalem. ASOR Annual Director Kermit Schoonover hosted a dinner party for him and Mrs. Albright, Nelson Glueck, and G. Ernest Wright, together with all the appointees for that year. Many old "war stories" were told, with Glueck and Albright each trying to outdo the other. In the course of that evening Albright noted that he had wanted to come back to the School, especially to see how it looked, and to see how it was doing now that Jerusalem had been reunited. He then said that he was glad to note that nothing had changed.

W. F. Albright (right) holding his Eretz-Israel Festschrift during a reception following its presentation on March 13, 1969. With Albright (left to right) G. Ernest Wright, Nelson Glueck and Israel President Zalman Shazar.

(RJS)

"Nothing had changed." Albright's comment provides the springboard for this study of the history of ASOR's Jerusalem School, now called the W. F. Albright Institute of Archaeological Research (AIAR). On one level, certainly, Albright was correct. The building and the grounds had weathered the 1967 Six-Day War virtually unscathed, and the people at the School were, in the main, the same people who had worked and studied there before the war. I believe that if Albright could come back today, in the year 2001, he could make exactly the same comment — the building and the people appear largely the same. On another level, however, Albright was wrong. Everything has changed. The Six-Day War initiated a series of events that dramatically altered and transformed the very nature of ASOR and the role of the Jerusalem School/Albright Institute as a scholarly entity.

Everything has changed. To understand this, it is necessary to describe something of the nature and character of the Jerusalem School as it emerged within ASOR prior to the Six Day War. Given Philip King's comprehensive coverage of this early era (see KING and articles from 1975) and Eric Meyers' study of ASOR in this volume, I begin here with only a brief background sketch. From 1967, however, and in greater detail, the history of the Jerusalem School/Albright Institute will be examined in two sections, one covering the period from 1967 to 1980 and the second the period from 1980 to date. Together, these three sections will attempt to highlight the growth and development of the Jerusalem School/Albright Institute, along with a few bumps in the road, tracing the implementation of a vision that began in 1900 and has been modified many times in order to adapt to changes in two worlds: political and economic, and intellectual and scholarly. Finally, this history will conclude with a more-or-less full account of what the Albright Institute is today and with a few thoughts on the directions in which growth may continue in the future.

Background: The Jerusalem School 1900–1967

The Founding Years 1900–1920

On June 13, 1895 J. Henry Thayer, President of the Society of Biblical Literature (SBL), proposed to that organization that they initiate a program to establish a school for study and research in Palestine. In 1900 this dream became a reality when the SBL, the American Oriental Society (AOS), and the Archaeological Institute of America (AIA) jointly founded the American School of Oriental Study and Research in Palestine.

For the first twenty-four years of its existence, the School rented space at a variety of locations. During these years it was largely a teaching and research institution. The staff and students conducted courses at the Institute and did extensive scholarly research. They also toured widely, taking photographs, making squeezes of inscriptions, and mapping sites. One of the primary goals of Charles C. Torrey, the School's first director, and of his successors, was to build a library. Within a few years they had been so successful that scholars such as R. A. S. Macalister, Frederick J. Bliss, Gottlieb Schumacher, and Ernst Sellin were using it for research. The development and growth of the library has been both a concern and a success of the institution for over a century.

World War I had a significant impact on the Jerusalem School, forcing it to close its doors from 1914 to 1917. However, during this interim, Mrs. James B. Nies (the former Jane Dows Orr) pledged $50,000 to ASOR to build a permanent home for the Jerusalem School on land that had been acquired in 1909. Attached to the gift were conditions: (1) that either AIA or some other incorporated body acquire title to the land purchased by ASOR in 1909; (2) that the building cost no more than $50,000; and (3) that she have the privilege of naming the structure. ASOR was incorporated in 1921 and in the same year construction of the Nies Building began. By 1924, although not yet fully complete, the Jerusalem School of ASOR had a permanent home at 26 Salah ed-Din Street, and, over time, this greatly affected the development of the organization.

> *"the main object of said School shall be to engage properly qualified persons to prosecute biblical, linguistic, archaeological, historical, and other kindred studies and researches under more favorable conditions than can be secured at a distance from the Holy Land."*
>
> (From Founding Resolutions, 1900)

The Jerusalem School in the first phases of construction, ca. 1922. (ASOR)

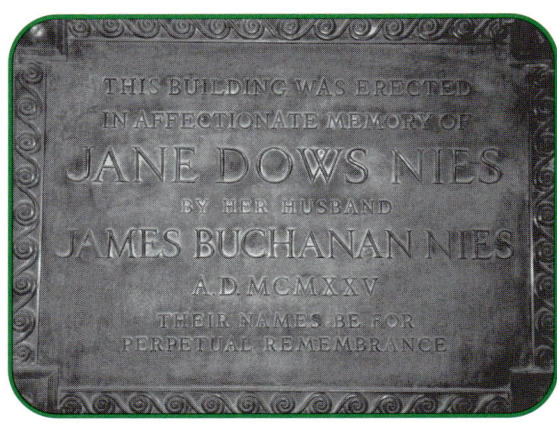

Nies building dedication plaque at the Institute's front entrance.

Following the Allied victory in World War I, Palestine ceased to be under Ottoman rule, and subsequently came under British Mandate. Thus the stage was set for dramatic change on another front. During Ottoman rule it had been difficult to obtain permission for archaeological work. With the advent of the British Mandate and the establishment of British antiquities laws, archaeology suddenly became a far more feasible enterprise. Within a few years, many major archaeological projects were conducted in Palestine. Soon, ASOR, through the Jerusalem School, became a dominant player in the archaeological enterprise. This occurred primarily because, during World War I, ASOR had recognized that growth and development of the organization in Palestine required the continuity provided by a long-term director. After serving a year as Thayer Fellow and part of a year as acting director, ASOR appointed William Foxwell Albright as the first long-term director at the Jerusalem School. He served from 1920 until 1929, and again from 1933–1936.

W. F. Albright in 1913 during service as principal and science teacher at a high school in Menno, South Dakota. The following year he began graduate study at Johns Hopkins University. (WFAF)

The W. F. Albright Years 1920–1930

Albright was a brilliant scholar whose ideas had a forceful impact. He was certainly the right person in the right place at the right time. His activities as director changed ASOR, the Jerusalem School, and the discipline of the archaeology of Palestine. Albright continued to adhere to the original goals of the Jerusalem School by promoting a wide range of research in Jerusalem. The scope of Albright's knowledge is a testament to this; he was considered an expert in the fields of archaeology, Semitic epigraphy, paleography, history, philology, and biblical geography. Today, if we look at the AIAR library, we see that its books dating to the 1920s and 1930s reflect all those fields. The ASOR fellows and students who used the facilities of the Jerusalem School and library prior to World War II were exposed to his great influence and collectively represent that same intellectual breadth.

By 1924, with the opening of the Nies building, Albright was in a position to expand the activities to which ASOR was originally dedicated, namely archaeological and biblical research. One way to do this was to expand the educational program. With a facility that could house the Director and the Annual Professor, and with ten rooms in which to house students and visiting scholars, he was able to increase the number of fellows in residence during the academic year and to introduce a summer school for a larger clientele. This was one manner in which the Jerusalem School became more economically self-sufficient and serviced the needs of the supporting institutions back in North America. This summer program, which began in 1925 after the hostel was completed and continued until the advent of World War II, included a lecture series, formal presentations on archaeology and biblical geography, and major tours/field trips throughout Palestine and Syria.

W. F. Albright in Jerusalem in 1924 with his wife Ruth Norton Albright and their two year old first son, Paul. (WFAF)

ASOR group on a field trip to Tell Beit Mirsim in 1924. (ASOR)

W. F. Albright shaving in front of his tent at the Tell Beit Mirsim expedition camp. (Undated photo, presumably 1932.) (WFAF)

Group at the Jerusalem School in 1935. (left to right) Back Row: Prof. G.R. Berry, Colgate-Rochester Divinity School (Honorary Lecturer); Mr. Noble (Assistant to Clarence Fisher); Prof. Elbert C. Lane, Hartford Seminary Foundation (Honorary Lecturer); Prof. W.F. Albright (Director, 1920–29; 1933–36); President Emeritus Warren J. Moulton, Bangor Theological Seminary (Honorary Lecturer; former Director, 1912–13); Mr. Edward P. Blair, Yale University; Dr. Harry M. Orlinsky, Dropsie College and the University of Pennsylvania (Nies Scholar). Middle Row: Rev. Arnold C. Schultz, University of Chicago; Prof. John W. Flight, Haverford College (Honorary Lecturer); Dr. Clarence Fischer (Professor of Archaeology, 1925–41); Dean C.C. McCown, Pacific School of Religion (Annual Professor; former Director, 1929–31); Rev. Y. Herman Sacon, Drew University; Rabbi Maurice Bloom, Newburgh, N.Y.; Dr. Abraham Bergman (Biran), Johns Hopkins University (Thayer Fellow) Front Row: Paul Albright, Mrs. Ruth Albright, Mrs. Blair, Mrs. Donya Orlinsky, Katherine Wamboldt, Mrs. Lane.

A second way in which the activities of the Jerusalem School expanded was through archaeology. Excavation had been largely impossible under Ottoman rule, but with the new openness of the British Mandate it was encouraged. In many ways the Jerusalem School was not optimally placed to undertake such a program, since no one associated with the school had archaeological experience, and field work required significant funding. Meanwhile, major and wealthy universities took the lead in initiating excavations. These included the University of Chicago at Megiddo; Harvard University, together with a British consortium at Samaria; the University of Pennsylvania at Beth-Shean; Yale University, the Department of Antiquities and the British School of Archaeology in Jerusalem, with some ASOR support in later years, at Jerash; the University of Liverpool and the Department of Antiquities at Jericho; and the Welcome-Marston Excavations at Tell ed-Duwier, Lachish. Even smaller institutions such as Haverford College at Beth-Shemesh and the Pacific School of Religion at Tell en-Nasbeh were able to mount significant projects staffed with Americans, and with a paid work force. But sponsorship of such major projects was closed to the Jerusalem School itself since it lacked both adequate finances and, at first, a director with field competence.

Ancient walls exposed in front of the Jerusalem School in 1927. (ASOR)

Fortunately, Albright understood well the significance of the archaeological endeavor. First he acquired the services of an advisor, Frederick Bliss, excavator for the Palestine Exploration Fund (PEF) before World War I, and second he became acquainted with the local cadre of archaeologists. These initially included Père Vincent of the Ecole Biblique, John Garstang the Director of Antiquities, and W. J. Phythian Adams of the British School of Archaeology in Jerusalem and the PEF, and finally Clarence S. Fisher, an experienced excavator who had learned field methods under George Andrew Reisner at Samaria beginning in 1909. Albright also realized that he could staff a project from among the fellows at the Jerusalem School. So in 1922, on a shoestring budget paid for by limited private grants, he was able to excavate at Tell el-Fûl, north of Jerusalem and, in 1923, at the four mounds at Malhah, southwest of Jerusalem. These projects helped Albright learn the basics of excavation technique, both through first hand experience and through Fisher's advice. He also learned the basics of ceramic analysis from Vincent. Very quickly Albright became an experienced archaeologist.

> In the 1920s and even the 1930s there wasn't much local archaeological work. Hebrew University had a small Department of Archaeology ... You had the Department of Antiquities of the Palestine government, which was not all that active ... Thanks especially to Albright, the American School raised the discipline to a professional level; he developed Palestinian archaeology.
>
> Avraham Biran, 1999

One of the senior fellows at the Jerusalem School in the early 1920s was Melvin Grove Kyle, President of Xenia Theological Seminary, later Pittsburgh Theological Seminary. Kyle was able to raise funds to pay for a modest excavation in association with Albright. They chose to excavate at Tell Beit Mirsim in four seasons between 1926 and 1932. This project established Albright as a leading archaeologist and the scholar who best understood ceramic chronology. The final reports, presented as the *Annuals* of ASOR, set new standards for publications in the discipline.

Even though Albright established himself as one of the leading archaeologists of the region in the 1920s and 1930s, he did not consider himself an archaeologist. To Albright, archaeology was simply a tool that could provide a certain type of information about antiquity — it could be used to date sites and structures. That information, in turn, could be used to refine historical or geographic issues. For Albright this was where significance was to be found — in a synthesis of a wide variety of data. It was with this open, synthetic, all-inclusive mind set — combining geography, history, epigraphy, paleography and archaeology to create a greater whole — that Albright ran the Jerusalem School, greatly influencing the scholars and students who passed through its doors in the 1920s and 1930s. The good name and respected reputation of ASOR and the Jerusalem School were established through his activities and leadership.

Dr. Clarence Fisher, Jerusalem School Professor of Archaeology 1924–1941. (ASOR)

The Nelson Glueck Era 1932–1947

After Albright left the Jerusalem School in 1929 to assume an academic position at The Johns Hopkins University, he was followed by several short-term directors. Then in 1932, Nelson Glueck, was appointed as a new long-term director. Glueck served as the director from 1932 to 1947, except for a three-year period in the mid-1930s when Albright returned, and in 1940–1941 when Clarence S. Fisher served as acting director while Glueck was in the United States. Glueck had learned archaeology from Albright at the excavations of Tell Beit Mirsim. Following Albright's model he initiated a series of long-term survey projects in Ammon, Moab, and Edom. During tenure as director he also excavated at Khirbet et-Tannur and Tell el-Kheleifeh. Later, between 1952 and 1964, he conducted further survey work in the Negev. Through the late 1930s, in the tradition of Albright, Glueck continued to direct and supervise the activities of the School, promoting education and research and doing archaeological survey and excavation work. During the second half of his tenure, however, the world was at war and the educational activities of the school were in abeyance. Through this period he managed the property and conducted his own extensive archaeological survey in TransJordan. In 1947 he completed his service as director and returned to the U.S. to take up responsibilities as President of Hebrew Union College in Cincinnati. Then, in 1948, when the Jerusalem School suddenly found itself in Jordan, it was not accessible to Glueck because of his Jewish faith.

Nelson Glueck (right) with Ali Abu Ghosh near Qasr Abu Rubbeh, September 1936. (NG)

Nelson Glueck in the Transjordan in the late 1930s. (NG)

Nelson Glueck at Sheikh Ibreik (Beit Shearim) in February 1939. (NG)

Nelson Glueck (right) and Sherif ed-Din in the desert in 1938. (NG)

Summary

This sketch of the Jerusalem School during the period 1900 to 1948 allows for two observations that are relevant to subsequent discussions. First, is the significant impact made by the two long-term directors, Albright and Glueck. Through their abilities and doggedness they shaped the Jerusalem School in a manner that was not possible when the School was run by annual directors, who were neither in a position to conceive of nor to implement longer-term plans. During their extended tenures both Albright and Glueck were able to enhance the stature and prestige of the Jerusalem School and, between the two World Wars, to create the dominant research institution in the region, something a series of annual directors could never have accomplished.

The second observation is that the growth and success of the Jerusalem School up to this point was predicated on cordial relations with the host country. Before World War I it enjoyed tolerance on the part of the Ottoman government, but after World War I Albright, Glueck and the other directors were to receive the active support of the officials of the British Mandate, a government, however, that was colonialist. As later history demonstrates, it was not at all representative of the local population. In contrast, because they were apolitical and not British, ASOR and the Jerusalem School developed many friends among the local population of Muslims, Jews, and Christians. Certain members of the local Jewish population (Benjamin Maisler/Mazar, Avraham Bergman/Biran, Eliezer Sukenik, Jacob Kaplan, Shemuel Yeivin, Immanuel Ben Dor, and Judith Marquet-Krause, to name some of the major figures) recognized the importance of recovering the region's heritage and became members of the Jerusalems School's archaeological community. To the Arab population, however, archaeology at the time was merely viewed as an interesting field that had nothing important to do with life other than providing jobs for skilled excavators and workmen. Of the non-Jewish local community, only Dimitri Constantine Baramki entered the archaeological ranks. To the foreign archaeologist from the time of Edward Robinson, the local Arab population served almost solely as informants, to provide place names or locations for archaeological sites, or as laborers. This was the extent of their involvement in archaeology, and this was to have significant repercussions in the future when compared with the fledgling Jewish archaeological community.

The Jerusalem School 1946–1967*

In Palestine the end of World War II was followed almost immediately by the end of the British Mandate, the War of 1948 and the establishment of the State of Israel and of the Hashemite Kingdom of Jordan. These were tumultuous years, but also important years in the history of archeological discovery and of the Jerusalem School. In 1946, still under the direction of Nelson Glueck who was then in his final year as director, the Jerusalem School reopened with hopes of reestablishing its pre-War programs, but that was not possible. It was not until 1947–48, under the leadership of director Millar Burrows — who was concurrently serving as President of ASOR — that the Jerusalem School attempted to re-establish a full program. The steadily deteriorating political environment as the British Mandate was drawing to an end caused the program to be curtailed, leaving only limited classes and a few research fellows. It was at this troubled time that the discovery of the Dead Sea Scrolls became public. (See also the ASOR history section and KING pp. 113-18 for further discussion of this most important topic.) Then war broke out.

A result of the War of 1948 was the division of Jerusalem into a western Israeli city and what became an eastern Jordanian city. The Jerusalem School was located in the eastern half a scant few hundred yards from the no man's land that until 1967 was to separate Israel and Jordan. This had a major impact on the School. No longer was it in the center of a united Palestine with unlimited travel possibilities. It was now located on the western edge of Jordan. Israel was viewed as a hostile neighbor. Travel there was largely forbidden to residents of the School, and those of Jewish faith now had no access to the eastern city. Therefore, contact with the emerging community of Jewish archaeologists in Israel was severely diminished and scholarly association could only occur in Europe and North America. These were the realities that faced the Jerusalem School starting in the summer of 1948.

*Editor's Note: During the Post World War II era from 1946 into the early 1970s, the histories of ASOR and of its Jerusalem School, which becomes the W. F. Albright Institute, are intimately intertwined. The editor and authors of the ASOR and AIAR histories have worked deliberately to minimize redundancies in reporting on these overlapping years while preserving a coherent story line for each section. Readers will of course find the fullest picture by reviewing both.

The Dead Sea Scrolls: Discovery and Research at the Jerusalem School

In the early spring of 1947 a Bedouin herdsman of the Ta'amireh tribe entered a cave in the cliffs of the northwest coast of the Dead Sea. There he found jars which contained leather scrolls wrapped in linen cloth.

John C. Trever photographing the Manual of Discipline manuscript at ASOR. (JT)

During the subsequent months, five of these scrolls were purchased by the archbishop of the Syrian Orthodox Monastery in Jerusalem, Mar Athanasius Samuel, and three others by E. Sukenik of the Hebrew University in Jerusalem. In February 1948, Father Butros Swomi and Archbishop Samuel brought several of the scrolls to the Jerusalem School where they were examined and photographed by Fellows John C. Trever and William H. Brownlee. Sample photographs were sent to W. F. Albright in Baltimore.

Albright immediately responded, hailing the scrolls as "the greatest manuscript discovery of modern times." Subsequently Archbishop Samuel brought his scrolls to the United States where in 1950 and 1951, four of them were published for ASOR in two volumes by Millar Burrows, with the assistance of Trever and Brownlee.

Meanwhile, the source of the original finds were traced back to the Dead Sea shores. In February and March 1949, Lankester Harding of the Department of Antiquities in Jordan and Roland de Vaux of the Ecole Biblique carried forward scientific investigations in Cave I. They estimated that the cave had concealed a library of as many as two hundred scrolls.

Scroll fragment from Cave I from the book of Daniel (1QD^a) (JT)

(left to right) P. Benoit and R. de Vaux of the Ecole Biblique in Qumran Cave I on a visit in the 1970s. (JDS)

Investigations in Cave I launched a wider search of caves, and manuscripts were discovered in another thirteen locations. These finds drew attention to the ruins at nearby Khirbet Qumran which was subsequently excavated by Harding and de Vaux in a series of campaigns from 1951 through 1956. Cave IV, located just opposite the Qumran settlement was discovered in 1952. It provided a wealth of manuscript fragments representing all of the books of the Hebrew Bible with the exception of Esther, along with many apocryphal writings, commentaries, liturgical texts and sectarian documents.

View of the Qumran plateau from the southeast. (JDS)

During the first decade after the discovery of the scrolls, all of the Cave I manuscripts were published, and from the mid-1950s international al teams of scholars continued research on the numerous scroll fragments from the other Qumran Caves. Through the mid-1960s much of this work was centered at the Rockefeller Museum in Jerusalem. During this period the Jerusalem School and the Ecole Biblique continued to be the principal centers for scrolls research.

Joe Seger inside Cave IV at Qumran in 1962. (JDS)

Manuscript fragment of Psalm 15:1–4. (JDS)

After 1967, control of the museum passed into Israeli hands. Since then ASOR scholars have continued to be engaged significantly in ongoing study and publication work. Much of this has involved the tedium of conserving and photographing fragments, and of translating and assembling documents from the numerous bits and pieces.

In recent decades the Albright Institute has hosted a continuing series of fellows engaged in scrolls research. These include John Strugnel (Harvard University), who until 1990 headed the American scrolls research team, Mark Smith (Yale University), Stephen A. Reed (Ancient Bible Manuscript Center, Claremont, CA), Sidnie White Crawford (Albright College, and now at the University of Nebraska at Lincoln), Susan G. Sheridan (University of Notre Dame).

Sidnie White Crawford, an NEH and Dead Sea Scrolls Fellow at the Albright Institute in the early 1990s, analyzing scroll fragments.

Activity at the School after 1948

No appointments were made to the Jerusalem School in 1948–49, except for that of the Annual Director Ovid R. Sellers who arrived in the summer. In his annual report to the Trustees he made the following observations:

> *The School's position near the front lines made it a target for a great deal of small arms fire and mortar shells. Many windows were broken and every room in the building received smoke damage. It is remarkable that while some thirty mortar shells fell in the grounds, not one struck the buildings. The greatest harm was done by a mortar shell which tore a hole in the front fence and by a mine which was placed in the vestibule of the main building.* (BASOR 116 p. 5)

For the next few years the directors worked deliberately to rebuild and maintain the Institute's physical plant that had been damaged in the War. From July 1948 to April 1949 much of the Jerusalem School was rented by the United Nations to serve as its base in Arab Jerusalem, and then from April 1949 until April 1951 much of the facility was rented to serve as the United States Consulate. Every year from that point through the 1980s directors would comment on fixing, repairing, painting and improving the physical plant. Each said that things were better and looked nice, but that more needed to be done.

(left to right) Directors Melvin G. Kyle and Ovid R. Sellers at Tell Beit Mirsim, August 10, 1930. (ASOR)

Ovid Sellers on his eightieth birthday during the 1964 season at Shechem. (ASOR)

In 1951, ASOR President Kraeling noted other needs of the facility:

"The fact that our entire plant in Jerusalem had gone without replacement and renovation of household and other equipment since the days of the depression and that in addition to what had been done by the Sellers, Kelsos, Clarks, and Winnetts more still will be needed to bring it up to standard form. The School should have either a piano or a record player with a good collection of records. It should have a radio. It needs for the dormitory rooms new bedsteads to replace the old white enamel things that went out of date in 1910 or thereabouts. It needs new darkroom equipment, good photographic and enlarging equipment. It needs some drafting tables and some camping and excavating equipment. It would be a great boon if we could install at least small wash-basins with hot and cold running water in each of the dormitory rooms to replace the old wooden stands with porcelain bowl and pitcher that are still in use there. We have a wonderful installation here at Jerusalem, recognized as one of the important schools of archaeology in the country. We ought to keep it abreast of the times in the elementary facilities it offers to visiting scholars and students. Nothing elaborate, to be sure, but at least the simple installations we today regard as standard in the American way of life."

(Carl Kraeling, April 10, 1951, ASOR Newsletter #7 1950–51, pp. 1–2.)

With the possible exception of the piano, all of these improvements were made over the next decade or so. For the record, the wash basins were finally installed in the hostel rooms in 1963–64 under the supervision of Director Paul Lapp at about the same time that the courtyard was covered with flagstone pavement.

The Beth-Zur Staff 1957. (back row left to right) Spiridion Joshshan (Foreman), Machtoaz (Formatore), Micky Funk, Emile Abu Diyyeh (Foreman), Katherine Sellers, Muhtadi (Surveyor); (front row left to right) Robert Funk, Paul Lapp, Ovid R. "Sandy" Sellers, Nancy Lapp, H. Neil Richardson and John McKenzie. *(NL)*

Academic life began anew in 1949, though on a much reduced scale. Together with a project to photograph manuscripts at the Greek Orthodox and Armenian Patriarchates in Jerusalem and at Saint Catherine's Monastery, the focus of the Jerusalem School became archaeological. In 1949 a joint excavation project organized by ASOR, the Pittsburgh Theological Seminary and the United Nations relief project was instituted under the direction of Director James Kelso at Tulûl el-`Alayiq and later also at Khirbet en-Nitla, near Jericho. These were the first ASOR excavations after World War II and also the first cooperative relief efforts involving ASOR whereby the United Nations paid the wages of the 150 unskilled workers. In 1950–51 archaeological research and excavation continued with further work at Tulûl el-`Alayiq and in a new effort at Dhiban. The tradition of excavation that began with Albright, primarily at Tell Beit Mirsim, and then continued under Glueck was thus renewed, and again became a regular component of the curriculum. Between 1950 and 1967 ASOR sponsored, co-sponsored, or supported, with both staff and financial contributions, projects at Tulûl el-`Alayiq, Dhiban, Tell es-Sultan, Khirbet Qumran, Bethel, the Buqe'ah, Petra, el-Jib, Shechem, Beth-Zur, Pella, Ghassul, Araq el-Emir, Ta'anach, Wadi edh-Dhaliyeh and Dhahr Mirzbaneh, Ai, Tell er-Rumeith, Tell es-Sa'idiyeh, Bab edh-Dhra' and on the grounds of the Jerusalem School itself. In addition various Islamic sites in Syria were excavated in a project led by Oleg Grabar. Since ASOR attempted to have these projects run serially through the year and not concurrently, by the mid-1950s the Jerusalem School was managing a wide variety of equipment that was used on a rotating basis.

In 1950–51, instruction resumed and the extensive trips and excursions organized by the School were re-established. These continued to be a regular feature of the Jerusalem School's program through 1967. The annual highlight was the fall trip to the north, which usually lasted two weeks and included parts of Syria, Turkey, Lebanon, and Iraq. Each year there were also many trips to sites and ongoing excavations in Jordan, always with a featured trip to Petra. These trips were viewed as essential components of the School's curriculum. By the late 1950s, however, the academic program of classes had largely been abandoned, apparently because it was no longer viewed as needed since most of the archaeological fellows and students were thought to have sufficiently advanced standing.

By the mid-1950s, archaeology had increasingly become the School's *raison d'être*. Starting with his work at Tell Beit Mirsim in 1926, Albright had trained a generation of Americans and those who later became Israeli archaeologists. For the most part, American excavation work in Palestine ended in the mid-1930s and did not resume again in Jordan until about 1949. In effect, these 15 to 20 years represent one generation of scholarship, so in 1949 when ASOR and the Jerusalem School returned to the field, one of the goals regularly noted by project directors was to train a new generation of field archaeologists.

In the early part of the 1950s American fieldwork was conducted in the manner that Albright and Fisher had conducted work in the 1920s and 1930s. During this period, however, Kathleen M. Kenyon initiated her work at Jericho with some annual financial and staffing support from ASOR and the Jerusalem School. Kenyon came from an excavating tradition different from that of Albright, and at Jericho she introduced a more refined stratigraphic process. Training in her techniques had an impact on many individuals, but for the history of the Jerusalem School, the influence on 1955–56 fellow, Lawrence E. Toombs, is the most notable. Toombs was at the Jerusalem School that year to learn archaeology and pottery in preparation for going into the field with the new Drew-McCormick Excavations at Shechem, a project directed by Albright's former student, G. Ernest Wright. During that year Toombs excavated with Kenyon at Jericho and learned her stratigraphic method.

As with other ASOR/Jerusalem School projects, one of Wright's goals in initiating the Shechem project was to train a new generation of archaeologists. Wright fully embodied the Albright tradition, bringing to the project expertise in ceramic analysis and in methods for synthesizing archaeological and historical data. Because of his training at Jericho, Toombs brought with him a fresh approach involving debris analysis that surpassed the strictly architectural method of stratigraphic analysis used by Fisher and Albright. At Shechem, with Toombs' insistence and Wright's support, the Albright and Kenyon approaches were melded and the new "American Method" of archaeology was born.

Lawrence Toombs supervising the excavation of an MB jar burial in Field VI at Shechem in 1962. (JDS)

Since the project was organized as a training dig, the "American Method" forged at Shechem came to be used on most ASOR/Jerusalem School/AIAR digs from the 1950s to the 1980s. Shechem students and staff who subsequently ran other projects included W. J. Bennett, Jr., Roger Boraas, Robert J. Bull, Joseph Callaway, Edward F. Campbell, Dan Cole, William G. Dever, John S. Holladay, Albert Glock, Siegfried Horn, H. Darrell Lance, Nancy R. Lapp, Paul W. Lapp, James F. Ross, Joe D. Seger, Lawrence Toombs and Henry Thompson. Within a few years of the start of the Shechem project, Paul Lapp was directing numerous projects on behalf of ASOR and the Jerusalem School, and Joseph Callaway was directing a new project at Ai.

Shechem Excavations Staff in 1962. (left to right bottom row) John Holladay, Kermit Schoonover, Alberto Soggin, G. H. R. "Mick" Wright, Stanley Chestnut, Sigfried Horn, Rafiq Dajani (Jordanian Antiquities Representative) and William Dever. (second row) James Ross, Joseph Callaway, Paul Lapp, Lawrence Toombs (Associate Director), G. Ernest Wright (Director), Edward Campbell (Assistant Director), Robert Bull, George Landes and Ovid R. "Sandy" Sellers. (third row) Roger Borass, Byron Hanes, Sara Callaway, David Voelter, Dan Cole, Murray Nichols, Vivian Bull, Carol Landes and Mia Soggin. (top row) Delbert Hillers, Carl Graesser, Albert Glock, Fuad Zoughbi, Joe Seger, H. Darrell Lance and Henry Thompson. *(Photo by staff photographer Lee Ellenberger)*

Joe Callaway (left center pointing) guiding a tour at Ai for the Shechem team in 1964. (right to left) Hank Thompson, Ernest Wright, Sigfried Horn, Kermit Schoonover, Sara Callaway and Mary Lou Ellenberger.

In 1963 Nelson Glueck, as President of the Hebrew Union College Jewish Institute of Religion, founded the Hebrew Union College Biblical and Archaeological School in Jerusalem. In many ways Glueck modeled the school after ASOR's Jerusalem School as a base for American scholars and researchers engaged in Near Eastern Studies in Israel. Within a year of the school's founding, it began long-term excavation at Gezer. In a role not affiliated with ASOR, G. Ernest Wright became the director of this project in association with his students William G. Dever and H. Darrell Lance. Given the directors' experience at Shechem, Gezer brought the "American Method" to Israel in another model training dig. This dig also incorporated student education and the interests of the natural sciences that were inspired by the "new archeology" in a manner heretofore unseen. The Gezer dig, representing the "American Method," challenged the "Israeli Method." Thus began an intense and vocal rivalry between the two methodological schools that continues to this day, although now more staid and tempered by shared experience and understanding.

(right to left) G. Ernest Wright, William G. Dever, and H. Darrell Lance at Gezer in 1971.

Yigael Yadin (right) in discussion with ASOR President Jim Sauer (left) and Albright Institute director Sy Gitin (center) at an AIAR reception in 1982.

> Interestingly, at the same time that Wright was developing an "American Method" with his students in Jordan, Yigael Yadin was creating and teaching an "Israeli Method" in his excavations at Hazor. The methods taught at Hazor were also based primarily on those of Albright and Fisher. However, unlike at Shechem, they were not modified by Kenyon's stratigraphic methods, but instead remained heavily influenced by a more architectural approach. Moreover, while the ASOR Jerusalem School was one of a few foreign schools that dominated the archaeology of Jordan, the Jewish students and colleagues of Albright were creating a national archaeological tradition in Israel. The contrast has considerable significance. Archaeology in Jordan at this period must be viewed as a foreign colonialist enterprise with little intellectual impact on the local population who only served as a work force; while in Israel an independent national archaeological tradition was developing as a palpable national pastime. Yadin, military hero, politician and archaeologist, was using archaeology to help create a modern and united Israel by hearkening back to and bringing to life the most glorious time in Jewish history, the Solomonic Period, with its palaces, temples, city walls, and gates. Yadin's model of a glorious past helped determine the future. By the late 1950s archaeology in Israel had become an integral part of this past/future process.

From Glueck's departure in 1947 until 1961 each director of the Jerusalem School was an annual director. The nature of the annual director's job was mostly that of a caretaker, maintaining the plant and program and working to implement policy and those changes that derived from the home office and the ASOR Board of Trustees. Their brief tenure provided no time in which to generate or implement any longer term vision for the Institute as had been possible under Albright and Glueck. The ASOR Trustees recognized this and in 1956 they noted that, unless they could find a new candidate to become a long-term director, irreparable damage would be done to the Institute. But they lamented the fact that just as the younger fellows learned what the Jerusalem School was all about, they were snapped up for jobs in the United States and couldn't return. However, in 1960 ASOR thought that just such a person to serve long-term had been found: a recent Harvard Ph.D., Paul W. Lapp.

Lapp was the first of a new generation of archaeologists who had been trained on digs in the 1950s. He was a student of Wright with a doctoral dissertation entitled *Palestinian Ceramic Chronology, 200 BC to 70 AD*. In 1960 he was hired to spend four years at the Jerusalem School, the first year as Annual Professor and then, from 1961 through 1964, as Director. In 1965 he received a contract to serve as Professor of Archaeology through 1968. Lapp jumped right into this job, initiating a rapid-fire program of excavations and salvage projects. In addition, as Director of the Jerusalem School he was in charge of facilitating the other ASOR affiliated projects: Shechem, Ai, Pella, el-Jib, and Tell es-Sa'idiyeh. It is clear from Lapp's reports as Director of the Jerusalem School, and those of the ASOR President, that this put a strain on analytical space, the shared use of excavation equipment, and available hostel space — some nights in the summer the hostel was so full that people slept on the porch in sleeping bags. Starting in about 1964 the hostel was running at full capacity through the entire year, and in 1966 ASOR President G.E. Wright noted that there simply was not enough working space at the Jerusalem School. This was becoming a serious problem.

Paul W. Lapp (right) and Albert Glock (below left) with Awani Dajani, Director of the Jordanian Department of Antiquities (second right) and other representatives at Taanach in the mid-1960s. Lapp directed major excavations there from 1963 to 1968. (NL)

In 1964, the U.S. Agency for International Development (USAID) pressured ASOR President Detweiler to have ASOR, through the Jerusalem School, assist them in helping the Jordanian government stabilize and prepare its archaeological tourist sites for increased tourism. This program was to help the Jordanian government raise long-term tourist dollars. Although ASOR initially did not want to become involved, it represented the sole qualified group of American archaeologists in the region, and therefore Detweiler finally agreed that ASOR would help USAID. As a result, in the fall of 1964 Lapp went on leave from his position to oversee this program and a number of younger fellows were hired by USAID through the Jerusalem School. Once the program began it was clear that USAID wanted Lapp and his staff to move too swiftly to maintain what Lapp, and consequently ASOR, deemed as reasonable archaeological standards. In August 1965 this contract was terminated by ASOR.

Paul Lapp at Araq al-Amir in 1962. (NL)

The mid-l960s illustrate a dilemma that continued to haunt the School. With Lapp excavating so many sites, bringing staff into the field for these projects and then using most of the analytical space available at the School, the directors and staffs of the other ASOR projects ceased to enjoy the freedom that had been traditional in their use of the School's facilities. The School became overcrowded and cramped, especially during the spring and summer seasons. This led to a re-evaluation of the directorship situation, and when Lapp returned from work on the USAID project a new management structure was instituted. Some people concluded that no long-term director of the Jerusalem School should also direct major projects since this could create conflicts of interest in terms of the equitable use of facilities, the availability of the Director's time, and in the raising of support funds.

Paul Lapp (left) with American Ambassador to Jordan, William Macomber (center) and the director of the Palestinian Archaeological Museum, Yusef Saad in 1965. (NL)

Thus on July 1, 1965, when Lapp returned to the Jerusalem School on a full time basis, it was no longer as Director. He was appointed Professor of Archaeology and for the remainder of his contract the Jerusalem School was run by a series of annual directors. Having been relieved of his administrative tasks, Lapp was able to devote all his time and energies to completing the publication of the projects he had undertaken.

Summary

In the 1920s, with his vast and widely dispersed expertise, Albright was able to nurture the School and create a model research institution in biblical, linguistic, archaeological, historical and other kindred studies, just as the ASOR charter had sought. Starting in 1948, ASOR attempted to reimplement Albright's model in running the Jerusalem School. It established a program of classes and education for fellows, field trips, and archaeological projects, all under annual directors. The ASOR board knew that having annual directors was not the most effective way to run the school, but they were unable to find a suitable and qualified long-term director. Thirteen years of this resulted in a sort of "intellectual drag." All classes had ceased, the field trips became far more archaeological, and the focus narrowed to teaching archaeological methods in order to allow the staff, fellows, and students to participate in one or more of the three or four ASOR projects that took place during the year. By the early 1960s the school had become moribund.

The attempt to reinvigorate the Jerusalem School in 1960 with the long-term appointment of Paul Lapp did not work. Lapp was a brilliant and innovative archaeologist who, had he lived longer, would probably have revolutionized archaeological methods and theory, but unlike Albright he was not a synthesizer of the wider range of disciplines. In any event the times and circumstances of the era weighed heavily against his attempts to rejuvenate ASOR and to rebuild the Jerusalem School program.

In 1966, the President and Trustees of ASOR reached a new and unique juncture in the history of the Jerusalem School. It was determined that the School's facilities were inadequate to meet the needs being placed upon it. In addition, the character of East Jerusalem had changed significantly over the preceding eighteen years. In 1948 the facilities of the Jerusalem School were located in an almost rural environment, but with the division of Jerusalem the area around the School grew dramatically and the facility soon found itself located on the main street of downtown East Jerusalem. By 1966 this meant a disturbing rise in noise levels, but far more importantly, a dramatic rise in real-estate values. It was estimated that the facility's worth was over $1,000,000, far more than the rest of all ASOR's assets combined. The ASOR Trustees concluded that for this $1,000,000 they should sell the facility, move to the edge of East Jerusalem, build a new facility that would better meet their needs, and deposit the balance as a cash resource. It seemed to be the optimal solution.

Therefore, in 1966–67, protracted negotiations were conducted regarding the sale of the School and property and the acquisition of space at a new location. These negotiations were conducted by Annual Director John Marks and a variety of ASOR officers. By April 1967 an offer was in hand. They had identified rental space available to serve the institution for two years. They had also found land that was located just ten minutes from the current facility, and had engaged an architect to prepare preliminary plans for a new building. At the ASOR Trustees' meeting in April 1967 it was voted to implement this plan and sell the Salah ed-Din Street facilities.

What happened next significantly altered the history of ASOR. During 1966 and early 1967 tensions between Israel and the neighboring Arab states had been escalating. In the spring of 1967, both sides were girding for war. And by May the prospective purchaser of the building was experiencing problems generating the needed cash — his backers saw the war clouds more plainly than ASOR. Nonetheless, in early June 1967, Marks had an uncashed check in his hands and ASOR had sold the property. At the same time, people were being evacuated from Jerusalem and by the morning of June 5th only Director Marks, Siegfried Horn, and the Lapps remained at the Jerusalem School. Just before the shelling of Jerusalem started, Marks, his family, and Siegfried Horn left the city, scurrying to Jericho. The Lapps also departed. The Jerusalem School was left empty except for major-domo and cook Omar Jibrin, who had faithfully worked for the school for over thirty years, and who stayed on by himself to guard the facilities.

Friends are like gold, they never get rusty. Omar Jibrin, 1999

Omar Jibrin in the Institute's kitchen in the early 1980s.

The Creation of the Albright Institute 1967–1970

> *I told Omar, who I remembered from before, "Put the American flag up!" I thought, "there is war and you never know what is going to happen in the case of war." They did put up the American flag and that at least ensured that neither the Israeli army nor the Jordanian army would do any damage to the school.*
>
> Avraham Biran, 1999

> *During the 1967 War and the immediate aftermath, I was the only remaining American archaeologist in Jerusalem, at the Hebrew Union College in the new city. A few days after the war ended, Nelson Glueck arrived in a state of euphoria… Glueck wanted to go immediately to the American School, where he had been Director… I drove us there, and at the front gate we met Omar Jibrin, the legendary cook and major-domo, who had remained at the school alone during the war and secured the property, at great risk to himself. Glueck… had not seen him in nearly 20 years. I watched silently as these two grand old men — one a Jordanian Muslim Arab, the other an American Jewish rabbi — fell on each other's necks weeping. That was a moment I will never forget. It spoke volumes about the unique ecumenical character of the Jerusalem School and the way it has profoundly affected the lives of so many people.*
>
> William G. Dever, 1999

The Six-Day War began at 11:26 a.m. on Monday June 5, 1967. The Jerusalem School had just been vacated and Omar Jibrin alone was left to guard it. By the morning of Wednesday June 7, Jerusalem had been reunited under Israeli control. Miraculously, the School had sustained no serious damage. Later, Annual Director William Van Etten Casey, S.J. listed 56 broken windows, a broken drain pipe, some bullet holes, and one mortar crater — by far the least damage to any structure in the area. The property had not been used by the Jordanian military, and, therefore, had not been a target of Israeli shelling. On the morning of June 7, Avraham Biran, Director of the Department of Antiquities of the State of Israel, a former student of Albright's and 1935–36 Thayer Fellow at the School, came to investigate its fate. He found the School safe and sound in the custody of his old friend Omar. This news was quickly passed on to William Dever, at that time the Director of the Hebrew Union College Biblical and Archaeological School, who cabled this information to ASOR President Wright — although the cable didn't arrive for a week. Dever, acting on behalf of Wright and with the blessing of Biran, turned the Jerusalem School over to the American Consulate General for its temporary use since its own building nearby had been badly damaged. By Thursday (June 8) an official US flag was flying over the building and it was safe from any further depredations of war.

Back in the U.S., as the war broke out Wright and Hebrew Union College Jewish Institute of Religion President Glueck were worried about the fate of the Jerusalem School and that of the Hebrew Union College Biblical and Archaeological School. With the sponsorship of William Macomber, Under Secretary of State and a former Ambassador to Jordan, and U.S. Representative Robert Taft, Glueck arranged to go to Israel for an on the spot investigation. Glueck arrived in Israel late on Monday June 12, one week after the war began. The next day Glueck, Dever, and Ezra Spicehandler managed to reach the School and confirm what Biran had seen a week earlier. Glueck officially took control of the facility, under the specific orders of Wright, until the arrival of Director Casey. Glueck confirmed Dever's actions and then returned to the other side of town. Later that week, on June 16, Glueck declared that all the School's employees were to be retained.

On June 2 Marks had sent an emergency cable to incoming Annual Director William Van Etten Casey, requesting his immediate presence in Jerusalem. Casey quickly responded and after much delay, arrived in Tel Aviv on the evening of June 16. With Glueck's help, Casey received a pass allowing him to go to the Jerusalem School the next morning. Omar met him at the door and Casey's term as Annual Director formally began.

For the next three months, until September, Casey was the only ASOR-related official in residence, since the School was still being used by the American Consulate. The former local staff remained intact except for the School's second cook, Mohammed Adawi, who did not return after the war and who subsequently became the cook in Amman for the fledgling American Center for Oriental Research (ACOR). In July Casey hired a new executive assistant to the director, Munira Said, who today, 33 years later, remains associated with the School. Casey oversaw the immediate repair of the building and the cleanup of the grounds and quickly acquainted himself with the new situation in Jerusalem. In mid-September the American Consulate moved back to its own quarters. This allowed Casey to prepare the facility for the coming academic year. Then, at the end of September, Casey took a trip around Europe in a successful attempt to locate and reclaim the Jerusalem School's new car. The car was found in Liverno, Italy, in the custody of the shipper. Casey rerouted it to arrive in Ashdod, not Beirut. By mid-October the Jerusalem School had its new vehicle, a Plymouth.

While Casey was dealing with the realities of the new situation on the ground, ASOR President Wright and the ASOR Trustees were also attempting to determine how to deal with the new reality. In an *ASOR Newsletter* dated June 19, 1957 Wright wrote, "I see only problems ahead and few solutions at the moment." One thing was quickly made clear: the facilities of the Jerusalem School had not been sold. The check had not been cashed, nor could it be, because the buyer had stopped payment. By mid-July, Wright and the ASOR Executive Committee had decided that "no decision about the future of the Jerusalem School be made for a year or until some clarity in the political situation emerged."

Munira Said at her desk in the Institute office in 1988. (POS)

The decision to sell the Jerusalem School property was not based on the long-term goals of the organization, but rather as a solution for short-term problems — a shortage of money and overcrowding. The war forestalled this particular plan, and in its aftermath a variety of issues suddenly arose. These included the question of long-term use of the Jerusalem facility and the direction and course that ASOR should follow *vis-à-vis* research in Israel, Jordan, Lebanon, Syria, and Iraq. In the fall of 1966, when ASOR was just beginning to formulate plans to sell the School property, ASOR former-President Detweiler had gone to Jerusalem to investigate matters. During this trip he had asked for reactions from the fellows at the Jerusalem School. Their concerns had more to do with the heart and soul of ASOR than with the question of an immediate and economically-motivated sale of the property.

One of the first questions to face ASOR after the Six-Day War was where ASOR as an entity was to work. Depending upon how things were resolved, would it be possible to work both in Israel and in the Arab world? ASOR had been founded to work in the Holy Land —Palestine — but this had later been enlarged to include all of the Middle East in accord with Albright's all inclusive Orientalist perspective. Should ASOR now retreat to Israel alone, to the West Bank, or to Jordan? These were the questions that framed the dialogue from the summer of 1967 as options were weighed and discussed. Wright described the discussion:

> Some members have thought that ASOR's only future was to cast its lot with the Arabs. Others have urged that because of our financial situation and because of the great influence upon the organization of Albright and Glueck we should narrow our scope and become entirely Israeli oriented. Yet Albright and Glueck, themselves, not to speak of a number of American and Israeli Jewish scholars, have been the first to protest such a radical reduction in our cultural interests and service activity.
> (G. Ernest Wright *ASOR Newsletter* #8 April 1970 p. 5.)

> *The question of relocating the School needs to be explored in the light of answers to other questions: what is and should be the nature and extent of our cooperation with the other archaeological institutions in Jerusalem? What is the purpose of the American School itself? Is it a resident research center? A home for archaeological expeditions? A teaching institution? What type of building(s) and what organizational structure will be best suited to its future? Considerable sentiment was expressed that Old Testament interests have long dominated the School's activity and that more structured relationships with institutions in the United States for the training of students might be created. The possibility of doing much more in Islamic studies and Arabic was enthusiastically suggested as well, though few people today are specializing in Islamic art and archaeology. The same situation to an even greater extent exists in the field of Crusader studies.*
>
> (John Marks, *ASOR Newsletter* #3 1966–67, pp. 3–4)

On December 27, 1967, President Wright addressed the ASOR Board of Trustees, saying, "we have to move as promptly as possible, extending our resources to the very limit to activate American historical and cultural activities, particularly in those lands where our organization has a primary responsibility: Iraq, Syria, Jordan, Lebanon, Saudi Arabia and other countries at the tip of Arabia" (G. Ernest Wright *BASOR* 189 p. 6). In other words, the Jerusalem School would remain the ASOR presence in Israel and ASOR would attempt to open new facilities in the neighboring countries as money and the respective political situations allowed. On May 3, 1968, the Board of Trustees established an Amman Committee, headed by John Marks, which joined the supervisory committees for the Jerusalem School and the Baghdad School. In 1969 a committee to plan for a Beirut School was organized. On December 29, 1969, both the ASOR Trustees and its Corporation supported a formative and far reaching resolution that encouraged these committees to incorporate themselves as institutes independent of ASOR. (See the text of Wright's summary statement in the ASOR history section.) This marked one of the most significant turning points in the history of the organization.

Wright and the ASOR Board decided that the best way to deal with the changing political world of the Middle East was to have separate and independent Schools in as many countries as possible, starting with Jerusalem and Amman, hopefully continuing in Baghdad, and adding Beirut. These independent schools would chart their own future to continue and expand ASOR's commitment "to prosecute Biblical, linguistic, archaeological, historical, and other kindred studies and researches under more favorable conditions than can be secured at a distance from the Holy Land." They would remain affiliated with ASOR which would assist the various Schools both financially and organizationally. Since each institute would have its own identity as they were incorporated, each needed a new name, and the Committee of the Jerusalem School chose for itself "The William Foxwell Albright Institute of Archaeological Research in Jerusalem" (AIAR). On May 8, 1970, AIAR completed its incorporation proceedings. In addition to President Edward F. Campbell, Jr., Vice-President Frank M. Cross, Jr., Vice-President H. Darrell Lance, and Secretary-Treasurer Philip J. King, there were eighteen founding trustees. The letters of incorporation stated:

Edward F. Campbell, Jr., first president of the W. F. Albright Institute 1970–74 (ASOR)

(right to left) Edward F. Campbell, Jr., with G. E. Wright and Mustafa Tawfeek on Tell er-Ras overlooking Shechem in 1964. (JDS)

The purposes for which the corporation is formed are to promote the study and teaching and extend the knowledge of the geography, history, archaeology, and languages and literatures of ancient Israel and other lands of the Near East by affording educational opportunities to faculty and students of American and Canadian colleges and universities, and to other qualified faculty and students.
(KING p. 196.)

Although the goals were virtually identical to those of ASOR when it was founded in 1900, a new era had been born. The new AIAR was technically debt free and independent. In addition its trustees had a five-year renewable lease on the Jerusalem building and facilities at a cost of only $1 per year. The land and building, however, continued to be owned by ASOR.

Just after the fighting ceased in mid-July 1967, when Wright and the Executive Committee of ASOR began to deal with the long-term impact of the Six-Day War, they also implemented the following practical actions: the ASOR appointees for the 1967–68 year should proceed to the Jerusalem School as planned before the war; scholarly projects previously planned for the year should be carried through whenever possible; and plans for excavations scheduled in 1968 should continue. Accordingly, by early October 1967, a smaller than normal community of scholars began to arrive, leaving plenty of room in the School's hostel for short-term guests throughout the year. Much of the time many rooms were empty. Nonetheless, the School's activities were renewed. Lectures and soirees resumed at the School, as did a series of field trips to sites not visited on School trips since 1940: Masada in a tour led by Yadin and Sinai in a tour led by Dever, in addition to sites from Dan to Beer-Sheva. On the other hand, the annual fall trip to Egypt, Syria, Lebanon and Iraq, or Turkey became impossible. The various fellows went to work and the School again became a functioning research institution. After running a brief "rescue operation" at Suwwanet eth-Thaniya (near Jericho) in the winter, the School prepared for the ASOR digs of the spring and summer of 1968: Shechem, Tell er-Ras, Ai, and Taanach.

Kermit Schoonover served as the Annual Director of the Jerusalem School for the academic year 1968–1969. After the tumultuous years leading up to and following the Six-Day War, this year can only be viewed as calm. Five appointees as well as their families made up the core of the School's community, but since all fellows were married, two of them had to find apartments away from the School. Therefore, — for the first time in years, there was plenty of available, and often unused — space in the facility during the winter. A variety of social and academic functions took place at the school, highlighted in March by the visit of William and Ruth Albright as mentioned earlier. In the fall, Robert Boling conducted a short season of excavation at Tananir, above Schechem and the Balatah village. A variety of field trips around Israel rounded out the major events. The year ended with the Ai and Shechem projects each coming back for another field season.

David Noel Freedman served as the Annual Director of the Jerusalem School for the academic year 1969–1970, in charge of a core school community of five and a few students. Again, virtually all the fellows had families, with some finding apartments in the nearby Kaloti building and elsewhere away from the School. At the start of the year in September, Annual Professor Carl Graesser and other appointees organized a two-week survey of the Jenin-Megiddo region. Once the actual academic year began, they organized one of the most extensive and intense program of field trips in many years, visiting eight sites under excavation. In addition, they went to many other sites that were not currently being excavated where the respective directors gave special tours. They participated in other trips in conjunction with Hebrew Union College, and even managed a seven-day trip to the Sinai. It was Freedman who, along with Joe Seger, Director that year of the HUC Biblical and Archaeological School, and Avraham Biran, Director of the Department of Antiquities, organized an annual English language archaeological lecture series that was held at the Rockefeller Museum. This was to continue for the next twenty-seven years as one of the main lecture series for the reporting of recent archaeological excavations and research in Israel.

Noel Freedman (center) with staff and family being interviewed by Abe Rabinowitz of the Jerusalem Post in the Albright courtyard in 1969.

Regarding the facilities themselves, Casey, Schoonover and Freedman all worked on maintenance of the building, and early in Freedman's term it was noted that the School looked as good as it had in many years. Freedman cleaned and repaired the water system, improved the electrical system, and for the first time paved the driveway all around the building. As part of his program of improvements, he also converted the School's garage into an archaeological workroom, dedicated as "The George Ernest Wright Archaeological Laboratory." This workroom relieved some of the facility's problems by providing analytical space for its associated projects. Another key moment in Freedman's term came in May 1970, when the Jerusalem School officially became the William Foxwell Albright Institute of Archaeological Research.

The George Ernest Wright Archaeological Laboratory 1988. (ASOR)

Munira Said at the Albright Institute front gate.

The ASOR front gate sign freshly painted and installed in the rear garden of the Institute in 1970.

Immediately after the Six-Day War, the Jerusalem School suffered dramatic financial impacts. First, the standard of living in Israel was higher than in Jordan, hence expenses were 35% higher. Second, with the reunification of Jerusalem in late June 1967, Israel viewed East Jerusalem as part of a united Israeli Jerusalem. Thus the employees at the Jerusalem School became subject to the Israeli Social Security Law. While this law worked for the long-term benefit of the employees, it and the new Israeli taxes placed a new financial burden on ASOR.

Another financial problem grew out of the more limited usage of the hostel. Between 1967 and 1970 room occupancy dropped dramatically. Not only were fewer people spending long periods of time at the School, but many of those who were coming were married with families, and the School's hostel could not accommodate them. This may have been a result of an enhanced quality of life that made families more welcome in the Jerusalem environs, but it was detrimental to the School's financial wellbeing.

These financial problems aggravated an ongoing problem. During World War II ASOR had built up a small cash reserve. It was this reserve that had covered ASOR's and the Jerusalem School's small annual deficits from 1948 to 1967. Overall, the balance sheet had not been affected because of growth in the value of securities held in the endowment, but by 1967, the existing surplus had been exhausted. Thus with the increased cost of living, social security and taxes, and a drop in occupancy of the Jerusalem School's hostel, a real deficit developed. This became apparent at the same moment that ASOR expanded and created ACOR, which also had to be funded. ASOR's capacity to support its new range of initiatives was thus severely tested.

Because of the Six-Day War, all ASOR-related archaeological field projects for the summer of 1967 were canceled. But by the summer of 1967, it was already clear that there would be no similar impediment in 1968. Four projects planned field seasons for that summer: the combined Drew-McCormick work at Shechem and Tell er-Ras, along with those at Ai and Taanach. A major problem facing each of these projects was funding. ASOR President Wright anticipated this problem and requested help from the United States government. In November 1967, Wright and ASOR Administrative Director Thomas Newman submitted a proposal to the Smithsonian Institution for counterpart funds (excess U.S. government foreign currency funds being disposed by the Smithsonian Institution under Public Law 480) to support these excavation projects. Funding was granted immediately, totaling $80,000 to be divided between the excavation projects at Taanach $28,800, Ai $18,050, Shechem-Tell er-Ras $25,270, and Lapp's previous ASOR digs $4,000, with $3,800 for ASOR administrative expenses. This support enabled these projects to come close to completing their work. Funding was continued in the summer of 1969 when an additional $45,000 was awarded to support another major season at Ai. In addition the Smithsonian provided another $5,000 to ASOR for administration, an important cash infusion to help fight the tide of red ink.

Notably, in 1968 and 1969 all ASOR digs affiliated with the Jerusalem School were located in the West Bank, more or less closing down work begun prior to 1967. There was, however, a problem working in the West Bank, which was viewed as occupied territory by Israel, Jordan, and UNESCO. What governing agency was to be responsible for authorizing this work? In 1968 each of the field projects, Taanach, Ai, Shechem, and Tell er-Ras obtained excavations permits from the Department of Antiquities of Israel, the Department of Antiquities of Jordan, and UNESCO. This practice of multiple excavation licenses appears to have been continued in 1969 for work at Shechem and Ai but later that year Jordan ceased to issue such permits. With this development, for the most part, ASOR/AIAR research in the West Bank ended. It was not until 1970 that new ASOR/AIAR projects would begin for the first time outside of the West Bank, in Israel proper.

(left to right) G. Ernest Wright with William Dever at Gezer in 1971. (JDS)

Shechem staff on a visit to Gezer in 1968. (left to right) Lawrence Toombs, Anita (Furshpan) Walker, Dewey and Marion Beagle, Joe Seger, Carol Meyers (behind), Gerald Lindell, G. E. Wright, John Holladay, and James Ross. (JDS)

AIAR and the Big Digs 1970–1980

By the summer of 1970, ASOR and the newly independent AIAR were facing a grave crisis. Expenses had greatly outstripped income and both organizations were drawing more and more on ASOR's endowment in order to survive. As a new entity, AIAR had no endowment or assets. It also had no corporate support beyond that of ASOR, which had an endowment and a valuable asset in the Jerusalem facility. Thus ASOR bore the responsibility for the expenses of running the overall organization and publications, as well as for providing money to its institutes, AIAR and ACOR. Without a drastic reduction in expenses and/or the generation of additional operating gifts or endowment, the future for all parties was at best uncertain. This fact weighed heavily on ASOR president G. E. Wright, who at various times continued to suggest that the existing Jerusalem facility be sold, and that AIAR move to a less expensive location. For example in April 1974, Wright expressed the opinion that, "at the moment, our main problem is the building and property with which most scholars identify the American Schools — The Albright Institute of Archaeological Research in Jerusalem." With a declining endowment, he did not know how to justify keeping a property valued then at up to $2,000,000, and which not only did not generate much income, but actually cost $50,000 per year to run and maintain. He suggested that the property was a hindrance to scholarship and should be sold to create an endowment, the income of which could be used to support programs. Somehow Wright had to keep the dream alive. From 1966 to the late 1970s this solution was considered many times, but, except for the aborted sale just before the Six-Day War in 1967, it never generated the requisite support to carry the day.

The biggest surprise of the 1970s is that ASOR and AIAR survived their combined financial turmoil intact and in the original Jerusalem facility. Clearly the greatest success engendered by ASOR and AIAR in this period was its program of excavations. The "Big Digs" organized by or affiliated with ASOR and AIAR changed the face of archaeology in the region; in a larger sense all of these digs are Wright's progeny.

In the 1950s the Shechem project set the archaeological standard for ASOR. Wright designed this project in part to teach a new generation of archaeologists how to do field work. Within a few years its alumni were initiating large new projects in Jordan: Paul Lapp at Tell Taanach and Tell er-Rumeith, Joseph Callaway at Ai and Radanna, and Siegfried Horn at Tell Hesban.

Gezer Field School contingent in 1971. Phase I Core staff seated in front row (left to right) Joe Seger, Dan Cole, Darrell Lance (Associate Director), William Dever (Director), Anita (Furshpan) Walker and John S. Holladay. (JDS)

In 1963/64, when Wright and Glueck organized the Gezer project in Israel on behalf of the Hebrew Union College Biblical and Archaeological School in Jerusalem and the Harvard Semitic Museum, they found themselves in a more expensive world than they had known and still existed in Jordan. As one means of overcoming the financial burdens, Gezer followed the precedent set by Yadin at Masada and established a field school for students who would pay for the privilege of slaving away digging in the hot sun. These were not just graduate students in training to be leaders in the field (although this was clearly one major goal and one of Gezer's most significant contributions to the discipline), but college students and other volunteers who could come and experience the excitement of archaeology in Israel. This melding of the goals of Shechem with the volunteerism of Masada formed the first "Big Dig" at Gezer — there was even a movie made with that title. Gezer was to establish the norm for all future American work in Israel. Even though it was not an ASOR project, it was one of Wright's projects and it was the father or grandfather of virtually all subsequent ASOR work in Israel. The first evident success of Wright's program was the assignment of W. G. Dever and H. D. Lance as co-directors at Gezer, with a Core Staff including Dan Cole, John S. Holladay, Joe D. Seger and Anita (Furshpan)Walker. Gezer's alumni include, among others, Oded Borowksi, Volkmar Fritz, Pamela Gaber, Lawrence Geraty, Seymour Gitin, Larry Herr, Paul Jacobs, John Matthers, Carol Meyers, Eric Meyers, Suzanne Richard, Lawrence Stager, James F. Strange, and John E. Worrell. Every one of these scholars directed an excavation project in the 1970s, 1980s or 1990s. Thus, a new generation of scholars had been created based on Wright's vision first implemented at Shechem in 1956, and then furthered through the Gezer project and his years as president of ASOR.

(left to right) Lawrence Stager, John Worrell (Director) and Philip King at Tell el-Hesi in summer 1970. (ASOR)

In 1969, when ASOR president Wright was organizing the first ASOR digs in Israel, he had to look no further than the model developed at Gezer for structuring the new excavations. Find a group of American and Canadian universities, colleges, and seminaries to jointly sponsor a dig and then use their students to do the actual excavation in return for college credit. Other, unaffiliated, student and adult volunteers were also welcome to participate. This is how the first two ASOR projects to excavate in Israel, the Joint Expedition to Tell el-Hesi and the Joint Expedition to Khirbet Shema', were organized, and it is how most other ASOR projects were structured throughout the 1970s. It was a model that worked. This inaugurated the era of the "Big Dig," and whether big or not, projects like Caesarea Maritima, Meiron, Lahav, Nabratein, Gush Halav, Be'er Resisim, and Tell Jemmeh all followed this basic model.

(left to right) Dean Moe and Eric Meyers (Director) at Khirbet Shema' in summer 1970. (ASOR)

At this same time, in the late 1960s, Wright was deeply influenced by what was going on in archaeology beyond the Middle East. It was clear to him that the "New Archeology" and the work of people like Lewis Binford and David Clarke were having a major impact on his students, and he saw that archaeologists could get more information out of the archaeological record than just chronostratigraphy. Dever and his team had begun to bring "specialists" to Gezer in the late 1960s. It was Wright and his student Lawrence Stager, however, who insisted, when the Tell el-Hesi expedition was formed, that a full cadre of specialists — botanists, geologists, pottery, lithics and neutron activation specialists, and faunal and human osteologists — be present in the field to analyze all aspects of material culture being recovered so that their interpretation could have an immediate effect on excavation strategy. This soon became a model for American digs throughout the region, and almost immediately Wright, Stager and Anita Walker were off to Cyprus to apply it at ASOR's new project at Idalion. Wright's last major edited works dealt with anthropology and archaeology — "The Tell: Basic Unit for Reconstructing Complex Societies of the Near East"; and "The 'New' Archaeology." These were something quite apart from his theological work of the 1940s, but still reflected his humanistic approach to archaeological research.

With the advent and development of ASOR's archaeological program in Israel in the late 60s and 70s American archaeology in the Middle East ran into a phenomenon that it had not encountered before. The archaeological work of ASOR in Palestine during the British Mandate and subsequently in Jordan between 1948 and 1967 was that of a foreign archaeological community doing its research in an area where, in the main, the local community was uninvolved at an intellectual level. This was true except for the nascent Jewish archaeological community that developed in Palestine in the late 1920s and 1930s, but this was a small group that only grew after Israel achieved independence in 1948. On the whole, therefore, and until its entry into archaeological work in Israel in the mid-1960s, the archaeologists of ASOR, as well as the archaeologists of some of the other foreign schools, were dominant in an isolated sphere. The new generation of archaeologists created in Jordan at Shechem in the late 1950s and early 1960s were trained in this isolation of the Biblical Theology movement and they were only challenged from within. Starting at Gezer, however, ASOR left the splendid isolationism of colonialism and began to face competition and challenges from outside its own intellectual world.

Robert J. Bull, director of the Caesarea Excavations, using the excavation's, slide collection in the Albright Institute library in 1987.

Gus Van Beek (right), director of the Tell Jemmeh Excavations, with staff member at Jemmeh in spring 1973. (JDS)

Similarly, the other American digs of the late 1960s and early 1970s in Israel — Hesi, Shema, Caesarea, and Van Beek's excavations at Tell Jemmeh — also entered a world in which a strong and dynamic local archaeological community had developed. In the mid-1950s, the vast majority of the leading Israeli archaeologists had worked together at Hazor under Yadin, where they had developed archaeological methodologies, practices, and assumptions that were different from those that, at the same time, ASOR was developing in the West Bank and Jordan. Thus, ASOR, instead of providing a dominant and authoritative role (the benevolent colonialist), now found itself involved in vibrant and at times heated conversation about the nature of archaeology. This was something new, and it was stimulating. The debate took place on two levels — methodological (Israeli versus American) and cultural (secular/nationalistic versus biblical). In concert, the late 1960s and the 1970s saw the demise of the biblical theology movement, which in itself spelled the end of biblical archaeology as envisioned by Wright. It was at the end of this period that W. G. Dever began his attempt to transform biblical archaeology into a secular and scientific discipline called Syro-Palestinian archaeology, an arch-aeology quite at home in the "New Archeology" and eventually in the post-processual movement. The debate over this transformation filled numerous pages in *BASOR*, *Biblical Archaeologist*, *Eretz Israel*, and in Hershel Shanks' new magazine *Biblical Archaeology Review*. It is within this context in the early 1970s that AIAR developed out of ASOR.

Immediately after the Six-Day War, ASOR needed to come to grips with the vast cost-of-living differences between Jordan and Israel. Again following on the experience at Gezer, where U.S. counterpart funds under Public Law 480 had been acquired for excavation support, ASOR president Wright identified a source of support that in all likelihood allowed ASOR and AIAR to make its transition and survive into the mid-1970s The source was in the program of excess currency grants administered by the Smithsonian Institution. This provided a means by which the U. S. government could foster scholarship in regions where it was acquiring too much local currency through the repayment of loans and interest. Monies beyond U.S. governmental need in the involved countries were made available for grant support. Beginning in 1967 Wright and the ASOR offices successfully applied for some of this money on behalf of the ASOR digs. From these annual grants, which ASOR continued to receive through December 1973, ASOR received a management fee, and the various digs supported by the grants hired services and rented work and living space from the Jerusalem School/Albright Institute. These grants, involving awards totalling around $600,000, advanced the excavation and publication of many projects — Taanach, Ai, Shechem, Tell er-Ras, Khirbet Shema', and Tell el-Hesi — and of this ASOR received over $100,000 during those six years. It cannot be claimed that this money balanced the ASOR and AIAR budgets, but it was a financial life raft during the first lean years of divestiture and expansion.

From the incorporation of AIAR, by agreement with ASOR and ACOR, only ASOR was to do the majority of the fund-raising and then allocate the funds among the institutes. Therefore, in the early years of AIAR (1970–1976), the Institute was fully reliant on ASOR, except for designated gifts and direct donations from its own trustees. By 1976, however, AIAR could seek funds on its own, as long as it was not competing with ASOR or ACOR. Over the next two years, AIAR secured $52,000 in gifts from the Merrill, Helena Rubenstein, and Pew Foundations. These were the largest direct and independent gifts that, until that time, had been received from sources outside of the AIAR Board of Trustees.

By 1980, it was clear that in order for AIAR to build a strong independent school, it needed a long-term director. Interestingly enough, this idea had already been expressed a decade earlier. In 1969, Delbert Hillers, chairman of ASOR's evaluation committee, pointed out that "there are real and obvious advantages in making longer-term appointments for director, both for the sake of the School's standing in the scholarly community in Jerusalem and for the sake of effective administration." (*BASOR* 197, p. 9)

Albright Institute Directors in the 1970s

1969/70	*David Noel Freedman*
1970/71	*Robert J. Bull*
1971–1975	*William G. Dever*
1975/76	*Eric Meyers*
1976/77	*David Noel Freedman*
1977–1980	*Albert Glock*

In the meantime, because of the Institute's circumstances and, most importantly, the lack of funds, annual directors were still appointed —David Noel Freedman in 1969/1970 and Robert J. Bull in 1970/1971. Freedman's and Bull's tasks focused on maintaining the aging facilities. They were also responsible for promoting the school, and encouraging as many contacts as possible, within both the Israeli and East Jerusalem communities.

On the academic level, Bull continued the joint Hebrew Union College-AIAR English lecture series at the Rockefeller Museum that had been begun the year before by Freedman in cooperation with HUC Archaeological Director Joe Seger and Israel Department of Antiquities Director Avraham Biran. Through the most difficult of times, this series was a staple of AIAR's program, and it became the back-bone of the Institute's more comprehensive academic program in the 1980s. With a number of fellows in residence, both in the AIAR facility as well as in the nearby Kaloti Building, AIAR was a hub of archaeological activity. A number of these fellows were supported by the Smithsonian grants for work on various ASOR Projects. Field trips to major sites in Israel, including a long trip to Sinai, were organized with the help of Annual Professor Keith Beebe. The trip to Turkey, however, was the first major out of country trip since the Six-Day War, but it now required traveling by boat, since driving there from Jerusalem was impossible. This was the last major out-of-country field trip taken by AIAR fellows for many years. Bull also hosted a number of parties for both the Israeli and East Jerusalem archaeological communities, at times bringing together people who had not socialized in over twenty years.

> *The annual director has his problems: you come here and you are gone within the year and a new person comes on. On the other side, the annual director comes here with a kind of confidence that others who are longer term people did not have. The short-term annual directors usually came here on sabbatical. They were assured of a job and back in the States they were still in the academic track. If you moved out of it for more than two years and went back, you could not fit yourself into it because jobs were not that plentiful or you had lost the kind of seniority that you may have had.*
> Robert J. Bull, 1999

Robert J. Bull, Annual Director of the Albright Institute in the Albright garden in 1971.

Even though Bull had completed his planned work at Tell er-Ras in 1968, a call from Avraham Biran, the Director of the Israel Department of Antiquities, took Bull and James F. Strange back to Tell er-Ras for a few weeks in 1970 to excavate a cistern that was being looted. Strange also undertook salvage work at French Hill. Bull's contacts with Biran also resulted in Bull's organization of one of the "Big Digs" of the 1970s, the Joint Expedition to Caesarea Maritima, one of the first ASOR/AIAR projects after World War II to excavate a major, urban New Testament/Roman-Byzantine-Islamic archaeological site. As director of AIAR, Bull also helped facilitate the ASOR/AIAR excavations at Ai/Radanna, Shema, and Tell el-Hesi in the summers of 1970 and 1971.

During the 1970–71 academic year, the AIAR trustees found a candidate to become a long-term director in Jerusalem — William G. Dever, a former student of Wright's who had trained at Shechem. In 1964, together with Wright and H. Darrell Lance, he began excavating Gezer. In 1966 Dever became the Director and Lance the Associate Director of the project. After seven years at Gezer, which included four years as director of the Hebrew Union College Biblical and Archaeological School, Jerusalem (HUCBASJ), he resigned both positions to become the director of AIAR. Dever began his new position at one of the most difficult times in the School's history; the budget was more than halved for his first year. On one level, it was his job to save AIAR, and during his four years at the helm, there were dramatic changes at the Institute. In 1975, Dever left AIAR to assume a position at the University of Arizona.

William G. Dever at Gezer in the late 1960s. (JDS)

The Dever Directorship 1971–1975

Although during Dever's term AIAR/ASOR enjoyed the support of Smithsonian money, most of it went to the digs. At the same time, the hostel was mostly empty, since many of the fellows had families and lived in the Kaloti Building or elsewhere. Both to reduce expenses and increase income, Dever and AIAR turned half of the hostel into offices, labs and a photography facility which could be rented out to the ASOR digs that were receiving Smithsonian grants. This strategy worked in the short-term and every available work space was rented. AIAR had become a dig house. Since that meant fewer hostel guests, Dever released two of the kitchen staff, keeping only Omar to cook for the few residents. In addition, Dever secured donations from the major projects of the day to help refurbish and refurnish rooms. These were then assigned names in honor of the donor projects: Caesarea, Gezer, Taanach, Shechem, Shema, and Hesi. Dever also remodeled the kitchen in the Director's House and refurbished other parts using money saved from his moving allowance and employing his own carpentry skills. These skills were also used at various other times in his four-year tenure as he assisted in maintenance and repair of the Institute structure.

One task of the director of AIAR was to help facilitate ASOR's archaeological field projects. In 1971 Dever assisted the Ai/Radanna, Tell el-Hesi, Shema, and Caesarea Maritima projects; in 1972 the Shema and Caesarea Maritima projects; in 1973 the Tell el-Hesi, Caesarea Maritima, and Meiron projects; in 1974 the Caesarea Maritima and Meiron projects; and in 1975 the Tell el-Hesi, Caesarea Maritima, and Meiron projects. The experience of facilitating these digs, preparing their equipment, helping to procure their excavation permits, housing their staffs, hosting them before and after the seasons, and working with their staff in the off-season as part of the Smithsonian support, as well as frequently visiting the sites during the excavation seasons, provided Dever with an overall perspective on what the ASOR/AIAR archaeological community was doing. From this vantage point, he pressed ASOR to institute and enforce standards both in fieldwork and in publication, and to create a more professional American archaeological presence.

In 1971 the financial situation of ASOR and AIAR was such that the sole funded fellow was Thayer Fellow Thomas Schaub. Subsequent years saw the refunding of the annual professor and of a number of other fellowships, but ASOR/AIAR money remained very tight throughout Dever's tenure. The dig staffs renting space in the AIAR facility created the community, but in 1971 there was no money for field trips, seminars, or training digs, and recovery during the subsequent years was limited.

When AIAR duties did not consume all his time, Dever was able to do research and write up his work at Gezer, as well as write articles on other subjects. In 1972 and 1973, with a minimal budget, Dever also managed to conduct two small seasons of clean-up at Shechem, adjacent to the northeast gate. There he found a Middle Bronze Age II temple, which he soon published, but this was the only fieldwork of his tenure. In 1973 the "Yom Kippur War" occurred, and this was a trying time at the school. Despite all these difficulties, however, these years were among the most productive of Dever's scholarly career.

One way in which both Bill and Norma Dever contributed to a greater awareness of the presence and the local activities of ASOR and the Albright Institute was to host numerous dinners, soirees, and parties. Their guest lists were a veritable who's who of the archaeological and biblical studies community. With the Institute's scant budgets, the Devers prepared and served many of these public relations meals themselves in order to make them affordable. Bill Dever also lectured on two major tours in the United States and Canada on behalf of ASOR and AIAR in the hopes of raising money for both of the organizations.

Norma Dever with Omar Jibrin at an Albright Institute garden reception in 1973.

> There was the head man at the American University in Beirut. He was well-known among the country and all the people. They asked him whether to make a stone wall around the [Jerusalem] School. Some agreed and some did not agree. He said, 'We have to have a vote to see how many would say yes and how many say no.' They voted. They voted and that man, the director of the university in Beirut, was against it. Everybody else agreed and they said, 'Why are you against it? You have to tell us why.' He said, 'Yes' This was after 1948. He said, 'You know what you did for the Arabs and you know what you have done for Palestine. There is no danger, everything is well known. I think if you will keep the School now, like this, everybody will see your axes, **mijafin** [hoes], **goufa** [baskets], all like this, bones. But, if you build a wall around, and trucks come, people outside say will say 'pss pss pss pss... bringing guns and arms.' They will not think you are bringing **fukhar** [potsherds]. So, I believe you should leave it open as it is. And everybody on the street is aware; he comes down and he comes to visit and he sees it is **fukhar**.' Everybody believes and changed their mind [and the current fence stayed]. A very wise man. I agree with him, because the people think, 1948, we used to have a lot of trouble on Salah ed-Din. They came and checked on the School, inside... [it was okay].
>
> Omar Jibrin, 1999

> We are getting to the point where the School is known to the local people, by the population of the Arab universities. There is a mixture of contact with the staff and students, and one can notice that this has grown and grown and grown. The people are becoming more aware of what the Albright is doing, which for a long time was shut in. The local people did not know what was going on. By allowing Arab students and teachers to come from the universities and attend those lectures which involve AIAR fellows, especially those who are proper Arab teachers at other universities, has created an interest in the local public... Now there are more people who are interested in archaeology, but who do not belong to the Albright community, but who are interested in coming to the lectures. They are learning now that there is an institution which could be helpful in this. Including the people outside is a very important factor for the life of the School.
>
> Munira Said, 1999

AIAR: Rebuilding the School that Albright Built — A History of the W. F. Albright Institute of Archaeological Research by Jeffrey A. Blakely

During the Dever years AIAR's operation was dependent on ASOR at virtually every level, except for the awarding of fellowships and the day-to-day management of the Institute. But these activities were also conducted within guidelines set by ASOR. During this period, two major changes occurred at the corporate level. In 1974 Edward F. Campbell completed his term as AIAR president and was replaced by Philip J. King. Soon afterward ASOR president Wright, who had seen ASOR through eight troubled years from 1966 died in August, 1974 and was succeeded by Frank M. Cross. By the time of his death, Wright had achieved a number of goals. He had dramatically changed ASOR by creating independent schools in Israel and Jordan. These were actively working to conduct archaeological research in their respective countries, with ASOR providing the neutral meeting ground where scholarly discussion and interchange could continue to occur. Also, between 1956 and 1974, Wright had fostered a new generation of archaeologists to conduct work in what had been Palestine. By the time of his death, his students were already directing AIAR and ACOR, and from 1982 to the present, others have served as presidents and officers of ASOR. In addition, a number of the students and junior staff members on Wright's Shechem, Gezer, Hesi, Shema, and Idalion digs have gone on to direct archaeological projects in Canada, Cyprus, Egypt, Israel, Jordan, Saudia Arabia, Tunisia, the United States and Yemen.

(left to right) Philip King, AIAR President, with Glenn Rose and Kevin O'Connell S.J. of the Tell el-Hesi excavation team in the Albright garden in the mid-1970s.

AIAR Directors 1975–1980

Eric M. Meyers assumed the annual directorship of AIAR for the academic year 1975/1976. The transition occurred during the celebration of ASOR's 75th Anniversary in Jerusalem and its associated festivities. One of the long-term objectives Meyers undertook during his interim appointment was the normalization of the Institute's financial situation and the greater accountability regarding budgetary expenditures. A main issue during the year of Meyers' tenure was the plan of the Municipality of Jerusalem to condemn part of the AIAR facility in order to build a road to ease traffic congestion in the area. After much discussion in a variety of venues, the plan was "dropped," although it continued to be raised again and again over the next decade. It was also at this time that AIAR began the process of applying for tax-exempt status from the State of Israel, which it had received from Jordan prior to 1967. This saga, too, continued to be played out into the late 1980s, albeit without successful resolution.

With fifteen appointees in 1975/76, once again the AIAR program began to develop. Trips to many sites, including those in the Sinai, lectures in the continuing Rockefeller series, and a brief field campaign directed by Eric Meyers and Ehud Netzer of the Hebrew University at Herodian Jericho made this a busy year. At the end of the academic year, preparations were made to assist the new Lahav/Tell Halif excavations organized by Joe Seger as well as Bob Bull's continuing Caesarea Maritima project. When Meyers completed his year as director, the Institute could look forward to greater financial stability, and to the coming two-year directorship of David Noel Freedman. The transition of the presidency for both AIAR and ASOR also occurred at this time, as Frank Cross stepped down as president of ASOR to be succeeded by Philip J. King. Consequently, King resigned his position as AIAR president and was replaced by Ernest S. Frerichs. Both King and Frerichs served in their new capacities from 1976 to 1982.

Eric Meyers, Annual Director of the Albright Institute 1975–76. (ASOR)

(left to right) Joe Seger (Director) with Mary Elizabeth Shutler and Dan Cole at Lahav/Tell Halif at the start of excavations in 1976. (POS)

(left to right) Ernest S. Frerichs, Philip J. King, Edward F. Campbell, Jr., Nancy Lapp, and Albert Glock in the living room of the Director's apartment in the late 1970s.

Ernest S. Frerichs AIAR President 1976–82.

(left to right) Ernest S. Frerichs with Expedition Director Glenn Rose, John Wilkinson, Director of the British School of Archaeology in Jerusalem, Bob Bull and Ted Campbell at Tell el-Hesi in 1981.

The expected two-year directorship of David Noel Freedman was cut short because he had to return to the University of Michigan to resume academic responsibilities in the summer of 1977. During Freedman's year, the Rockefeller lecture series continued, as did the fellows' tours of archaeological sites in the region, although there were far fewer fellows in 1976/77. In the summer of 1977, as Freedman was preparing to return to Michigan, he assisted the Hesi, Lahav, and Meiron/Gush Halav projects to prepare for the field. Much of Freedman's energies, and those of his successor, Albert E. Glock, were spent in dealing with attempts to obtain tax-exempt status for the Institute and the ever increasing, volatile inflation rate then beginning in Israel.

In the summer of 1977, Albert E. Glock was appointed Interim Director of AIAR to fill in for Freedman. Once it became clear that Freedman would not be able to return, Glock was appointed director to complete the second year of Freedman's original tenure. In the following year, Glock was appointed to an additional two-year term as director, thus extending his service as director to three years.

During Glock's years at AIAR, the Institute came under extreme financial pressure, and, while there was a variety of appointees each year, the number never exceeded six. Nevertheless, field trips were conducted each year, usually to sites under excavation, and the appointees also participated in a series of lectures in which they presented their research. In addition, the Rockefeller Museum's English lecture series held in conjunction with HUC, now named the Nelson Glueck School of Biblical Archaeology, continued. A highlight of the spring of 1980 was a visit by Helen Glueck, during which she regaled the fellows with stories of the Jerusalem School in the 1930s.

Albright Institute Presidents through the 1970s

1970–1974   Edward F. Campbell, Jr.
1974–1976   Philip J. King
1976–1982   Ernest S. Frerichs

Al Glock speaking with Carol Meyers at an AIAR reception in the late 1970s.

AIAR Director Al Glock (left) leading a tour of the Taanach project laboratory at the Albright Institute in 1977.

The Albright Institute library in 1969.

The Albright Institute library in the mid-1980s.

With a tight budget, Glock decided to focus his energy on three projects. First, he endeavored to maintain the infrastructure of the Albright as much as possible. Second, he worked to foster a closer relationship with the East Jerusalem community and held meetings and informal get-togethers with neighbors and long-term friends as a way of reaffirming the organization's commitment to the neighborhood. Third, Glock felt it vital to maintain and reinvigorate the library. He therefore worked diligently to fill gaps in the existing book and periodical collections. In the last year of his tenure, he worked with the AIAR trustees to secure funds to hire Joan Kendrick as a full-time librarian, whose responsibility was to re-catalogue the library in accordance with the Library of Congress system. At this time, the library of Edmund Gordon, containing two thousand volumes and offprints, was acquired as a gift from Gordon's heirs. The collection related mostly to the field of Assyriology and included his personal papers. This filled a major gap in the Albright's collection.

The major focus of Glock's life from the mid-1970s, however, was his commitment to the development of a local Palestinian archaeological community. As a result, he taught a wide variety of archaeological courses at Birzeit University, helping to develop the Department of Archaeology, the precursor of the Birzeit University Palestinian Institute of Archaeology. Prior to Glock's appointment as AIAR director, in the spring of 1977, at the behest of then AIAR director Freedman, Glock initiated a series of salvage excavations in Jenin in conjunction with Birzeit University. While Glock kept these aspects of his activities separate from his AIAR work, he continued these and other activities during and after his years as director of AIAR. When Glock left the AIAR in 1980, he noted that the Institute needed a strong long-term director and that the AIAR trustees should work to remove the economic obstacles that kept the director and the Institute from flourishing.

A more positive period of growth at the Institute developed in the 1980s. It had its beginning, in part, in 1979 when ASOR and Brandeis University began a three-year joint archaeological collaboration, the Brandeis University/ASOR archaeological semester in Israel. The Hyatt and Albright Institutes in Jerusalem conducted the program, which provided an outstanding undergraduate educational experience in archaeology and the history and culture of ancient Israel, including a series of field trips and a three-week excavation. The program was organized and co-directed by Seymour Gitin, then AIAR Annual Professor, who, in the second year of the program, began his long-term tenure as AIAR director. Gitin also held a joint appointment from Brandeis as an Adjunct Assistant and then Associate Professor. The co-directors of the program with Gitin were the directors of the Hyatt Institute, G. Wiener, and his successor, B. Levy. Tel Dor was the site of the first year's excavation directed by Gitin in cooperation with Ephraim Stern of the Hebrew University. The second and third year's excavations were conducted at Tel Miqne-Ekron, and represented a pilot project for the long-term Albright Institute/Hebrew University excavations under the direction of Gitin and T. Dothan. The Brandeis/ASOR program was clearly a success, with a number of students going on to do graduate work in archaeology and anthropology, and some eventually even to direct their own excavations in Israel, Jordan and the United States. The program was not continued, however, as Brandeis University under new leadership had begun the process of closing down the Hyatt Institute, the center of its overseas programs in Israel.

Summary

Before the Albright could develop a comprehensive program, partly emulating the "golden age" of archaeological research of the 1920s and 1930s, it had to confront two major problems. The first involved the effects of Wright's decision to deal with the aftermath of the Six-Day War by expanding and creating ACOR, CAARI, and the Carthage School during the 1970s. This action may well have been the proper response to the times at an intellectual level, but it clearly exacerbated the financial problems of AIAR in Jerusalem and almost caused the entire enterprise to sink on more than one occasion. The second was the complicating factor of AIAR having lost the high profile and position of intellectual leadership that it had attained fifty years earlier under Albright and Glueck. At that time, the Jerusalem School had developed into a multi-disciplinary Institute with a program, in-house scholars in a wide variety of fields, and a facility that could support a broad spectrum of research. By the late 1950s, however, the School had ceased to run a program and by the mid-1960s through the 1970s, it had become little more than a dig house to facilitate the various ASOR archaeological projects in the region. By the late 1970s, ASOR/AIAR had been unable to fund book and journal acquisitions to maintain a top research library even in archaeology, just as it had been unable to fund the maintenance of its building. While it facilitated American archaeological research in Israel, the Institute itself had become a minor player in an archaeological arena dominated by the indigenous archaeological community of Hebrew University, Tel Aviv University, and the Israel Department of Antiquities. Thus, the situation facing AIAR in the late 1970s was not enviable. AIAR needed to consider its purpose and goals carefully, and to design and implement a workable plan to survive, recover and flourish.

The Albright Institute 1980–2000
Establishing a Vision

By 1980, AIAR was at its lowest point in sixty years, with the Institute functioning almost solely as a service organization and dig house for a small clientele, and with no clear agenda other than survival. AIAR and ASOR recognized that to effect a major change in this situation, a long-term director was needed. As a result, Seymour (Sy) Gitin was appointed the fifth long-term director in the history of ASOR/AIAR, beginning an initial three-year contract on July 1, 1980. During the next twenty years, his contract was renewed at regular intervals and he continues to serve as the new century begins. Gitin, a graduate of HUC-JIR had been Nelson Glueck's student until Glueck's death in 1971. He then continued his doctoral research on the first millennium B.C. pottery from Gezer under W. G. Dever, and was, therefore, already part of the Albright/ASOR tradition. Taking the long-term view, Gitin believed that the first step in revitalizing AIAR was the restoration of the Institute's intellectual environment within the context of the local scholarly communities and the needs of American research projects. He concluded that four areas needed to be addressed: program, fellowships, excavations and outreach/information-sharing. Each of these had the potential of recreating a *raison d'être* for the Institute beyond just providing services in support of ASOR field work. Also, each area was to some degree dependent upon the other, and each needed the support of a strong infrastructure, including staff, facility, finances and library.

Sy Gitin at Gezer in 1973.

Seymour Gitin, AIAR Director 1980 – present.

Staff

The lean years of the 1970s had also taken their toll on the staff at AIAR. With inflation running rampant in Israel, staff wages were lagging far behind. In 1980, Gitin determined that the staff's wages were below those of comparable positions at neighboring institutions, and in the summer, he reorganized the staff structure and the Institute's system of financial management. With the concurrence of the trustees, a 25% wage hike was instituted immediately as a way of raising staff moral, and, within six months, it was decided that staff salaries would be calculated in dollars, rather than in local currency. The AIAR trustees also agreed to provide medical insurance coverage for the staff and to establish a reserve for payment of severance, as required by Israeli law. By 1986, a recommendation for establishing an employee pension plan was also accepted by the trustees. These changes encouraged a more positive staff attitude and increased productivity, but in order to help balance the budget in the face of these additional expenses, the Institute cut back on some of the less essential food services for residents.

For the first year, Gitin ran the facility with the help of the existing staff, but in 1981, an assistant to the director was appointed. Ann Roshwalb served in this capacity for four years, and after her departure in 1985, the position was reconfigured into that of an assistant director. This position was held by Thomas E. Levy for two years. With Levy's departure in 1987 the position reverted to that of assistant to the director and Edna Sachar was hired, first on a part-time basis. Then, as the Albright's program tripled in size, she began working full-time During her twelve-and-a-half years, Edna was a most positive force in supporting the growth of the Institute's activities. She was succeeded for a brief time in 1999 by Helene Roumani. The position is now filled by Helena Flusfeder.

Thomas E. Levy and wife Elena outside the Garden Apartment entrance in 1986. Levy served as Assistant Director from 1985 to 1987. (POS)

Edna Sachar in 1999. She served as Assistant to the Director from 1987 to 1999. (POS)

Helena Flusfeder became Assistant to the Director in 2000.

Omar Jibrin in 1988. (POS)

Omar Jibrin, AIAR's head cook and major-domo was ASOR/AIAR's longest serving staff member. Omar, who had first been hired by Clarence Fisher during Nelson Glueck's term as ASOR director in 1939, was for 56 years one of the mainstays of the American School/Albright Institute in Jerusalem, befriending generations of American, Palestinian and Israeli students and scholars. In the difficult political environment of Jerusalem, Omar steadfastly maintained a positive presence at the school, providing it with a strong sense of continuity and stability. His love for his work and the people he met at the school helped create a friendly and warm atmosphere, which greatly contributed to the success of the Institute and its program. Omar retired for the first time on June 30, 1983, but three months later, at Gitin's instigation, he returned to work at AIAR and continued to function as head cook until 1995. After a long period of illness, Omar died at home in Bethany on December 15, 1999. He was succeeded by the current cook, Hisham M'farreh (his nephew), who continues to develop new and exciting menus to the delight of all residents and fellows.

Formal picture of ASOR/AIAR group at celebration of Omar Jibrin's 50th anniversary as an employee of the Jerusalem School/Albright Institute. (left to right back row) Philip J. King (Past-AIAR and ASOR President), John Spencer (AIAR Treasurer, now Vice President), Eric Meyers (former AIAR Director, then President-elect ASOR), Joe D. Seger (President AIAR) and Sy Gitin (Director AIAR). (front row) Edward F. Campbell, Jr. (First AIAR President, former ASOR Vice President), Robert J. Bull (former AIAR Director), Vivian Bull (AIAR Trustee), Omar Jibrin (AIAR Cook and major-domo), Norma Kershaw (AIAR and ASOR Trustee), Richard J. Scheuer (AIAR and ASOR Trustee), and William G. Dever (former AIAR Director and ASOR Vice President).

The Facility

Although all the AIAR directors worked to repair and improve the physical plant, in an old building this task is never-ending and given the lack of sufficient resources, by 1980 the maintenance of the structure and its grounds was falling in arrears. Gitin and maintenance man Said Freij accordingly instituted short- and long-term plans for plant improvement and annual general maintenance and repairs, which have continued to the present time. When the facility was built in 1925, it had its own water system, complete with cisterns. By the 1980s, most of these cisterns were no longer needed and Gitin solicited special funds from the trustees to convert two of them into archaeological laboratories that could then be rented out to ASOR-affiliated projects. Eventually, one became the Miqne lab and the other was first used by the Ashkelon project and is currently the Sepphoris lab. Gitin also organized the funds for a new drainage and sewer system that created a suitably dry environment in the basement of the main building to enable it to be transformed into the library journal room, effectively doubling the capacity of the library.

View of the Albright courtyard from outside the Director's house in the late 1970s.

(left to right) Richard J. Scheuer Fellow J. P. Dessel discussing pottery from Lahav/Tell Halif with Lahav Project Director Joe D. Seger in the Miqne Lab in 1985. (POS)

(left to right) AIAR Director Sy Gitin with Lawrence Stager and Douglas Esse, Director and Associate Director of the Leon Levy Ashkelon Excavations. Stager is receiving keys to the Ashkelon Lab in late spring 1985.

AIAR: Rebuilding the School that Albright Built — A History of the W. F. Albright Institute of Archaeological Research by Jeffrey A. Blakely

AIAR Director Gitin with pneumatic drill initiates the repair of the Institute fence.

New shelving inside the G.E. Wright Lab with Miqne Formatore Moshe Ben Arie at work in the background in 1988. *(POS)*

Throughout the 1980s and 1990s, the Albright facility continued to undergo major improvements. Among other things, the roofs of the Director's House and Annual Professor's apartment building were replaced, funded mainly by gifts from trustees Norma Kershaw and Richard J. Scheuer. The Garden Apartment was repainted thanks to a gift from Lydie Shufro and the bathrooms and showers of the Director's House and hostel were renovated. Funds raised by the annual alumni drive, under the leadership of trustee Norma Dever, paid for the renovation of the laundry room, for new window shutters, and, in part, for the rebuilding of the Institute's perimeter fence. The remaining funds for the fence project were contributed in memory of former trustee Miriam Ross by her family and friends. Most recently, the Annual Professor's apartment was renovated, funded by gifts given in memory of Jean H. Charlesworth and from Trustee Richard J. Scheuer. The G.E. Wright Lab, fitted with new shelving and a heating and air-conditioning unit, a gift of the Miqne project, was converted into a year round pottery restoration and research facility.

Besides the physical expansion of the library mentioned above, the greatest impact on the Albright as a research center was the development of the Institute's computer facilities. While computers had been used at the Albright since 1985, as a result of a gift solicited by Gitin from Hewlett-Packard, it was only in 1997 that a comprehensive plan for the computerization of the library and the Albright as a whole was implemented. This came as a benefit from the $100,000 providing for enhanced computer facilities included as a portion of the NEH grant received that year. The acquisition by the Albright of its own server provided a computer network with connections to every room in the facility, allowing immediate and simultaneous access to the World Wide Web for all of the Albright's resident fellows and staff. At the same time, a computer center for the fellows, with several computers, printers and a scanner, was established in the library periodical room.

AIAR Trustee and Miqne staff member Walter Aufrecht entering computer data at the Institute in the late 1980s. (POS)

(left to right) Miqne Fellow Garth Gilmour, Barton Fellow Ed Mahar and USIA Fellow Jonathan D. Lawrence in the new journal room and computer center for fellows in 2000.

AIAR: Rebuilding the School that Albright Built — A History of the W. F. Albright Institute of Archaeological Research by Jeffrey A. Blakely

The Albright Institute and its Governing Board

The Albright's success has been, and continues to be, based on the support and encouragement of the Institute's officers and Board of Trustees. With a long-term director, the manner in which the AIAR Board of Trustees oversaw the management of the AIAR facility changed from what it had been under short-term directors. Together, the trustees and Gitin established long-term policy and the annual budget. The director in turn planned and implemented the program, oversaw the management of the facility, helped in fund raising, and carried out his own research program.

Joseph A. Callaway, AIAR President 1982–88, (center left) with Albright Institute Trustees (left to right) Mildred Freed Alberg, Joy Ungerleider Mayerson, William E. McClure, Carol Meyers, and Edward Cohen at an exhibit reception in the Russell Senate office building in Washington, D.C., during ASOR and AIAR Board of Trustees Meetings on April 22, 1985. Cohen became AIAR's first Board Chairperson in 1988. He was succeeded by Joy Ungerleider Mayerson who served from 1989 to 1994. (ASOR)

Changes involving the presidency of AIAR had also occurred by 1980. With the new corporate and financial structure, the AIAR President's position achieved more prominence, displacing the role formerly played by the President of ASOR in the management of AIAR activities. The presidency of Ernest S. Frerichs, which ended on July 1, 1982, provided the critical transition. Frerichs was responsible for helping to formulate the job description for the long-term directorship and for creating the basis of the new working relationship between Gitin and the Board of Trustees. He was succeeded by Joseph A. Callaway, who served until May 1988. During his term, Callaway helped the Albright to stay afloat financially, shepherding AIAR interests involved in a major NEH Challenge grant received by ASOR, and thus securing the fund basis for the establishment of an independent endowment for AIAR. This prepared the way for the successful transition to the great growth period of the Albright in the 1990s. Joe D. Seger succeeded Callaway as president, and it was during his tenure from 1988–1994 that Albright monies were moved from the ASOR portfolio to AIAR's own endowment account. Seger also labored in other ways to clarify the legal separation from ASOR and, most notably, was successful in negotiating arrangements for the transfer of the Jerusalem property from ASOR into AIAR hands. In addition, he also helped to secure sustainable funding from the U.S. government — specifically, from the NEH, the United States Information Agency (USIA) and the Department of Education (DoE) — for fellowships and administrative support. J. Maxwell Miller, who served as president for one year in 1994–1995, made a significant effort to broaden the financial support base for the Institute from the private sector. He was followed by Patty Gerstenblith who took over the presidency at a critical point in the life of the Institute and helped to stabilize its operation. In 1997 she successfully oversaw the award of a two-million dollar NEH Challenge grant primarily for endowment enhancement. She also helped finalize the long-ongoing efforts of Joe Seger, AIAR Board Chair Joy Ungerledier Mayerson and Director Gitin for the transfer of the Institute property from ASOR to AIAR hands. In July 2000 Sidnie White-Crawford succeeded her as AIAR's eighth president.

J. Maxwell Miller, AIAR President 1994–95, (third from left back row) with Albright Institute trustees, fellows and staff at Tell Miqne in 1995. To his left Barry Gittlen, John Spencer, Trude Dothan, Lydie Shufro and Edna Sachar (seated) with Director Sy Gitin standing behind.

AIAR: Rebuilding the School that Albright Built — A History of the W. F. Albright Institute of Archaeological Research by Jeffrey A. Blakely

Joe D. Seger, AIAR President 1988–94. (POS)

Patty Gerstenblith, AIAR President 1995–2000, in the Miqne Lab at the Institute in the late 1990s. (POS)

Sidnie White Crawford who became AIAR President in 2000.

AIAR Trustees at a meeting in the Director's house in 1997. (left to right) Bernard J. Bell, Director Sy Gitin, Lydie Shufro, Lee Seeman, John Spencer, Lawrence Stager, Ernest S. Frerichs, Shalom Paul, Richard J. Scheuer, President Patty Gerstenblith, Thomas Cox, Norma Dever, Mark Smith, Barry Gittlen and Jodi Magness.

Joy Ungerleider Mayerson.

Edward Cohen was elected the first AIAR Chairman of the Board in 1988 and he immediately initiated an open line of communication with the Director. Joy Ungerleider Mayerson succeeded him in 1989. During her term she provided exceptionally strong leadership, vision and support without which the Institute would not have enjoyed such positive development in the early 1990s. After her death in 1994, the current chairperson, Daniel Wolk, assumed Board leadership. Wolk's commitment to, and support of the Institute has been similarly unequivocal. Throughout the past two decades, a number of other officers and trustees have also made major contributions to the success of the Institute and its programs. Among these, Richard J. Scheuer stands out as the most dedicated and supportive. Dick Scheuer's many contributions to the AIAR and ASOR are honored in the acknowledgments at the beginning and elsewhere within this volume.

Joy Ungerleider Mayerson, Chairman of the AIAR Board of Trustees 1989–94, with (left to right) Director Sy Gitin, Millard Lind, Jonas Greenfield and Jerry Murphy O'Connor in the Director's house in the early 1980s. At the time Joy Ungerleider Mayerson was First Vice President of the Albright Board of Trustees.

AIAR: Rebuilding the School that Albright Built — A History of the W. F. Albright Institute of Archaeological Research by Jeffrey A. Blakely

At the beginning of the 1980s, the operation of AIAR was almost totally dependent on ASOR's subsidy. In 1984, however, ASOR was forced to reduce its support until it barely covered essentials. Therefore, AIAR had to raise additional funds, and, simultaneously, begin to build its own endowment. In 1981 ASOR was awarded a 1:3 NEH matching grant with part of the money pledged to AIAR. AIAR trustees Richard J. Scheuer and Joy Ungerleider Mayerson together pledged a total of $300,000 to help establish an AIAR endowment as part of the required match. Others also contributed and, by the end of the grant period in 1987, the AIAR endowment fund within ASOR stood at about $550,000. This provided some new stability for AIAR in meeting its expenses. Throughout this period, annual contributions for operating expenses, plant maintenance, and plant improvement were made by various trustees. Of particular importance were the contributions of Richard J. Scheuer, Joy Ungerleider Mayerson, Arnold Flegenheimer, Elizabeth Bechtel, Estanne Abraham and Norma Kershaw.

Dan Wolk, Chairman of the AIAR Board of Trustees 1994–present.

Support for infrastructure and general operations from outside the AIAR Board of Trustees also provided essential assistance. Gitin made a number of fund-raising trips throughout the United States where he lectured extensively and also met with potential individual contributors and foundations. Fund raising thus evolved as one of the major jobs of the Director, especially in conjunction with the AIAR presidents Seger and Gerstenblith and with AIAR treasurer John Spencer, preparing grant proposals. As a result successful requests for support were submitted to the Abraham, Hewlett-Packard, Kress, Lipper, Littauer, Revson, Billy Rose, B. Rose, R. Rose and Helena Rubenstein Foundations, as well as to the NEH, the USIA, the DoE and others.

John Spencer ably served as AIAR Treasurer from 1988 to 1997. From 1997 to present he has continued his service as AIAR Vice President.

Two major but related issues facing AIAR in the 1980s were the continuing question of whether the Municipality of Jerusalem was going to condemn part of the AIAR property in order to build a road, and how to secure the long-term use of the AIAR facility and property, which was owned by ASOR. ASOR by 1985 had cut greatly into its endowment, and since the AIAR property was its largest asset, and its own viability was of great concern, there remained the possibility that ASOR might have no choice but to sell the property. Regarding the former issue, in order to preclude the road building project, Gitin oversaw the plans for a new building on the back lot of the property, which were drawn up by the Albright's architect Moshe Gary and approved by the city planning commission. This and the direct intervention of the mayor of Jerusalem, Teddy Kolleck, effectively put an end to the road issue. This issue of ownership of the facility was successfully negotiated with ASOR in 1994, and after pursuing legal options in Israel, it was finally resolved with the formal transfer of the property from ASOR to AIAR in 1996.

Library

The maintenance and growth of the Institute library formed essential elements in the 1980s plan for developing the Albright. While there was a sound basis on which to build, the history of the library shows that over the years it had not had a consistent and well-funded acquisitions policy or binding program, and had not been run by a long-term, full-time library staff.

When the Jerusalem School was founded in 1900, one of the first priorities of the directors was to create a quality research library. They were highly successful through the early years, and, until World War II broke out, the library flourished through journal exchanges, donations, and the purchase of books. After World War II, the costs associated with the Jerusalem School mounted and library acquisitions declined. Throughout the 1950s and much of the 1960s, with no budget and no long-term director to motivate acquisitions, the library languished, receiving only ASOR journal and book exchanges and some donations, along with only a few purchases. On the positive side, however, was the donation in 1966 of a state-of-the-art steel shelving system from H. Dunscomb Colt.

After the Six-Day War, the situation was further exacerbated by the lack of a librarian. The directors and Institute Secretary Munira Said oversaw the library, but ASOR recognized that the lack of a librarian and of a budget was a serious problem. An evaluation of the situation was conducted in 1967 by Elvire Hilgert, the Associate Librarian at McCormick Theological Seminary, and in 1968, a Library Committee was appointed to administer all ASOR libraries. To assist in the management of the Jerusalem School library, Trustee Elizabeth Bechtel donated $3000 to hire Yusef Saad, formerly of the Palestine Archaeological Museum. He ran the library on a part-time basis from April 1969 until March 1971. In December 1970 the Library Committee initiated an annual donation to the library of the Ecole Biblique to promote a relationship with that library and indicate "our appreciation for past cooperation on the part of the Ecole Biblique, and our hope for a larger commitment in the future." This relationship is still in effect today, allowing AIAR fellows regular access to the Ecole library.

With the appointment of Dever in a long-term position in 1971 the ASOR Library Committee was disbanded and the responsibility for running the library returned to the director. Soon thereafter, in the summer of 1972, Dever appointed Pablo Figueras to serve as part-time librarian, funded by a grant from the Merrill Foundation. Figueras continued to serve as part-time librarian until 1976. An evaluation of the library showed an inventory of about 15,000 monographs and journals with a value of about $200,000 — a very significant asset. From 1976 to 1979 the library was run by the directors and volunteers, and it was during this period that the Edmund Gordon Assyriological library was acquired by AIAR. In 1979, as mentioned previously, Joan Kendrick was hired to convert the library to the Library of Congress classification system. A PEW grant and a gift from Richard J. Scheuer greatly helped with this transformation. In June 1982, the new librarian, Annette Magnus, completed the job. She also began a new program for journal binding, and for improving the journal exchange program with ASOR. In addition, duplicate journals and monographs were donated to the new libraries of ACOR and CAARI.

During the early years of Gitin's tenure, the Institute's artifact collection of six thousand items, begun by Albright in the 1920s, along with its map collection, were also re-catalogued and incorporated into the library. The space problem for the growing library was temporarily solved by a plant improvement grant from Trustee Richard J. Scheuer, which provided for the conversion of the archaeological storage area in the basement of the main building into the library's journal room. This provided ample space for the growth of the library for the next fifteen years. Throughout this period, annual grants from private sources, like those from the Littauer Foundation, and later, long-term support from the U.S. Department of Education (DoE), allowed the Albright to gradually increase its library holdings. Other additions came in 1986, with the donation of the library of former Albright NEH Fellow Daniella Saltz, and in 1993 with the bequest of the library of Douglas Esse, a former Barton Fellow and Albright trustee.

AIAR Director Sy Gitin in his office in the mid-1980s. On the right is a new exhibition case with artifacts from the Institute study collection.

Fellows at work in the library carrels in 1988. (POS)

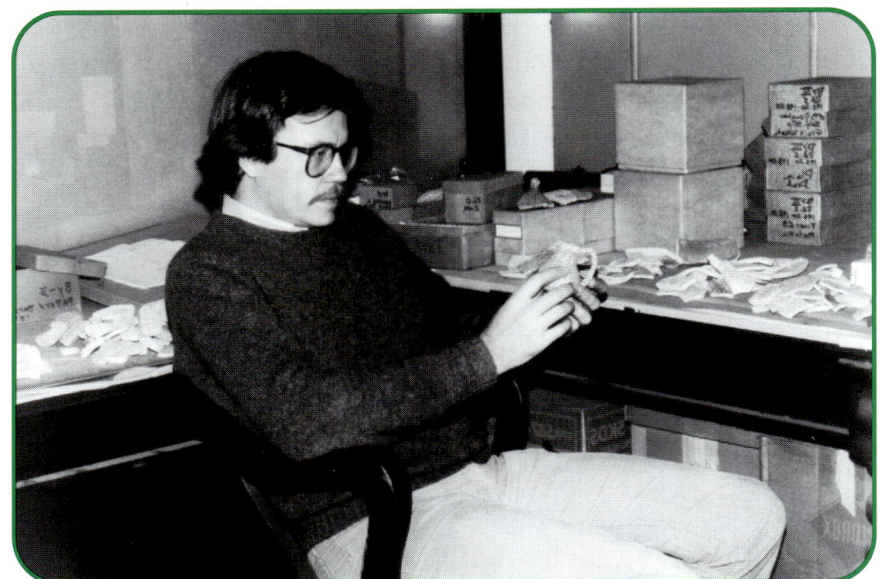

Douglas Esse, Albright Barton Fellow, analyzing pottery in the Institute's basement lab in 1980. Esse served as Associate Director of the Ashkelon Excavations through the mid-1980s and was an AIAR Trustee from 1990 until his untimely death from cancer in 1992.

Douglas Esse (left) with Miriam Tadmor, Curator of the Israel Museum (right) at an Institute reception in 1984. In the background are Helen Merrillees, wife of then Australian Ambassador to Israel and now Director of CAARI in Nicosia, Robert Merrillees, and Pierre de Miroschedji of the French Archaeological Mission.

Although the library was well managed throughout this time, insufficient funds precluded the employment of a full-time librarian. Serving as part-time librarians during these years were Annette Magnus (1982–83), Leah Alexander (1983–85), Hanna Caine (1985–87, 1989–93), Bella Greenfield (1989–2000) and Marina Zolinsky (2000–present). From 1996, with the increased funding provided by the grant from DoE, the Albright was finally able to appoint a long-term head librarian. Sarah Sussman was hired for the post and, with Bella Greenfield continuing in a part-time position, a new phase in the library's development was initiated. In 1997, a three-year Getty Trust grant of $141,000, obtained with the help of Trustee Lydie Shufro, provided continuing support for the head librarian and for two part-time assistants, and tripled the Albright's acquisition and binding budgets. This allowed the library to fill important gaps in its monograph and periodicals collections, as well as to expand the scope of its holdings in the areas of Prehistory, Classical, and Islamic studies. In preparation for these new holdings, the library journal room was again renovated to accommodate an additional 4,500 books and periodicals. The library currently holds 28,500 volumes.

Librarian Annette Magnus discussing library matters with Munira Said in the Institute's main office in 1982.

Leah Alexander Librarian 1983–85.

Bella Greenfield Librarian 1989–2000. (POS)

Sarah Sussman Chief Librarian 1996 to the present. (POS)

Also in 1997, the Albright was awarded a $2,000,000 challenge grant by the National Endowment for the Humanities of which $900,000 was for the library endowment, and $100,000 for computerizing the library and library security. These funds provided for the purchase of a highly sophisticated, state-of-the-art library computer software program, Tech-Lib developed by OCLC. It also suported librarian training in the use of the new computer program and technical support. Increased security for rare and out-of-print volumes was provided by the purchase of a number of locking cabinets, for restricted access. In 1999, Gitin solicited a matching grant from the Council of American Overseas Research Centers (CAORC) to provide funds for a computer specialist in MARC library cataloging, which further advanced the program for computerizing the library. Also in 1999, Cecile Lyons, the wife of the late Albright trustee Dr. Melvin Lyons, established the Melvin Lyons Library Resource Endowment in his memory. Mel Lyons served throughout the 1970s and early 1980s as the ASOR medical consultant for excavations. In May, 2000 the library collection was named in honor of Trustee Richard J. Scheuer in recognition of his special interest in and generous support of library development through the years.

AIAR Treasurer Marian Scheuer Sofaer at the May 2000 naming of the Institute's library collection in honor of her father, long-time ASOR and AIAR Trustee Richard J. Scheuer.

Program

Starting in 1980, Gitin also initiated steps to develop the Albright's educational program in conjunction with, and as an integral part of, the Institute's fellowship offerings. Consequently, the role of AIAR began to change from being primarily a service organization for excavation projects to one that was program-oriented in support of research, and this is reflected in the rebirth of an annual program of activities. In 1980, in addition to an occasional lecture given at the Institute and periodic field trips, the sole institutionalized aspect of program was the still ongoing joint AIAR-HUC English-language archaeological lecture series held at the Rockefeller Museum. This high-profile lecture series served for twenty-seven years as a valuable venue for presenting new archaeological results and interpretations. By 1996, however, largely because of the success of these lectures, other institutions had created their own series, generating a proliferation of lecture programs at archaeological institutes and museums in Jerusalem. This, coupled with the loss of parking facilities at the Rockefeller Museum and the change in the local environment of East Jerusalem resulting from the *Intifada*, brought an end to the AIAR-HUC series.

> *The Albright's primary goal is to maintain itself as a research institution. It should provide an opportunity not only for graduate students in archaeology, the professionals of tomorrow, but also for undergraduate students in both the humanities and sciences. This is important as it will enhance undergraduate studies by deepening young students' appreciation of the role of archaeology in historical, sociological and anthropological recoveries of the past and the relationship between the past and the present. I see that kind of dual role for the Albright.*
>
> Ernest S. Frerichs, 1999

One of the first aspects of the traditional program to be reinstituted was a year-long series of field trips in Israel and the West Bank. These trips were reminiscent of those led by Albright in the 1920s and 1930s, but instead of week-long excursions on horseback, they were day-long trips in a van. The goal, however, remained the same: to acquaint the fellows with the topography and geography of ancient Israel and the historical sites of all periods. These trips, conducted two to three times a month, became so popular that, by the 1990s, as the number of fellows increased, a second (or third) van was sometimes required to accommodate the appointees and guests. Besides the local trips, annual or semi-annual trips abroad were again organized. These trips, to Crete, Cyprus, Egypt, Greece, Jordan, Lebanon and Turkey, like those led earlier by Albright and others, were concentrated on the archaeology of the specific region or country.

Group picture of AIAR fellows in 1983/84. (left to right back row) Aileen Baron, Ann Killebrew, Daniella Saltz, Mark Smith, J. Kenneth Eakins, James Ross, Jack P. Lewis, A. M. Lewis and Director Sy Gitin. (front row) Elizabeth Bloch-Smith, Marion Eakins, Miriam Ross, Gloria London and Miriam Chernoff. Not in the picture Baruch Halpern and J. Cheryl Exum.

Avraham Biran, Director of Excavations at Tel Dan, giving a tour to an AIAR/ASOR group in the mid-1980s. (left facing Biran, right to left) Bill Bruton, Dan P. Cole and Ernest Ferichs.

Baruch Halpern (right), NEH Fellow 1984/85, with Emmanuel Marx, Ben Gurion University anthropologist on an AIAR field trip to the Negev.

AIAR field trip to Turkey 1985. (left to right) Annual Professor Walter Aufrecht, Marilyn Hershfield and NEH Fellows Philip King and Richard Hess.

Albright fellows and friends trip to Crete 1994 (left to right top row) Sidnie White, Louise Hitchcock and Dan Crawford. (middle) Anne Killebrew, Trude Dothan and Sy Gitin. (bottom) L. Byrne, Beatrice St. Laurent and Walter Aufrecht.

Group at AIAR Appointees' Colloquium at ACOR, Amman in 1999. (left to right top) AIAR Director Sy Gitin and Shimon Gibson. (middle) Ann Killebrew, Sandra Blakely, Laura Mazow, and Patricia Bikai (ACOR Associate Director). (bottom) Robert Schick, Robert Mullins, Justin Lev-Tov, and Pierre Bikai (ACOR Director).

Iron Age Research group of international scholars at the Institute in 1982. (left to right back row) Sy Gitin (AIAR Director), Gabriel Barkai, Ami Mazar, Brian Hesse, Moshe Dothan, Steven Rosen and Douglas Esse. (front row) Lawrence Stager, David Ussishkin, Arlene Rosen, Paula Wapnish, Trude Dothan and Pierre de Miroschedji.

With the growth in the number of fellows also came an increasing diversity of their research interests. Accordingly, new complementary components to the Albright's program were added to meet their needs. The program also took into account the growing interest and involvement of the other foreign and local archaeological communities in AIAR activities. This greatly enriched the experience of the Albright fellows, bringing them into contact with an ever-expanding circle of scholars and broadening their academic horizons. By the early 1990s, a number of Israelis and Palestinians, as well as American and European scholars teaching or doing research at other local institutions, became Associate Fellows at the Institute and regularly participated in and contributed to the Albright program. Overall, these activities benefited significantly from the Albright's open-door policy. The Institute's tradition of service as a meeting ground for researchers from all of the foreign schools, as well as from Israeli and Palestinian institutions, was greatly expanded. This policy also affected the use of the library, attracting an increasing number of local researchers to the Institute. The Albright's proximity to the French, British and German schools of archaeology, the Israel Department of Antiquities at the Rockefeller Museum, the Institute of Archaeology at the Hebrew University, the Institute of Islamic Archaeology and Department of History and Archaeology of Al-Quds University, also has been a contributing factor in attracting participation from a broad range of scholars and students. Thus, even during the early years of the *Intifada* between 1987 and 1990, and during the Gulf War in 1991, the Albright was able for the most part to maintain a regular program schedule.

AIAR fellows and staff with gas masks at the outbreak of the Gulf Crisis in 1991. (left to right) Jane Waldbaum (Dorot Research Professor), Said Freij, Sy Gitin (Director), Robert Haak (NEH Fellow), Mark Meehl (James A. Montgomery Fellow), Edna Sachar and Labiba Saleh.

By 1984, most of what comprises the Albright's current annual program of events had been established. This included the Institute's weekly series of seminars, reports and workshops, the monthly dinners with guest scholars, biweekly local field trips and annual study trips abroad, and, until 1996, the AIAR-HUC Archaeological Lecture Series. In order to ensure that the program would be responsive to the research needs and interests of the Albright fellows, the director initiated the tradition of holding an orientation and planning meeting with the fellows at the beginning of the academic year, during which the year's program is discussed. To formalize and publicize the schedule of events, an annual program brochure is printed, and currently two thousand copies are distributed both locally and abroad.

In 1981, Albright fellows conducted the first regularly scheduled series of Seminars, which serve primarily as forums for appointees to share their research with their AIAR colleagues and with the wider community of scholars from other institutions. In the following year, the series of Reports was inaugurated, in which local and foreign excavators present their most recent archaeological research in the region. In recent years, this series has been expanded to include reports on sites in Jordan (such as the presentation by Hans Nissen on Basta, jointly sponsored with Birzeit University; Michele Piccirillo on Umm al-Rasas; Peter Fischer on Tell Abu al-Kharaz, Ain Abda, and Saham; and Konstantinos Politis on Zoar), as well as reports on sites in the Palestinian entity (such as the presentations by Hamdan Taha on Khirbet Belameh, Marwan Abu Khalaf, Hani Nur el-Din and Robert Schick on Khirbet Shuwayka, and Jean-Baptiste Humbert on his excavation in Gaza.

> The number of Albright Fellows and the broad range of their research, has increased dramatically during the past ten years. Today the hostel and apartments are filled with more and more young scholars doing serious and important research. The Institute's program has also developed beyond its traditional parameters to include a greater focus on both Pre-history, Classical and Islamic Studies. Today, not only are we partners in excavation and research projects with Israeli, but also with Palestinian institutions. The emphasis on developing joint projects with both local archaeological communities is the direction in which the Albright should be headed in the future.
>
> Robert Haak, 1999

The Director's and Appointees' Workshops, which subsequently became the Workshop series, were initiated in 1984. An in-house program, the workshops afforded appointees the opportunity to test theories and to share the progress of their research with other AIAR fellows in an informal setting. Also in 1984, the first monthly series of Annual Professor's and Appointees' Evenings with Guest Scholars was held. Now the responsibility of the Program Coordinator, these evenings include a dinner and an informal discussion with resident and non-resident Albright fellows and a local or visiting scholar selected by the fellows. They offer a unique opportunity for AIAR fellows to become acquainted with senior scholars working within a wide spectrum of ancient Near Eastern studies.

Andrea M. Berlin, Samuel H. Kress Fellow 1984/85 lectures to fellows and friends in 1985.

During these years, two very successful short-term programs were also developed. From 1983 through 1986, Conversations in Archaeology were held on a bimonthly basis. These involved senior local archaeologists discussing their experiences and their role in the development of archaeology from the Mandate period to the present. These sessions were audio-taped and transcribed, and the tapes and manuscripts are now part of the Albright archives. Participants in the series included, among others, Avraham Biran, Ruth Amiran, Joseph Aviram, Moshe Dothan, Trude Dothan, Benjamin Mazar and Yigael Yadin. Sometimes, these sessions were less formal, such as when the excavator of Megiddo, Geoffrey Shipton, visited the Albright in 1986 and reminisced about the archaeological excavations at the site in the 1920s and 1930s. Also, from 1983 until 1988, annual multi-day seminars on Jerusalem were conducted by Dan Bahat.

Another important part of the current program, the Guest Lecturer from Abroad series, was initially scheduled only intermittently because of insufficient funding. Stuart Swiny, the director of CAARI, was the first lecturer in 1983. In 1990, an exchange of lectures was organized between Sy Gitin and William Coulson, then director of the American School of Classical Studies at Athens. In 1993, the W.F. Albright Lectureship in Ancient Near Eastern Studies was funded by a one-time grant from USIA, and the lecturer was William Ward of Brown University. In 1994, with limited funds, lecturers included Janine Bourriau of the Institute of Archaeology of the University of London (jointly sponsored with the British School of Archaeology in Jerusalem); Donald Whitcomb of the Oriental Institute of the University of Chicago; and Susan Rotroff of Hunter College (jointly sponsored with the American School of Classical Studies at Athens).

AIAR Director Sy Gitin with Brown University Professor of Egyptology William Ward in the AIAR courtyard in 1993.

When regular funding was made available in 1998, the Lecturer from Abroad program was expanded and developed into two annual series. The first of these was a series of exchange lectures between the Albright director and the directors of other schools of archaeology in the Mediterranean basin. To date, this series has included directors from ACOR, CAARI, the American School of Classical Studies at Athens, and the IV University of Barcelona (Pompeu Fabra). The second program was the Trude Dothan Lectureship in Ancient Near Eastern Studies established by an endowment from the Dorot Foundation. The lectureship, honoring Dothan's award of the Israel Prize in Archaeology in 1998, was established at the Albright to support and encourage the Institute's role in advancing the dialogue between the Israeli, Palestinian and foreign archaeological communities in Jerusalem. Under this program, each year a senior scholar from abroad is invited to lecture at the Albright, the Hebrew University and Al-Quds University. The first lecturer, in 1999, was Wolf Dietrich Niemeier of Heidelberg University; and the second, in 2000, was Sir John Boardman of Oxford University.

Professor Wolf Dietrich Niemeier (second left) of Heidelberg University with (left to right) Barbara Niemeier, Trude Dothan (Professor emerita Hebrew University), H. Marwan Abu Khalaf (Director of the Institute of Islamic Archaeology, Al-Quds University) and Sy Gitin (AIAR Director) on the occasion of the first Trude Dothan Lecture in 1999.

Fellowships and Appointees

The second major aspect of Gitin's long-term agenda for improving the intellectual environment at the Albright was the enhancement of the fellowship program. In the 1979/80 academic year, there were five appointees at AIAR, but, at that time, few of these positions were supported by AIAR fellowships. The Annual Professorship provided room-and-board, but no stipend, and the Professor of Archaeology, who was not in residence, was funded by the Brandeis/ASOR program. The only regularly funded fellowships available at AIAR were the Barton Fellowship (an endowed award), and the Montgomery and the ASOR W.F. Albright Fellowships, both of which were funded by ASOR on an annual basis and could be used either at AIAR or at one of the other ASOR institutes. Starting in 1980, one of Gitin's top priorities was the establishment of new fellowships and the creation of a program that would attract the most highly qualified candidates to fill these positions.

Ralph W. Doermann of Trinity Lutheran Seminary (right) with Benjamin Mazar of Hebrew University at Tell el-Hesi in 1983. Doermann was James A. Montgomery Fellow at AIAR in 1969–70, Annual Professor in 1976–77, and an NEH Fellow and Annual Professor in 1984–85.

AIAR Appointees 1967 – 2000

Academic Year	Number Per Year
1967–1968	8
1968–1969	6
1969–1970	3
1971–1972	5
1972–1973	4
1973–1974	12
1974–1975	8
1975–1976	15
1976–1977	7
1977–1978	4
1978–1979	4
1979–1980	5
1980–1981	8
1981–1982	7
1982–1983	7
1983–1984	18
1984–1985	21
1985–1986	15
1986–1987	25
1987–1988	21
1988–1989	27
1989–1990	29
1990–1991	26
1991–1992	25
1992–1993	28
1993–1994	31
1994–1995	40
1995–1996	52
1996–1997	48
1997–1998	51
1998–1999	57
1999–2000	51

From 1980 through 1999, the AIAR successfully gained regular renewals of the National Endowment of Humanities Fellowships first granted in 1979, secured nine long-term and three short-term annual appointments, and established an Associate Fellowship program for which thirteen Associate Fellow annual fee grants were obtained from the USIA. In association with AIAR presidents and trustees, Gitin also arranged for fifty-seven other short and long-term fellowships funded through or in association with the Institute. By 1999, the number of annual appointees had reached fifty-two, including thirty with Albright stipends and Associate Fellowship fee grants, and twenty-two additional Associate Fellows. By 1998, the total annual appointees/fellowship offerings had increased to $238,000.

Walter Rast from Valparaiso University at work on Bab ed-Dhra' reports. In 1982–83 Rast served for a half year as Annual Professor and for a half year as an NEH Fellow. He was Annual Professor again in 1994–95.

In 1983–84 Jack Lewis of Harding College (left) and James Ross of Protestant Episcopal Seminary in Virginia (right) were Senior Fellows at the Institute.

Richard Hess of Loyola University, 1985 AIAR NEH Fellow, exploring the spring area at Ein Gedi on a field trip.

The first of the new long-term fellowships, which Gitin organized was established in 1983, the ten-month Samuel H. Kress Fellowship for pre-doctoral research in architecture, art history, and archaeology. In 1990, the twelve-month post-doctoral position of Dorot Research Professor was created at the initiation of then Board Chair Joy Ungerleider Mayerson. After three years, funding for this award was redirected to support and then endow, as part of the 1997 NEH challenge grant, the Dorot Director and Professor of Archaeology, the position currently held by Gitin. Awards for three ten-month USIA Junior Research Fellowships, and thirteen Associate Fellow annual fees grants began in 1993. USIA also provided a grant for a senior appointee, which helped to initiate the funding for the Annual Professor's stipend and room-and-board costs. These funds were matched by a grant from the Horace Goldsmith Foundation obtained with the help of AIAR Board Chairman Daniel Wolk. This significantly upgraded the award, making it equal to the NEH Fellowship award.

AIAR Director Sy Gitin (left) with 1986–87 Post Doctoral Fellow Arlene Rosen (Miqne and Ashkelon Projects) and NEH Fellow Steven Rosen (Negev Archaeological Survey) at a 1987 reception. Arlene Rosen was an NEH Fellow at the Institute in 1987–88.

Also in 1993, the first post-doctoral twelve-month Islamic Studies Fellowship was funded. Over the years, support for this fellowship has come from USIA, NEH, the Horace Goldsmith Foundation, the Cudahy Foundation (arranged by AIAR president Patty Gerstenblith), and the Abraham Fund. In 1995, the first award was made for the 10-month, pre-doctoral Samuel H. Kress Joint Athens/Jerusalem Fellowship for dissertation research in architecture, art, archaeology and Classical studies. This was organized with the assistance of William Coulson, then director of the American School of Classical Studies at Athens. In 1996, the first short-term annual appointments were made for two three-month Andrew W. Mellon Fellowships for post-doctoral research, open to scholars from the Czech Republic, Hungary, Poland and Slovakia. These were arranged with the assistance of Mary Ellen Lane, the Executive Director of the Council of American Overseas Research Centers (CAORC). A year later, this program was expanded to three regularly funded fellowships, with a fourth award depending on the availability of funds. Eligibility for these fellowships was also expanded to include scholars from Bulgaria and Romania.

Jodi Magness of Tufts University USIA Summer Scholar in Residence in 1996 at work in the AIAR library. Magness was a James A. Montgomery Fellow in 1985–86 and a Samuel H. Kress Fellow in 1986–87.

AIAR: Rebuilding the School that Albright Built — A History of the W. F. Albright Institute of Archaeological Research by Jeffrey A. Blakely

In 1997, the James A. Montgomery Fellow/Program Coordinator, previously awarded on an occasional basis, became a regular part of the Albright Appointees' program. Since 1999, this position has been supported by a new endowment — the endowment for the Ernest S. Frerich Program for Albright Fellows — established initially by the Dorot and Scheuer Foundations. This endowment supports all aspects of the Fellows program. It was established in honor of the Albright's long-time trustee and past president, Ernest S. Frerichs, whose guidance and wisdom over the years have been a key factor in the success of the Institute.

The fifty-seven additional short- and long-term, for the most part project-specific, fellowships awarded since 1983 included thirty-seven appointments funded by, among others, the Dorot, Scheuer, Bloomingdale and Grant private foundations. These are mostly Associate Fellowships for pre-doctoral research in ancient Near Eastern studies, Dead Sea Scrolls research and for the preparation of archaeological publications. Non-private funding agencies provided twenty fellowships for pre- and post-doctoral research in ancient history and literature, Islamic Studies and anthropology. From 1994–98, eleven of these fellowships were funded by CAORC's Advanced Multi-Country Research Fellowship program, and from 1995–97, nine fellowships were awarded by the Social Science Research Council.

AIAR Appointees, Residents and Staff in 1998–99. (back row left to right) AIAR Director Seymour Gitin, Adam Gitin, Post Doctoral Fellow Mahmoud Hawari, Miqne Research Fellows Danielle Steen and Justin Lev-Tov, Islamic Studies Fellow Robert Schick, USIA Junior Research Fellow Seth Sanders, NEH Fellow David Reese, Miqne Researcher Anna de Vincenz, Research Fellow Baruch Brandl, Miqne Architect J. Rosenberg, Research Fellow Khader Salameh and Miqne Research Fellow Tanya McCullough. (middle row) Munira Said, Cherie Gitin, Nuha Khalil Ibrahim, Research Fellow Azriel Gorski, AIAR Librarian Sarah Sussman, James A Montgomery Fellow and Program Coordinator Robert Mullins, Research Fellow Issa Sariei, USIA Junior Research Fellow Lisa Cole, Samuel H. Kress Joint Athens/Jerusalem Fellow Brien Garnand, Post-Doctoral Fellow Gary Long, Research Fellows Markus Roehling, Stephen Pfann and Ann Killebrew, Hisham M'farreh, Said Freij and Research Fellow Nava Panitz-Cohen. (seated) AIAR Assistant to the Director Edna Sachar, Fulbright Fellow Rebeccah Sanders, Research Fellows Jennie Ebeling and Theodore Burgh, George A Barton Fellow Benjamin Saidel, Reka Balla Soos, Andrew W. Mellon Fellow Marta Balla, Anna Balla Soos, USIA Junior Research Fellow Tristan Barako, Samuel H. Kress Fellow Laura Mazow, AIAR Institute Manager Nadia Bandak, Nawal Ibtisam Rsheid. (front row) Miqne Researcher Pia Babendure, Senior Fellow Samuel Wolff, Intern Gayle Adler, Senior Fellows Linda Ammons and John Worrell. (appointees not in photograph) Annual Professor James Charlesworth, NEH Fellow Sandra Blakely, Samuel H. Kress Fellow Michael Homan, Andrew W. Mellon Fellows Laszio Hunyadi and Peter Vargyas, Senior Fellows Marwan Abu Khalaf, Oded Borowski, Theodore Carruth, Thomas Dozeman, Volkmar Fritz, Barbara Johnson, Ralph Klein, Susan Sheridan and Hamdan Taha, Post-doctoral Fellows Aaron Brody, Yosef Garfinkel, Shimon Gibson, Sejin Koh and Hani Nur-el-Din, Research Fellows Tracy Alsberg, Joanne Clarke, Michael Daise, Alison French, Mohammad Ghosheh, Amir Golani, Haythem Ratrout and Iman Saca, and USIA/CAORC Multi-Country Fellow Michelle Bonogofsky.

This greatly expanded fellowship program now includes students and scholars from North America, Europe, the Middle East (Israelis and Palestinians), South Africa, Australia and the Far East. The increase in the number of fellows and the diversity of nationalities, cultural backgrounds and research interests have significantly enhanced the international environment of the Albright and broadened the scope of research conducted at the Institute. Consequently, Prehistory, Classical and Islamic studies have become common fields of research, side by side with the traditional subjects for which the Albright has been well-known — Bronze and Iron Age archaeology, ancient Near Eastern languages, literature, history, religion, and biblical studies. What also attracts so many students and scholars to the Albright is the unique experience of being able to find in the local academic community opportunities to discuss and test their research ideas with members of one of the most comprehensive, in-depth groups of scholars in ancient Near Eastern studies in the world.

Excavations

In working to transform the Albright into an Institute with a comprehensive year-around program, Gitin also recognized the need to maintain and expand the services provided to ASOR-affiliated excavation projects, not just in facilitating seasonal field work, but also with opportunities for the use of the Institute throughout the year. To accomplish this goal, the Albright enhanced its facilities for artifact analysis and restoration by creating two archaeological labs in the main building and by refurbishing the Wright lab in the back lot to make it an all-weather work space. A fully equipped publication studio was also established. The storage areas in the attic and in the back-lot shed were expanded and reorganized, and a number of shipping containers were acquired for additional storage. These improvements were undertaken together with efforts to refurbish parts of the hostel and the Garden Apartment, the renovation of the Annual Professor's apartment, and the creation of the Porch Apartment as a new residence space. Improvements also included the reorganization and enhancement of the library and of its holdings in response to the greatly expanded fellowship program. The cumulative effect was a dramatic increase in the use of the Institute by field and publications projects throughout the year. Specifically, the expanded fellowship program, with more and larger grants, attracted a greater number of excavation staff members to the Albright for project-related research and publications preparation. And the improved research and storage space brought to the Albright long-term rentals of the labs by the Miqne, Ashkelon, and Sepphoris (Duke University) projects and storage space by the Sepphoris (University of South Florida), Caesarea, Meiron, Shema, and Nabratein projects, among others.

Bob Mullins, James A. Montgomery Fellow and Program Coordinator, explains cultic activity inside the Philistine temple at Tell Qasile.

Vivian and Robert Bull, both AIAR Trustees working on Tell er-Ras pottery in back of the Institute in 1998. Bob Bull was Director of Tell er-Ras Excavations from 1964–1970 and AIAR Director in 1970–71.

By 1999, most of the twenty-four ASOR-affiliated and Albright-assisted excavation and publications projects working in Israel, the West Bank and the Palestinian Entity had come to use the Albright's resources in one way or another.

1999 AIAR Assisted Excavations
(* = ASOR/CAP Affiliated — for ASOR/CAP affiliates from 1970–2000 see appended list.)

Field Projects

Ashkelon (Leon Levy Expedition/Harvard University and the Semitic Museum), L.E. Stager Director

Combined Caesarea Expeditions* (Universities of Maryland and Haifa), K.G. Holum and A. Raban Directors

Khirbet Cana* (University of Puget Sound), D. Edwards Director

Tel Kedesh (University of Michigan), S. Herbert and A. Berlin Directors

Lahav/Tell Halif Phase III* (Cobb Institute of Archaeology, Mississippi State University), P. Jacobs Director

Rekhes Nafha 396* (Harvard University and Ben-Gurion University of the Negev), B. Saidel and S. Rosen Directors

Sepphoris* (University of South Florida), J. Strange Director

Zeitah* (Pittsburgh Theological Seminary), R. Tappy Director

Publications Projects

Tell Balatah/Shechem* (Drew-McCormick Expedition), E.F. Campbell Director

Caesarea Maritima Vault Project* (University of Maryland), J. Blakely and J. Bennett Directors

Tell el-Hesi (Joint Archaeological Expedition), J. Blakely Principal Investigator

Jericho-Jordan Bank Site, R. Schick Director

Lahav /Tell Halif Phases I–II* (Cobb Institute of Archaeology, Mississippi State University), J.D. Seger Director

Lahav/Tell Halif Phase III* (Cobb Institute of Archaeology, Mississippi State University), P. Jacobs and O. Borowski Directors

Meiron/Nabratein* (Duke University), E. Meyers and C. Meyers Directors

Tel Miqne-Ekron* (W.F. Albright Institute of Archaeological Research and the Institute of Archaeology of the Hebrew University), S. Gitin and T. Dothan Directors

Nahal Tillah* (University of California-San Diego), T. Levy Director

The Neo-Assyrian Empire in the Seventh Century B.C.E. Research Project* (Albright Institute/Council of American Overseas Research Centers), S. Gitin Director

Sepphoris Ein Zippori* (Duke University), E. Meyers and C. Meyers Directors

Sepphoris Regional Project* (Duke University), E. Meyers and C. Meyers Directors

Joint Sepphoris Project* (Duke University and the Hebrew University), E. Meyers, C. Meyers, E. Netzer and Z. Weiss Directors

Shiqmim* (University of California-San Diego), T. Levy Director

Tell Taannek* (Palestinian Institute of Archaeology, Birzeit University and the American Schools of Oriental Research), K. Nashef and W.E. Rast Directors

As the number of ASOR-affiliated excavations increased over the years, the Albright's involvement in logistical support for these projects also increased, including procuring excavation, recording and camp equipment and recommending technical and excavation supervisory staff. Working closely with ASOR's Committee on Archaeological Policy and the local antiquities authorities, the Albright helped to solve research-related and administrative problems for a number of American field projects. Gitin also played a significant role in the creation of new American field projects and gave special assistance to excavation and publication projects directed by younger American archaeologists.

From the beginning of his tenure, Gitin was convinced that to restore the Albright's scholarly credentials as an archaeological institute, it was essential for the director to develop his own excavation project as had most of the Institute's other long-term directors. He was also committed to making such an excavation a teaching dig, continuing the tradition of training American students and scholars in fieldwork that began with Albright and Wright. In establishing a new field project, Gitin had two primary research goals. The first was to broaden his Iron Age II ceramic study, based on his work at Gezer, into an inter-regional project that would address the questions of the mutual impact of Israelite and Philistine material culture and its effect on the process of urbanization. The second was to create a joint project with an Israeli colleague that would demonstrate that American and Israeli methodological approaches to field work, then the subject of an intensive debate, were not mutually exclusive, but in fact complementary.

To achieve these goals, Gitin and Trude Dothan, with the help of then AIAR president Ernest S. Frerichs organized the joint American/Israeli Tel Miqne-Ekron excavation project. It was sponsored by the Albright Institute and the Hebrew University, and eventually received support from twenty-two United States, Canadian and Israeli institutions, as well as from the Dorot, Berman and other private foundations. Tel Miqne, identified as Ekron, one of the Philistine capital cities, is known from both biblical and non-biblical texts. One of the largest Iron Age sites in Israel, it was selected as the focus of both Dothan's and Gitin's research because it was located on the ancient border between Philistia and Judah. As a frontier site, it offered the best possibilities of measuring and evaluating inter-cultural contact and its effects on the process of urbanization.

AIAR: Rebuilding the School that Albright Built — A History of the W. F. Albright Institute of Archaeological Research by Jeffrey A. Blakely

Joy Ungerleider Mayerson (left), Director of the Dorot Foundation and then First Vice President and later Chairperson of the Albright Institute Board of Trustees at the 1984 inauguration of Camp Dorot the Tel Miqne/Ekron excavation camp, with directors Sy Gitin (center) and Trude Dothan (right).

Co-directors of the Tel Miqne/Ekron excavations Hebrew University Professor Trude Dothan and and AIAR Director Sy Gitin discussing field strategy in the early 1980s.

Miqne Project directors discuss excavation progress with visitors to the site in 1982. (left to right) Avraham Malamat, Trude Dothan, Norma Dever (behind), William Dever and Sy Gitin.

Information-Sharing and Outreach

The establishment of an information-sharing and outreach program was also a critical part of the plan to revitalize the Albright. It was designed to help reestablish the Institute as a major archaeological center by providing students, scholars and interested amateurs, both locally and abroad, with an over-all view of archaeological activities in Israel. In 1984, with a grant from the Billie Rose Foundation, and later with funds arranged for by Avraham Biran from the Nelson Glueck School, Gitin established a joint pilot project for the publication of a new journal, *Excavations and Surveys in Israel*. Other partners in this project were the Israel Exploration Society (IES) and the Israel Department of Antiquities (IDA). The journal — the English translation of the Hebrew *Hadashot Arkheologiyot*, the Archaeological Newsletter of the IDA — was edited by Ann Roshwalb the assistant to the Albright director, and Gitin, and presented an annual summary of all archaeological projects in Israel. By 1991, the journal had become financially viable and responsibility for its publication, together with its assets, including a bank account and inventory of back issues, were turned over to the IDA.

Also in 1991, with the support of AIAR trustee Norma Kershaw, Gitin helped to initiate an annual news feature, "Archaeology in Israel," published in the *American Journal of Archaeology*. The article, which offers a yearly review of archaeological and research activities in Israel, is written by Albright Senior Fellow Samuel Wolff, a senior archaeologist at the Israel Antiquities Authority. Gitin also helped in the organization of a number of symposia in the United States and Israel and edited and contributed to their publications. These included Recent Excavations In Israel: *Studies in Iron Age Archaeology*, with W.G. Dever (*AASOR* 49, 1989); *Recent Excavations in Israel: A View to the West* (Archaeological Institute of America Monograph 1, 1995); *Mediterranean Peoples in Transition* (the Trude Dothan Festschrift), with A. Mazar and E. Stern (IES, 1998); and *The Practical Impact of Science on Near Eastern and Aegean Archaeology*, with S. Pike (Monograph of the Wiener Lab of the American School of Classical Studies at Athens, 1999).

> *In 1984 the Israel Exploration Society decided that we should have an International Congress here on biblical archaeology. We did not know if it would work, but we decided in 1984 to do it. On the whole the Albright was a very important force in organizing this and on the committees organizing it. I was very much surprised that 450 participants came from outside of Israel. It was a big success, and we published a volume. Of course since it was such a big success we decided in 1990 to have a second one, for which the Albright was again a big help. This conference had a full week of lectures and discussions, and a conference volume was also published.*
>
> Josef Aviram, IES President, 1999

For the past twenty years, the Albright's program brochure and library acquisitions list have been distributed annually, both locally (in the Middle East) and abroad, in mailings that reached more than 2000 by 1999. From 1985 through 1990, the Albright offered an Annual Subscription Program for colleagues abroad, which provided information on the Albright's program and research activities and local archaeological news. Also, for the past decade, the abstracts of Albright fellows and summary reports of the fellows' projects have appeared annually in the *ASOR Newsletter*. Expanded versions of some of these reports, as well as the director's annual reports on Albright activities, appear in the AIAR newsletter, *Albright News*, now edited by trustee Lydie Shufro. In addition, the *Bibliography of Appointees*, a selection of fellows' publications produced as a result of their research at the Albright, is printed and distributed every four years. In the early 1990s, Gitin also organized and edited two series of articles that appeared in the *Biblical Archaeologist*, "Current Archaeological Research in Israel," and "Profiles of Archaeological Institutes."

*The first issue of an Albright Institute newsletter was produced in Fall 1995 by AIAR trustee Barbara (Babs) Miley. Publication was resumed in May 1997 under the title **Albright News** edited by trustee Lydie Shufro and has appeared annually since that time.*

A major part of the Albright's Information Sharing Program includes outreach education activities both locally and abroad. Since in the early 1980s, the director and senior Albright appointees have regularly lectured at Israeli and Palestinian archaeological institutions, and the director also lectures each summer in a number of educational programs conducted by ASOR-affiliated and Israeli excavation projects. Recently, the Albright initiated an annual Internship in Archaeology Program for six to ten interns from the Rothberg School for Overseas Students of the Hebrew University. The program provides a practicum for which students can earn four university credits, while they offer assistance to research projects conducted at the Albright. In the year 2000 the Internship program was extended to include students from Al-Quds University; and a bi-weekly lecture program for these students was established, with lectures given by AIAR Fellows.

In the 1990s, with the growth of Palestinian archaeological institutes, the Albright extended its outreach activities to excavation projects run by the Institute of Islamic Archaeology of Al-Quds University and the Palestinian Institute of Archaeology of Birzeit University. One of the primary responsibilities of the Albright's Islamic Studies Fellow has been to teach regular courses at Palestinian universities and give periodic lectures at Israeli and Palestinian institutions, as well as co-directing excavation projects for Palestinian students. The director and staff of the Albright also served as a major resource for organizing and planning the renewed excavation program at Birzeit University. Gitin also organized funding from the American, French and German schools in Jerusalem for the Jericho-Jordan Bank site project, the Institute of Islamic Archaeology's first excavation. In addition, some of the Palestinian students who were trained in the field school of the Tel Miqne-Ekron excavations served as staff for the first excavation licensed by the Palestinian Authority in 1994, at a site adjacent to Hisham's Palace (Jericho).

(left to right) Michal, Adam, Cherie and Talya Gitin in the Albright courtyard in 1981.

With respect to outreach program efforts abroad, Gitin has regularly given a number of lectures at the Albright each year for visiting academic and lay groups, mostly from the United States. He has also lectured extensively in North America and Europe, giving 77 presentations in nineteen years. Most recently, he was the Archaeological Institute of America's Charles Eliot Norton Lecturer, and one of the Mellon Foundation lecturers in Eastern Europe.

On the social side, summer receptions, an Albright tradition for decades, were graciously hosted by Cherie and Sy Gitin through most of the 1980s, bringing to the Institute each year hundreds of local and foreign scholars, students and dignitaries. More recently, the summer receptions have been limited to celebrating special occasions, among others, the 1989 reception honoring the fifty years of service of Omar Jibrin; the 1997 celebration of fifty years of Dead Sea Scrolls research; and the 1998 reception in honor of the publication of the Trude Dothan Festschrift. In May 2000, the Albright hosted a lavish reception at the close of the three-day international symposium celebrating the Centennial of ASOR and of the Jerusalem School. (See also the ASOR Part Three centennial in this volume).

U.S. Ambassador to Israel Samuel Lewis (left) with Sy Gitin and Munira Said at an AIAR reception in the early 1980s.

(left to right) Munira Said with Michael Bergoyne of the British School of Archaeology and 1982–83 Annual Professor Walt Rast at an AIAR reception in the early 1980s.

Distinguished Guests at an Albright Reception in the mid-1980s. (left to right) AIAR/ASOR Trustee Norma Kershaw, Honorable Thomas Pickering, U. S. Ambassador to Israel, Eleanor and John Newark, and Marsha Eisenberg.

Battya de Miroschedji and Jean Perrot of the French Archaeological Mission at an AIAR reception in the late 1980s.

Over the years, the Albright has also continued the tradition of having afternoon tea and coffee in the garden for residents and guests, and of holding special tea-receptions before and after the weekly seminar, report and workshop programs. This too has greatly contributed to the spirit of conviviality and openness for which the Albright has always been known, and which has made the Albright uniquely suited as a place to bring together members of all the archaeological communities in Jerusalem.

On May 31, 2000, the AIAR courtyard was formally dedicated as the "Kershaw Garden" with the installation of a commemorative marker, in honor of the outstanding service and many contributions of AIAR Honorary Trustee Norma Kershaw and her husband Reuben.

Garden reception at the AIAR-ASOR Centennial celebration May 31, 2000.

Thoughts on the AIAR's Future

American-led research at the Albright will continue to have an important impact on local archaeological activities, as the Institute maintains its traditional scholarly goals and helps to advance the discipline of ancient Near Eastern archaeology. The Institute will no doubt have to confront similar issues to those it has faced during various difficult transitions since its founding in 1900, especially those that occurred after 1967. Its future success lies in part in expanding contacts and developing new relationships with the Palestinian, Jordanian and Israeli academic communities, as well as with the various foreign institutions in Jerusalem that serve the international community of scholars. The success of the Albright and of archaeological research in Israel and in the West Bank area are interdependent. Effectiveness in advancing scholarship in Near Eastern studies will be dependent upon the extent to which each of these academic communities can respond to the variety of challenges that they will have to face together in the future.

Joe D. Seger, 1999

I see the Albright Institute as a neutral meeting place, an oasis, where people of all different nationalities can meet. In the short-term, we have a special role to play in responding to the emerging needs of the developing Palestinian archaeological community in an appropriate, respectful, and helpful way, by sharing our expertise and knowledge. We will, of course, deepen our close ties with the Israeli archaeological community, while expanding our research activities wherever possible to include academic communities in neighboring countries. This should be our goal for the future as increasingly, archaeology ceases to be defined and limited by modern political boundaries.

Patty Gerstenblith, 1999

The overall mission of the Albright has been to provide a research home for archaeologists and biblical scholars enabling them to live and work in Jerusalem, to have access to archaeological sites throughout the Middle East and to enjoy opportunities to interact with academics in other institutions in the region. We serve as a forum in which scholars from around the world can get together and speak to each other. Developing our involvement with the fledgling Palestinian academic community is very important, as is maintaining our strong ties with the Israeli archaeological community. Working to forge better ties with scholars in Jordan, Cyprus, Greece and the larger Mediterranean world, should also be one of our primary objectives. The Albright's role in excavations and publications will continue to be among its top priorities as will its role as a research institution for both archaeologists and text scholars. Our goal for the future is to continue the pursuit of our historic mission with deliberate vigor, responding positively to the challenges and opportunities that lie before us in the twenty-first century.

Sidnie White Crawford, 1999

The Albright Institute in the New Century

Since the Albright became an independent institution thirty years ago and began to develop beyond the resources and program of ASOR, it has made significant progress in becoming a more comprehensive research institute. In some ways it has successfully emulated W.F. Albright's and Nelson Glueck's ASOR of the 1920s and 1930s, and in others, it has developed its own distinctive research character, with a forward-looking program more suitable for the twenty-first century. Currently it enjoys recognition as having one of the largest and most productive of all pre- and post-doctoral research programs in ancient Near Eastern studies. In 1992, it received recognition and accolades from the United States Information Agency:

Along with the American Institute of Indian Studies [in Delhi, India], the Albright is one of the most eminent of the [14] American Overseas Research Centers funded by USIA. (A.R. Devereux, American Overseas Research Centers, A Profile and Evaluation, Bureau of Educational and Cultural Affairs, USIA, 1992:50).

Devereux described the Albright as an Institute with strong ties to other centers in the region, which enables it to carry on an unparalleled approach to Middle Eastern archaeology, history and culture (p. 56). Devereux adds that "the Albright is considered a part of the fundamental archaeological scene. One cannot imagine what it would be like without the Albright" (p. 70). Perhaps one of the best measurements of the Institute's success is the achievements of its alumni, who make up a large percentage of past and current faculty of biblical, religious, Judaic, and Near Eastern archaeological studies at major universities and seminaries in the United States and Canada. Many of these alumni are among the leading scholars in their fields.

As we stand at the threshold of a new millennium and of the second century in the history of the Jerusalem School, the Albright Trustees, under the firm continuing leadership of its officers and Director Gitin, have re-affirmed their commitment to the continuing role of the Institute as a beacon of American scholarship in the Middle East. The current changes in the geo-political landscape in the area offer a tremendous potential for research in the entire region. With the Institute's support for the newly established archaeological program at Al-Quds University, its ongoing association with Hebrew University in the Tel Miqne/Ekron excavation and publication project, the international project "The Neo-Assyrian Empire: A Study of Center and Periphery" co-sponsored by CAORC, and its continued backing of American researchers and of ASOR's excavation and publications projects, the future of the Albright Institute as a premier center for Middle East research is most promising.

AIAR
APPENDED LISTS

Officers

Board of Trustees

Staff

Appointees

Assisted Research Projects

Mosaic detail from the "Treading of Grapes" panel of the fourth century A.D. Dionysos Mansion at Sepphoris in Israel. EMM

AIAR Board Chairmen 1988–2000

Edward Cohen	1988–1989
Joy Ungerleider Mayerson	1989–1994
Daniel Wolk	1994–

AIAR Presidents 1970–2000

Edward F. Campbell, Jr.	1970–1974
Philip J. King	1974–1976
Ernest S. Frerichs	1976–1982
Joseph A. Callaway	1982–1988
Joe D. Seger	1988–1994
J. Maxwell Miller	1994–1995
Patty Gerstenblith	1995–2000
Sidnie White Crawford	2000–

AIAR Directors 1969–2000

David Noel Freedman	1969–1970
Robert J. Bull	1970–1971
William G. Dever	1971–1975
Eric M. Meyers	1975–1976
David Noel Freedman	1976–1977
Albert Glock	1977–1980
Seymour Gitin	1980–

AIAR Officers *(Current during 2000)*

Chairman	Daniel Wolk
President	Patty Gerstenblith –2000
	Sidnie White Crawford 2000–
Vice-President	John R. Spencer
Treasurer	Thomas R. Cox –2000
	Marian Scheuer Sofaer 2000–
Assistant Treasurer	David Marrus 2000–
Secretary	Sidnie White Crawford –2000
	Jodi Magness 2000 –

AIAR Staff *(Current during 2000)*

Dorot Director	Seymour Gitin
Assistant to the Director	Helena Flusfeder
Institute Manager	Nadia Bandak
Chief Librarian	Sarah Sussman
Librarians	Bella Greenfield
	Ludmila Kovalevsky
	Mariana Zolinsky
Chef	Hisham M'farreh
Maintenance Man	Said Freij –2000
	Ashraf Hanna 2000 –
Administrative Consultant	Munira Said
Business Manager (U. S.)	Samuel Cardillo

AIAR Board of Trustees (Members current during 2000)

Walter E. Aufrecht	University of Lethbridge
Robert J. Blinken	New York, NY
Joan R. Branham	Providence College
Vivian Bull	Linfield College
John A. Coleman	White Plains, NY
Thomas R. Cox	Stamford, CT
Sidnie White Crawford	University of Nebraska-Lincoln
Norma Dever	Tucson, AZ
Ray Frankel	Los Angeles, CA
Ernest S. Frerichs	Dorot Foundation
Patty Gerstenblith	DePaul University
Eugene M. Grant	New York, NY
Robert D. Haak	Augustana College
Sharon Herbert	University of Michigan
Jodi Magness	Tufts University
David E. Marrus	Rumson, NJ
Philip Mayerson	Mamaroneck, NY
Carol Meyers	Duke University
Barbara Miley	La Jolla, CA
Shalom Paul	Hebrew University
Jonathan P. Rosen	New York, NY
Richard J. Scheuer	Larchmont, NY
Lee R. Seeman	Great Neck, NY
Lydie Shufro	New York, NY
Mark S. Smith	Saint Joseph's University
Marian S. Sofaer	Palo Alto, CA
John R. Spencer	John Carroll University
Jane C. Waldbaum	University of Wisconsin-Milwaukee
J. Edward Wright	University of Arizona
Daniel Wolk	Rye, NY
Ziony Zevit	University of Judaism

AIAR Honorary Trustees

Robert J. Bull	Drew University
Edward F. Campbell, Jr.	McCormick Theological Seminary
Edward E. Cohen	Philadelphia, PA
William G. Dever	University of Arizona
David Noel Freedman	University of California-San Diego
Norma Kershaw	Mission Viejo, CA
John H. Marks	Princeton University
George E. Mendenhall	University of Michigan
Eric M. Meyers	Duke University
Kevin G. O'Connell, S.J.	The Jesuit Center, Amman, Jordan
Joe D. Seger	Mississippi State University
Lawrence E. Stager	Harvard University
Paul Steinberg	Hebrew Union College/JIR

AIAR: Rebuilding the School that Albright Built — A History of the W. F. Albright Institute of Archaeological Research by Jeffrey A. Blakely

AIAR Offices

In the United States:

AIAR President's Office
Dr. Sidnie White Crawford
Department of Classics
236 Andrews Hall
University of Nebraska-Lincoln
Lincoln, NE 68588

Phone: 402 472 4475
Fax: 402 472 4481
E-mail: scrawford@unlserve.unl.edu

AIAR Fellowships Office
Dr. John R. Spencer
Department of Religious Studies
John Carroll University
20700 North Park Blvd.
University Heights, OH 44118

Phone: 216 397 4705
Fax: 216 397 4478
E-mail: spencer@jcu.edu
Web address: www.aiar.org

AIAR Business Office
Mr. Sam Cardillo
P.O.B. 40151
Philadelphia, PA 19106

Phone: 215 238 1290
Fax: 215 238 1540
E-mail: cardillo@sas.upenn.edu

In Israel:
AIAR (W. F. Albright Institute)
26 Salah ed-Din Street
P.O. Box 19096
91190 Jerusalem
Israel

Phone: 972 2 628 2131
Fax: 972 2 626 4424
E-mail: director@albright.org.il

The Kershaw garden at the Albright Institute. The view is from the director's appartment looking toward the annual professor's apartment and kitchen.

AIAR Appointees 1970–2000

Abbreviations of Appointments:

Ashkelon	Ashkelon Fellow
AD	Acting Director
AP	Annual Professor
ASOR/W. F. Albright	ASOR W.F. Albright Fellowship
Barton	George A Barton Fellow
Bloomingdale	Bloomingdale Foundation Fellow
CAORC-Multi	Council of American Overseas Research Centers Advanced Multi-Country Fellow
DFT	Director of Field Trips
Dorot	Dorot Foundation Fellow
DorotRP	Dorot Research Professor
DSS	Dead Sea Scrolls Fellow
EBR	Endowment for Biblical Research Grantee
Fulbright	Fulbright Hayes Fellow
Glueck	Nelson Glueck Fellow
HRA	Honorary Research Associate
HRP	Honorary Research Professor
HU	Hebrew University
HUIAS	Hebrew University Institute of Advanced Studies
Islamic	Islamic Studies Fellow
Kress	Samuel H. Kress Foundation Fellow
Kress/Joint	Samuel H. Kress Joint Athens/Jerusalem Fellow
Mellon	Andrew W. Mellon Fellow
Merrille	Merrille Foundation Fellow
Montgomery	James A. Montgomery Fellow
Miqne	Miqne Excavation Fellow
NEH	National Endowment for the Humanities Fellow
PA	Professor of Archaeology
PC	Program Coordinator
PD	Post Doctoral Fellow
RA	Research Associate
RF	Research Fellow
RP	Research Professor
Scheuer	Richard J. Scheuer Fellow
SIR	Scholar in Residence
SF	Senior Fellow
SSRC	Social Science Research Council Fellow
Thayer	J. Henry Thayer Fellow
UG	Undergraduate Fellow
USIA Junior	United States Information Agency Junior Research Fellow
USIA Summer	United States Information Agency Summer Scholar in Residence
VS	Visiting Scholar

Appointees

Thomas Abowd	*(Columbia University)*	1996–97	SSRC
Avriel Adler	*(Hebrew University)*	1992–93	RF
Abbas Alizadeh	*(Harvard University)*	1990–91	PD Ashkelon
Mitchell Allen	*(University of California - Los Angeles)*	1989–90	Ashkelon
		1991–93	RF
Susan Heuch Allen	*(Brown University)*	1988–89	Barton
Tracy Alsberg	*(Oriental Institute, University of Chicago)*	1998–99	RF

Linda Ammons	(Assumption College)	1993–95	SF
		1998–99	SF
Francis I. Anderson	(Macquarrie University)	1976–77	HRP
Ronald D. Anderson	(Heritage Arts Foundation)	1994–95	PD
Eyal Ben Ari	(Hebrew University)	1989–90	Bloomingdale/Miqne
Adele Asher	(University of South Africa)	1993–94	RF
Melissa M. Aubin	(Florida State University)	1999–2000	USIA Junior
Walter Aufrecht	(University of Lethbridge)	1983–84	Senior
		1985–86	AP
		1990–92	SF/SSHR
Carolina A. Aznar	(University Compultense of Madrid)	1995–97	RF
Jere L. Bacharach	(University of Washington)	1994–95	CAORC-Multi
Dan Bahat	(Bar Ilan University)	1989–90	RF
'Isa Baidun	(Institute of Islamic Archaeology, Al-Quds University)	1996–97	RF
Marta Balla	(Technical University of Bucharest, Hungary)	1998–99	Mellon
Miriam Balmuth	(Tufts University)	1980–81	NEH
Tristan Barako	(Harvard University)	1997–98	RF
		1998–99	USIA Junior
Uzi Baram	(University of Massachusetts)	1993–94	Barton
Carol Bardenstein	(Dartmouth College)	1995–96	CAORC-Multi
		1995–96	SSRC
Aileen Baron	(California State University at Fullerton)	1983–84	NEH
Eleanor Ferris Beach	(Gustavus Adolphus College)	1992–93	PD
		1994–95	Barton
Keith Beebe	(Independent Scholar)	1970–71	AP
Celia Bergoffen	(New York University)	1986–87	RF
		1987–88	Kress
		1988–89	RF
		1990–91	PD
Andrea M. Berlin	(University of Michigan)	1984–85	Kress
Carel Bertram	(University of California – Los Angeles)	1995–96	CAORC-Multi
John Betlyon	(Smith College)	1987–88	VS
Piotr Bienkowski	(Liverpool Museum)	1999–2000	AP
Gerald M. Bilkes	(Princeton Theological Seminary)	1997–98	USIA Junior
Roni Binder	(Hebrew University)	1993–94	RF
Brenda Blakeburn	(Wake Forest University)	1994–95	Fulbright
Jeffrey A. Blakely	(University of Wisconsin-Madison)	1996–97	AP
Sandra Blakely	(University of Southern California)	1996–97	Barton
		1998–99	NEH
Elizabeth Bloch-Smith	(University of Chicago)	1983–84	Barton
		1986–87	RF
Hanswulf Bloedhorn	(German Protestant Institute of Archaeology)	1999–2000	SF
Joanne Bloom	(Bryn Mawr College)	1982–83	Barton

Francis Boelter	(Garrett Theological Seminary)	1976–77	HRA
Michelle Bonogofsky	(University of California - Berkley)	1998-99	CAORC-Multi
Oded Borowski	(Emory University)	1987–88	AP
		1991–92	Dorot RP
		1995–96	AP
		1998–99	SF
Nancy Bowen	(Earlham School of Religion)	1995–96	PD
Robert Bowling	(McCormick Theological Seminary)	1975–76	RP
		1980–81	AP
Baruch Brandl	(Israel Antiquities Authority)	1997–2000	RF
Aaron Brody	(Harvard University)	1992–93	Barton
		1993–94	Dorot
		1995–96	USIA Junior
	(White-Levy Program for Archaeological Publications)	1998–99	PD
Steven Brooke	(Miami, FL)	1996–97	RF
Carolyn Brown	(Hebrew University)	1988–89	RF
Raymond E. Brown	(Union Theological Seminary, NY)	1978–79	AP
Dan Browning	(Batash-Timnah Excavation Project)	1988–89	RF
William H. Brownlee	(Claremont Graduate School)	1977–78	AP
Nicolo Bucaria	(Institute of Jewish Studies, Salemi, Sicily)	1994–95	RF
Stephanie L. Budin	(University of Pennsylvania)	1997–98	Kress/Joint
Robert J. Bull	(Drew University)	1974–75	AP
		1980–81	NEH
Wilfred F. Bunge	(Luther College)	1994–95	SF
Theodore Burgh	(University of Arizona)	1998–99	Fulbright
Nefi Bushman III	(University of Arizona)	1986–87	Kress
Joseph Callaway	(Southern Baptist Theological Seminary)	1976–77	HRP
Theodore R. Carruth	(David Lipscomb University)	1998–99	SF
Charles E. Carter	(Duke University)	1989–90	Kress
James H. Charlesworth	(Princeton Theological Seminary)	1998–99	AP
Miriam Chernoff	(Brandeis University)	1983–84	RF
Joanne Clarke	(British School of Archaeology, Jerusalem)	1997–98	RF
	(Council for British Research	1998–99	RF
	in the Levant, Jerusalem)	1999–2000	PD
Kelley Coblentz	(Harvard University)	1994–95	RF
Catherine L. Cockerham	(Gordon-Conwell Theological Seminary)	1994–95	RF
Joelle Cohen	(Hebrew University)	1989–90	RF
Susan Cohen	(Brown University)	1991–93	Dorot/Miqne
Dennis Cole	(New Orleans Baptist Theological Seminary)	1992–93	SF
Lisa M. Cole	(University of Arizona)	1998–99	USIA Junior
Eugene Collins	(Malone College)	1984–85	SF
John Collins	(University of Minnesota)	1995–96	SSRC
Michael D. Coogan	(Unaffiliated)	1975–76	PA
Robert Cooley	(Southwest Missouri State University)	1979–80	AP

James J. C. Cox	(Andrews University)	1977–78	AP
Bruce Cureton	(Hebrew University)	1997–98	RF
Michael Daise	(Princeton Theological Seminary)	1998–99	RF
Claudine Dauphin	(Centre National de Recherche Scientifique)	1988–89	SF
Jean Davidson	(University of Vermont)	1981–82	RA
J.P. Dessel	(University of Arizona)	1985–86	Scheuer
Tomas Dezso	(Eotvos L. University, Hungary)	1997–98	Mellon
F.W. Dobbs-Allsopp	(Yale University)	1997–98	NEH
Ralph Doermann	(Trinity Lutheran Seminary)	1969–70	Montgomery
		1976–77	AP
		1984–85	AP/NEH
Trude Dothan	(Hebrew University)	1994–95	SF
	(Hebrew University Emerita)	1995–2000	SF
Thomas B. Dozeman	(United Theological Seminary)	1998–99	SF
Elizbieta Dubis	(Jagiellonian University, Poland)	1997–98	Mellon
Julie A. Duncan	(Harvard University)	1987–88	Barton
J. Kenneth Eakins	(Golden Gate Baptist Theological Seminary)	1983–84	AP
Jennie R. Ebeling	(University of Arizona)	1998–99	Fulbright
Douglas Edwards	(University of Puget Sound)	1992–93	SF
Robert Eisenman	(California State University - Long Beach)	1985–86	NEH
Nadia Abu El-Haj	(Duke University)	1991–92	Fulbright
James Engle	(Eastern Mennonite Seminary)	1992–93	SF
Lewis Eron	(Unaffiliated)	1975–76	RF
Itzhak Eshel	(Timna Valley Project)	1989–90	PD
Douglas Esse	(University of Chicago)	1979–80	Barton
		1985–87	PD
Gregory Etter	(Harvard University)	1990–91	RF
J. Cheryl Exum	(Boston College)	1979–80	NEH
Steven D. Fraade	(Yale University)	1984–85	PD
Ilana Feldman	(University of Michigan)	1998–99	CAORC-Multi
Zbigniew T. Fiema	(Unaffiliated)	1999–2000	NEH
Steven Fine	(UCLA)	1988–90	RF
Edwin Firmage	(University of California - Berkeley)	1987–89	RF
Alysia Fischer	(University of Arizona)	1995–96	EBR
		1996–97	USIA Junior
Amy L. Fisher	(Emory University)	1993–94	Dorot
Paul Fitzpatrick	(Ecole Biblique)	1995–96	RF
Jaroslav Folda	(University of North Carolina)	1974–75	RA
Rebecca M. Foote	(Harvard University)	1994–95	CAORC-Multi
James N. Ford	(Hebrew University)	1997–98	RF
Robert Fortna	(Vassar College)	1978–79	AP
Andrew Cousins	(Emory University)	1995–96	SSRC

Benjamin R. Foster	(Yale University)	1976–77	ASOR/W. F. Albright
		1983–84	PD
Rafael Frankel	(Haifa University)	1997–98	SF
Alison French	(James Madison University)	1997–99	Miqne
Ernest Frerichs	(Brown University)	1982–83	AP
Richard E. Friedman	(University of California - San Diego)	1997–98	SF
Glenda Friend	(Baltimore Hebrew University)	1995–96	EBR
		1996–97	USIA Junior
Ann Fritschel	(Emory University)	1996–97	RF
Volkmar Fritz	(German Protestant Institute of Archaeology)	1998–99	SF
Ida Frohlich	(Pazmany Peter Catholic University, Hungary)	1996–97	Mellon
Neil Shozo Fujita	(Iona College)	1990–91	SF
Diana Furmanik	(Unaffiliated)	1975–76	RF
Yossi Garfinkel	(Hebrew University)	1989–90	Grant/Miqne
		1990–91	RF
		1991–92	Bloomingdale
		1997–99	PD
Brien Garnand	(University of Chicago)	1998–99	Kress/Joint
Barbara Geller	(Unaffiliated)	1975–76	RF
Avriel Genesen-Yarus	(Hebrew University)	1986–88	RF
		1990–92	RF
Lawrence T. Geraty	(Harvard University)	1970–71	Thayer
Patty Gerstenblith	(Harvard University)	1975–76	Fulbright
Marcia Geyer	(Union Theological Seminary - New York)	1988–89	RF
Mohammed Ghosheh	(Institute of Islamic Archaeology, Jerusalem)	1997–98	RF
	(Arab League University, Cairo)	1998–2000	RF
Shimon Gibson	(Palestine Exploration Fund/ Israel Antiquities Authority)	1996–98	PD
	(Israel Antiquities Authority)	1998–99	PD
	(Unaffiliated)	1999–2000	PD
Mordechai Gichon	(Tel Aviv University)	1993–94	SF
Garth H. Gilmour	(Hebrew University)	1990–91	RF
	(University of Oxford)	1994–95	Barton
Gary Ginsberg	(Brown University)	1983–84	Dorot
Seymour Gitin	(Hebrew Union College)	1975–76	Glueck
	(Nelson Glueck School of Biblical Archaeology)	1979–80	AP/PA
Barry Gittlen	(University of Pennsylvania)	1969–70	ASOR/W. F. Albright
	(Baltimore Hebrew University)	1988–89	NEH
Kathryn Gleason	(University of Pennsylvania)	1995–96	NEH
Albert E. Glock	(Concordia College)	1971–72	RP
	(Concordia Teachers' College - Riverside, CA)	1973–76	RP
Amir Golani	(Hebrew University)	1990–91	RF
		1991–93	Bloomingdale
		1993–97	RF
	(Israel Antiquities Authority)	1998–2000	RF

Victor R. Gold	(Pacific Lutheran Theological Seminary)	1986–87	AP
Jonathan Golden	(University of Pennsylvania)	1995–96	USIA Junior
Robert M. Good	(Yale University)	1978–79	Montgomery
Avner Goren	(Israel Antiquities Authority)	1993–97	RF
Azriel Gorski	(Hebrew University, Weizmann Institute of Science Fellow)	1996–97	RF
	(Hebrew University)	1997–2000	RF
Norman Gottwald	(Graduate Theological Union - Berkeley)	1973–74	RA
Carl Graesser, Jr.	(Christ Seminary - Seminex at Pacific Lutheran Seminary at Berkeley)	1983–84	AP
Susan L. Graham	(University of Notre Dame)	1997–98	Barton
Jonas Greenfield	(Hebrew University)	1993–95	SF
David C. Greenwood	(University of Maryland)	1973–74	RA
George D. Groeneman	(Graduate Theological Union - Berkeley)	1984–85	RF
Dennis Groh	(Garrett Theological Seminary)	1974–75	Montgomery
		1981–92	AP
S. Vida Grubisha	(Wake Forest University)	1994–96	RF
Ronald D. Guengerich	(University of Michigan)	1976–77	Thayer
Robert Haak	(Augustana College - Rock Island, Illinois)	1990–91	NEH
		1992–93	AP
		1997–98	AP/AD
David Hague	(London Bible College)	1992–93	SF
Rachel Hallote	(University of Chicago)	1991–92	Barton
David Halperin	(University of California – Berkeley)	1973–74	Montgomery
		1974–75	RA
Baruch Halpern	(York University)	1983–84	NEH
Wael H. Hamamreh	(Yarmouk University)	1999–2000	RF
Paul Hanson	(Harvard University)	1969–70	Thayer
James W. Hardin	(University of Arizona)	1994–95	USIA Junior
Michael Hasel	(University of Arizona)	1995–96	Kress
Frances Hasso	(University of Minnesota)	1995–96	SSRC
Mahmoud Hawari	(Institute of Islamic Archaeology Al-Quds University)	1998–99	PD
Sharon Herbert	(University of Michigan)	1981–82	RA
Larry G. Herr	(Canadian Union College)	1993–94	AP
Richard Hess	(Loyola University)	1985–86	NEH
Brian Hesse	(University of Alabama at Birmingham)	1984–85	NEH
Paula S. Hiebert	(Harvard Divinity School)	1989–90	RF
Theodore Hiebert	(Harvard Divinity School)	1989–90	NEH
Craig Hinrichs	(Miami University)	1988–89	Barton
Nicolle Hirschfeld	(University of Texas - Austin)	1995–96	Barton
Barry Hoberman		1975–76	RF
Steven W. Holloway	(American Theological Library Association)	1993–94	Barton
Kenneth Holum	(University of Maryland)	1990–91	SF/HU Lady Davis Fellow

Michael M. Homan	(University of California - San Diego)	1998–99	Kress
Salah H. Houdalieh	(Jerusalem Archaeology Department)	1993–94	RF
Bett Houston	(Hebrew University)	1995–96	RF
Horace Hummel	(Concordia Seminary)	1992–93	SF
Melvin Hunt	(University of California - Berkeley)	1979–80	Merrille
		1980–81	RA
Patrick Hunt	(Simpson College)	1987–88	RF
Laszlo Hunyadi	(Janus Pannonius University, Pecs, Hungary)	1998–99	Mellon
Andrea Jacobs	(University of Texas - Austin)	1995–96	SSRC
Paul F. Jacobs	(University of St. Thomas)	1984–85	NEH
Longina A. Jakubowska	(Bryn Mawr)	1986–87	Barton
John Jarick	(University of Melbourne)	1987–88	RF
		1988–89	PD/Golda Meir Felllow HU
		1989–90	Barton
Lena Jayyusi	(University of Pennsylvania)	1995–96	SSRC
William Jobling	(University of Sydney)	1991–92	SF
		1992–93	Dorot RP
Alexander Joffe	(University of Arizona)	1987–89	RF
		1989–90	Barton
		1991–92	PD
Barbara L. Johnson	(Ashkelon Excavation)	1987–88	DFT
		1987–88	NEH
	(Harvard Research Associate)	1988–96	SF
	(Jerusalem)	1996–98	SF
	(Albright Institute)	1998–99	SF
	(Unaffiliated)	1999–2000	SF
Samantha Joo	(Brandeis University)	1994–95	RF
Lisa C. Kahn	(University of Tulsa)	1993–94	Barton
		1995–96	USIA Junior
Susan Kahn	(Harvard University)	1995–96	SSRC
John Kampen	(Payne Theological Seminary)	1991–92	AP
		1992–94	SF
Maureen Kaplan	(Unaffiliated)	1975–76	ASOR/W. F. Albright
Marwan Abu Khalaf	(Institute of Islamic Archaeology Al-Quds University)	1996–98	SF
Ellen Kenney	(New York University)	1997–98	Kress
		1997–98	CAORC-Multi
Ann Killebrew	(Hebrew University)	1983–84	Dorot
		1984–85	RF
		1985–86	RA
		1986–92	Dorot/Miqne
		1992–93	Montgomery
		1993–94	USIA Junior
		1994–95	Kress
		1995–97	RF
	(Haifa University/Hebrew University)	1997–99	RF
	(Haifa University)	1999–2000	PD

Philip J. King	(Boston College)	1985–86	NEH
Ralph Klein	(Lutheran School of Theology at Chicago)	1998–99	SF
Frederich W. Knobloch	(University of Pennsylvania)	1984–85	RF
SeJin Koh	(Institute of Holy Land Studies, Jerusalem)	1995–97	PD
	(Jerusalem University College, Jerusalem)	1997–2000	PD
Jayanth K. Krishnan	(University of Wisconsin)	1998–99	CAORC-Multi
David Kurtzer	(Yale University)	1996–97	RF
Robert D. Lamberton	(Washington University, St. Louis, MO)	1999–2000	SF/HUIAS
H. Darrell Lance	(Colgate-Rochester Divinity School)	1973–74	AP
Hayim Lapin	(University of Maryland - College Park)	1996–97	NEH
		1996–97	Kress/Joint
Eric C. Lapp	(Duke University)	1992–93	Kress
		1993–94	RF
		1994–95	USIA Junior
Eric Larson	(New York University)	1992–93	Dorot/DSS
Egon H.E. Lass	(Ashkelon Excavation Project)	1986–88	RF
	(Harvard Research Associate)	1988–89	RF
		1989–94	Ashkelon
Scott Layton	(University of Chicago)	1988–89	NEH
Zvi Lederman	(Harvard University)	1991–92	Barton
Gunnar Lehmann	(German Protestant Institute of Archaeology, Jerusalem)	1994–95	PD
		1996–97	PD
		1999–2000	SF
Werner E. Lemke	(Colgate-Rochester Divinity School)	1972–73	AP
Mark Levine	(New York University)	1996–97	SSRC
Justin Lev-Tov	(University of Tennessee)	1996–97	USIA Junior
		1997–99	Miqne
Thomas Levy	(Museum of the Negev, Beersheba, Israel)	1982–83	NEH
Jack Lewis	(Harding College)	1983–84	SF
Abigail Limmer	(University of Arizona)	1999–2000	RF/Foreign Language
Lowndes Lipscomb	(Unaffiliated)	1975–76	Fulbright
Gloria London	(University of Arizona)	1983–84	Kress
Gary A. Long	(Jerusalem University College, Jerusalem)	1997–99	PD
Rosa Lowinger	(New York University)	1983–84	Zion Research Fellow
Jack R. Lundbom	(University of California - San Diego)	1997–98	SF/NEH
	(Center of Theological Inquiry, Princeton)	1999–2000	SF
Ellen Louise Lyons	(Duke University)	1986–87	Barton
D. Bruce MacKay	(University of Toronto)	1993–94	Kress
John R. MacRay	(Middle Tennessee State University at Memphis)	1972–73	RA
Jodi Magness	(University of Pennsylvania)	1984–85	Barton
		1985–86	Montgomery
		1986–87	Kress
		1987–88	Mellon
		1988–90	RF
	(Tufts University)	1996–97	USIA Summer

Dale Manor	(University of Arizona)	1988–89	Kress
Pierce Matheney	(Midwestern Baptist Theological Seminary)	1987–88	SF
Richard Mattersdorff	(University of Maryland)	1992–93	RF
Brenda May	(Union Theological Seminary)	1988–89	RF
Philip Mayerson	(New York University)	1987–89	VS
Gabi Mazar	(Israel Department of Antiquities)	1986–87	RF
Laura B. Mazow	(University of Arizona)	1997–98	USIA Junior
		1998–99	Kress
		1999–2000	Miqne
Thomas McCollough	(Centre College)	1991–94	SF
David W. McCreery	(Pittsburgh Theological Seminary)	1977–78	ASOR/W. F. Albright
Tanya McCullough	(University of Toronto)	1999–2000	Miqne
Neil McEleney	(St. Paul's College, Washington)	1973–74	RA
Susan E. McGarry	(Episcopal Divinity School, Cambridge)	1987–88	RF
	(University of Michigan)	1997–98	RF
Mark Meehl	(Johns Hopkins University)	1988–89	Kress
		1989–90	Montgomery/PC
Petr Melmuk	(Charles University, Czech Republic)	1997–98	Mellon
Esther Menn	(University of Virginia)	1999–2000	PD
Stefan Meyer	(Henry Ford and Washtenaw Community Colleges, Michigan)	1997–98	CAORC-Multi
Carol Meyers	(Unaffiliated)	1975–76	Thayer
Lester Meyers	(Concordia Seminary, St. Louis)	1973–74	RA
Jacob Milgrom	(University of California - Berkeley Emeritus)	1995–97	SF
Robert D. Miller II	(University of Michigan)	1995–96	RF
		1996–97	Kress
		1997–98	Montgomery/PC
Jolanta Mlynarczyk	(Research Centre for Mediterranean Archaeology, Polish Academy of Sciences, Warsaw)	1999–2000	Mellon
David B. Monk	(Princeton University)	1991–92	Kress
James M. Monson	(Jerusalem)	1994–97	RF
James Muhly	(University of Pennsylvania)	1981–82	NEH
Kenneth V. Mull	(Aurora College)	1973–74	Thayer
		1988–89	AP
Robert A. Mullins	(Hebrew University)	1997–98	USIA Junior
		1998–2000	Montgomery/PC
Elaine Myers	(University of Toronto)	1996–97	RF
		1999–2000	Barton
Tami Nahmias	(Hebrew University)	1990–91	RF
Khaled Nashef	(Birzeit University)	1995–98	SF
Yehuda Nevo	(Ben Gurion University of the Negev)	1986–87	RF
Thomas Noonan	(University of Chicago)	1972–73	Montgomery
Hani Nur-el-Din	(University of Strasbourg)	1989–90	Miqne
		1990–93	RF
	(Jerusalem Department of History and Archaeology Al-Quds University)	1993–97	RF
		1997–2000	PD

Kevin O'Connell	(Unaffiliated)	1980–81	AP
John W. Olley	(Baptist Theological College of Western Australia)	1985–86	SF
Steven M. Ortiz	(American Institute of Holy Land Studies)	1989–90	RF
	(University of Arizona)	1994–95	USIA Junior
		1995–96	Barton
David Owen	(Cornell University)	1988–89	NEH
Nava Panitz-Cohen	(Hebrew University)	1989–90	Grant/Miqne
		1990–93	RF
		1997–2000	RF
Shalom Paul	(Hebrew University)	1996–98	SF
Miriam Peskowitz	(Duke University)	1992–93	Kress
Leo Perdue	(Vanderbilt University)	1973–74	Glueck
Claire Pfann	(Graduate Theological Union, Berkeley)	1984–85	RF
Stephen J. Pfann	(Hebrew University)	1984–85	RF
		1984–85	EBR
		1997–2000	RF
Ben F. Philbeck	(Southeastern Baptist Theological Seminary)	1984–85	SF
James L. Phillips	(University of Illinois - Chicago)	1996–97	NEH
		1999–2000	AP
Tom Pierce	(American Institute of Holy Land Studies)	1989–90	RF
Tomasz Polanski	(Jagiellonian University, Cracow, Poland)	1999–2000	Mellon
Thea Politis	(University of Reading, UK)	1999–2000	Kress/Joint
Benjamin Porter	(University of Wyoming)	1996–97	RF
Aref Abu Rabia	(Tel Aviv University)	1986–87	RF
Pavol Raka	(Charles University, Czech Republic)	1996–97	Mellon
Walter E. Rast	(Valparaiso University)	1971–72	RP
		1982–83	AP/NEH
		1994–95	AP
Haythem F. Ratrout	(An-Najah National University, Nablus)	1997–99	RF
Stephen A. Reed	(Ancient Biblical Manuscript Center, Claremont)	1989–90	PD/Dorot
		1990–91	Dorot/DSS
David Resse	(Field Museum of Natural History, Chicago)	1998–99	NEH
Alexandra Retzleff	(University of North Carolina - Chapel Hill)	1999–2000	Kress
Suzanne Richard	(Johns Hopkins University)	1974–75	Glueck
Austin Rittenspach	(Elizabethtown College)	1973–74	RA
Markus Roehling	(University of Bonn)	1998–99	RF
Gary O. Rollefson	(University of Arizona)	1978–79	ASOR/W. F. Albright
D. Glenn Rose	(Phillips University)	1981–82	AP
Arlene M. Rosen	(Geological Survey of Israel)	1985–87	PD
	(Unaffiliated)	1987–88	NEH
	(Israel Department of Antiquities)	1988–89	PD
	(Ben Gurion University of the Negev/ Weizmann Institute of Science Fellow)	1996–97	SF
Steven A. Rosen	(Negev Archaeological Survey)	1985–86	PD
		1986–87	NEH
Michael Rosenbaum	(Brandeis University)	1996–97	PD

Ann Roshwalb	(Brandeis University)	1975–76	Montgomery
	(Unaffiliated)	1985–86	PD
	(Miqne Publications)	1986–87	PD
		1987–88	SF
James F. Ross	(Virginia Theological Seminary)	1970–71	PA
	(Protestant Episcopal Seminary in Virginia)	1983–84	SF
Joan Rothman	(Brown University)	1982–83	RF
Susan I. Rotroff	(Washington University)	1999–2000	SF
Alwyn R. Rouyer	(University of Idaho)	1993–94	SF
Yorke M. Rowan	(University of Texas - Austin)	1994–95	CAORC-Multi
	(University of Georgia)	1999	NEH
		2000	USIA Junior
Iman N. Saca	(University of Illinois - Chicago)	1998–99	RF
		1999–2000	USIA Junior
Benjamin A. Saidel	(Harvard University)	1993–94	USIA Junior
		1998–99	Barton
	(Harvard-Ashekon Expedition)	1999–2000	PD
Yasir Sakr	(University of Pennsylvania)	1995–96	USIA Junior
Khader I. Salameh	(Awqaf Administration, Islamic Museum, Jerusalem)	1993–94	RF
		1997–98	RF
	(Islamic Museum, al-Harem al-Sharif, Jerusalem)	1997–2000	RF
Hamed J. Salem	(Birzeit University)	1999–2000	RF
Daniella Saltz	(Harvard University)	1974–75	ASOR/W. F. Albright
		1975–76	RF
	(Hebrew University)	1984–85	NEH
	(Unaffiliated)	1984–86	SF
Rebecca Sanders	(University of Notre Dame)	1998–99	Fulbright
Seth L. Sanders	(Johns Hopkins University)	1998–99	USIA Junior
Todd K. Sanders	(Harvard University)	1996–97	RF
Issa Sarie'	(Department of History and Archaeology - Al-Quds University)	1998–2000	RF
Victor Sasson	(New York University)	1977–78	Thayer
James Sauer	(Harvard University)	1971–72	ASOR/W. F. Albright
Thomas Schaub	(University of Pittsburgh)	1971–72	Thayer
Robert Schick	(Institute of Islamic Archaeology, Jerusalem)	1995–96	NEH
		1995–96	USIA Islamic
		1996–97	NEH
		1996–97	Islamic
		1997–98	Islamic/AP
		1998–2000	Islamic
David Schloen	(University of Chicago)	1997–98	NEH
Brian Schmidt	(University of Michigan)	1995–96	CAORC-Multi
Frederick W. Schmidt	(St. George's College, Jerusalem)	1994–95	SF
William Schniedewind	(Brandeis University)	1992–94	PD
	(University of California - Los Angeles)	1996–97	PD
Ulrike Schorn	(University of Erlangen, Germany)	1990–91	RF
Nicola Schreiber	(University College, London)	1995–96	RF

Eileen Schuller	(Harvard University)	1980–81	Barton
	(McMaster University)	1995–96	SF
Stuard D. Sears	(University of Chicago)	1994–95	CAORC-Multi
Choon Leong Seow	(Princeton Theological Seminary)	1986–87	NEH
Byron Shaffer	(Forham University)	1973–74	RA
Sariel Shalev	(Tel Aviv University)	1986–87	RF
Abier Z. Shamma	(University of California - Los Angeles)	1994–95	RF
Ilan Sharon	(Hebrew University)	1986–87	RF
Lewis Shaw	(Yale University)	1981–82	Barton
Susan G. Sheridan	(University of Notre Dame)	1997–98	NEH
		1998–2000	SF
Stephen J. Shoemaker	(Florida State University)	1999–2000	NEH
Vikesh Singh	(Brown University)	1995–96	Fulbright
Ilona Skupinska-Lovset	(University of Lodz, Poland)	1999–2000	Mellon
Kathryn Slanski	(Tel Aviv University)	1999–2000	PD
Susan Slyomovics	(Brown University)	1994–95	CAORC-Multi
David B. Small	(Unaffiliated)	1984–85	NEH
Mark S. Smith	(Yale University)	1983–84	RF
		1985–86	AP
		1988–90	PD
		1990–91	Dorot/DSS
Walter Sorge	(Eastern Illinois University, Charleston, IL)	1994–95	SF
John R. Spencer	(John Carroll University)	1984–85	AP
		1995–96	USIA Summer
Beatrice St. Laurent	(Wellesley College)	1992–93	NEH
		1993–94	USIA Junior
	(Jerusalem)	1994–95	SF
David Stacey	(Institute of Archaeology, London)	1988–89	RF
Larry Stager	(Harvard University)	1972–73	Thayer
Deborah Starr	(University of Michigan)	1997–98	CAORC-Multi
Danielle Steen	(University of Colorado)	1998–2000	Miqne
Rebecca Stein	(Stanford University)	1995–96	SSRC
Daniel Sterman	(Brown University)	1983–84	Dorot
James F. Strange	(Union College)	1970–71	Montgomery
	(University of South Florida)	1996–97	SF
Frederick M. Strickert	(Wartburg College)	1995–96	SF
John Strugnell	(Harvard University)	1981–82	NEH
Sandra Sufian	(New York University)	1996–97	SSRC
Michael O. Sugerman	(Harvard University)	1995–96	Kress/Joint
James Swauger	(Carnegie Museum of Natural History, Pittsburgh)	1979–80	AP
Marvin A. Sweeney	(University of Miami)	1987–88	PD
		1993–94	Dorot RP
Hamdan Taha	(Palestine Department of Antiquities)	1996–2000	SF
May O. Talbot	(University of California - Los Angeles)	1994–95	Kress

Lynn W. Tatum	(Duke University)	1983–85	RF
J. Glenn Taylor	(Yale University)	1985–86	Barton
Thord Thordson	(Lund University, Stockholm)	1995–96	PD
Lawrence E. Toombs	(Wilfrid Laurier University)	1975–76	AP
Phyllis Trible	(Andover Newton Theological Seminary)	1974–75	RA
Tamas Turan	(Center for Jewish Studies, Hungarian Academy of Sciences, Hungary)	1997–98	Mellon
Francois Valla	(Centre de Recherche Francais de Jerusalem)	1986–87	SF
Peter Vargyas	(Janus Pannonius University, Pecs, Hungary)	1998–2000	Mellon
Andrew G. Vaughn	(Princeton Theological Seminary)	1993–94	Fulbright
Anna de Vincenz	(Hebrew University)	1999–2000	PD
Benedict T. Viviano	(Duke University)	1971–72	Montgomery
Jane C. Waldbaum	(University of Wisconsin - Milwaukee)	1989–90	NEH
		1990–91	DorotRP
Paula C. Wapnish	(Smithsonian Institution)	1984–85	NEH
William Watters	(University of Iowa)	1973–74	RA
Darren Weening	(Lethbridge University)	1991–92	UG/Dorot/Miqne Computer Fellow
George Whipple	(Ohio Northern University)	1976–77	HRA
Sidnie Ann White	(Albright College)	1989–90	NEH
		1990–91	Dorot/DSS
		1991–92	DSS
Theodore Williams	(University of Arizona)	1999–2000	Fulbright
E. Jan Wilson	(Hebrew Union College - Cincinnati)	1989–91	RF
		1993–95	PD
Bonnie Wisthoff	(University of Arizona)	1985–86	Kress
		1986–87	Montgomery
Samuel R. Wolff	(University of Chicago)	1987–88	NEH
	(Harvard Research Associate)	1988–89	PD
		1989–90	PD/Ashkelon
	(Ben-Gurion University of the Negev)	1990–91	PD
	(Israel Antiquities Authority)	1991–93	PD
		1993–2000	SF
Timothy Woodard	(Lethbridge University)	1991–92	UG/Dorot/Miqne Computer Fellow
John Worrell	(United Church Board of World Ministries)	1993–95	SF
	(Old Sturbridge Village, Sturbridge, MA Emeritus)	1998–99	SF
David P. Wright	(Hebrew University)	1989–90	SF/Fulbright
Haddon Wright	(MacQuarie University, NSW, Australia)	1995–96	RF
		1996–97	SF
J. Edward Wright	(Brandeis University)	1986–87	Thayer
	(University of Arizona)	1995–96	PD

Stephen V. Wyrick	(California Baptist College - Riverside, CA)	1992–93	SF
Nadia Yaqub	(University of California - Berkeley)	1995–96	SSRC
William Yarchin	(Claremont Graduate School)	1980–81	RA
John Y. H. Yieh	(Yale University)	1989–90	Barton
Ziony Zevit	(University of Judaism - Los Angeles)	1986–87	NEH
		1994–95	SF/Guggenheim
Mark Ziese	(Andrews University)	1996–97	RF
Jeffrey Zorn	(University of California - Berkeley)	1990–92	Kress
		1994–95	PD
		1995–96	NEH

The "Mona Lisa with pieta" mosaic from the fourth century A.D. Dionysos Mansion at Sepphoris in Israel. EMM

AIAR Assisted — ASOR/CAP Affiliated Projects Current 1970–2000
(Initial date indicates year first affiliated with ASOR/CAP)

In Israel

1968–81	Tel Anafa	Sharon C. Herbert	University of Michigan
1970–	Joint Expedition to Tell el-Hesi	John E. Worrell	Hartford Seminary Foundation
		D. Glenn Rose	Phillips University
		Valarie M. Fargo	
		Jeffrey A. Blakely	Archeological Assessments, Inc.
1971–	Joint Expedition to Caesarea Maritima	Robert J. Bull	Drew University
1974–91	Meiron Excavations	Eric M. Meyers	Duke University
		Carol Meyers	Duke University
		James F. Strange	University of South Florida
1976–	Lahav Research Project Phases I–II	Joe D. Seger	University of Nebraska-Omaha / Mississippi State University
1977–91	Gush Halav Project	Eric M. Meyers	Drew University
		Carol Meyers	Drew University
		James F. Strange	University of South Florida
1978–94	Central Negev Highlands Project	William G. Dever	University of Arizona
1980–91	Khirbet en-Nabratein	Eric M. Meyers	Duke University
1981–	Excavations at Tel Miqne-Ekron	Seymour Gitin	W. F. Albright Institute
		Trude Dothan	Hebrew University
1982	Galilee Surface Survey	James F. Strange	University of South Florida
1982–87	Joint Sepphoris Project	Eric M. Meyers	Duke University
		Carol Meyers	Duke University
		James F. Strange	University of South Florida
1983–91	Caesarea Ancient Harbor Project	Robert Hohlfelder	University of Colorado
1983–94	Shiqmim	Thomas E. Levy	AIAR/University of California-San Diego
1984–91	Gezer Late Bronze Defenses	William G. Dever	University of Arizona
1986–89	Beth Shan Valley Project	Nephi W. Bushman II	University of Arizona
1986–94	Tell Wawiyat Excavations	William G. Dever	University of Arizona
		Beth Alpert Nikhai	
		J. P. Dessel	
		Bonnie Wisthoff	
1988–94	Joint Sepphoris Project	Eric M. Meyers	Drew University
		Carol Meyers	Drew University
		Ehud Netzer	Hebrew University
1989–91	Mt. Carmel Caves Amino Acid	Paul J. Hearty	
1989–	Combined Caesarea Expedition	Kenneth G. Holum	University of Maryland
		Avner Raban	University of Haifa
1989–91	Tell Yaqush	Douglas L. Esse	University of Chicago
1991–	Ashkelon: Leon Levy Expedition	Lawrence E. Stager	Harvard University

1992–	Lahav Research Project Phase III	Paul F. Jacobs	*Mississippi State University*
		Oded Borowski	*Emory University*
1993–	Caesarea Maratima Vault Project	W. J. Bennett	*Archeological Assessments Inc.*
		Jeffrey A. Blakely	*Archeological Assessments Inc.*
1993	Tel Beth Shemesh Excavations	Zvi Lederman	*Ben Gurion University*
		Shlomo Bunimovitz	*Tel Aviv University*
1994–	Neo-Assyrian Project	Seymour Gitin	*AIAR/CAORC*
1995–	Nahal Tillah Project	Thomas E. Levy	*University of California-San Diego*
1995–	Promontory Palace, Caesarea	Kathryn Gleason	*University of Pennsylvania*
			Cornell University
		Barbara Burrell	
1995–	University of South Florida Sepphoris Excavations	James F. Strange	*University of South Florida*
1995–	Sepphoris Regional Project	Eric M. Meyers	*Duke University*
		Carol Meyers	*Duke University*
1997–	Sepphoris Ein Zippori	Eric M. Meyers	*Duke University*
		Carol Meyers	*Duke University*
		J. P. Dessel	*University of Kentucky*
1999–	Khirbet Cana	Douglas R. Edwards	*University of Puget Sound*
1998	Tell Yaqush	David Schloen	*University of Chicago*
		Timothy Harrison	*University of Toronto*
1999–	Rekhes Nafha Project	Benjamin A. Saidel	*Harvard University*
		Steve Rosen	*Ben Gurion University*
1999–	Zeita Excavations	Ronald E. Tappy	*Pittsburgh Theological Seminary*
1999–	Tel Kedesh Excavation	Sharon Herbert	*University of Michigan*
		Andrea Berlin	*University of Minnesota*
2000–	Sepphoris Acropolis Excavation	Jonathan L. Reed	*University of La Verne*

In West Bank

1956–	Expedition to Shechem	G. Ernest Wright	*Harvard University*
		Edward F. Campbell Jr.	*McCormick Theological Seminary*
		Robert J. Bull	*Drew University*
1962	Tell er-Ras Excavations	Robert J. Bull	*Drew University*
1962–	Taanach Excavations	Paul W. Lapp	*Pittsburgh Theological Seminary*
		Nancy Lapp	*Pittsburgh Theological Seminary*
		Albert Glock	*AIAR/Birzeit University*
1962–	Joint Excavations at Ai and Khirbet Raddana	Joseph A. Callaway	*Southern Seminary*
1995	Jordan Bank Project	Robert Schick	*AIAR*

ACOR

The ACOR Odyssey

A History of the
AMERICAN CENTER OF ORIENTAL RESEARCH

Amman, Jordan

by Nancy Lapp

1968–2000

Author's Preface

This essay is not intended to present a complete history of the American Center of Oriental Research. Much of this has already been most adequately presented in the center's twenty-fifth anniversary publication, *ACOR: The First Twenty-Five Years; The American Center of Oriental Research, 1968–1993*, compiled and edited by Branwen Denton and Patricia Bikai. That work, as well as Bert de Vries' summary of the first twenty years, in *ACOR Newsletter* #4, were starting points in compiling this photographic story, and much credit must be given to these authors. Other *ASOR* and *ACOR Newsletters* were also key sources for the text. Photos and images come from collections in the ASOR Boston office, from ACOR in Amman, and from individual dig directors who responded to our request for photographs. As a result, while we will not present a fully detailed history, it is hoped that indeed "a picture is worth a thousand words," and that the photographic collection which has been assembled will in its own way be expressive of the course by which ACOR has passed from its founding to its present maturity.

Credits

Particular thanks for help in assembling the photographs for this section on ACOR's history go to Pierre and Patricia Bikai for access both to the ACOR archives in Amman and their personal collection, to Rudolph Dornemann for access to the ASOR archives in Boston, and to Donald Keller for the photographs in the ACOR archives in the Boston office. Photographs have also been reproduced from the *ACOR anniversary publication, ACOR: The First Twenty-Five Years*, and the *ASOR* and *ACOR Newsletters*. All pictures otherwise not referenced come from these sources.

Other individuals who have provided photographs include: Ruth L. Boling (RLB), Robin Brown (RB), Robert Coghenaur (RC), Michele Daviau (MD), Rudolph Dornemann (RD), Joe Greene (JG), Timothy Harrison (TH), Donald Henry (DH), Artemis Joukowsky (AJ), Martha Sharp Joukowsky (MJ), Nancy Lapp (NL), Anita Marks (AM), David McCreery (DM), Patrick McGovern (PM), Suzanne Richard (SR), Gary Rollefson (GR), Thomas Schaub (TS), Patty O. Seger (POS), Robert H. Smith (RS), and Randy Younker (RY). Pictures are referenced as indicated in parentheses.

ACOR
The ACOR Odyssey
A History of the American Center of Oriental Research
Amman, Jordan
1968–2000

by Nancy Lapp

Mosaic "greeting" at the front door of ACOR in Amman. Copy of the "Personification of Spring" from the southern aisle of the Petra Church.
(POS)

The present vision and purpose of the American Center of Oriental Research is best expressed in its Mission Statement as adopted by its Board of Trustees in 1994.

The ACOR Mission Statement

"The American Center of Oriental Research (ACOR) in Amman, Jordan, was founded in 1968 to promote the study and teaching and extend the knowledge of the geography, history, art, archaeology, and languages and literatures of ancient Jordan and other lands of the Near East by affording educational opportunities to faculty and students of U.S. and Canadian colleges and universities, as well as to other qualified faculty and students and by the prosecution of original research, excavation and exploration.

In its first quarter century ACOR has provided a vital link between Jordanian academic and government institutions (including the Department of Antiquities) on the one hand, and scholars from the U.S. and other nations pursuing research in the Arab World, on the other. ACOR provides a variety of facilities and fellowships — to professional academics from major universities engaged in advanced research, and to educators who wish to conduct study projects in Jordan to enhance their teaching in their home communities. ACOR also supports students who wish to participate in archaeological excavations and related projects. In addition, ACOR assists both small and large field projects in archaeology. ACOR provides advice, coordination, equipment, research and laboratory facilities, a library of 20,000 volumes, residential accommodation, and lecture/meeting rooms, as well as an academically stimulating and personally congenial environment.

ACOR's mission for the next quarter century will be to support scholarly research, with special emphasis on archaeology, on the past and present human condition in Jordan and the surrounding region. The mission also includes: continued development of the ACOR Library for advanced research; broadening ACOR's function as a meeting place for both international scholarly exchange and instruction on subjects related to Near Eastern archaeology and civilization; and continued cooperation with Jordanian institutions of higher education."

Adopted by the ACOR Board of Trustees March 24, 1994

I
ACOR: THE FOUNDING YEARS

The founding of an American Center in Amman, Jordan was authorized by resolution of the American Schools of Oriental Research in 1968. This immediately followed the 1967 Arab-Israeli war, which resulted in the closing off of opportunities for Americans to continue work in Arab countries from the ASOR School (now the W. F. Albright Institute) in Jerusalem. Leaders in ASOR were responding to an urgency to continue the American archaeological presence in the wider Near East region, both through excavation and through assistance to the indigenous institutions; in Jordan these include the Department of Antiquities and the University of Jordan.

Rudolph H. Dornemann was appointed as Annual Professor in Amman for 1968–69, responding to the request from the University of Jordan to assist in their Department of Archaeology. His primary responsibilities were the teaching of courses at the University and serving as a consultant to the Director General of Antiquities.

Rudolph H. Dornemann

The new organization was called the American Research Center in Amman and a committee, chaired by John Marks, was appointed to supervise it by ASOR President G. E. Wright.

The First Amman Center Committee

John Marks, President
Roger Boraas
Siegfried Horn
James B. Pritchard
William L. Reed
Bastiaan Van Elderen

Presidents of the ACOR Board of Trustees

1970–78	John Marks
1978–82	Walter Rast
1982–86	Gough Thompson
1986–88	Edgar Harrell
1988–92	Robert Coughenour
1992–	Artemis Joukowsky

John Marks, Chairperson of the Amman Center Committee. From 1970 he also served as the first President of the Board of Trustees. (AM)

The headquarters for the new center was near the First Circle in Amman on the first floor of this building.

By 1969 rental space was found near the Third Circle with more ample living and work space.

The Dornemann's with their young sons were the first of several families to occupy the Third Circle residence. (RD)

Backyard of the 1969 ACOR rental property.

Mohammed Adawi, who left his home near Jerusalem and his work at the American School in Jerusalem during the 1967 fighting, was subsequently retained by ASOR and has served as the cook throughout ACOR's existence in Amman.

The Adawis and their young family celebrate the holidays with the Dornemanns.
(RD)

(left to right) Siegfried Horn, Rudy Dornemann, and Mohammed Adawi outside the Third Circle ACOR.

(left to right) Mohammed Adawi with Henry O. Thompson. Thompson was ACOR Annual Professor/Director in 1971–72.

The USAID program of archaeological work, which Rudy Dornemann had headed in Amman before 1967, included clearance and excavation of the Amman theater and colonnaded street. Following 1967 this program was gradually phased out.

The Amman Theater after clearance and reconstruction. (RD)

In the early years the primary responsibilities of the directors and other appointees involved teaching at the University of Jordan and consultation with the Department of Antiquities.

Rudy Dornemann lecturing at the University of Jordan.

Early budgets were around $20,000 a year, with large contributions from the United States Department of State which was anxious to support the American cultural presence in Jordan.

Rudy Dornemann's earlier excavation work at the citadel in Amman were joint projects for the training and employment of Jordan's archaeologists, and this type of cooperation continued with the excavations directed by Roger Boraas, Bastiaan Van Elderen, and Henry O. Thompson.

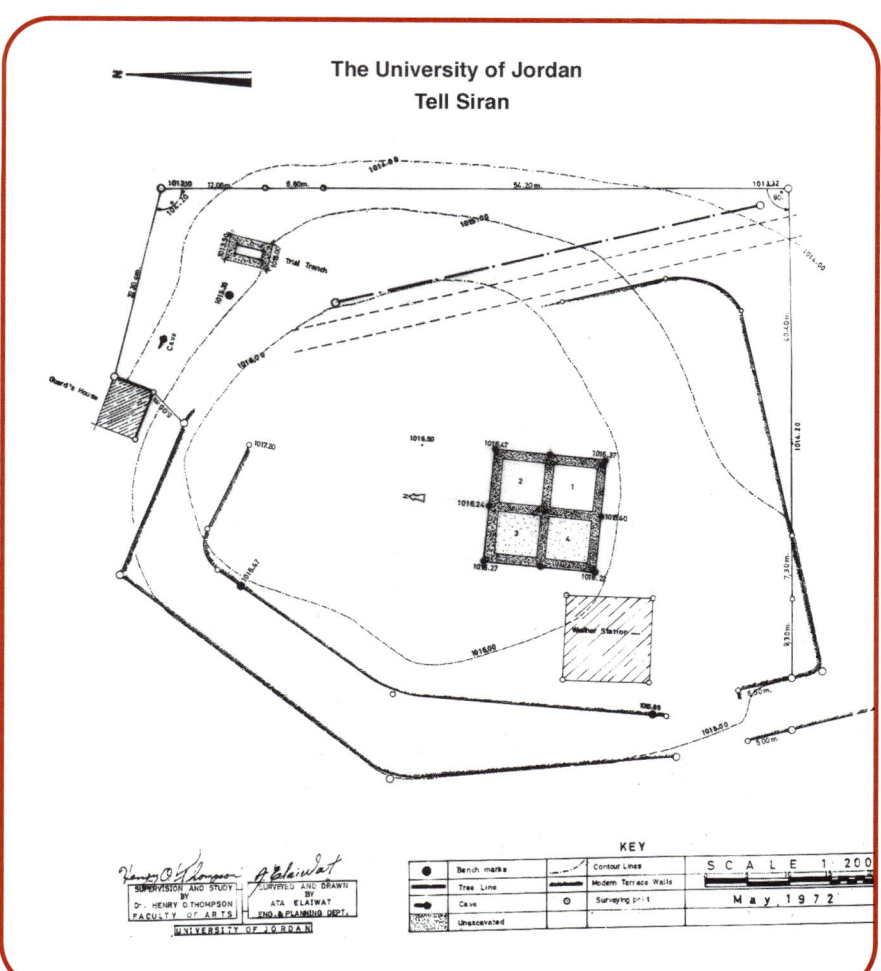

Site map of Siran. Henry O. Thompson Supervisor.

Inscribed bottle from Siran.

In the late 1960's it became increasingly evident within ASOR that a more deliberate separation between the work in Amman and that in Jerusalem was necessary. Accordingly the structures of ASOR were reorganized in 1970. ASOR would continue in the United States with its endowment and corporate membership, and with its program of publications and fellowships, but sponsorship of centers in the Near East would belong to newly formed corporations charged with management of their own programs and budgets. The Amman Committee was thus incorporated as the "The American Center of Oriental Research in Amman." Formal affiliation with ASOR continues through membership within the ASOR Corporation and with a representative member of the ASOR Board of Trustees. ASOR serves as an umbrella organization for membership, ASOR publications, and voluntary certification of archaeological projects.

During the founding years, from 1968 through 1975, ACOR was served by directors appointed each year. Unitl 1972 they also served as Annual Professors.

Annual Professor/Directors

1968–69	Rudolph Dornemann
1969–70	Murray Nicol
1970	Bastiaan Van Elderen
1970–71	Siegfried Horn
1971–72	Henry Thompson
1972–74	Bastiaan Van Elderen
1975	George Mendenhall

Murray Nicol, ACOR Director 1969–70, discusses ACOR's relationship to the Department of Antiquities, with Jacoub Oweis, its Director.

George Mendenhall (center) has remained active in ACOR projects through the 1990's. He is seen here with Patricia Bikai (left) and Denyse Homes-Fredericq of Belguim who is the excavator of Lehun.

ACOR: The ACOR Odyssey 1968–2000 — *A History of the Americaan Center of Oriental Research by Nancy Lapp*

ACOR's service as a base for American dig groups began with the pioneering excavations at Tall Hisban in 1968. The Tall Hisban work continued through several seasons until 1976, when it became the founding arm of the Madaba Plains Project which succeeded it.

Excavation Director Siegfied Horn of Andrews University (right) showing visiting dignitaries around at Tall Hisban; in top center is Dr. Moawiyah Ibrahim, later head of the Institute of Archaeology at Yarmouk University.

In 1972 Bert de Vries began an architectural survey of Umm el-Jimal. Excavation and reconstruction followed and he has continued project efforts there until the present.

Bert de Vries (right) discusses strategy in the field with Scott Ralston (center).

249

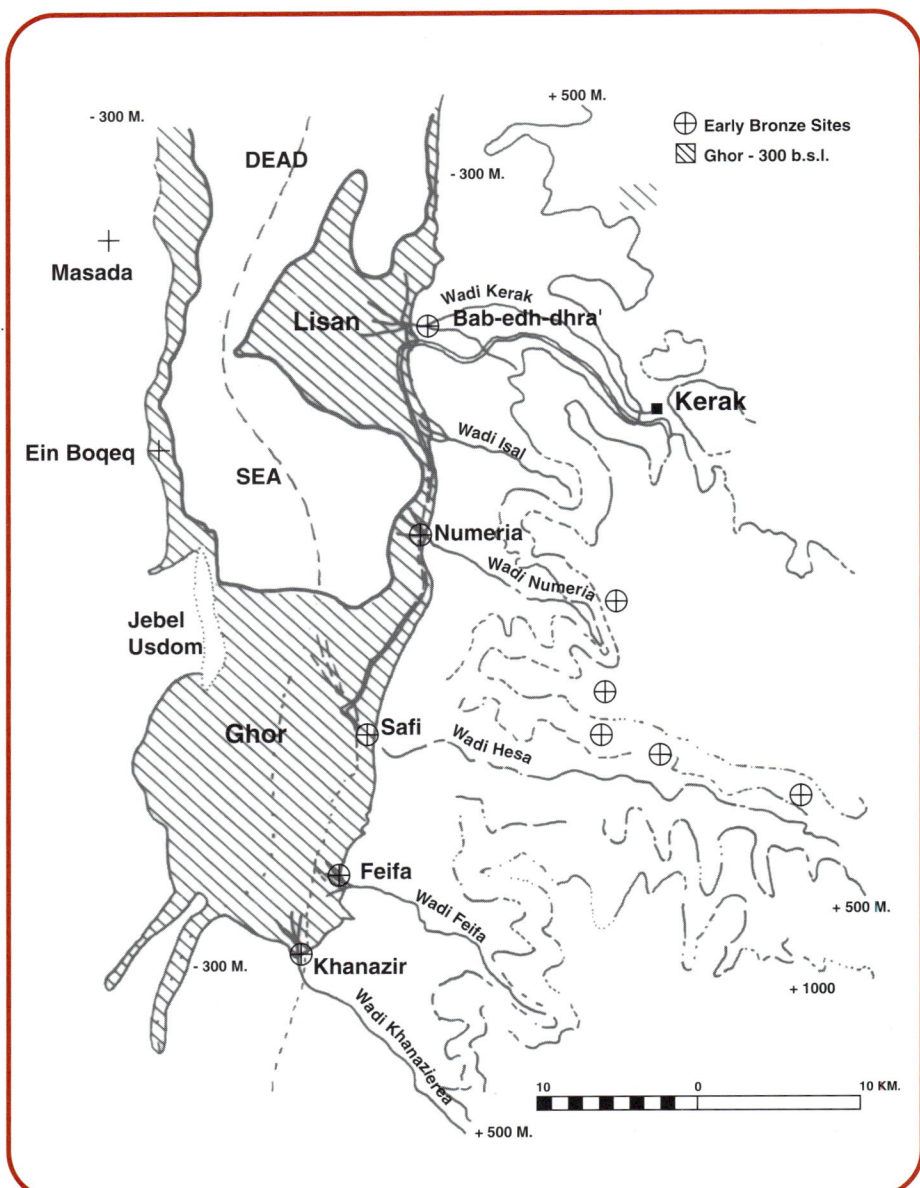

Map of the Dead Sea Plain area in central Jordan.

Excavations at Bab edh-Dhra' were first conducted during three seasons (1965–67) by Paul W. Lapp. After Lapp's untimely death in 1970, Walter Rast and Thomas Schaub took over responsibility for the publication of the Bab edh-Dhra' materials. In 1973 and following they undertook renewed work with a survey of the Dead Sea Plain area. Five major Early Bronze sites were identified: Bab edh-Dhra', Numeira, Safi, Feifa and Khanazir. This initiated the Expedition to the Dead Sea Plain Project whose excavation and publication efforts are still continuing.

Tom Schaub washes pottery collected on the Dead Sea Plains survey at project headquarters in Kerak. (TS)

II
YEARS OF GROWTH 1975–1981

The first longer-term Director at ACOR was James A. Sauer. He was appointed to the post and continued to serve the institute until the summer of 1981. At that time he returned to the United States for an academic position at the University of Pennsylvania and to begin his first term as newly elected President of ASOR.

The succeeding Directors of ACOR 1975 — Present

1975–81	**James Sauer**
1981–88	**David McCreery**
1988–91	**Bert de Vries**
1991–	**Pierre Bikai**

James A. Sauer, Director of ACOR 1975–81. He was President of ASOR, 1982–88 and President of the ACOR Board of Trustees, 1991–92.

Director Sauer (center) with Ghazi Bisheh (left) and Fawzi Zayadine of the Department of Antiquities.

During Jim Sauer's term close cooperation with the University of Jordan and the Department of Antiquities continued, and a joint project of intensive survey in the Jordan Valley was initiated.

In 1977 ACOR moved once more, renting a new building between the Fifth and Sixth Circles.

In this building study areas were available for visiting scholars, and several NEH (National Endowment for the Humanities) and ASOR W.F. Albright Fellows were attracted to the more adequate hostel accommodations.

ACOR headquarters in 1977.

Entrance of ACOR headquarters in 1977.

NEH Fellow R. Thomas Schaub at work at ACOR.

ACOR: The ACOR Odyssey 1968–2000 — *A History of the Americaan Center of Oriental Research by Nancy Lapp*

(Left to right) Tom Schaub and Walt Rast discuss Bab edh-Dhra' excavations in the expanded library.

Mohammed Adawi continues to work faithfully.

Mohammed is sometimes joined by his son Said as activity at the Center increases.

Under Jim Sauer's leadership the Center in Amman began to reach out to Syria to assist ASOR in its interest in developing archaeological efforts among Jordan's neighbors.

Jim Sauer (center) provides an explanation of the Temple of Bel at Palmyra during an ASOR Trustee visit. Philip King, President of ASOR, is standing on the far left.

Beginning in 1972, in addition to the Director, a second scholar as Annual Professor was appointed at the institute whenever possible.

Annual Professors 1972–1989

1972–73	Henry O. Thompson (as "Visiting Professor")
1973–77	James A. Sauer
1977–78	William J. Fulco
1978–79	Edwin Schick
1979–80	Burton MacDonald
1981–82	Gary O. Rollefson
1983–84	Prescott H. Williams
	Robert G. Boling
1985–86	Keith Beebe
	Robert Coughenour
1986–87	Burton MacDonald
1987–88	Brian Byrd
1988–89	William Jobling
	Robert Schick

In Syria in 1977, Jim Sauer looks for an elusive site on Phase I of ASOR's Archaeological Survey of Syria. These efforts would ultimately culminate in the initiation of excavations at Tell Qarqur.

In 1977, and during the years following, Patrick McGovern of the University of Pennsylvania directed excavations and survey work in the Baq'ah Valley, a well-watered area fifteen kilometers northwest of Amman.

(left to right) Helen Schenck and Baq'ah Valley Project Director Patrick McGovern look for sites. (PM)

Pat McGovern admires an Iron I juglet just recovered from the cave excavations. (PM)

(left to right) Robin Brown and Jane Mohawi excavating a cave in the Baq'ah Valley, 1977. (PM)

From the mid-1970's excavations at the Bab edh-Dhra' town site and at Tell Numeira were conducted as part of the Expedition to the Dead Sea Plain. The Early Bronze age towns and the huge Bab edh-Dhra' cemetery were excavated in 1975, 1977, 1979, and 1981.

Walt Rast (center) and Bruno Fröhlich (right) review an Early Bronze I burial with Ghazi Bisheh.

Area Supervisor Alberic Culhane admires the Bab edh-Dhra' Early Bronze age pottery.

Nancy Lapp studying the finds from a Bab edh-Dhra' EB IV tomb. (NL)

The excavations at Pella had been interrupted by the 1967 war, but were resumed in 1979 under the auspices of the College of Wooster, the University of Sydney in Australia, and the Department of Antiquities of Jordan. The project was directed by Robert Smith.

Pella of the Decapolis with excavations in progress. In the center is the civic center church, probably Pella's main cathedral with the columns of the atrium and of the north porch restored. (RHS)

(left to right) Pella of the Decapolis Director Robert Smith with Area Supervisor Leslie Preston Day and Foreman Badri Madi discussing the excavations in the civic center. (RHS)

Between 1978 and 1983 J. Maxwell Miller and Jack M. Pinkerton directed a survey on the Kerak Plateau. This involved three summer seasons of fieldwork establishing grid coordinates, preparing descriptions, and sampling surface pottery. Four hundred forty-three sites were examined from the southern rim of the Wadi el-Mujib to the northern rim of Wadi el-Hasa, and from the desert fringe on the east to the edge of the Dead Sea escarpment to the west.

The Nakhl temple, Site 420, of the central Moab survey. (RB)

Other projects included the investigation of iron smelting sites at Abu Thawwab and Wadi Wardeh by Robert Coughenour and a sounding inside the Qasr at Araq el-Emir by Robin Brown.

Robin Brown in the area she excavated at Araq el-Emir in 1976. (RB)

In March 1980 the First International Conference on the History and Archaeology of Jordan was held at Oxford in England. This initiated a series of tri-annual international conferences that have continued up to the present.

The conference was organized by the Jordanian Department of Antiquities assisted by an international committee and under the patronage of the Royal Family. Crown Prince Hassan (front center) participated in many of the sessions.

(left to right) Jim Sauer and Bert de Vries were among the participants representing ACOR at the Oxford Conference.

ASOR, from before 1967, and ACOR, since its founding, have assisted the "Friends of Archaeology" in Jordan in their efforts to foster better understanding and appreciation of the culture heritage of the country.

Jerry Mattingly (center) describes the remains at Baluah for a Friends of Archaeology field trip.

Tom Parker (with clipboard) tells about Lejjun, one of the Roman border forts he excavated as a part of his Limes Arabicus Project.

Tom Schaub (at sign) interprets the Early Bronze site of Bab edh-Dhra' for visitors.

III
Years of Stability Lead to Permanency 1981–1988

David McCreery became the Director at ACOR in 1981. He led the institute in its programs of scholarship and outreach for the next seven years. The increased program activity at ACOR cried out for a larger facility, and David spent much of his time during his first several years in negotiating, raising money, and overseeing the construction of a more permanent home for ACOR.

David and Linda McCreery.

Thanksgiving at ACOR in 1982. Around table left to right: Walter Rast, Colin Gillete, Laura Hess (Brian Byrd and Tom Schaub behind), David McCreery, Linda McCreery (standing), Tom Parker, Gary Rollefson and Jerry Mattingly.

During these years archaeological activity in Jordan continued to increase.

The Jerash International Project was launched by teams from several different countries in 1982.

Mrs. Crystal Bennett and Dr. Peter Parr of the British School at Jerash in October 1982.

The North Theater

The American team under the leadership of Vincent Clark excavated in the North Theater and a church to the east.

ACOR mounted an emergency "salvage" project in 1982 at Umm al-Bigal where tombs were uncovered during a construction project.

David McCreery examines a jar from one of the Umm al-Bigal tombs. (DM)

Scott Ralston removes roof fall from the articulated skeleton of an 18-year old female from an Umm al-Bigal tomb. (DM)

Volunteers Laura Hess (at the top) and Brian Byrd (with the pick) come to the rescue. Linda McCreery is out of sight behind Brian. (DM)

Between 1982 and 1985 Steve Falconer and Bonnie Magness-Gardiner surveyed and excavated the Early Bronze IV – MB II site of Tell el-Hayyat.

(left to right) ASOR President Phil King, Pat Fall, Steve Falconer, and Bob Erskine look over the site in 1982.

The group examines surface finds. ASOR President King stands in back center.

Glen Peterman, a staff member at Tell el-Hayyat in 1985.

ACOR: The ACOR Odyssey 1968–2000 — A History of the Americaan Center of Oriental Research by Nancy Lapp

Along with digging, diplomacy and development work, scholars at the center in the early 1980's also enjoyed other activities including tours and social events that provided for the growth of the community spirit at ACOR.

(left to right) Tom Parker and Linda McCreery provide some entertainment at ACOR, December 1982.

Social activities in this period included celebration of the wedding of Gary Rollefson and Ilse Kohler.

ACOR group at a picnic overlooking Araq el-Emir in 1982. (left to right), ACOR Librarian Pam Mattingly, Administrator Laura Hess, NEH Fellows Tom Parker and Jerry Mattingly, ASOR W.F. Albright Fellow Cheri Lenzen. (in back) Tom Schaub (NEH Fellow), Linda McCreery and former Administrator Scott Ralston.

Excavations began at `Ain Ghazal in northeast Amman in 1982. This work revealed uninterrupted Neolithic occupation covering a span of at least 2000 years.

In 1983 the first group of astounding cultic finds appear: plaster statues (ca. 90 cm high) and busts (ca. 45 cm) dated to 6750–6500 B.C.

Gary Rollefson, Director of the `Ain Ghazal Project. (GR)

(left to right) Gary Rollefson and NEH Fellow Albert Leonard inspect superimposed plaster floors. (GR)

ACOR: The ACOR Odyssey 1968–2000 — A History of the Americaan Center of Oriental Research by Nancy Lapp

(left to right) Dani Petocz and Conservator Kathy Tubb wrap the `Ain Ghazal plaster statues in foil in preparation for lifting. (GR)

A box was prepared in order to lift the statues and to ship them to London for preservation. Shown (left to right) are Alison Betts, Svend Helms with Brian Bowen behind him, and Ted Banning. (DM)

The final wrapping up of the statues for shipment and signing of papers took place at the Queen Alia Airport. In the group (left to right) are David McCreery, Wa'el Rashdan, Lutfi Khalil and Nasmieh Rida. (DM)

Since 1968 Roger Boraas had supervised a number of ACOR related field projects. In 1982 he was called upon once again, this time to help with excavation work at Khirbet Iskander.

Roger Boraas at Khirbet Iskander. (SR)

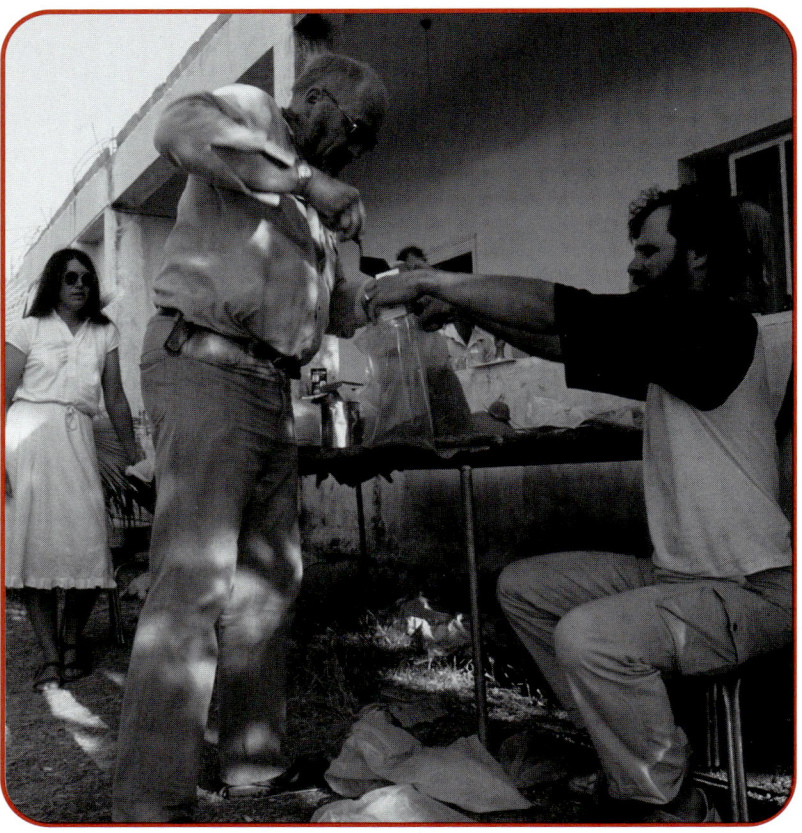

Roger Boraas (center) working on flotation with Jesse Long (right) and Bonnie Wisthoff. (SR)

(left to right) Suzanne Richard and Jesse Long, directors of the Khirbet Iskandar excavations, with restored Early Bronze IV pottery. (SR)

Robert and Jean Boling were frequent residents at ACOR where Bob had appointments in 1983–84 (Annual Professor), 1984–85 (NEH Fellow), and 1994–95 (USIA Fellow). Just before they were to leave Jordan in December 1994 they lost their lives in a tragic automobile accident on the way to Aqaba. Bob had been a member of the ACOR Board of Trustees and he chaired a committee to raise money from ACOR alumni/ae for the new building.

Jean and Bob Boling are part of the Halloween festivities in 1983.

(left to right) Jean and Bob view a site with Bert de Vries on an ACOR outing.

Robert and Jean Boling
(RLB)

A fund-raising campaign had been initiated by James Sauer already in 1979 for the purpose of establishing permanent quarters for ACOR. David McCreery worked throughout his term to plan and supervise the construction of a new building, and then to initiate activity in the new facility. These efforts were supported in the U.S. by the Board of Trustees under the leadership of ACOR's successive Presidents Walter Rast (1978–82) and Gough Thompson (1982–86).

ACOR building line drawing.

Walter Rast, President of the ACOR Board of Trustees, looks over the site chosen for the new ACOR in 1982.

Khirbet Salameh, with Late Byzantine, Roman, Hellenistic and perhaps Iron age remains, is located on the northern edge of the site.

With $1.2 million raised, a ground-breaking ceremony at the new ACOR building site was held on August 6, 1984.

"The Big Dig" gets underway.

David McCreery (standing) supervises Prince Ra'ad!

H.R.H. Prince Ra'ad bin Zeid (with shovel) and friends at the Foundation Laying Ceremony.

(left to right) Mohammed Asfour, Prince Ra'ad, and others tour the building site..

Prince Ra'ad at the "Topping-out" Ceremony, October 31, 1985.

The completed ACOR building was inaugurated on July 17, 1986 when Prince Mohammed Ibn Talal cut the ribbon.

The New ACOR Building.

In 1986, with the building project completed, Dave McCreery and the ACOR staff turned to the tasks of moving in and initiating program activities in the new facility. Also in 1986 Edgar Harrell succeeded Gough Thompson as ACOR President.

David McCreery, Scott Ralston, and others moving the map case from the old building.

Fellow Glen Peterman at work in one of the new carrels. (NL)

The new library. (NL)

During the succeeding years field work activities continued to increase.

In 1986-87 Robin Brown, ASOR W. F. Albright Fellow, excavated at the Crusader castles at Shobak, Wu'eira, and Kerak.

Robin Brown (right) and Abdullah (Abu Ashjar) at Qasr Shobak. (RB)

Thomas Parker directed the Limes Arabicus Project from 1976–89, including excavations at Tell Lejjun. Parker currently directs excavation work at Roman Aqaba.

Jennifer Groot in her supervisor duties at the Lejjun Roman fort. (RB)

S. Thomas Parker

Tom Parker at the Aqaba excavations.

Jennifer C. Groot (RB)

Jennifer Groot, a young and talented archaeologist, died in 1987 after a short illness. As a field supervisor and object specialist she served on the staff of excavations at Hesban, Umm el-Jimal, the Limes Arabicus, and assisted with the publication of objects from Araq el-Emir. Other publications also resulted from her work on these excavations, particularly her reports from Lejjun. She excelled in her abilities as a stratigrapher, an analyst of small finds, and as a teacher in the field.

After her death colleagues established the Jennifer C. Groot Fellowships to assist beginning archaeologists in excavations and related project work, usually by covering their travel expenses. The first Jennifer C. Groot Fellowship was offered in 1989. By 1999 the endowment had grown so that it was possible to offer three Groot Fellowships per year.

Recipients of the Jennifer C. Groot Fellowship

Year	Recipient(s)
1989–90	Benjamin F. Hartsell
1990–91	Brenda Strickland
1991–92	Kelly Low
1992–93	Denine Dudley Judith Mitchell
1993–94	Megan Perry Janet King
1994–95	Elizabeth Anne Pollard Lisi Elizabeth A. Stephens
1995–96	Mary Barbara Reeves Angela Hummel
1996–97	Carol Frey Pauline Ripat
1997–98	Brian Brown Christian Rata
1998–99	Robin Armstrong Joseph McClain Warren Wood
1999–2000	Valerie Batt John Dekle Melissa N.C. Nevillis

Jennifer Groot in the objects laboratory at Umm el-Jimal in 1977. (RB)

In 1988, Bert de Vries, former ASOR W. F. Albright Fellow, member of the ACOR Board of Trustees, and Director of the excavations at Umm el-Jimal, became ACOR Director. At the same time Robert Coughenour assumed responsibilities as President of the ACOR Board.

Bert de Vries.

Around the table left to right Amar Khamash, Gaetano Palumbo, Bert de Vries, Cynthia Schartzer and Tom Dailey enjoy dinner at ACOR. (Sally de Vries, not shown, was hostess for the occasion.)

(right to left) Doris Miller, Robert Coughenauer, Prince Ra'ad bin Zeid, Mohammed Asfour, Khair Yassin, Charles Miller, Bert de Vries, Burton MacDonald, Anne Ogilvy, Rudolph Dornemann (behind), Wadad Kawar and Michel Marto. (RC)

On occasion the ACOR Board of Trustees holds its spring meeting in Jordan. One-third of ACOR Board Members are now Jordanian citizens. Trustee Judy Zimmerman took the photograph seen above at the July 1990 Board meeting in Amman.

Ghazi Bisheh (right) studying the master plan for the Amman Citadel.

Under a grant from USAID in 1987, ACOR, in cooperation with the Jordanian Department of Antiquities, initiated a pilot Cultural Resources Management (CRM) Project, concerned with long-range planning for conservation and management of archaeological and historical sites threatened by modernization in the country.

Donald Whitcomb began excavations at Islamic Aqaba in 1986. His work was to benefit from the CRM Project.

(left to right) Bert de Vries, Zbigniew Fiema, and Don Whitcomb, with a sign for Islamic Aqaba, prepare for tourism as part of the CRM project. (DW)

Don Whitcomb (left) discusses his work at Aqaba with Ghazi Bisheh (right) of the Department of Antiquities. (DW)

James Flanagan and David Mc-Creery began excavations at Tell Nimrin as Co-Directors in 1989.

James Flanagan (standing) and David McCreery examine the road cut at Tell Nimrin. Department of Antiquities representative Sa'ad Hadidi is standing under the tree. (DM)

Dave McCreery drawing a section in square N30/W20. (DM)

In 1989 Michele Daviau directed excavations at Tell Jawa as part of the Madaba Plains Project team. In 1991 and 1992 she continued this work as a separate project. In 1996, she initiated a survey in the Wadi ath-Thamad and excavations at Khirbet al-Mudayna.

Clean up in Building 800 at Tell Jawa. (MD)

(left to right) J. Andrew Dearman and Michele Daviau in a cistern found in the Wadi ath-Thamad Survey. (MD)

Pierre Bikai

IV
Years of Developing Programs and Resources 1991–2000

In 1991 Pierre Bikai became the third long-term Director of ACOR and Jim Sauer became President of the ACOR Board. In 1992 Sauer was succeeded by Artemis Joukowsky. This initiated another decade of growth in program activities and in the development of support resources for the center.

Reception for out-going Director Bert de Vries and in-coming Director Pierre Bikai in 1991. (left to right) Tom Schaub, Patricia Bikai, former Director and ACOR President Jim Sauer, Sally deVries, Bert de Vries and Pierre Bikai.

(right to left) Pierre and Patricia Bikai with Ghazi Bisheh of the Department of Antiquities.

The number of fellowships available for scholars and students increased greatly in the 1990's. In addition to the Shell, Teagle, Winnett, Dodge, ASOR W. F. Albright, and Kress Fellowships, some of which continued for a number of years, government funds became available through the Arabic Speaking Academic Immersion Program and the Mellon Foundation (ASAIP) and the United States Information Agency (USIA) including support from the Near and Middle East Research and Training Act (NMERTA) through efforts of the Council of American Overseas Research Centers (CAORC). To date ACOR has had thirty NEH (National Endowment for the Humanities) Fellows. Occasionally Fulbright scholars have also been in residence. Student travel and support awards now include the Groot, Russell, Harrell, and Pierre and Patricia Bikai Fellowships. The Harrell Fellowship is a gift from the Harrell family and now has a small endowment. The Bikai Fellowship, made possible by Pierre and Patricia, was first offered in 1999. It offers residency at ACOR for several weeks and a small stipend for a student who has travel funds from another source. (See Appended Listing of Appointees). In addition various CRM (Cultural Resource Management) projects brought staff and archaeologists to ACOR.

ASAIP Fellows in 1993. (left to right) Charlene Constable, Marion Katz, Timothy Gianotti and Lynn Killean.

Thomas Schaub was a Fulbright Scholar in the summers of 1989 and 1991. He is seen here (left) donating a sherd storage cabinet for the Early Bronze age study collection to Pierre Bikai at ACOR.

(left to right) Zbigniew Fiema (USIA Fellow, 1991–92, 1993–94), Glen Peterman, (USIA Teagle Fellow 1989–90 and USIA Fellow 1991–92) and Gaetano Palumbo (CRM archaeologist, 1991–94).

Projects researching the prehistory of Jordan began in the 1980's. They continue to the present, now particularly in the desert regions.

Donald Henry, Director of the excavation of the Middle Paleolithic shelter of Tor Faraj, near Ras en-Naqb, talks with Mr. Faraj about his use of water sources and pasturage. (DH)

Don Henry pointing out superimposed petroglyphs ranging in date from Epipaleolithic to Thalmudic on the back-wall of the Epipaleolithic site of Jebel Hamra, near Quwweira. (DH)

The Neolithic site at Tabaqat al-Burma in northern Jordan was excavated by Ted Banning and Ian Kuijt as part of the Wadi Ziqlab Project. (DH)

During the 1990's the Temple of Hercules Project on the Amman Citadel was funded by USAID. It is part of a comprehensive site development plan to create an archaeological park on the Citadel.

The Hercules Temple before restoration.

The capital of the second column of the Hercules Temple is restored.

(Left to right) Chrysanthos Kanellopoulos, author of **The Great Temple of Amman: The Architecture**, displays a copy of the book with Sharkir Dotta, master printer who supervised the production of this book and **The Mosaics of Jordan**.

A CRM Conference was held in Amman in September 1992 to appraise the results of efforts till that time and to plan the future. The focus was upon ways to adjust the needs of development to those of heritage preservation. Participants included officials of the Department of Antiquities, faculty of Jordanian universities, representatives of non-govermental organizations (NGO's), as well as representatives of the USIA which had provided the grants.

Participants at the 1992 CRM conference.

*Gaetano Palumbo, CRM archaeologist (center left), presents **JADIS** registration cards to Safwan Tell, Director of the Department of Antiquities (center right), and members of his registration staff. JADIS (**Jordan Antiquities Database and Information System**) locates archaeological sites not only to assist archaeologists but also to help developers and contractors for planning construction projects.*

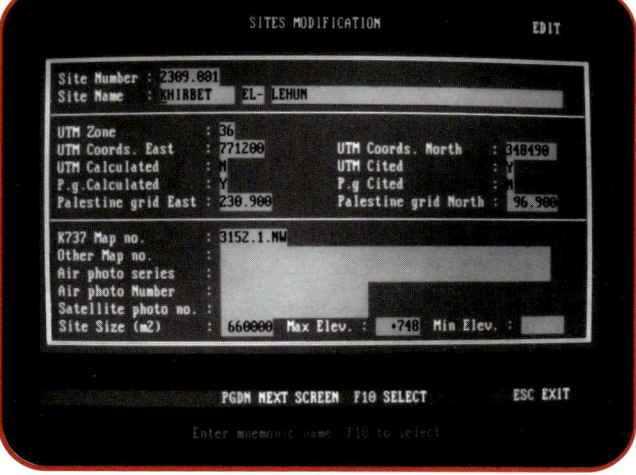

Kenneth W. Russell had worked on the ACOR projects at the Amman Citadel and at Islamic Aqaba. However his first interest was in the history and archaeology of Petra and in ethnoarchaeology studies of the Bidul Bedouin living there. On May 10, 1992 just as he was about to begin directing the excavations of the Byzantine complex at Petra he died unexpectedly. He was 41 years of age.

In Russell's honor a memorial trust was set up to provide travel fellowship support for students for archaeological and related research, scholarships for education in archaeology and related fields for residents of Jordan, and to provide assistance for the education of the children of the Bidul Bedouin.

Recipients of Russell Fellowship Support

1992	**Bedul school in Um Sayhoun**
1993–94	**Fatma Marii**
1996–97	**Edith Dunn**
1997	**Bedul school in Um Sayhoun**
1998–99	**Linah Ababneh**
1999–2000	**Sarah E. Whitcher**

Kenneth W. Russell (RB)

(left to right) Muhammad Najjar, Pierre Bikai and Ken Russell on the Amman Citadel, 1991. (RB)

The continuing discovery of mosaics in Jordan have created an urgent need that provisions be made for their preservation. Restoration efforts and the construction of protective shelters are an essential part of the Madaba Archaeological Park project initiated in 1991 by the Ministry of Tourism and Antiquities, ACOR, and USAID (United States Agency for International Development).

The shelter under construction at the Church of the Virgin and Hippolytos Hall in Madaba.

Cleaning and repairing the mosaics in the Church of the Virgin.

The Church of the Virgin shelter following its completion.

ACOR launched the *ACOR Newsletter* in 1989. Published from Amman twice a year, it presents up-to-date news of the projects, fellows, and the varied activities of ACOR. In addition ACOR produces the *ACOR Newzette*, a limited, usually a one page publication for ACOR residents, staff, trustees, and a few friends. The *Newzette* is published nine to twelve times a year.

*A variety of logo images, representing various ACOR projects and activities have been used for the **Newsletter** and **Newzette** mastheads.*

ACOR Newsletter
أخبــار أكــور

Vol. 9.2 — Winter 1997

ACOR Newzette
أخبــار أكــور

Vol. 7.2 — Winter 1995

ACOR's archaeological publication series was launched in 1992 with the volume, *The Mosaics of Jordan*, by Michele Piccirillo. This volume, with 303 pages of full color, details Jordan's rich historic heritage in Roman, Byzantine and Umayyad mosaics. The publication was made possible by a grant from USAID to assist in the development of high-quality printing in Jordan. Income from the sales has been used for the publication of other works on the art and archaeology of Jordan.

Other ACOR Publications

JADIS: The Jordan Antiquities Databas and Information System: A Summary of the Data; edited by Gaetano Palumbo, 1994

The Great Temple of Amman: The Architecture; by Chrsanthos Kanellopoulos, 1994

The Great Temple of Amman: The Excavations; by Anthi Koutsoukou, Kenneth W. Russell, Mohammed Najjar, and Ahmed Momani, 1997

ACOR: The First 25 Years, The American Center of Oriental Research: 1968–1993; by Branwen Denton and Patricia M. Bikai, 1993

Madaba: Cultural Heritage; edited by Patricia M. Bikai and Thomas A. Dailey, 1996

Ancient Ammonites & Modern Arabs: 5000 Years in the Madaba Plains of Jordan; edited by Gloria A. London and Douglas R. Clark, 1997

The 150th Anniversary of the United States' Expedition to Explore the Dead Sea and the River Jordan; by Robert E. Rook, 1998

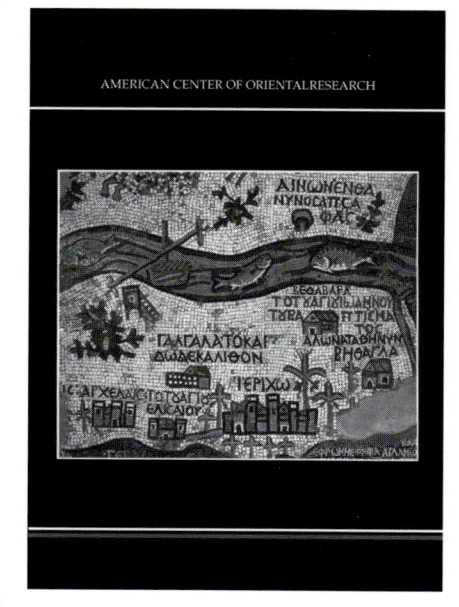

*Front and back covers of **The Mosaics of Jordan**.*

At Petra, excavations and investigations at the site of the Byzantine Ecclesiastical Complex began in the early 1990's. Four stages of development have been revealed: pre-church use phases; a church complex constructed in the early to mid-fifth century A.D.; a major remodeling probably in the sixth century; and evidence of plans for another remodeling of that structure before its destruction by fire at the end of the sixth century.

Church with mosaics of the second phase.

Pierre Bikai observes excavations within the church.

Cleaning the mosaics in the Petra Church.

Suggested restoration of first phase church.

On December 5, 1993 fragments of burnt papyrus scrolls were discovered among ash in the northeast room of the Petra Church. Since then a rigorous and deliberate program of preservation, study, and preparation for publication has been underway. Both American and Finish scholars are participating in this work.

Deborah Kooring looks on as the scrolls are being excavated.

*A group of burnt scrolls **in situ**.*

Suggested restoration of the room where the scrolls were found, representing the phase before the scrolls were stored there.

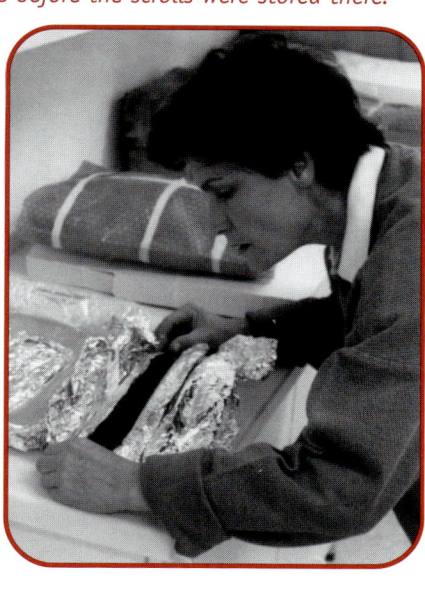

Conservator Catherine Vanlentour at work with scrolls in ACOR laboratory.

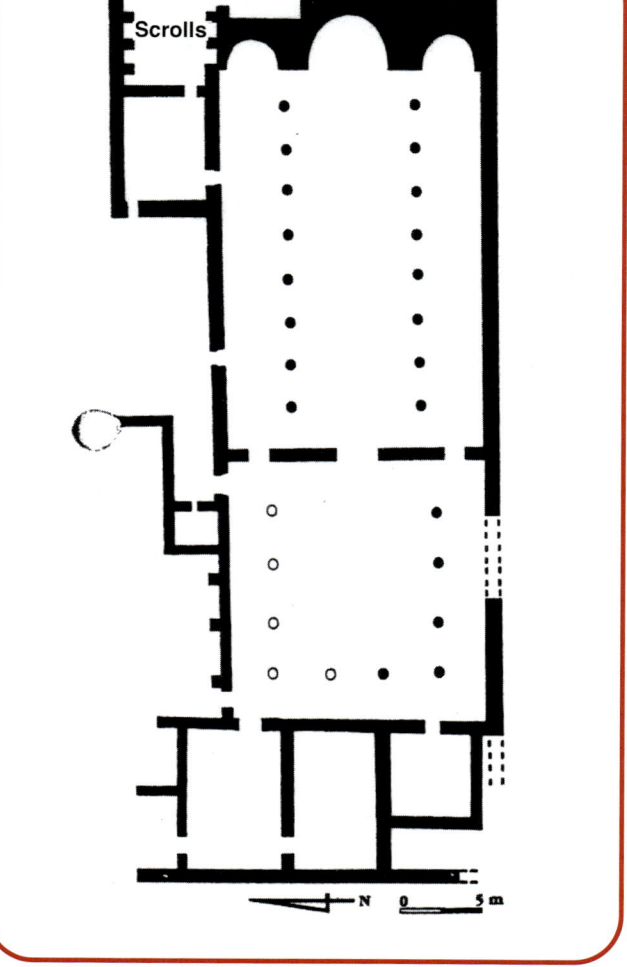

Plan locating the room where the scrolls were found.

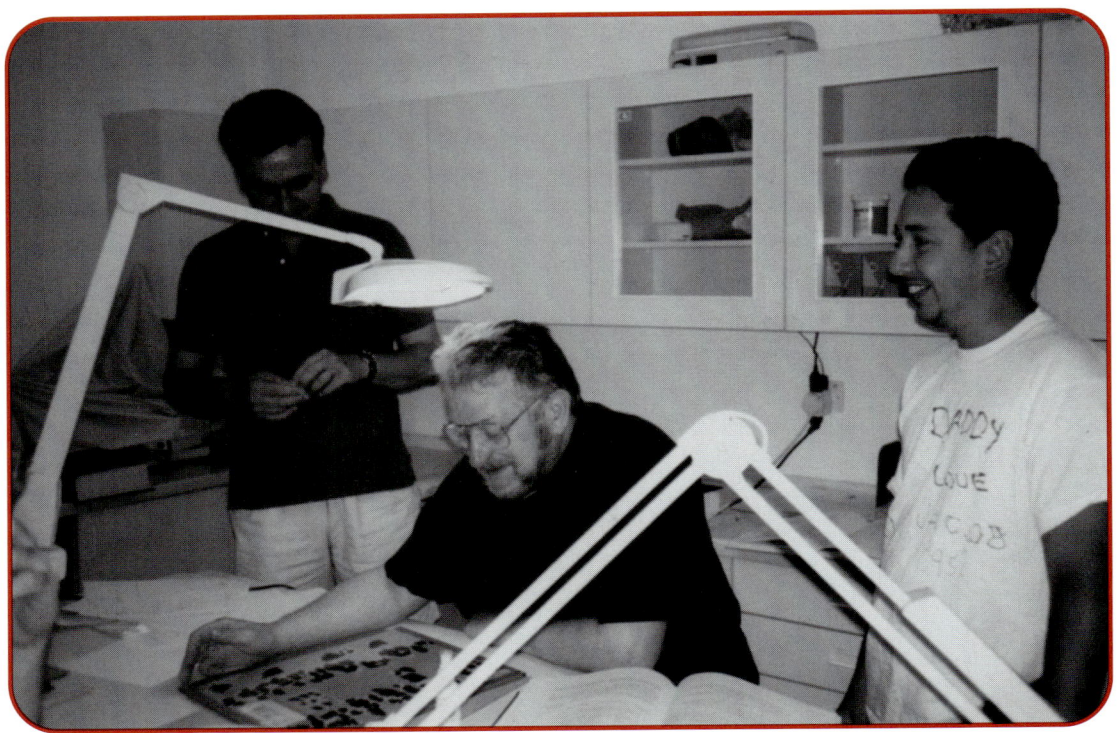

(left to right) Traiano Gagos, Ludwig Koenen, and Matthew Kraus in the ACOR Conservation Laboratory.

Robert W. Daniel of the American team.

Ludwig Koenen, from the University of Michigan, (left) head of the American scroll team, and Zbigniew Fiema, one of the excavators of the church.

A scroll with text that recalled King Hussein's peace efforts was named for the King and Queen: "Papyrus Petra H.M. King Hussein bin Talal and H.M. Queen Noor al-Hussein."

Jaakko Frösén, organizer and leader of the Finnish team for conservation of the scrolls. Frösén helped to obtain support for the conservation work in Finland.

Clem Kuehn explains to Queen Noor the high-tech resources available for the interpretation of the scrolls.

Steven Booras, with Omar Kamal (left) and Gene Ware (seated right) from Brigham Young University presenting scanning equipment for the scroll project. Looking on in the center (left to right) are Ghazi Bisheh, Pierre Bikai, Marjo Lehtinen, and Robert Daniel.

The Byzantine Church of St. George on Jebel Weibeh was excavated by Pierre Bikai in 1993. The house on the site now serves as a center for art, "Darat al-Funun" of the Shoman Foundation.

Pierre Bikai gives Her Majesty Queen Sofia of Spain a tour of the Church. Patricia Bikai is to the left, with Abdul Hameed Shoman on the right.

In 1995 Pierre Bikai received the Abdul Hameed Shoman Foundation Award "in recognition of his efforts and accomplishments" in conservation and culture preservation.

(left to right) Patricia and Pierre Bikai with Mr. Shoman.

ACOR: The ACOR Odyssey 1968–2000 — A History of the Americaan Center of Oriental Research by Nancy Lapp

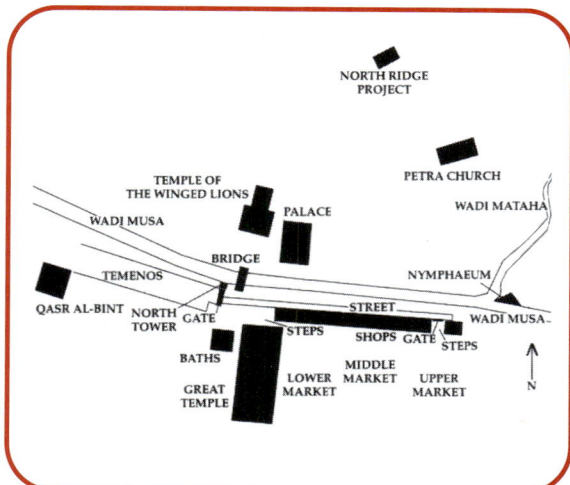

Schematic plan locating the Petra Church, the North Ridge Project, the Great Temple, and the Colonnaded Street and Shops.

Shelter over the church at Petra.

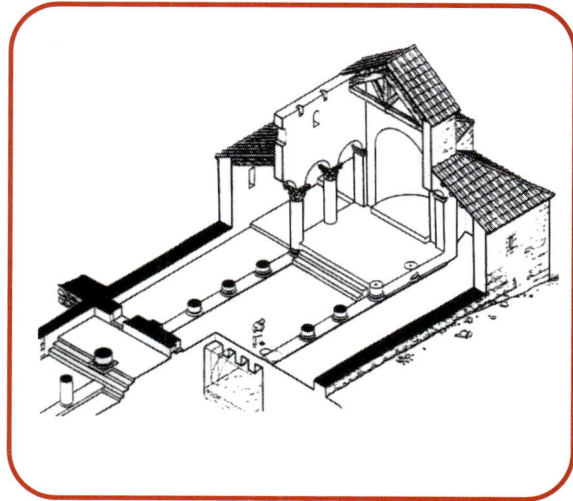

Line drawing of a projected restoration of the Ridge Church with the cistern below shown as a cutaway.

As the decade draws to a close ACOR related projects still continued at Petra. These include investigations of the North Ridge Church by Patricia Bikai, and the Great Temple project directed by Martha Joukowsky. A major endowment, provided ACOR by USAID in 1997, will assure the continuation of its efforts to further explore and preserve remains at the site well into the twenty-first century.

Her Majesty Queen Noor officially inaugurated the Petra Ecclesiastical Church on July 8, 1998. The site is now open to public view by visitors to Petra.

Her Majesty Queen Noor (left) visiting with Martha Sharp Joukowsky at the Great Temple Site. (MJ)

The Great Temple excavations directed by Martha Sharp Joukowsky re-erect a column in the Great Temple lower temenos triple colonnade. (MJ)

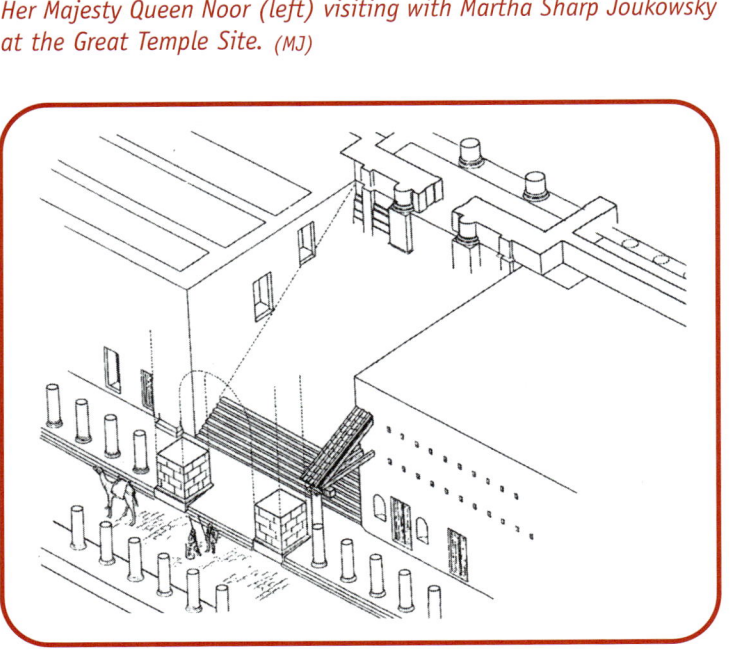

Line drawing of a projected restoration of the shops and steps leading down to the colonnaded street in front of the Great Temple.

In 1999 the ACOR Library included 12,918 volumes and around 12,000 individual journal numbers, plus an extensive map collection. The holdings include materials in Near Eastern archaeology, anthropology, Arabic language and culture, history and political science (especially Jordan and the region), history of art and architecture, geography, geology, and related studies.

The library reading and service areas with stacks in the background.

Librarian Humi Ayoubi at work.

The library stacks.

Through the decade of the 1990's ACOR has experience exponential growth. It provides services to an ever increasing population of research scholars and students. Significant during these years were the successful retirement of the mortgage debt on the new building and the initiation of a broad ranging program of other funding initiatives. A successful proposal in 1996 to the National Endowment for the Humanities for matching funds encouraged the generation of endowment support. Stimulated by a major lead gift from President Joukowsky the ACOR Board is now near the goal of completing this challenge program. As the century closes, ACOR's overall endowment, including over $1 million in the Petra fund for site investigation and preservation, is now in excess of $2.7 million.

Artemis A. W. Joukowsky (AJ)

Support for ACOR programs and activities throughout the 1990's continued to be provided in major portion through grants and contracts from USAID, USIA, U.S. Department of Education, NEH and other U.S. government sources, as well as by funds from private foundations; this support is largely through the efforts of Pierre and Patricia Bikai. In 1998 ACOR also received support contributions totaling $100,000 from ASOR, through the generosity of its Board Chairman P.E. MacAllister.

The successes of ACOR during this period are due in large part to the leadership provided by its President, Artemis A. W. Joukowsky. Artie's good business sense and ability to generate loyal support has provided a framework of confidence within which ACOR has pressed steadily forward.

Today ACOR looks to the twenty-first century with anticipation and hope. ACOR arrives at this juncture with a strong leadership team in place. It is expected that the scope of its support for archaeological research and other programs in Jordan will continue to expand. ACOR's 1994 Mission Statement provides a guiding vision for the coming decades.

ACOR
APPENDED LISTS

Officers

Board of Trustees

Staff

Appointees

Assisted Research Projects

Aquatic bird mosaic detail from the West Panel of the sixth century A.D. Hippolytus Hall in Madaba, Jordan.

ACOR Presidents 1970–2000

John H. Marks	1970–1978
Walter E. Rast	1978–1982
Gough W. Thompson, Jr.	1982–1986
Edgar C. Harrell	1986–1988
Robert A. Coughenour	1988–1991
James A. Sauer	1991–1992
Artemis A. W. Joukowsky	1992–

ACOR Directors 1968–2000

Rudolph H. Dornemann	1968–1969
Murray B. Nicol	1969–1970
Bastiaan Van Elderen	1970
Siegfried H. Horn	1970–1971
Henry O. Thompson	1971–1972
Bastiaan Van Elderen	1972–1974
James A. Sauer	1974 (Fall)
George Mendenhall	1975 (Spring)
James A. Sauer	1975–1981
David McCreery	1981–1988
Bert de Vries	1988–1991
Pierre Bikai	1991–

ACOR Officers (Current during 2000)

President	Aretmis A. W. Joukowsky
First Vice President	H.R.H. Ra'ad bin Zeid
Second Vice President	Lawrence T. Geraty
Secretary	Anne Ogilvy
Treasurer	Randolph Old

ACOR Staff (Current during 2000)

Director	Pierre Bikai
Associate Director	Patricia Bikai
Assistant Director (Amman)	Kurt Zamora
Assistant Director (Boston)	Donald Keller
Hostel Manager	Kathy Nimri
Accountant	Nisreen Shaikh
Chef	Mohammed Adawi
Procurement Manager	Sa'id Adawi
Facility Maintenance	Abed Adawi
Housekeeping	Vicki Libio
Housekeeping	Caesar Octavio
Librarian	Carmen Ayoubi
Assistant Librarian	Patricia Masri
Facility Maintenance Assistant & Night Manager	Hani Moussa

ACOR Board of Trustees (Members current during 2000)

Mohammed Asfour	Amman, Jordan
J. Carl Brown	Princeton University
Henry (Terry) Christensen III	New York, NY
Nicholas Clapp	Los Angeles, CA
Bert de Vries	Calvin College
Harold Forshey	Miami University of Ohio
Nancy (Nan) Frederick	West River, MD
Lawrence T. Geraty	La Sierra University
Sami Habayeb	Amman, Jordan
Donald O. Henry	University of Tulsa
Artemis A. W. Joukowsky	Brown University
Widad Kawar	Amman, Jordan
Oystein (Sten) S. LaBianca	Andrews University
Nancy Lapp	Pittsburgh Theological Seminary
Michel Marto	Amman, Jordan
Anne Ogilvy	Philadelphia, PA
Randolph Old	Severna Park, MD
John Oleson	University of Victoria
S. Thomas Parker	North Carolina State University
Gaetano Palumbo	Los Angeles, CA
Leila Sharaf	Amman, Jordan
Joe D. Seger ex officio	Mississippi State University
Neil A. Silberman	Branford, CT
James Wiseman	Boston University
H. R. H. Ra'ad bin Zeid	Amman, Jordan
Judy Zimmerman	Camas, WA

Khirbet Salameh opposite ACOR.

ACOR Offices

In the United States:

ACOR
at Boston University
656 Beacon Street, Fifth Floor
Boston, MA 02215-2010

Phone: 617 353 6571
Fax: 617 353 6575
E-mail: acor@bu.edu
Web address: www.bu.edu/acor

In Jordan

ACOR
P.O. B. 2470
Amman 11181
Jordan

Phone: 962 6 534 6117
Fax: 962 6 534 4181
E-mail: acor@go.com.jo

ACOR Appointees 1971–2000

Academic Year	Number Per Year
1971–72	1
1972–73	1
1977–78	1
1978–79	1
1979–80	1
1980–81	5
1981–82	3
1982–83	4
1983–84	5
1984–85	5
1985–86	4
1986–87	3
1987–88	5
1988–89	2
1989–90	6
1990–91	1
1991–92	14
1992–93	25
1993–94	20
1994–95	36
1995–96	28
1996–97	28
1997–98	17
1998–99	22
1999–2000	19

ACOR Appointees 1971–2000

Abreviations for Fellowships

ASOR/W. F. Albright	ASOR W. F. Albright
NEH	National Endowment for the Humanities
ASAIP	Arabic Speaking Academic Immersion Program, Mellon Foundation
USIA	United States Information Agency
NMERTP	Near and Middle East Research Training Program
NMERTP Pre	NMERTP Pre-Doctoral
NMERTP Pst	NMERTP Post-Doctoral
NMERTP Sr	NMERTP Senior Research
NMERTP Ed	NMERTP Senior Educator
Groot	Jennifer C. Groot
Harrell	Harrell Family
Russell	Kenneth W. Russell
Bikai	Pierre and Patricia Bakai

Appointees

(* denotes Fellowship used in the U. S.)

Linah Ababneh	1998–99	Russell
Linda Adams	1992–93	USIA
Erin H. Addison	1994–95	NMERTP Pst
Fida Adely	1994–95	ASAIP
Marie Alanen	1993–94	USIA
Nicholas Alexander	1992–93	USIA
Michael Alcorn	1985–86	Shell
Betty S. Anderson	1994–95	USIA
John W. Anderson	1999–2000	NMERT Pst
Sharon K. Araji	1994–95	NMERTP Pst
Robin Armstrong	1998–99	Groot
Najma Bachelani	1994–95	NMERTP Pre
Salman el-Badour	1992–93	ASAIP *
Edward Banning	1981–82	ASOR/W.F. Albright
Deirdre Grace Barrett	1999–2000	Bikai
Valerie Batt	1999–2000	Groot
Elizabeth Anne Beal	1994–95	NMERTP Pre
Leigh-Ann Bedal	1998–99	NMERTP Pre
Amy Bentley	1993–94	ASAIP
Thomas Berger	1996–97	USIA
Robert G. Boling	1984–85	NEH
	1994–95	USIA
Michelle Bonogofsky	1997–98	NMERTP Pre
Karen Brostad	1998–99	USIA
Bruce Borthwick	1993–94	ASAIP
	1997–98	NMERTP Sr
Laurie Brand	1992–94	USIA
Colin Brooker	1986–87	NEH

Michaelle Browers	1997–98	NMERTP Pre
Brian Brown	1997–98	Groot
Carl Brown	1991–92	ASAIP
Robin M. Brown	1986–87	ASOR/W.F. Albright
	1987–88	Teagle
G. Wesley Burnett	1995–96	USIA
Brian F. Byrd	1984–85	Shell
	1987–88	NEH
Frederic Cadora	1991–93	ASAIP
Louise Cainkar	1994–95	USIA
Robert Caldwell	1998–99	NMERTP Pre
Campion Carruthers	1998–99	Harrell
Patricia Carter	1997–98	NMERTP Sr
David Clark	1996–97	NMERTP Pre
Douglas Clark	1998–99	NMERTP Sr
Vincent A. Clark	1979–80	ASOR/W.F. Albright
Nancy Coffin	1994–95	ASAIP
Nancy R. Coinman	1999–2000	USIA
Nora Ann Colton	1994–95	USIA
Douglas C. Comer	1999–2000	NMERTP Pst
Charlene Constable	1992–93	ASAIP
Julia Costello	1993–94	USIA
John Creed	1994–95	USIA
Karla J. Cunningham	1994–95	NMERTP Pre
Robert Daniel	1996–97	NMERTP Sr
Bryan Daves	1996–97	USIA
Caroline Davies	1995–96	USIA
Rochelle Anne Davis	1996–97	USIA
James Deemer	1988–89	NEH
John Dekle	1999–2000	Groot
Owen Dickens	1994–95	NMERTP Pst
Benjamin Dolinka	1998–99	NMERTP Pre
Beshara Doumani	1995–96	NMERTP Sr
Dinnine Dudley	1992–93	Groot
Edith A. Dunn	1992–93	USIA
	1996–97	Russell
Jennie R. Ebeling	1999–2000	USIA
Patricia L. Fall	1989–90	ASOR/W.F. Albright
Joy Lehman Farmer	1997–98	USIA
Zbigniew Fiema	1991–92	USIA
	1993–94	USIA
	1995–96	NMERTP Sr
Brian Fitzgerald	1992–93	USIA
James W. Flanagan	1980–81	NEH
Ellen Fleischmann	1998–99	NEH

Paula Flemming	1995–96	NMERTP Pst
Rebecca Foote	1991–92	ASOR/W.F. Albright
	1999–2000	NMERTP Pst
Carol Frey	1996–97	Groot
Timothy Gianotti	1992–93	ASAIP
	1995–96	USIA
James L. Gillespie	1994–95	NMERTP Pst
Elizabeth Gittings	1996–97	NMERTP Pre
Robert L. Gordon	1980–81	NEH
David F. Graf	1980–81	NEH
Andrew J. Graham	1999–2000	Harrell
Joseph A. Greene	1985–86	NEH
Scott Greenwood	1995–96	USIA
Jay Guikema	1991–92	USIA
Mohammed Hafez	1998–99	USIA
Cathlene Hanaman	1994–95	NMERTP Pre
Julie Hansen	1995–96	NMERTP Sr
David Harris	1993–94	ASAIP
Timothy Harrison	1992–93	USIA
	1996–97	NMERTP Sr
Benjamin Hartsell	1989–90	Groot
Sarah Harvey	1996–97	USIA
Waleed Hazbun	1997–98	USIA
Donald O. Henry	1983–84	NEH
Elizabeth Hess-Almubarak	1993–94	USIA
James Hill	1998–99	NMERTP Pre
Michael Homan	1998–99	USIA
Russell Hopley	1991–92	ASAIP
Najib Hourani	1997–98	NMERTP Pre
Angela Hummel	1995–96	Groot
Stephen Infantino	1995–96	NMERTP Pst
Linda Jacobs	1981–82	NEH
David M. Jacobson	1983–84	Shell
Kimberly Katz	1996–97	USIA
Marion Katz	1992–93	ASAIP
Marjorie Kelly	1994–95	USIA
Ellen Kenney	1998–99	Kress
Fawwaz Khraysheh	1993–94	USIA*
Lynn Killean	1991–93	ASAIP
	1992–93	USIA
Janet King	1993–94	Groot
Barbara Kingsley	1994–95	NMERTP Pre
Ronald Kirkwood	1995–96	NMERTP Ed
Frank L. Koucky	1987–88	NEH
Clement Kuehn	1995–96	NMERTP Sr

Dmytro Roman Kulchitsky	1999–2000	NMERTP Pre
Oystein LaBianca	1980–81	ASOR/W.F. Albright
	1989–90	NEH
Andrea Lane	1988–89	Teagle
Eric Lapp	1992–93	USIA
Nancy Lapp	1986–87	NEH
Cherie Lenzen	1982–83	ASOR/W.F. Albright
	1984–85	NEH
Albert Leonard, Jr.	1981–82	NEH
	1984–85	NEH
Elizabeth Pollard Lisi	1994–95	Groot
Jesse C. Long, Jr.	1994–95	NMERTP Pst
Kelly Lowe	1991–92	Groot
Sherry Lowrance	1995–96	USIA
Russell Lucas	1997–98	USIA
Ellen Lust-Okar	1996–97	USIA
Mark Lynch	1994–95	USIA
Jonathan Mabry	1987–88	Shell
Burton MacDonald	1991–92	Dodge
Abdo Malki	1992–93	USIA
Zeid el-Mannouri	1991–92	ASAIP *
Fatma Marii	1993–94	Russell
Donka Markus	1997–98	NMERTP Pre
Gerald L. Mattingly	1982–83	NEH
Jan McAuliffeq	1993–94	ASAIP
Joseph McClain	1998–99	Groot
David McCreery	1977–78	ASOR/W.F. Albright
Robin McGrew-Zoubi	1996–97	NMERTP Pst
David Mehall	1991–92	ASAIP
William Mierse	1996–97	NMERTP Pst
Doris Miller	1985–86	NEH
Judith Mitchell	1992–93	Groot
Mansoon Moaddel	1996–97	NMERTP Sr
Amiya Mohanty	1996–97	NMERTP Sr
Pete Moore	1995–96	NMERTP Pre
Maggi Morehouse	1994–95	NMERTP Pre
Nihad al-Musa	1992–93	USIA
Maysoon Al-Nahar	1996–97	Harrell
Stefanie E. Nanes	1999–2000	NMERTP Pre
Michael Neely	1992–93	USIA
	1998–99	USIA
Melissa N.C. Nevillis	1999–2000	Groot
Alan Olson	1996–97	NMERTP Pre
Thomas Paradise	1992–93	USIA
	1996–97	NMERTP Pst
Andrew J. Parasiliti	1994–95	NMERTP Pre

	1995–96	USIA
Christopher Parker	1999–2000	USIA
S. Thomas Parker	1982–83	NEH
Megan A. Perry	1993–94	Groot
	1994–95	NMERTP Pre
	1997–98	USIA
Glen Peterman	1989–90	Teagle
	1991–92	USIA
Jane Peterson	1992–93	USIA
	1998–99	USIA
Joseph Pimentel	1993–94	ASAIP
Anne Pirie	1996–97	NMERTP Pre
Phillip Posey	1995–96	NMERTP Pst
David Priess	1995–96	NMERTP Pre
Joseph Purello	1994–95	NMERTP Pre
	1995–96	USIA
Leslie Quintero	1998–99	USIA
Albert Randall	1994–95	NMERTP Pst
Walter Rast	1983–84	NEH
Christian Rata	1997–98	Groot
Carol A. Redmount	1989–90	Shell
David S. Reese	1983–84	Shell
Mary Barbara Reeves	1995–96	Groot
Michael Reimer	1996–97	NMERTP Sr
Charles Reineke	1997–98	NMERTP Pre
Alexandra Retzleff	1998–99	Kress
Suzanne Richard	1984–85	NEH
Pauline Ripat	1996–97	Groot
John Roberts	1992–93	USIA
Leonard Robinson	1996–97	NMERTP Pre
Marie-Jeanne Roche	1992–93	Dodge
Tori I. Rohl	1999–2000	NMERTP Pre
Gary O. Rollefson	1978–79	ASOR/W.F. Albright
	1980–81	NEH
	1998–99	NEH
Robert Rook	1994–95	NMERTP Pre
Bruce Routledge	1993–94	Winnett
Yorke M. Rowan	1994–95	USIA
Kenneth W. Russell	1989–90	NEH
Ahmed Sadri	1996–97	NMERTP Pst
Benjamen Saidel	1997–98	USIA
James A. Sauer	1971–72	ASOR/W.F. Albright
Sandra Scham	1995–96	USIA

R. Thomas Schaub	1982–83	NEH
Robert Schick	1987–88	Shell
	1993–94	USIA
Erika Schluntz	1997–98	Kress
Denise Schmandt-Besserat	1994–95	USIA
	1996–97	NMERTP Sr
Ingrid Schneider	1995–96	USIA
Irfan Shahid	1993–94	USIA
Trent Shipley	1996–97	NMERTP Pre
Andrew Shryock	1997–98	NEH
Gwendolyn Simmons	1995–96	NMERTP Pre
Steven R. Simms	1994–95	USIA
Ranjit Singh	1991–92	ASAIP
	1999–2000	NMERTP Pre
Susan Slyomovics	1993–94	USIA
Andrew M. Smith II	1992–93	USIA
	1994–95	USIA
	1998–99	USIA
Susan Smith	1999–2000	USIA
Beatrice St. Laurent	1994–95	USIA
Cheryl S. Steele	1994–95	NMERTP Pre
Alan Harris Stein	1994–95	NMERTP Pre
Elizabeth A. Stephens	1994–95	Groot
Richard Stephenson	1995–96	NMERTP Pst
Suzanne Stetkevych	1983–84	NEH
Brenda Strickland	1990–91	Groot
Eric Thompson	1995–96	NMERTP Pre
Lara G. Tohme	1999–2000	Kress
Sara Toomajian	1991–92	USIA
William Turpen	1995–96	NMERTP Ed
Jeffrey VanDenBerg	1995–96	NMERTP Pre
Susan Gail Vander Heide	1994–95	USIA
Bert de Vries	1972–73	ASOR/W.F. Albright
Bethany Walker	1999–2000	NEH
Peter Warnock	1992–94	USIA
Catherine Warrick	1997–98	USIA
Timothy Werner	1993–94	ASAIP
Sarah E. Whitcher	1999–2000	Russell
Donald Whitcomb	1985–86	NEH
Quintan Wiktorowicz	1996–97	NMERTP Pre
Allison Wilke	1996–97	USIA
Philip Wilke	1998–99	NMERTP Sr
Charles Wilkins	1995–96	USIA
Warren Wood	1998–99	Groot
Elise G. Young	1994–95	USIA

ACOR Assisted Archaeological Projects

(DAJ — Department of Antiquities of Jordan; USAID — United State Agency for International Development
CRM — Cultural Resource Management   *Indicates ASOR/CAP affiliation)

1968–73	*Tall Hisban	Siegfried Horn	Andrews University
1968	Amman Citadel	Rudolph Dornemann	ACOR
		Saffwan Tell	DAJ
		Aida Suliman	University of Jordan
		Fawzi el Fakhrani	University of Jordan
1969	Rujm el-Malfuf	Roger Boraas	Upsala College
1970	Swafiyeh	Bastiaan Van Elderen	ACOR/DAJ
1971	Tell Masuh	Bastiaan Van Elderen	ACOR/DAJ
1972	Khirbat el-Hajjar	Henry Thompson	ACOR/DAJ
1972–	*Umm el-Jimal	Bert de Vries	Calvin College
1972–73	Tell Siran	Henry Thompson	ACOR/University of Jordan
1973–76	*Tall Hisban	Lawrence T. Geraty	Andrews University
1973	Rujm el-Malfuf South	Henry Thompson	ACOR/DAJ
1973–	*Dead Sea Plain Project	Walter Rast	Valparaiso University
		R. Thomas Schaub	Indiana University of Pennsylvania
1975–76	Jordan Valley Survey	James Sauer	ACOR/University of Jordan
		Khair Yassine	
		Mo'awiya Ibrahim	
1976	Abu Thawwab	Robert Coughenour	ACOR/Western Seminary
1976*	Araq el-Emir	Robin Brown	ACOR
1976	Khilda	James Sauer	ACOR/University of Jordan
1976–79	*Wadi Wardeh Excavation	Robert Coughenour	ACOR/Western Seminary
1976–89	*Limes Arabicus Project	S. Thomas Parker	North Carolina State University
1977–83	*Numeira	Michael Coogan	Harvard University
1977	*Amman Airport	Larry Herr	Andrews University
		Lawrence Geraty	
1977–79	*South Ghor Survey	David McCreery	ACOR-USAID
1977–81	*Ras en-Naqb Survey	Donald Henry	University of Tulsa
1977–78 1980–81	Jebel el-Hawayah, Jebel El-Qesir	Patrick McGovern	University of Pennsylvania
1978*	Baq'ah Valley Project	Patrick McGovern	University of Pennsylvania
1978–79	*Yarmuk Project	John Lundquist	Brigham Young University
1978–82	*Kerak Plateau Survey	Maxwell Miller	Emory University
		Jack M. Pinkerton	
1979–80	*Wadi Hisma Survey	David Graf	ACOR
1979–81	*Qasr Kharana Architectural Survey	Stephen K. Urice	Harvard University
1979–84	*Wadi el-Hasa Survey	Burton MacDonald	St. Francis Xavier University

1979–89	*Pella	Robert Smith	Wooster College
		Basil Hennessey	University of Sydney
1980	Rujm el-Henu East/West	Patrick McGovern	University of Pennsylvania
1980–81, 1986	Khirbet Um ed-Dananir	Patrick McGovern	University of Pennsylvania
1980–82	*'Ain el-Assad	Gary Rollefson	ACOR
1980–81	*Tell edh-Dhahab el-Gharibi	Robert Gordon	ACOR/DAJ
1982–95	*Tell Abila	Harold Mare	Covenant Seminary
1981–95	*Wadi Ziqlab Survey	Ted Banning	University of Toronto
1981–	*Humeima	John Oleson	University of Victoria
1981	*Jordan Valley Village Project	J. Jones	Arizona State University
		Steve Falcones	
		Pat Fall	
1981–82	Wadi Bayir Survey	Scott Rolston	ASOR
1981–82	Um ed-Dananir	Patrick McGovern	University of Pennsylvania
1981–92	*Kataret es-Samra	Albert Leonard, Jr.	University of Missouri
1982–87	*Khirbet Iskander	Susanne Richard	Drew University
1982–	*Tell Safut	Donald Wimmer	Seton Hall University
1982	Wadi Isal Survey	Linda Jacobs	ACOR
1982–	*'Ain Ghazal	Gary Rollefson	San Diego State University 'Ain Ghazal Institute
		Albert Leonard, Jr.	University of Arizona
		Alan Simmons	University of Nevada at Las Vegas
		Zeidan Kafafi	Yarmouk University
1982–86	*Tell el-Hayyat	William G. Dever	University of Arizona
		Steve Falconer	
		Bonnie Gardiner	
1983–87	*Humayma Region Survey	John W. Eadie	
1983–84	*Irbid/Beit Ras Survey and Excavations	Cherie Lenzen	ACOR
1983–95	Aqaba/Ayla	Donald Whitcomb	University of Chicago/ ACOR-USAID/DAJ
1984–	*Madaba Plains Project	Lawrence T. Geraty	Andrews University LaSierra University
	*Tall Hisban	Oystein S. LaBianca	Andrews Univeristy
	*Tall al-'Umayri	Larry G. Herr	Canadian Union College
	*'Umayri Survey	Gary Christopherson	University of Arizona
		Douglas R. Clark	Walla Walla College
	*Tall Julul	Randall W. Younker	Andrews University
	*Tall Jawa (1989)	Michele Daviau	Wilfred Laurier University
1984–93	*Wadi el-Hasa Paleolithic Project	Geoffrey Clark	Arizona State Univeristy
1985, 1996–97	*Tell Abu en-Ni'aj	Steve Falconer	University of Arizona
		Bonnie Gardiner	
1985	*Tafila-Busayra Archaeological Survey	Burton MacDonald	St. Francis Xavier University

1985–86	*Southern Ghor and Northeast Arabah Survey	Burton MacDonald	St. Francis Xavier University
1985–86	*Jerash Mapping Project	Carol A. Meyer	University of Chicago
1985	Khirbet Salameh	Cherie Lensen Allison McQuitty	ACOR/University of Jordan
1986	Wadi Kafranja Survey	Joseph Greene	ACOR
1986–91	Petra Ethnoarchaeological Project	Kenneth Russell	ACOR
1986	Shobak Castle	Robin Brown	SUNY Binghamton
1986	Naur Survey	Robert Coughenour	ACOR-USAID
1986	al Qesir	Patrick McGovern	University of Pennsylvania
1987	al-Wueira	Robin Brown	SUNY Binghamton
1987	Kerak Castle	Robin Brown	SUNY Binghamton
1987	Amman Citadel Salvage Excavations	Joseph Green Mohammed Najjar	ACOR-USAID/DAJ/CRM
1987–92	*Wadi el Yabis Survey and Excavations	Jonathan Mabry Gaetano Plaumbo	University of Arizona University of Rome
1987–94	Cultural Resources Management Project	Joseph Greene Khairieh 'Amri Ernesta Kraszkiewicz Ruba Kana'an Cynthia Shartzer Gaetano Palumbo	ACOR-USAID/DAJ
1988	Tor Hamar	Donald Henry	University of Tulsa
1988	Greater Amman Survey	Joseph Greene Abdul-Samaía Abu-Dayyah	ACOR-USAID/DAJ/CRM
1988–89	*Wadi Shu'eib	Alan Simmons Gary Rolleffson Zidan Kafafi	Desert Research Institute Yarmuk University
1988	Wadi Shu'eib Survey	Karen Wright	Yale University
1988	Tell Handaquq	Jonathan Mabry Ian Kuijt Meredith Chesson	ACOR Harvard University
1989–	*Tell Nimrin	David McCreery James Flanagan	Willamette University Case Western Reserve
1990–95	*Tell Jawa	Michele Daviau	Willfred Laurier University
1989–91	Iraq ed-Dubb	Ian Kuijt	Harvard University
1989–90	Amman Citadel - 'Ain Ghazal Feasibility	Rudolph Dornemann	ACOR-USAID/CRM/ University of Jordan
1990–	Temple of Hercules	Rudolph Dornemann Khair Yassine Mohammed Najjar Kenneth Russell C. Kannellopoulos Anthi Koutsoukou Pierre Bikai	ACOR University of Jordan DAJ ACOR-USAID/ Ministry of Tourism and Antiquities ACOR

1991–	Madaba Archaeological Park Project	Michele Piccirillo Cheri Lenzen Ghazi Bisheh Ammar Khammash Timothy Harrison Pierre Bikai Leen Fakhoury	ACOR-USAID/Ministry of Tourism and Antiquities
1991–	*Kerak Regional Project	Gerald Mattingly	Johnson Bible College
1991–94	*Abu Hudhud/Wadi el-Hasa	Gary Rolleffson	'Ain Ghazal Institute
1992–	Petra Church Project	Kenneth Russell Pierre Bikai Zbigniew Fiema Robert Schick Khairieh 'Amr C. Kanallopoulos Robert Shutler	ACOR-USAID/DAJ/Ministry of Tourism and Antiquities
1992	Jerash Road Roman Fort Emergency Excavation	Gaetano Palumbo Ali Musa	ACOR-USAID/DAJ/CRM
1992	Tuwaneh Survey	Zbigniew Fiema	ACOR-USIA
1992–93	Balloon Project	J. W. and E. Meyers	ACOR/Ministry of Tourism
1992–94	Khirbet Salameh	Pierre Bikai	ACOR/University of Jordan
1992–94	*Wadi al-Heidan Survey	Glen L. Peterman	
1993	Tor Faraj	Donald O. Henry	University of Tulsa
1993	Tell Handaquq South	Meredith Chesson Ian Kuijt	Harvard University
1993	Khirbet et-Tannur	Marie-Jeanne Roche	ACOR
1993–94	*Levantine Mousterian Project	Donald Henry	University of Tulsa
1993–	*Petra Great Temple Project	Martha Joukowsky	Brown University
1993	Tell Madaba Archaeological Survey	Timothy Harrison	Unversity of Chicago
1993–94	Jebel al-Webdeh, Church of St. George	Pierre Bikai	ACOR/Shoman Foundation
1994	Qatrana Master Plan	Leen Fakhoury	ACOR-USAID/Ministry of Tourism and Antiquity
1994	Um er-Rasas Archaeological Park	Michele Picarillo	USAID/Ministry of Tourism and Antiquities
1994	*Via Militaris in Arabia	David Graf Fawzi Zayadine	University of Miami
1994–	*Khirbet Iskander	Suzanne Richard Jesse Long	Gannon University Lubbock Christian University
1994–	Lehun	Denyse Homes-Fredericq	Vrije Universiteit Brussels
1994–98	Southern Arabah Regional Survey	Andrew W. Smith	University of Maryland
1995–	Petra Roman Streets and Shops	C. Kanallopoulos Zbigniew Fiema	ACOR-USAID/Ministry of Tourism and Antiquities
1995–	Petra North Ridge Project	Patricia Bikai	ACOR-USAID

1995–	Petra Mapping Project	Pierre Bikai Patricia Bikai	ACOR-USAID/Hashemite University
1995–	Petra Papyrus Project	Pierre Bikai Ludwig Koenen Jaakko Frosen	ACOR University of Michigan University of Helsinki
1995	Petra Ethnoarchaeological Project	Steve Simms	ACOR
1995	Deir 'Ain Abata/Lot's Cave Conservation Project	Konstantinos Politis Pierre Bikai	ACOR-USAID/Ministry of Tourism and Antiquities
1995–96	Jasr el-Bint	Pierre Bikai	ACOR-USAID/Ministry of Tourism and Antiquities
1995–96	Ayyubid Tower Restoration	Antoni Ostrasz	ACOR-USAID/ Ministry of Tourism and Antiquities
1996–	*Wadi ath-Thamad Survey	Michele Daviau	Wilfrid Laurier University
1996	*Wadi Ramm Recovery Project	Dennine Dudley Barbare Reeves Vicki Karas	University of Victoria
1996–	*Tell Madaba Excavations	Timothy Harrison	University of Toronto
1996–	*Aqaba/Ayla	S. Thomas Parker	North Carolina State University
1996–	*Wadi Feinan (Ghwair)	Alan Simmons Mohammad al-Najjar	University of Nevada at Las Vegas/DAJ
1996–	*Khirbat al-Mudayna	Michele Daviau	Wilfred Laurier University
1996–97	Mafraq District Bioarchaeological	Jerry Rose Mohammad al-Najjar	University of Arkansas Yarmouk University of Sa'ad
1997–	Eastern Hasa Late Pleistocene Project	Nancy Coinman Deborah Olszewski	Iowa State University Bishop Museum
1997–	*Wadi Fidan Archaeological Project	Tom Levy Russell Adams	University of California-San Diego University of Sheffield
1997	Wadi Arabia Earthquake Project	Tina Niemi	University of Missouri
1997	Cartigraphical and Computerizing Research around Jebal Harun	Jaako Frosen	Academy of Finland
1997	Dhban Plateau Regional Survey	Chang Ho C. Ji	Andrews University
1997	Kerak Castle	Jack Lee	St. John Fisher College
1997–	*Bir Madkhur Excavation and Survey	Megan Perry Andrew M. Smith II	University of New Mexico University of Maryland
1997	Azraq Wetlands Prehistory and Paleoenvironmental Project	Richard Watson Rusty Low Douglas Schnurrenberger	San Juan College
1998	*South Arabah Survey	Donald O. Henry	University of Tulsa
1998–	Qastal	Erin Addison Stefania Dodoni	Hollins College
1998	Tell es-Saad	J. C. Ross	ACOR

1998–	Bawwah el-Ghazal	Leslie Quintero Gary Rollefson Philip Wilke	University of California - Riverside
1998*	Khirbet Muday Nat'aliya	Bruce Routledge	University of Pennsylvania
1998–	*Ghwair I	Alan Simmons Mohammad Najjar	University of Nevada at Las Vegas
1999	*Bioarchaeology of Byzantine of North Jordan	Jerry Rose	University of Arkansas
1999–	*Archaeology and Environment of the Dead Sea Plain	P. Edwards Steve Falconer Pat Fall P. Macumber	Arizona State University
1999–	*Middle Paleolithic of Northwest Jordan	J. J. Shea	SUNY Stony Brook
2000–	*'Ain Abu Nekheileh	Donald O. Henry	University of Tulsa

Roosters with an amphora mosiac panel from the sixth century A.D. in the Chapel of the Martyr Theodore in the Cathedral in Madaba, Jordan.

CAARI
The House of the Dancing Bird
A History of the
CYPRUS AMERICAN
ARCHAEOLOGICAL RESEARCH INSTITUTE
Nicosia, Cyprus

by Stuart Swiny

1978–2000

Authors Preface

The CAARI "Dancing Bird" logo was adapted by me from a Cypriot "Free Field" vase of Iron Age date early in my term as director and received ready acceptance by the CAARI trustees. The "Free Field" style of decorating vessels with human, animal, avian or vegetable motifs displays the uniquely Cypriot ability to blend traits from foreign and indigenous artistic traditions into an harmonious whole. The logo is thus an apt reminder of both Cypriot history and the CAARI mission. The image is of a wading bird, a type that frequents the seashore to hunt for fish in the shallows. The original version, from a vase now in the Cyprus museum, had a fish dangling on its beak. I believe that "The House of the Dancing Bird" thus provides a good title for this celebration of CAARI's establishment and early history.

Credits

Work in preparation of this section on the history of CAARI was assisted by the cooperation of Nancy Serwint who was Director of the Institute at the time when the manuscript was being prepared. Her help in providing access to the Institute's photographic archives is gratefully acknowledged. The special consideration of Vath-oulla Moustoukki for lending several unique photographs from the "Cast of CAARI" board in her office also deserves mention. With one exception all photographs reproduced here either come from the archives at the Institute or belong to the author. Ellen Herscher is to be thanked for providing the second to last picture of President Oliver and Director Merrillees. Robert Merrillees, Andrew Oliver and David Dietrich are likewise to be thank-ed for their assistance in providing the lists and materials included in the several appendices. Last but not least, the good help of Lydie Shufro, who, like in the old days, worked with the author on editing the final draft, is most gratefully acknowledged.

CAARI
The House of the Dancing Bird
A History of the Cyprus American Archaeological Research Institute
Nicosia, Cyprus
1978–2000

by Stuart Swiny

Throughout recorded history the island of Cyprus has played a politically marginal, but economically and strategically central position in Near Eastern affairs. Indeed, as perceptively noted by the German archaeologist Gustav Hirschfeld in 1880,

He who would become and remain a great power in the East must hold Cyprus in his hand(Deutsche Rundschau, XXIII, 1880:270).

This statement certainly holds true from the fourteenth century B.C. to the close of the twentieth century A.D., so much so that the dust jacket of the first volume of Sir George Hill's monumental work, *A History of Cyprus* published in 1940, proclaimed with little exaggeration "that the story of Cyprus, resolves itself, in some degree, into the story of the comings and goings of its colonists and conquerors." These words, which just happened to appear the year before the fall of Crete to Axis paratroopers, proved to be only too true in terms of real-politic, and the island braced itself for a German onslaught. But that never came. Had Cyprus been taken, the history of the island in particular, and the Middle East in general would have followed a very different course these last fifty years. Throughout the era of the Cold War, and during the Gulf War in 1991, Cyprus remained an important player in the region, like a giant, unsinkable aircraft carrier with all the rich human drama expected of a multiracial, multicultural crew. Today it harbors new interests of Russian and Balkan origin. Tomorrow? Who knows? But one fact is certain, Cyprus will remain, as it has since the dawn of history, a vibrant player in the eastern Mediterranean community of nations.

Early Explorations in Cypriot Archaeology

Archaeological exploration on the island goes back to the mid nineteenth century when French scholars first showed an interest in the distinctly Greek style of sculpture with its intriguing Near Eastern and Egyptian traits. But systematic investigation of ancient Cypriot cultures only began in the 1920s with the arrival of the Swedish Cyprus Expedition led by Einar Gjerstad. Work prior to this had mostly involved antiquarians digging for objects of either artistic or monetary value. This was particularly notable in the late Ottoman period when the brothers Louis and Alexander di Cesnola were active. These depredations of the island's cultural heritage provided abundant Cypriot antiquities for display in the great museums of the world, but did little to foster interest in the island's past for its own sake. Cypriot art was viewed primarily as a provincial imitation of a superior Aegean culture. Thus the need for a "School of Cypriot Studies" modeled on those European or American establishments in Athens, Jerusalem or Baghdad never arose.

Prior to the establishment of the Cyprus Republic in 1960, the Swedes seem to have been content with renting houses wherever they worked; only the American expedition sponsored by the University of Pennsylvannia at Kourion built a dig house at Episkopi and the French built one at Enkomi. In the wake of independence others would follow with French and Canadian missions investing in permanent premises at Salamis and Soli. After the Episkopi-based University of Missouri's excavation was interrupted by the EOKA (National Organization of Cypriot Fighters) struggle for union with Greece in 1955, the first American team to resume excavations was the University of Pennsylvania's Kyrenia shipwreck project in 1968. The following year Paul Lapp of the Pittsburgh Theological Seminary visited the island with a brief to establish a joint ASOR/University at Albany expedition to ancient Idalion. We met at the Cyprus Museum and he engaged me to deal with Late Bronze and Iron Age ceramics about which I had acquired good first-hand knowledge while working with Claude Schaeffer at Enkomi and Vassos Karageorghis at Kition. It was, tragically, to be our only meeting, since on his next visit to start up work at Idalion in the early summer of 1970 he drowned in a swimming accident near Kyrenia.

Expanding American Interests in the 1970s

From 1964 onwards, thanks to the enlightened policies of the Department of Antiquities, directed by Vassos Karageorghis, the number of foreign teams investigating the island's archaeological sites grew steadily, peaking at twenty in 1974. Six of these were American, including the Idalion Expedition sponsored by the American Schools of Oriental Research.

How then had ASOR, with its traditional focus of the lands of the Bible, become involved with Cyprus? In fact the religious connection between the two areas is strong. After all, thanks to the mission of St. Paul and St. Barnabas, Cyprus became the first province known to be governed by a Christian when the Roman governor, Proconsul Sergius Paulus, converted. So Cyprus certainly falls within the general sphere of ASOR interests. Despite the presence of so many excavations, the necessity for a foreign school or center was not considered until its need became evident to George Ernest Wright, President of ASOR and Director of the Idalion project. As a result, he proposed to establish the "East Mediterranean Institute of Archaeological Research" on the island. But again, destiny intervened. The July 1974 Coup d'Etat leading to the overthrow of President Makarios and the ensuing Turkish invasion resulting in the division of the island, as well as Wright's sudden death in August, caused all plans for a school to be abandoned.

New Initiatives for a Cyprus Center 1978

The American Schools of Oriental Research had weathered other storms of equal magnitude in the past, and three years later a revitalized organization, under the Presidency of Philip J. King, reconsidered its Cypriot options. The Government of Cyprus remained supportive of an American school and the concept was actively promoted by the United States Ambassador in Nicosia, William Crawford. As a result, at the 1978 Spring Meeting of the ASOR Board of Trustees, the Very Reverend Charles Harris offered a resolution to found the "Cyprus Archaeological Research Institute". The motion was passed, and as a result the *ASOR Newsletter* for April 1978 (No. 7 for that year) carried the first official mention of a Cyprus center.

Cyprus Archaeological Research Institute

In response to the invitation of the Department of Antiquities of the Republic of Cyprus, the American Schools of Oriental Research has decided to establish an institute in Nicosia to facilitate American archaeological work on Cyprus.

This institute is envisioned as functioning like other ASOR institutes throughout the Near East and the Mediterranean area. It will serve both as a research center and a depot for excavations. All American expeditions and individual researchers will be eligible to use the services of the institute to a greater or lesser extent, depending on the degree on which they choose to affiliate with ASOR. By sharing services of specialist personnel, dig equipment, archaeological reference collections, e.g., sherds and bones, and other resources, needless duplication will be avoided and American archaeological research in Cyprus will be enhanced.

In view of these objectives, the Department of Antiquities welcomes and supports the establishment of this new institute in Cyprus.

ASOR Newsletter No. 7 1978:11

Thus, a special committee was established, chaired by Norma Kershaw, and a handful of dedicated ASOR trustees began to study ways and means to establish a new center. This was to be a farsighted and bold endeavour because ASOR could hardly afford to bear alone the burden of yet another school, and the degree of interest that could be expected from the small Cypriot constituency in the United States was an unknown factor. Norma Kershaw was the ideal choice to lead the Committee since she had got to know the island well in the course of several visits which included excavating with Vassos Karageorghis at Kition. Her executive position with the Archaeological Institute of America would, it was hoped, help to cement a relationship with Classicists. It should never be forgotten, however, that the one constant source of support in those early years was the United States Information Agency and the Fulbright Commission, without which CAARI could hardly have survived beyond infancy.

Cyprus is unlike other Near Eastern countries where other foreign schools are located – with the possible exception of Israel. It is small enough for a person to make a return trip to any part of the island in a day. And its Department of Antiquities under the Directorship of Vassos Karageorghis had always provided full access to its collections and fine library to bona fide researchers. Permits delivered by the Department of Antiquities directly to the excavation directors were always received on time and quality accommodations for expeditions were everywhere inexpensive and plentiful. Under these favourable circumstances there was hardly a demand for a school located in the capital in order to facilitate access to the antiquities authorities or to provide accommodation and logistical services to incoming teams. Indeed, after 1974, the country's airport moved from Nicosia to the seaside town of Larnaca. Thus many expedition members never visited the capital at all!

CAARI's First Director

In the spring of 1978, immediately in the wake of the ASOR Board's enabling resolution, Anita Walker of the University of Connecticut was appointed first Director of the Institute. It was now named the Cyprus American Archaeological Research Institute (American having been inserted in the title at the request of the Government of Cyprus). She immediately set about following up the letter which she had sent in February of that year to scholars

Anita Walker CAARI Director 1978–79.

The people depicted in this historic photograph, taken in 1979 in front of the recently founded CAARI, played an important role in the early years of the Institute. (left to right) Anita Walker (first Director of CAARI), Philip King (President of ASOR), Norma Kershaw (first President of CAARI), Ted Campbell (Vice President of ASOR), Joan Scheuer and Dick Scheuer (ASOR Trustee).

involved in Cypriot studies, outlining how the Institute planned to find a building near the Cyprus Museum. This would provide a place for archaeologists to meet, hostel accommodation and work space with reference collections. Some library holdings were also planned, as was the purchase of some more expensive excavation equipment for general use. This all sounded like a commendable idea, but it was also a facility that seasoned Cypriot researchers, field archaeologists and graduate students, like me, did not urgently require. On the other hand, for newcomers to the field, especially students, an archaeological center would prove a distinct advantage. And, indeed, over the years I have observed with pleasure how student involvement has grown from a mere trickle in the 1970s to the steady flow of the 1990s. Today young researchers visiting CAARI are numbered in the hundreds per year.

CAARI's First Residence Inaugurated

Anita Walker fulfilled her pledge, and CAARI soon moved into the well-suited premises of an ex-maternity clinic (!), at 41 King Paul Street, a mere five-minute walk from the Department of Antiquities. The facilities were inaugurated in July 1978. By coincidence, the first long-term residents were French and Brazilian scholars finishing projects in biblical studies. The new Institute's first tangible impact on the Cypriot archaeological scene was the hosting of a one day "Archaeological Workshop" held at the American Center in August 1978. All expeditions, both Cypriot and foreign, were invited to provide reports of work in progress, and thus started a grand CAARI tradition. Initially biannual, this Workshop program is now held each summer at the Cultural Foundation of the Bank of Cyprus. It is considered the archaeological event of the summer and attracts a large audience of professionals and nonspecialists alike. During her term Anita Walker also organized a popular lecture series "Cypriot Archaeology: Perspectives and Retrospectives" which included such eminent speakers as Einar Gjerstad and Joan du Plat Taylor.

At that time Cyprus had no University, indeed no institute of higher learning. The local community of scholars involved with archaeology and Cypriot Studies consisted of a mere eight or nine professionals employed by the Department of Antiquities, two to three historians at the Cyprus Research Center and a handful of independent scholars. That was all. Apart from periodic international symposia organized by Cypriot government agencies and the occasional lecture, most archaeological activity focussed on excavation and publication, with little to no interest being shown in more theoretical approaches.

The Second Directorship 1979

In 1979 Ian Todd of Brandeis University was appointed to replace Anita Walker as Director. Despite the chronic shortage of funds, he nevertheless managed to complete furnishing the Institute and to expand its reference collection of sherds, geological and metallurgical specimens considerably. I well remember spending a night there with my family and breakfasting with Christine Kondoleon (later to become a CAARI Trustee). We found it most comfortable, but for the huge mosquitoes!

Towards the end of the 1970s a new archaeological methodology was being adopted by missions operating in Cyprus. For example, Ian Todd's Vasilikos Valley Project along with Larry Stager and Anita Walker's American Expedition to Idalion were the first problem-oriented, multidisciplinary regional projects to operate on the island. Since both were ASOR sponsored, CAARI now stood in the forefront of these new approaches to Cypriot archaeology.

The entrance to CAARI at 41 King Paul Street with Vathoulla Moustoukki in her minuscule office known as the "klouvi" (rabbit hutch)!

Unfortunately, Todd's directorship was to be short lived as he was recalled by his university just one year after taking office. There ensued another crisis for the fledgling center, to be resolved temporarily by his wife Alison South who offered to act as caretaker until a new director could be found. Daniel Potts, a specialist in ancient Near Eastern studies applied for the position along with several others. The situation was complicated by the fact that the two principal funding bodies, ASOR and the Fulbright Commission, had differing views on a potential director's qualifications and a stalemate ensued.

CAARI: The House of the Dancing Bird — A History of the Cyprus American Archaeological Research Institute by Stuart Swiny

CAARI's Third Director 1980–1995

Having recently completed my Ph.D. on the Middle Bronze Age of southern Cyprus at the Institute of Archaeology (University of London), I offered to run the Institute in Alison South's place, until a new director was appointed. A few months at CAARI close by the Cyprus Museum library suited me well. Previously, CAARI's directors had received their salaries in the form of Fulbright Fellowships. Thus, it was impossible for me as a non-US citizen to submit my candidacy. However, to my surprise and pleasure I was informed a few weeks later by Renos Kamenos, the Administrative Director of the Cyprus American Scholarship Program, that a compromise had been reached and that I could indeed be eligible for the directorship. And that is how I came to apply for a position that would captivate me for the next fifteen years. It was also the beginning of a close friendship and enjoyable working relationship with Vathoulla Moustoukki, the versatile Secretary of CAARI.

With his return to the United States, Ian Todd took over from Norma Kershaw as President of the CAARI Board. He would continue the struggle both for recognition within ASOR and for funding from a Cypriot expatriate community that considered that its meager resources should be channelled towards the plight of fellow Cypriots suffering from the events of 1974, rather than to an American institution with the potential backing of a vast and wealthy nation.

*The hall of the old CAARI looking towards the Common Room with the Director's and Librarian's offices on the right, staircase and kitchen on the left. The Lapithos chest to the right was donated to CAARI by James R. Stewart's widow Eve along with many rare books, including the **H.H. Kitchener Atlas** dated 1885, containing the first accurate and detailed map of Cyprus.*

One of the unsung heroes of these early years of CAARI's history is Philip King, who was then ASOR President. His interest in promoting the Institute's founding and unwavering support during the first impecunious years ensured its survival. *Evkarisó Kirie.*

My first priority as Director was to develop the Institute's role as a research center, a task that could only be achieved by a major expansion of the library. With the support of the Board, a library purchase line — albeit modest — was added to the budget. This, along with gifts from the Bank of Cyprus, the Cyprus Popular Bank, Barclays' Bank and several bequests, laid the foundations of a true research library.

October 1980 saw the first academic function organized on the premises of CAARI at 41 King Paul Street with Smithsonian Institution Researcher Theodore Wertime's provocative lecture "Man versus Goat: Deforestation in Antiquity." The event, which would be the first of many, was a great success, and it demonstrated that the Common Room had a carrying capacity of up to fifty persons! Other activities initiated around that time included "CAARI lunches" and site tours. These also, in due course, became an integral part of CAARI's modus operandi. About once a week — usually on Tuesdays — all residents and staff would eat at a local restaurant to socialize and generally get to know one another.

*The Albright Institute in Cyprus. Lunch at a **psestaria** (a restaurant serving grilled foods) in ancient Kition on the outskirts of Larnaca. (left to right) Ephraim Stern, Sarah Frerichs, Ruth Hestrin, Ernest Frerichs, Joan Rothman, Joanne Bloom, Stuart Swiny, Joan Todd (standing) and Claudia Guiliani. Early 1980s.*

The "Tuesday Lunch" was a much enjoyed tradition: CAARI residents and other interested persons would gather at a local restaurant to eat and exchange news. (left to right) Jim Ross, Michael Metcalf (Fulbright Fellow), Jane Barlow, Basil Hennessy, Linda Hulin, the late Miriam Ross, the late Gaynor West (a Fellow from the British School in Athens), Vathoulla Moustoukki, Kathryn Eriksson and Dorothy Metcalf. Spring 1988.

Occasionally, visiting scholars not using the Institute's facilities were invited to join, thereby providing a chance for CAARI users to make new acquaintances. The program of site tours made an effort to visit each excavation, both Cypriot and foreign, every time it undertook fieldwork, and had a dual purpose. First, it introduced the Institute, its staff, fellows and others to foreign teams, and second it enabled a comprehensive photographic record to be assembled for our slide collection. During my tenure as Director the archive of transparencies (slides) grew to more than five thousand and was even used on occasion by staff from the Department of Antiquities!

In the following year (1981) a CAARI excavation sponsored by ASOR began fieldwork at Sotira *Kaminoudhia*, an Early Bronze Age site in southern Cyprus. Apart from my personal interest in this little known period, I felt that an excavation would attract more researchers to the Institute and would also broaden its scope. Fortunately, these expectations turned out to be correct.

In June 1981 CAARI hosted the participants to the conference "Early Metallurgy in Cyprus." (left to right), CAARI Trustee Frank Kouchy, Robert Merrillees (seated on floor), Tamara Stech speaking with Spiros Iakovides (standing) and Anthony Snodgrass. (in the foreground) Jane Waldbaum, Mrs. Weisberger and Gert Weisberger.

CAARI excavations at the Early Bronze Age site of Sotira **Kaminoudhia**, Area A, August 1983. The characteristic coursed earthquake tumble is visible to the left of the wall foundations in the foreground, with Area B in the mid-distance to the right. The Ceramic Neolithic settlement of Sotira **Teppes**, excavated by the renowned Cypriot archaeologist Porphyrios Dikaios is, as its name indicates, the tell-like feature on the horizon.

The ASOR Committee on Archaeological Policy visit to Sotira **Kaminoudhia**, summer 1983. James Sauer at center discussing the project with (left to right) Rip Rapp (University of Minnesota), Stuart Swiny, Anne Ogilvy and William Dever. Helena (Laina) Swiny (with scarf) and Clark Walz (Site Supervisor, Drew University) are visible on lower left. Antigoni Zournatzi (Site Supervisor, University of California at Berkeley) squats with her back to the camera. The men in cloth hats are skilled laborers from nearby villages.

CAARI Receives USIA Support

Arguably the most significant single event at this stage in the history of CAARI was a visit by Ronald Ungaro, Chief of the Academic Exchange Program, United States Information Agency, in August 1982.

*Ronald Ungaro, Chief of the Academic Exchange Program, United States Information Agency, whose visit in the summer of 1982 marked a turning point in the history of CAARI. Alison South, Director of the Kalavasos **Ayios Demetrios** excavations, shows him the hole in the floor where an important cache of bronze weights was discovered. In the background (left to right) Anita Walker, Norma Kershaw and Cathy Schmidt (a volunteer who worked at CAARI).*

*United States Ambassador Raymond Ewing — with arms folded — and his wife Gerry visit the Late Bronze Age Maroni **Vournes** excavations directed by Gerald Cadogan standing to the left of the Ambassador. Autumn 1982. Raymond Ewing is a recently elected trustee.*

I invited Mr. Ungaro for an afternoon visit at the Institute to see for himself the role it played in Cypriot studies. It just so happened that a number of researchers were at CAARI that day. With a little orchestration on my part, they gathered in the Common Room for "lemonade and biscuits," and to meet our guest. David Pearlman enthused about *doukhanis* (threshing sledges), Liz Wheeler spoke on the choroplastic qualities of Red Polished pottery, Bill Fox unlocked the secrets of chipped stone and Steve Held told him how the pygmy elephants got to Aetokremnos (Vulture Cliff). Others, like Sheena Crawford, also came to show their support, and the collective enthusiasm for poor under- funded CAARI was tangible and infectious. To cap it off, I drove him, along with Norma Kershaw, Anita Walker and Kathy Schmidt, in the "White Hoax" (an immense old station wagon donated by the US Embassy) to attend an evening lecture by Vassos Karageorghis in the theatre at Kourion, and Karageorghis mentioned the work of CAARI several times. Later, we enjoyed a reception overlooking the magnificent moonlit cliffs below the Sanctuary of Apollo. Evidently, Ron Ungaro liked what he saw and what he heard. Soon after his return to Washington we received a $10,000 USIA grant for library purchases. His support of CAARI's program and its quest for permanent premises was to be central to this phase of the Institute's development.

The CAARI Common Room. in 1982. Doctoral student Joan Connelly (center — Princeton University) speaking with Brigitte Bourgeois (Louvre Museum). Lynn Bright (University of Edinburgh) is in the background next to the old wood-burning stove adapted from a British Army field kitchen stove! Simple, cheap and efficient, it kept the residents warm during the cold, damp winter months.

Four staunch supporters of CAARI at the inauguration of the Schaeffer Library. (foreground) James Sauer, (President of ASOR); (behind left to right) Daniel Howard Director of the American Center who was instrumental in obtaining the new Fulbright Fellowships and a grant for the library; Daniel Hadjitoffi, Executive Director of the Fulbright Commission in Nicosia who orchestrated these fellowships; and Gaynor West, the Institute's first Librarian.

In early April that same year my wife Helena (Laina) and I led a very successful tour of Cyprus sponsored by ASOR. The sheer beauty of the island, its atmosphere and of course its rich history captivated the participants. One of them, Lydie Shufro, was nominated and elected to be a CAARI Trustee later that month and would serve as its Vice President from 1985 to 1992.

CAARI Tour of Cyprus, April 1984. The guides relaxing on the steps of the House of Dionysius! (left to right) Dimitris Michaelides, Department of Antiquities Officer for the Paphos District, Yiannis Cleanthous, once Custodian of St. Hilarion Castle and Kyrenia Castle, now muktar of Lemba Village, Laina and Stuart Swiny.

Plans for a More Permanent Home, 1986

With the nucleus of a fine research library now straining the carrying capacity of our rented premises, the next requirement, logically enough, was to find a permanent home for the Institute. The stimulus for a financial undertaking of such magnitude was the providential receipt of a large gift in memory of J. R. Stewart that enabled the Trustees to seek more support from private sources, foundations and government agencies. In anticipation of a successful outcome to our fund-raising drive I undertook a search for a suitable building not only within easy reach of the Department of Antiquities and the Cyprus Museum but also close to the commercial center of town. In the summer of 1986, Dhemos Christou of the Department of Antiquities (later to become its Director) told me about a fine two storied, *arkhontiko spiti* (town house), for sale on Andreas Dhemitriou Street, within easy walking distance of the Cyprus Museum. I well remember wondering after my first visit one hot August afternoon in the company of Ellen Herscher, how the sturdy building with small rooms and superb terracotta tile floors could indeed be turned into an efficient institute. There was enough space for administrative and hostel purposes, but no single room of sufficient dimensions to accommodate the library holdings or seating for public lectures.

Famagusta Gate Cultural Center, November 1986. Traditional Cypriot potters gather to hear Fulbright Fellow Gloria London's lecture devoted to their dying craft. Although none of them spoke English, they did enjoy the slides! This venue, often used by CAARI, is part of the Venitian Defence Walls of Nicosia dating back to the 1560s. The event was sponsored jointly by CAARI and the Department of Antiquities. (back row right to left) Stuart Swiny and Gloria London, with village potters. (left background standing) Gerald Hennings, chairman of the Western Soverign Base Area Archaeological Society.

Nevertheless, the appealing character and location of the house were such that I urged the trustees to authorize an architectural survey in order to determine whether our space requirements could be fulfilled. The architectural firm Constantinos Fissentzides was engaged. Steve Held, who was a friend and professional archaeologist specializing in the early human colonization of Cyprus, drew up a plan that almost miraculously provided for all our needs. By amalgamating four rooms on the ground floor, a spacious library cum lecture hall was carved out of the existing maze. All the other pieces fell into place with ease and at last we had the ideal locale that would fulfill the demands of an efficient archaeological research institution. First of all it provided space — space for administrative purposes, space for laboratories, space for research, a library and lectures, living space and finally space to relax, indoors and out — and all of this in pleasant surroundings.

Not only were additional monies required to purchase the building, but the renovations and furnishings also had to be funded. The dream of ownership was achieved through the effort, dedication and generosity of the Institute's trustees and supporters, for which the present and future generations of scholars will be grateful. Members of the Board provided leadership gifts. Other trustees, like William Childs, contacted old school friends who were on the boards of major foundations. ASOR trustees were equally supportive. The whole operation was achieved without having to obtain a loan, and for that everyone involved in the project was justifiably proud. The fact that the complicated business of purchase, renovation and then furnishing progressed in a relatively timely manner and with few hitches, was in large part due to the tireless efforts of John G. Bartol, Chair of the Building Committee. For three years John, Laina and I worked closely together and it was a great sadness for us all when he passed away in 1992 without a chance to return to Cyprus to admire the New CAARI in all its splendor.

William Childs, Director of the Princeton excavations at Polis, relaxing at the dig house with a cup of tea.

The building was totally reorganized and enlarged, the plumbing upgraded and electrical installations rewired. As noted by our architect C. Fissentzides, projects of this type are more complicated and require greater supervision than simple construction from the foundations up. That the task was accomplished with few major problems says much about the architect's attention to detail and especially the ability and versatility of our contractor Christophis Nathanael and Son. His old-time stone masons were a joy to observe. They practised an art that may well disappear with their generation. Laina Swiny was engaged to undertake the interior decoration of the premises and its furnishing, which often meant "refurbishing" existing items and fittings. Her task was aided by a gift from Giraud Foster for the purchase of numerous items belonging to the island's traditional arts and crafts. The final result was a building with a comfortable, informal, yet sophisticated environment of distinctly Cypriot character. Nobody has ever accused CAARI of being institutional! If a dozen people are now able to live in relative harmony in the J. R. Stewart Residence, it is the result of the original careful planning for utilization of space. Jim Stewart, the well-known Australian archaeologist who excavated at Bellapais Vounous, Nicosia and elsewhere, and who contributed so much to Levantine Early and Middle Bronze Age studies, would have been pleased to know that his name is now a "household word" thanks to the support of his wife Eve for CAARI and its work.

The New CAARI Renovation project. The Fulbright Suite (lower right), Darkroom/Laboratory, and Hall Linen Cupboard, (upper left) September 1990.

The New CAARI Renovation Project. Architect Constantinos Fissentzides and assistant discussing the kitchen plans with Laina Swiny.

The New CAARI Renovation Project. The contractor, Mr. Christophis Nathanael, mixing cement in the future Library.

*Giraud Foster, President of the Board of Trustees, visited Cyprus several times during the renovation project. He is seen here together with Laina Swiny, in charge of the furnishing and decoration of the New CAARI, at Mosphiloti, the main source of ethnographic materials on the island. They are discussing, which objects to purchase. The **doukhani** (threshing board) the end of which is just visible on the right and the jar under scrutiny (dated 1824) were chosen for the CAARI Collection.*

While construction was underway, CAARI continued to develop on other fronts. In 1986, Vice President Lydie Shufro was instrumental in obtaining the first CAARI fellowship funded by a nongovernmental agency. Offered by the Pacific Scientific Corporation, this fellowship provided for travel support and accommodations at the Institute for at least a month each year, for a total of three years. Pacific Scientific Fellows David Reese, Tom Davies and John Leonard conducted their research on such diverse topics as Pleistocene fauna, the history of American Archaeology in Cyprus and Roman harbors and maritime activities. This was an excellent start as it brought the Institute to the notice of the grant-hungry student community.

The President of the Republic of Cyprus, H. E. George Vassiliou and Mrs. Androulla Vassiliou (center) visiting the Akrotiri Aetokremnos excavations in the summer of 1989 with Alan Simmons (with hat) of the Desert Research Institute, University of Nevada-Reno, the project Director. The President was much intrigued by the huge deposit of pigmy hippopotamus and elephant bones resulting from the slaughter of these animals by the first visitors to Cyprus some 12,000 years ago.

In addition, the Anita C. O'Donovan Fellowship was established in 1988 to provide travel funds and a stipend for a few weeks at the Institute, while other grants, such as the Charles. U. Harris Fellowship, were specifically intended for research on ASOR/Committee on Archaeological Policy affiliated excavations. The recipients of these diverse fellowships — among whom were Alice Kingsnorth and Joanne Clark — were for the most part aspiring young scholars at the time of this association with CAARI, but now are appearing on the staffs of universities and museums across Europe, North America and Australia. A good example is CAARI alumnus Joseph Greene, now the Assistant Director of the Semitic Museum at Harvard University and recently appointed trustee.

Three Old Timers enjoying a good laugh. (left to right) Nicole Hirschfeld, doctoral candidate, University of Texas at Austin, Linda Hulin, CAARI Research Fellow and Bonny Bazemore, doctoral candidate, University of Chicago, later to become CAARI Program Coor-dinator in Nicosia. Photo from late 1980s.

The New CAARI is Inaugurated

The eastern Mediterranean climate is such that much of the year it is possible to enjoy the relaxation of a garden. Here again CAARI, despite its location in the center of Nicosia, was fortunate to possess such an asset. Patty Wylde, a professional landscape architect, skillfully organized the space so that it could serve as an extension of the building. And it was in the paved and shady garden with its stone benches and lily pool that on the 10th of June 1991 the President of the Republic of Cyprus, Dr. George Vassiliou, came to inaugurate the new Institute. With him were Ministers and other members of the Government, including, of course, Michael Loulloupis, Director of the Department of Antiquities, and Vassos Karageorghis, Special Advisor to the President on Cultural Affairs. Also in attendance were many CAARI Trustees as well as several ASOR, Albright Institute and ACOR Trustees. Most distinguished among these were Charles Harris, then Chairman of the CAARI Board, Giraud Foster, its President, Lydie Shufro, its Vice President, James Sauer, President of ASOR, Carol Meyers, Vice President of the W. F. Albright Institute, and Pierre Bikai, then the new Director of ACOR in Amman. (Pierre had celebrated his half century birthday with all of us earlier that week.) Also present were Diana Buitron-Oliver, Andrew Oliver, Ken Hamma, Anne Melvin, Lillian Craig, Patricia Bikai, Eric Meyers, Sally and Bert de Vries, Tom Schaub and many others. Very special welcomes were also extended to Janet Harris and Caroline Foster, and to A. H. S. Megaw, former Director of the Department of Antiquities and Mrs. Elektra Megaw. In fact several hundred friends and supporters joined in on the celebration, requiring that the street outside be closed to traffic to accommodate the spillover of guests from the garden.

The New CAARI Renovation Project — the end result, spring 1992. Note the flowering "Bottle Brush" tree in foreground and the "Camel's Foot" tree behind. The CAARI lion (unfortunately stolen in 1999) is just visible standing guard at the top of the steps.

CAARI: The House of the Dancing Bird — A History of the Cyprus American Archaeological Research Institute by Stuart Swiny

On the 10th of June 1991 H. E. George Vassiliou, President of the Republic of Cyprus officially inaugurated the new premises. **Le tout** ASOR, CAARI and indeed Nicosia was present! A sampling (left to right) Ken Hamma, Linda Hulin, Lillian Craig, Anthea Garrod, Roy Smith, Vasilis and Diana Constatinides, Sophocles Hadjisavvas, Vassos Loizides, Ara Nigogosian, Nancy Hocking, Alison South, Tom Shaub, Pierre Bikai, Jim Sauer, Bert and Sally de Vries, Anne Melvin, Don and Nancy Flint, Andrew Oliver, Aris and Susan Sacorafos, Sarah Michaelides, Lygia Ieronimidou, Diana Buitron-Oliver, Janet Harris, Olga Demetriades, Giraud Foster, Speaker of the House Alexis Galanos, Gerald Hennings, Diana and Julian Whitehead, Pavlos Flourentzos, Susan Dain, Charles Harris, Eric Meyers, US Ambassador William Lamb, the Minister of Communications and Works, Stuart Swiny and President Vassiliou. Facing the podium (left to right lower right corner) Constantinos Fissentzides, David Dain British High Commissioner and (extreme right) Kevork Keshishian the author/editor of **Romantic Cyprus**.

An ASOR Mosaic: A Centennial History of the American Schools of Oriental Research

H.E. George Vassiliou, President of the Republic of Cyprus (left), being introduced to the Very Reverend Charles Upchurch Harris, Chairman of the CAARI Board (right) by Stuart Swiny at the CAARI Inauguration 1991.

Charles Harris and Vathoulla Moustoukki at the reception following the New CAARI inauguration in 1991.

Peter Megaw, former Director of the Department of Antiquities (center with white hat) is seen lecturing on a field trip to Paphos in October 1994, explaining many of the sites that he had excavated and preserved. The outing was organized in connection with CAARI's major first international conference "Res Maritimae: Cyprus and the Eastern Mediterranean from Prehistory to Late Antiquity."

The Move and the Movers

By 1991 it had already become a time-honored tradition for the CAARI staff, fellows and residents to get involved in activities above and beyond those specifically listed in their job descriptions! The inauguration was the best example of this practice and it would be churlish not to mention all participants in this official history, for the success of this great event, the most significant since the opening of the Institute twelve years earlier, was due to the special efforts of the following individuals: Assistant Director John Leonard and his wife Sherry Fox (now director of the Wiener Laboratory at the American School of Classical Studies in Athens), Secretary Vathoulla Moustoukki, Librarians Maria Stavrou and Diana Constantinides, Archivists Marita Anderson and Kay Ugeto, Fulbright Fellows Ellen Herscher and Ken Schaar, Leverhulm Fellows Michael Given and Molly Cotton, and Fellow Louise Steele.

Sherry Fox Leonard studying the "phaphologies," sic., of ancient Paphians! in the new CAARI Laboratory. Sherry was the first person to make use of these facilities after the move to the new premises.

Diana Constantinides in her ever shrinking "office" at the back of the Communications Room. She is central to the smooth operation of the Schaeffer library and much else besides. Diana's husband, Vasilis, accomplished "Brandy Sour" mixer, and master pork chop griller, has added a characteristic Cypriot flavor to many a "CAARI event."

Celebrating with beer (!) and caviar, the successful move of the Schaeffer Library from the Old to the New premises. Never again would food and drink be allowed within its hallowed book-lined walls! (left to right) Assistant Director John Leonard, Laina and Stuart Swiny, Archivist Kay Ugeto, Archivist (and supplier of the caviar!) Marita Anderson, Librarian Maria Stavrou and Sherry Fox Leonard. February 1991.

John Leonard was the Assistant Director responsible for running CAARI at the time of the move in 1991. He was the first person to occupy the Director's office in the new building. With characteristic energy, dedication, flair and good humor, he and Sherry did much to ensure that the transition from Old to New Premises went smoothly.

February 7, 1991: Moving out! Moving in! All the remaining furniture was moved from the Old CAARI to the New CAARI in "lorries" graciously supplied by the Mayor of Nicosia, Lellos Demetriades. Metal shelving from the Collections Room is lowered from the balcony. The Leonards' epic Volvo parked in front did more than its share of hauling in the move!

(left to right) Dr. Michael Given, Doreen and the late Roy Smith, who always ensured that the building and especially the garden at 11 Andreas Demetriou Street was kept in top notch condition. The term "handyman" acquired true meaning with Roy for whom no task was too difficult, too menial or too overwhelming.

John and Sherry Leonard deserve special credit for the time and effort, well beyond the call of duty, that they devoted first to overseeing "The Move," then "The Settling-In" and finally the Inauguration. From gingerly checking for broken roof tiles to hefting pig iron counterweights for ingenious contraptions such as the retractable stairs leading to the attic, John was always a willing helper. Likewise Roy Smith saw that the garden was spick and span while Georghia Nicolaou and Fotoulla Christodoulou kept the premises spotless, and all three did much else besides. Finally, from the beginning of the renovation project through to the opening ceremony, few could fully appreciate the extent to which Laina Swiny was involved. Often behind the scenes, she assisted in every aspect of the project, from laying out patterns of tile floors; to planting trees and shrubs in the garden; to overseeing delicate arrangements concerning protocol. For all of this she has my fullest gratitutde.

CAARI has always been fortunate to be cared for by a devoted staff. My brief to Georghia Nicolaou and her sister Fotoulla Christodoulou was to look after it as if it were their own home. And to their credit, they did. (left to right) Georghia next to her niece Tasoulla and sister Fotoulla. Together over the years they have contributed their fine cooking and Cypriot hospitality to numerous CAARI receptions. At the far right is Librarian Maria Stavrou, now the librarian of the Makarios III Foundation.

CAARI Moves On

With the inauguration behind us, life returned to its normal busy rhythm at CAARI, which in each succeeding year attracted ever more researchers. Through the initiative of Giraud Foster, CAARI applied for and received a prestigious National Endowment for the Humanities Fellowship in the amount of $30,000 to be offered annually. This in combination with the Janet and Charles Harris and the John Bartol Fellowships, all awarded on a yearly basis to researchers wishing to work in Cyprus, meant that the Stewart Residence was usually full, and that Schaeffer Library usage increased apace. Coincidentally, the first NEH Fellow was Nancy Serwint, a few years hence to be appointed as my successor.

*Charles U. Harris Fellow Alice Kingsnorth working on her study of the chipped stone from Sotira **Kaminoudhia** in the Communications Room. Summer 1991.*

CAARI Trustees Ken Hamma (left) and Nancy Serwint (right) "sneaking in" an ice cream cone treat (!) with Vathoulla Moustoukki at the fishing port of Latchi, near Polis.

(left to right) Shelby White, Jim Sauer and Lydie Shufro at the New York Institute of Fine Arts in November of 1985 where the first in a series of CAARI symposia in the U.S. was held.

Nancy Serwint was followed by a series of other distinguished NEH Fellows, including Pamela Gaber, Timothy Gregory and Michael Tomazou. At this time the library's holdings were further boosted by the receipt of a major grant from the J. Paul Getty Trust. This also provided for the cataloguing of the archives and computerization of the reference collection. Both projects were skilfully undertaken by our Archivist Marita Anderson.

Various programs had been routinely organized since the mid-1980s both for fund-raising purposes and to advertise the existence of the Institute. Starting in 1985 Lydie Shufro planned a series of highly successful events in the general New York area, while others took place as far afield as Washington DC, Los Angeles and San Francisco. From 1987, with Lydie Shufro and Trustee Pauline Albenda as co-editors, the CAARI News began to be published at regular intervals to inform and promote the mission of the Institute. In this same spirit Giraud Foster prepared a comprehensive manual for prospective trustees. This provided background information on the island and CAARI specifically for those trustees without a long-standing involvement with Cyprus.

Changes in 1993

In 1993 notable changes occurred within the Executive Committee of the Board of Trustees as Ellen Herscher was elected to be Vice President and Anne Melvin as Secretary.

For most of the academic year 1993/1994 I was on sabbatical leave at the American School of Classical Studies at Athens, and Jerry Vincent took over as interim-director of the Institute. During his stay in Nicosia he put his knowledge of bookkeeping to good use and worked hard on implementing a consolidated financial reporting system.

The new and larger premises enabled the expansion of CAARI's programmatic activities and as a result the position of Program Coordinator was added to the staff. Bonny Bazemore, completing her Ph.D. on the Cypriot syllabary held the position with distinction for three years; during the fourth year the responsibility was shouldered by Laina Swiny. In that time two symposia, several round tables, the annual summer archaeological workshop, a major exhibition and numerous public lectures were organized. Highlights during this period included "Making Pottery" in June 1993, which for two days brought together ceramicists from Jordan and Cyprus who were interested in ancient technology, and "The Practical Impact of Science on Field Archaeology", also a two-day symposium, organized by the Archaeological Research Unit of the University of Cyprus, CAARI and the American School of Classical Studies at Athens. The most ambitious project, however, was "Res Maritimae: Cyprus and the Eastern Mediterranean from Prehistory to Late Antiquity" held at CAARI in October 1994. Jointly organized by Trustee Robert Hohlfelder, University of Colorado at Boulder, and Conference Secretary Laina Swiny in Nicosia, the four-day international symposium included thirty-three contributions, two keynote speakers, a poster session and several field trips. The meeting was noted for the number of attendees visiting Cyprus for the first time and was characterized by the intermingling of established researchers, doctoral candidates and professionals with empirical knowledge. The proceedings, edited by S. Swiny, R. H. Hohlfelder and H. W. Swiny were published by ASOR in 1997 as the first volume in the CAARI Monographs Series.

Author, Stuart Swiny, taking notes at 40 meters depth for the Department of Antiquities, Cyprus on a possible wreck-site located off the northwest coast of the island October 1981.

CAARI has always promoted educational activities involving both school children and adults. The three photographs below record one such activity organized by the Program Coordinator in 1993 involving five staff members and fellows. The rapt young audience in all three pictures says it all! Spring 1993.

Fulbright Fellow Sherry Fox Leonard (right) explains her research on ancient human skeletal remains.

NEH Fellow and future Director of CAARI Nancy Serwint (right) preparing the large collection of terracottas from ancient Marion for publication.

CAARI Director Stuart Swiny explains the various uses of pottery from contemporary milking bowls (foreground) to Roman transport amphorae.

The last event organized during my directorship was the Institute's contribution to events celebrating Nicosia European Cultural Month in October 1995. The program included a comprehensive exhibit of traditional Cypriot pottery along with two demonstrations of pithos (large storage jar) making, one in English the other in Greek, as well at two fascinating lectures by Harriett Blitzer on traditional arts and crafts, also in both languages. It drew praise from the mayor of Nicosia, Lellos Demetriades, as the most typically Cypriot event of the whole celebration! It attracted large groups of people who came to view the lively, didactic exhibits organized by Laina Swiny both inside and out in the garden. Many of these visitors were school children totally unfamiliar with the culture of their grandparents.

The widely acclaimed exhibition "Traditional Cypriot Pottery" in 1995 attracted well over one thousand school children who came to view the crafts of their great-grandparents, which required skills now mostly forgotten. Two demonstrations of traditional crafts were organized for the general public with explanations in both English and Greek. On the left of this photograph the large clay cylinder that resembles a 50 gallon oil barrel is a dying vat for **vrakas** (traditional men's baggy black trousers), a pair of which are hanging up to dry. The CAARI garden is an ideal venue for such events. Autumn 1995.

(Above) The front hall of CAARI with didactic displays chronicling the history of "Traditional Cypriot Pottery." Representative items were borrowed mostly from the fine collections of Anna and Andreas Georghiades and the Theophanis Pilavakis Museum in Phini. Other objects came from the CAARI Collection.

(Left) Theophanis Pilavakis demonstrates how to manufacture a **pithos** (large storage jar), and explains the complexities of wine making as well as local customs concerning childbirth (note his wife in the bed behind). The Pilavakis family made the last traditional pithos in 1972.

CAARI People

Since the purpose of this ASOR centennial publication is not to produce a dry, monotonous chronicle of the various institutes' histories — that information is easily gleaned from the yearly Director's Reports — I wish to mention those who frequented CAARI over the years and who, in many instances have become lifelong friends. If people make a place, this is certainly true for the Cyprus American Archaeological Research Institute. First comes G. R. H. (Mick) Wright whose stature is only matched by his encyclopaedic knowledge and intellect, and who will surely be remembered by many for his appearance at a lecture one hot summer's night at 41 King Paul Street girt in a lungi and sporting his monocle. Jacques Claude Courtois was another figure who enlivened and enriched the Institute's early years at 41 King Paul Street. It was there that he prepared the artwork for his two volumes on Enkomi. Indeed, CAARI is the only legal *depositaire* (distributor) outside of France for one of his publications. We became friends after working together at Enkomi in 1969. His premature death in 1991 deprived CAARI of a staunch supporter. A fellowship in his name is planned for the future. Then there was Olivier Masson who, deep in discussion with his colleague Maurice Sznycer one morning at breakfast, inadvertently placed the electric kettle on the gas to boil! Joan Connelly too was a long-term resident during her dissertation days and served as our informal ambassador back in the United States, and there was Robert Morris, the "little Auzzie bleeder" with his incomparable sense of humour, or again Michael Given the veteran of many a sojourn during the writing of his thesis; both were always ready to lend a hand when needed. Other young "dissertation" scholars of the early, heroic years were Hartmut Matthäus and Andres Reyes who spent many a month shivering through those rather dank Cypriot winters at the "Old CAARI." Although the premises were simple and basic in terms of accommodations – and heating – they obviously satisfied the requirements of many a seasoned scholar who would visit time and time again: Michael Metcalf being a prime example, or the other Michael, this time, Heltzer. James Muhly too professed to enjoy the rather ascetic conditions at the Institute in winter. "Few distractions and good for work" he would note. The number of summers that Kenneth and Margaret Schaar have resided at CAARI I no longer recall, and they too have now become part of Institute folklore. Later in the "New CAARI" Joanna Smith and Danielle Parks helped define its character.

*Michael Given, long-term resident at both the Old and the New CAARI where he wrote most of his dissertation, checking the fit of a **stomion** (the entrance to a rock-cut tomb). Summer 1992.*

No record of CAARI's early history would be complete without a photograph of Napoleon, the Swiny's hound, well loved by most Institute visitors and residents, seen here assisting Danielle Parks on a "Roman Tomb Survey." Danielle, a Fulbright Fellow in 1994/95, also served as Assistant to the Director and was responsible for overseeing the Institute and especially the James R. Stewart Residence after office hours and on weekends.

They keep coming back! Barbara Kling, a Fulbright Fellow in the mid 1980's returns with her children Michael and Stephen on a National Endowment for the Humanities fellowship in 1996/97. Some of the photographs published in this history of CAARI were borrowed from the renowned "CAARI Cast" board visible on the wall behind Vathoulla Moustoukki (upper right) in her office.

Over the years many people stayed with us for shorter periods, scholars, special interest travellers, students, bishops, diplomats, soldiers, refugees, writers, artists and simple tourists with archaeological connections. Most had a story to tell and they certainly contributed to the congenial atmosphere at the Institute. For the Director of CAARI, life was never dull. Vathoulla Moustoukki and I always welcomed trustees who made a point of actually staying at CAARI to determine "how things were going." Most memorable were the Rosses. Jim Ross spent two sabbaticals with us, one each both before and after the move to the new premises. He and his wife Miriam always fostered a wonderfully congenial atmosphere and provided Laina and me with useful feedback on what it was like being "senior" inmates at the Institute. For me it was an added pleasure to have a mainland Early Bronze person *in situ* so to speak. Trustee Annemarie Weyl Carr has also been a regular visitor over the years; her enthusiasm and knowledge for late Byzantine art has been wonderfully refreshing to most of us specializing in earlier, usually much earlier, periods. Ken Hamma too would faithfully reserve a room at CAARI and spend time discussing recent developments despite his invariably tight schedule. Willy Childs sampled life at 41 King Paul Street and Ellen Herscher is a regular of the J. R Stewart Residence. And of course, I well remember the visits of Lydie Shufro who, on one occasion brought a magnum of champagne to a pre-inauguration dinner organized in honor of the long-suffering CAARI residents, and at another time flew in from Rome laden with succulent fresh Italian asparagus, prosciutto de Parma and superb fresh mozzarella di buffalo. Bravo!

Scholarly diversity and internationalism are amongst the great strengths of CAARI and it was interesting to observe American prehistorians such as Alan Simmons studying the very earliest human presence — and the extinction of pigmy hippopotami at Akrotiri *Aetokremnos* — in the library with English researcher Robert Holland writing a book on the British colonial period along with Israeli geologist Jacov Nir investigating the coasts of Cyprus.

One person who loomed large in the experience of running CAARI and working in Cyprus was Vassos Karageorghis. Few major lectures and colloquia sponsored by CAARI were not graced by his presence and it was always a pleasure to welcome him and his wife Jacqueline to the events marking the steady progression of the Institute towards what it is today. And of course, over the years we had many issues of mutual concern to discuss. As a friend and colleague — and it should not be forgotten that he was the Cyprus Government official to whom I had to report — I could always count on a quick and measured response to any matter brought to his attention. Without Vassos Karageorghis' staunch support, CAARI would hardly have seen the light of day, let alone reached its majority.

German scholar Armin Schopen, an expert on the early Islamic period, in the Collection Room demonstrates how the Arabs made ink: collect a few by-products from an abandoned copper mine, mix with oak galls gathered in the hills, brew gently over a low fire, decant, and you will have an indelible, never fading, jet black ink! Summer 1996.

Dr. Vassos Karageorghis, Director of the Department of Antiquities (1963–1989) addressing the audience at Fulbright Fellow Gloria London's lecture — jointly sponsored by CAARI and the Department of Antiquities — in 1986 in the historic Famagusta Gate.

Vathoulla Moustoukki organized a visit to the ruins of Leondari Vouno, a mighty medieval castle protecting the eastern approaches to Nicosia, in the spring of 1993. It is currently in a restricted military zone. On the far left Michael Given strikes an heroic pose while (left to right) Kay Ugeto, Vathoulla Moustoukki, Marita Anderson, Laina Swiny, Nancy Serwint, Diana Constantinides, Ian Todd, Despo Pilides, Linda Hulin, Julia Burnet and on the extreme right a National Guard soldier, listen intently to Bonny Bazemore standing in front of the Middle Bronze Age cemetery.

Vathoulla Moustoukki

Throughout my tenure at CAARI I was privileged to work with Vathoulla Moustoukki, a secretary whom I could totally trust and who knew me well enough to make time and time again the correct decisions in my absence. In addition to her normal and varied secretarial duties, Vathoulla would double as librarian, hostess, travel agent, counsellor or confidante, and during my overseas trips, as stand-in Director. Directors, Presidents and Trustees may come and go at CAARI, but Vathoulla stays on to provide the continuity and fount of knowledge that has guaranteed the ongoing success of the Institute. Working with Vathoulla was one of the great pleasures of my directorship. Not only did she give selflessly of her own time and energy to the Institute but her family and their wonderful house in Aglanja all became part of the CAARI experience both for my family and also for the many resident scholars.

CAARI: The House of the Dancing Bird — A History of the Cyprus American Archaeological Research Institute by Stuart Swiny

Running the Institute and turning it into a respected member of the ASOR triad of overseas center affiliates was an intensely personal experience which, *bon gré, mal gré*, was also imposed on my family. Few events did not include to some degree the guiding hand of Laina and many also required the assistance of our children, Philip and Alessandra. How many were the receptions and dinner parties organized at the Swiny home? Fortunately our house and garden were ideal for such activities, but one occasion bears specific mention. This was on Jim Sauer's first visit to Cyprus in the company of ASOR trustees. They included Philip King, Joy Ungerleider Mayerson and Phil Mayerson, along with Gough Thompson. Leon Levy and Shelby White were expected to join the group a day later when all were invited to a formal dinner in our garden. Everybody knows that in June it never rains on Cyprus so chairs, tables and settings were awaiting the thirty guests when a sudden thunder storm turned the garden into a swamp! Unperturbed, Laina and I moved everything into our front hall, fortunately large enough to accommodate such a crowd, and a good time was had by all … except for Leon and Shelby who unfortunately had to cancel their trip at the last moment.

The extended Swiny family in 1989 (left to right) Brave Mars held by Laina, Philip (Napoleon's rump is just visible behind to his left), Stuart holding Folly the cat from Sotira Village, Alessandra and the Land Rover — work horse of many a CAARI field trip.

*Still a good story! US Embassy staffers on a CAARI field trip being shown around Kalavasos **Tenta** by Ian Todd (right) who excavated the Neolithic settlement twenty years earlier. Todd was the second Director of CAARI. Autumn 1997.*

A Fourth Directorship 1995–1999

On the 1st of October 1995, after fifteen years to the day, I handed over the directorship to Nancy Serwint. I could review the excellent status of the Cyprus American Archaeological Research Institute with great satisfaction. It had developed from a small ten room apartment into a twenty-five room center with unique archaeological reference collections, a 10,000 volume library and a steady clientele of scholar/fellows supported by numerous fellowships. It was no longer that little known ASOR newcomer, but now stood as an internationally respected research institution and a major player in the growing field of Cypriot Studies. Above all, it still closely resembled my early vision of a small, friendly, vibrant, overseas school. What an achievement, often against stiff odds. For this everyone who shared in this venture can be justly proud!

With Nancy Serwint from the School of Art at Arizona State University taking over, first as Interim Director, and then a year later as Director, the Institute was to be in good hands. She knew Cyprus and CAARI well, both because she had resided in the J. R. Stewart Residence as the recipient of a National Endowment for the Humanities fellowship in 1983 and for having worked with the Princeton University excavations at ancient Marion regularly since that time. An art historian with a specific interest in Iron Age terracottas, her term as Director provided a healthy change from the more prehistoric focus of her predecessor. One of her major achievements was to take CAARI into the age of instant communication with access to the Internet and, with the assistance of Gerald Vincent, the creation of a CAARI web site (www.caari.org). Today one might wonder how such organizations ever existed without these communication amenities. But happily the day of the two week wait for a letter from the CAARI or ASOR head offices now belongs to another era!

At a Cyprus Museum Tour for Ambassador and Mrs. Kenneth Brill and Embassy staff led by Nancy Serwint (forward left), the group is seen viewing the Tamassos sphinxes outside the Conservation Laboratory with Chief Conservator Andreas Georgiades (to Serwint's immediate right).

Equally important, Nancy Serwint oversaw the implementation of a computerized accounting and billing system. Created by Charles Sohn, Gerald Vincent and her, it has now become a model for other ASOR affiliated institutes. Along with these developments went an increase in the number and quality of computers and other office equipment available for researchers. Throughout her term, the small but dedicated staff remained essentially the same with Vathoulla Moustoukki as Administrative Assistant and Maria Stavrou as Librarian, with Diana Constantinides replacing Bonny Bazemore as Program Coordinator.

The programmatic activities for which CAARI is renowned were continued and the spectrum of cultural activities expanded. In March 1998 Director Serwint and Diane Bolger organized the most significant event since Res Maritimae. This was in the form of an international conference assembling thirty five speakers. "Engendering Aphrodite: Women and Society in Ancient Cyprus" attracted much attention in Cyprus and abroad and provided a new approach to gender studies on the island. A photographic display with the theme "Images of Women in Ancient Cyprus" was held in the CAARI library to coincide with the conference. The field trips included a *de rigeur* visit to the Sanctuary of Aphrodite at Palaeopaphos.

The international conference "Engendering Aphrodite: Women and Society in Ancient Cyprus" organized by CAARI in March 1998 attracted well deserved attention in the local press. The presenters are assembled in the Cleopatra Hotel, conveniently located a few blocks from the Institute.

Many of the conference participants were long-time regulars of CAARI, such as Valerie Cook and Cecilia Beer sitting on either side of Charles Sohn and Nancy Serwint in the Common Room. The kilim hanging on the wall behind the sofa was donated to CAARI by Norma Kershaw. March 1998.

Renowned Cypriot poet Costas Montis (left) with National Endowment for the Humanities Fellow David Roessel who translated Montis' "Closed Doors" into English. Nicosia 1998.

The photographic exhibition "Women and Society in Ancient Cyprus" was mounted by request of the Cyprus Department of Town Planning and Housing, Ministry of the Interior, Polis. Autumn 1998.

Building an Endowment

In 1998 CAARI received the promise of a major gift which is sure to deeply influence the future of the Institute. Charles and Janet Harris, who played such a pivotal role in all major developments at CAARI from its inception (Charles Harris, in fact, as noted earlier, was responsible for its very creation) pledged half a million dollars towards its endowment. This news was announced by the then incoming President Edward Gilbert who during his term endeavoured to build on this magnificent gift. The effort was assisted by a subsequent contribution of $100,000 from ASOR Chairman P.E. MacAllister, half of which required dollar for dollar matching support from other trustees and CAARI friends. This challenge was quickly met. And in 1999 the Harris's pledge was completely fulfilled by contributions finally totalling $600,000. Over the years, CAARI has indeed been fortunate to have attracted such far-sighted and generous trustees and friends who have now helped ensure its long-term survival.

Meanwhile, CAARI continued to attract increasing numbers of young scholars. The fall and spring terms 1998/1999 provided a record occupancy of 250 for the J. R. Stewart Residence with scholars drawn from many different countries. Since its earliest days the Institute has been characterized by the international character of its researchers and scholar visitors, who have found in CAARI a home away from home. In June 1999 a section of the Greek Archaeological Society at Athens was inaugurated in Nicosia.

Braving the heat, enduring the dust, and ignoring their typically overloaded schedule, members of the ASOR Committee on Archaeological Policy cherish their on-site tours. Idalion, summer 1998 was no exception. With the broad sweep of hills framing the temple of Aphrodite in the background, one recognizes hidden under the obligatory hats and/or sunglasses (left to right) Carolyn Hoffman, Pamela Gaber (Director of the Idalion excavations), Walter Rast (ASOR CAP Chairman), Vathoulla Moustoukki, Ed Gilbert (President of the CAARI Board), Joe Seger (President of ASOR) and Nancy Serwint (CAARI Director).

When not involved in administrative or programmatic duties, Nancy Serwint concentrated on her publication of the huge corpus of terracottas from the Princeton excavations at Marion where she also continued to excavate. After four busy and productive years, on July 1, 1999, she in turn handed over the directorship to Robert S. Merrillees and returned to the School of Art at Arizona State University.

Sy Gitin, Director of the W. F. Albright Institute of Archaeological Research, Jerusalem, lectures at CAARI, March 1999 with Eric Lapp (right), CAARI NEH Fellow.

Trustees Andrew Oliver and Diana Buitron-Oliver join Cyprus based trustees and fellows for tea at CAARI. (clockwise from left) Aaron Brody (Fulbright), Lillian Craig (Trustee), Daniel Guill (Fulbright), Eric Lapp (NEH), Andrew Oliver, Maria Kyriakou (Trustee), John Leonard (Fulbright), Sherry Fox Leonard and Diana Buitron-Oliver. Autumn 1998.

Beginning a New Century

The new Director, Robert Merrillees, was no newcomer to Cyprus; in fact, few foreign archaeologists can boast with him of having first excavated there in 1961; in his case with J. R. Stewart who to most of us is but a much respected name. And neither was he a newcomer to CAARI, having lectured at 41 King Paul Street in the early 1980s. After earning a Ph.D. in Archaeology from the University of London, Merrillees chose a diplomatic career, becoming something of a twentieth century anachronism by combining fine scholarship with diplomacy. His postings as Ambassador of Australia to Israel, Sweden, and Greece enabled him to continue to pursue his academic work. The contributions of Robert Merrillees to Bronze Age Cypriot scholarship are considerable and varied; one might even say eclectic. He loves nothing more than to play Devil's Advocate with a commonly held opinion. From opium to the identification of Alashia, life around him is never dull. Although he will miss the fine library he and his wife Helen, a scholar in her own right, have at last shelved in France after their peripatetic existence, one can expect him to devote equal attention to CAARI's holdings and their *lacunae*, for he is a passionate bibliophile.

Challenges and Cyprus are perhaps synonymous. For Laina and me the move to America after so many years abroad was likewise a challenge, but a welcome one. It is with a shared and deep satisfaction that we both are able to continue to promote appreciation for that small island, which played such an important role in our lives. Laina is now the Curator of the Cesnola Collection at the Semitic Museum, Harvard University, and I serve as Director of the Institute of Cypriot Studies at the University at Albany. So we both remain as involved as ever with the life and history of Cyprus.

(left to right) Andrew Oliver and Robert Merrillees at ASOR Centennial Gala, in Washington D.C. in April 2000. At meetings of the CAARI Trustees on April 14, Drew Oliver was elected to succeed Ed Gilbert as CAARI President for 2000–2001.

Each of the four directors to have stood at CAARI's helm over the past twenty-one years has faced new challenges, which they have confronted and typically resolved with imagination and determination for the benefit of the Institute. The challenges currently faced by Robert Merrillees are old and new at the same time; old in that Cyprus remains divided into two major ethnic entities and extreme tact is required in a country where monumental issues are often viewed in black and white; new because most agree that the situation will change with the Republic of Cyprus's anticipated accession to the European Union; new because of the growing influence of the new University of Cyprus (which opened its doors to students in 1992) on local scholarship, and, finally, new because of changing attitudes towards archaeological excavation, site preservation and accessibility to the greater public.

One of the greatest rewards of our long sojourn on the island was the friendship we enjoyed with the Cypriots themselves. This photograph, taken by friend and colleague Ellen Herscher in 1991 while a Fulbright Fellow at CAARI, sums it up so well: Yiannis Cleanthous, onetime Custodian of St Hilarian Castle, then of Kyrenia Castle (where we first met in 1968,) later still of the Yeroskipou Folk Museum and now muktar (mayor) of Lemba Village, entertains us (Laina is to the right) under a spreading mulburry tree in his beloved garden. For those familiar with the recent history of Cyprus, his successive postings will be seen to echo the tragic events of the past decades, events that have failed to dampen either his, or his countrymen's, indomitable spirit.

A Promising Future

To sum up, the presence of the Cyprus American Archaeological Research Institute encourages Classicists and scholars specializing in the Aegean to associate themselves with the American Schools of Oriental Research. This, in my opinion, is one of the more healthy developments to occur within the larger ASOR organization since the founding of the American Center for Oriental Research in Amman. It has caused a westward shift in ASOR's otherwise more restricted and traditional focus on the continental Near East. We can in any case be confident that, as we move into the twenty-first century, CAARI will continue to encourage and support scholarship across the broad range of interests on the island, from the prehistoric era into early modern times, embracing study of Bronze Age and Classical archaeology, as well as of Byzantine, Crusader, Venetian, Ottoman, and British Colonial and Modern history.

Today's world is much changed from that which existed a century ago when those farsighted and pioneering scholars founded the American School of Oriental Research, but I am convinced they would have approved of the direction followed by their organization as it reaches the new millennium. Biblical Archaeology does not have the same meaning in 2000 as it did in 1900; the field has expanded, matured, and, like an intelligent, educated human being, it has broadened its horizon. Today, multidisciplinary and cross-cultural studies are in vogue, therefore the current trends in scholarship promote the dynamic role CAARI plays as one of the affiliated overseas centers of the American Schools of Oriental Research. Once again, Cyprus emerges as the stepping stone between the Orient and the Occident, and ASOR in various ways, is contributing to this phenomenon, as it looks forward to a second century of archaeological and historical research in these evocative regions of the eastern Mediterranean and the Near East.

CAARI
APPENDED LISTS

Officers

Board of Trustees

Staff

Appointees

Assisted Research Projects

Mosaic pattern detail from the sixth century A.D. Basilica of Chrysopolitissa, Cyprus.

CAARI Board Chairman

Charles U. Harris 1991–

CAARI Presidents 1978–2000

Norma Kershaw	1978–1979
Ian Todd	1980–1982
Andrew Oliver Jr.	1982–1984
Charles U. Harris	1984–1991
Giraud V. Foster	1991–1995
Andrew Oliver Jr.	1995–1997
Edward G. Gilbert	1997–2000
Andrew Oliver Jr.	2000–

CAARI Directors 1978–2000

Anita Walker	1978–1979
Ian Todd	1979–1980
Stuart Swiny	1980–1995
Nancy Serwint	1996–1999
Robert Merrillees	1999–

CAARI Officers (Current during 2000)

Chairman	Charles U. Harris
President	Edward G. Gilbert 1999/2000
	Andrew Oliver 2000/2001
Vice President	Annemarie Weyl Carr
Vice President for Development	Kate Herrod 1999/2000
Secretary	Robert Wozniak 1999/2000
	David Detrich 2000/2001
Treasurer	Andrew Oliver 1999/2000
	William Andreas 2000/2001
Assistant Treasurer	Gerald L. Vincent
Clerk	Julie Hansen

CAARI Staff (Current during 2000)

Director	Robert S. Merrillees
Deputy Director and Librarian	Diana Constantinides
Administrative Assistant	Vathoulla Moustoukki

CAARI Board of Trustees *(Members current during 2000)*

William S. Andreas	Sudbury, MA
Diana Buitron-Oliver	Chevy Chase, MD
Annemarie Weyl Carr	Southern Methodist University
Linda M. Clougherty	Rolling Hills Estates, CA
Lillian Craig	Nicosia, Cyprus
David A. Detrich	Mattituck, NY
Raymond C. Ewing	Ammendale, VA
Giraud V. Foster	Baltimore, MD
Gustave Feissel	Scottsdale, AZ
Joseph A. Greene	Harvard Semitic Museum
Timothy E. Gregory	Ohio State University
Julie Hansen	Boston University
Charles U. Harris	Delaplane, VA
Kate Herrod	Falls Church, VA
Ellen Herscher	Washington, DC
Maria Kyriacou	Nicosia, Cyprus
Eric M. Meyers	Duke University
Andrew Oliver Jr.	Chevy Chase, MD
Joe D. Seger ex-officio	Mississippi State University
Nancy Serwint	Arizona State University
Joanna S. Smith	Bryn Mawr College
Stuart Swiny	University at Albany (SUNY)
Michael K. Toumazou	Davidson College
Gerald Vincent	Cortez, CO
F. Bryan Wilkins	Washington, DC
Robert J. Wozniak	Washington, DC
Bruce Zuckerman	University of Southern California

Mosaic pattern detail from the sixth century A.D. Basalica A at Ayios Yeoryios of Peyai, Cyprus.

CAARI Offices

In the United States:
CAARI
at Boston University
656 Beacon Street, Fifth Floor
Boston MA 02215-2010

Phone: 617 353 6570:
Fax: 617 353 6575
E-mail: caari@bu.edu
Web address: www.caari.org

In Cyprus:
CAARI
11 Andreas Demitriou St.
Nicosia 1066,
Cyprus

Phone: 357 2 670 832
Fax: 357 2 671 147
E-mail: director@caari.org.cy

CAARI Appointees 1983–2000

Susan Heuck Allen	1988–89	Fulbright
Jane Barlow	1988–89	Fulbright
Uzi Baram	1993–94	A. C. O'Donovan
Cecilia Beer	1993–95	John G. Bartol
Patricia Bikai	1984–85	Fulbright
Aaron Brody	1998–99	Fulbright
Rebecca Bryant	1994–95	Fulbright
Mauriusz Burdajewicz	1996–97	J. P. Getty
Joanne Clarke	1990–91	J. R. Stewart/Sydney University
Julia Clarke	1992–94	John G. Bartol
Boldizsar Csornay	1989–90	Cyprus/Hungarian Government Cultural Exchange
Derek Counts	1997–98	A. C. O'Donovan
Thomas Davis	1987–88	Pacific Scientific
Carin Deslex	1994–95	Leventis Foundation
Lita Diacopoulos	1995–96	Charles and Janet Harris
William Duba	1999–2000	Fulbright
Richard Dunn	1995–96	Charles and Janet Harris
Elizabeth Doering	1997–98	Fulbright
Glynnis Fawkes	1999–2000	Fulbright
Marian Feldman	1994–95	Charles U. Harris
Sherry Fox-Leonard	1992–93	Charles and Janet Harris
	1993–94	Fulbright
Smiljka Gabelic	1984–85	Cyprus/Yugoslavia Government Cultural Exchange
Pamela Gaber	1985–86	Fulbright
	1995–96	NEH
Rickey Gann	1985–86	Leventis Foundation
Joseph Greene	1986–87	Fulbright
Michael Given	1989–90	Cambridge University
	1993–96	Leverhulme Trust
Basil Gomez	1994–95	John G. Bartol
Timothy Gregory	1994–95	NEH
Daniel Guill	1998–99	Fulbright
Julie Hansen	1983–85	Fulbright
Ellen Herscher	1990–92	Fulbright
James Hester	1993–94	Fulbright
Nicolle Hirschfeld	1995–96	Fulbright
Craig Hinrichs	1987–89	Pacific Scientific
	1989–90	Fulbright
Louise Hitchcock	1999–2000	Fulbright
Barbara Holz	1993–94	Charles and Janet Harris
Gloria Igosi	1987–88	Pacific Scientific

Priscilla Keswani	1990–91	Fulbright
Alice Kingsnorth	1990–91	Charles and Janet Harris
Barbara Kling	1983–84	ASOR/W. F. Albright
	1987–88	Fulbright
	1996–97	NEH
A. Bernard Knapp	1987–88	Fulbright
Eric Lapp	1998–99	NEH
John Leonard	1988–90	Pacific Scientific
	1995–96	A. C. O'Donovan
	1997–98	Fulbright
Gloria London	1985–86	Fulbright
	1999–2000	NEH
Glenn Markoe	1986–87	Fulbright
Murray McClellan	1985–86	Fulbright
Carole McCartney	1995–96	John G. Bartol
Kaelyn McGregor	1994–95	Leventis Foundation
Robert Morris	1988–89	J. R. Stewart/Sydney University
Michael Mueller	1996–97	Fulbright
James Muhly	1987–88	Fulbright
George Papasavvas	1993–94	Leventis Foundation
	1995–96	Leventis Foundation
Daniell Parks	1990–91	A.C. O'Donovan
	1993–94	Kress
	1994–95	Fulbright
	1995–96	Charles U. Harris
Joseph Parvis	1996–97	Fulbright
Karl Petruso	1984–85	Fulbright
Nicholas Stanley Price	1997–98	NEH
David Reese	1988–89	Pacific Scientific
	1991–92	Fulbright
	1993–94	Charles and Janet Harris
David Roessel	1993–94	Fulbright
	1997–98	NEH
David Rupp	1987–88	ASOR/W. F. Albright
Kenneth Schaar	1989–90	Fulbright
Nancy Serwint	1992–93	NEH
Lauren Silver	1995–96	Fulbright
Joanna Smith	1991–92	Fulbright
	1993–94	Whiting
	1995–96	NEH
Michael Toumazou	1994–95	NEH
Ian Todd	1986–87	Fulbright
Pippa Vanderstar	1993–94	Fulbright
Bethany Walker	1994–95	Fulbright
Clark Walz	1984–85	Fulbright
Antigoni Zournatzi	1988–89	Berkeley University
	1993–94	NEH

CAARI Assisted Excavation and Survey Projects Current During 2000

(* indicates ASOR/CAP affiliation)

Athienou-Malloura	Michael Toumazou	Davidson College
Agios Georghiostis Pegias-Yeronisos	Joan B. Connelly	University of Missouri-Columbia
*Idalion	Pamela Gaber	University of Arizona
*Kalavasos-Kopetra Project	M. Rautman	University of Missouri-Columbia
	M. McClellan	Boston University
*Kalavasos-Ayios Demetrios	Ian Todd	Kalavasos, Cyprus
	Alison South	
*Kholetria-Ortos	Alan Simmons	University of Nevada at Los Vegas
*Kourion-Amathus Gate Cemetery	Danielle Parks	University of Missouri-Columbia
*Larnaca Hinterlands Project	Albert Leonard, Jr.	University of Arizona
*Mitsero-Politiko Regional Survey	A. Bernard Knapp	University of Glascow
Marion/Arsinoe	William A.P. Childs	Princeton University
*Politiko Phorades Excavation	A. Bernard Knapp	University of Glascow
Rantidi Forest-Lingrintou Dhigeni	Bonny Bazemore	Chicago, IL
*Sotira-Kaminoudhia	Stuart Swiny	University at Albany (SUNY)
*Vasilikos Valley Project	Ian Todd	Kalavasos, Cyprus
	Alison South	

CAARI Assisted — ASOR/CAP Affiliated Projects 1981–2000

(Initial date indicates year first affiliated with ASOR/CAP)

1981	Idalion	Anita Walker
		CAARI
1981–2000	Sotira-Kaminoudhia	Stuart Swiny
		CAARI
		University at Albany (SUNY)
		Rip Rapp
		University of Minnesota (1983)
1981–2000	Vasalikos Valley Project	Ian Todd
		Brandeis University
		Kalavasos, Cyprus
1984–86, 1993–96	Canadian Paliapaphos Survey	David Rupp
		Brock University
1985–87, 1990–94	Kourion	David Soren
		University of Arizona
1986–90, 1993–94	Kourion Archaic	Diana Buitron
		Chevy Chase, MD
1987–88, 1990	Akrotiri-Aetokremnos	Alan Simmons
		University of Nevada at Reno
1987–88, 1992–2000	Kalavashos Kopetra	Marcus Rautman
		University of Missouri-Columbia
		Murray McClellan
		Boston University
1989–90	Idalion	Lawrence Stager
		Harvard University
1991, 1996–2000	Idalion	Pamela Gaber
		University of Arizona
1991–96	Paphos Harbor Explorations	Robert Hohlfelder
		University of Colorado
1992–96, 1999–2000	Kholetria-Ortos	Alan Simmons
		University of Nevada at Las Vegas
1992–98	Sydney Cyprus Survey	A. Bernard Knapp
		Sydney University
		University of Glasgow

1995–2000	Kalavasos-Ayios Demetrios	Ian Todd & Alison South
1997	Sotira Archaeological Project Survey	Stuart Swiny University at Albany (SUNY)
1998–2000	Politiko Phorades Excavation	A. Bernard Knapp Sydney University University of Glasgow
1999–2000	Mitsero-Politiko Regional Survey	A. Bernard Knapp University of Glasgow
1999–2000	Kurion-Amathus Gate Cemetery	Danielle Parks University of Missouri-Columbia
2000	Larnaca Hinterlands Project	Albert Leonard, Jr. University of Arizona

Medallion with an allegorical bust of Ktisis holding a Roman building measure. A fifth century A.D. mosaic representing the founding spirit of the baths belonging to the Eustolios Complex at Kourion in southern Cyprus.
Photo credit: Harry C. Heywood, Chairman, Western Sovereign Base Archaeological Society, Cyprus.